Kevin D. Ray

Romans

Romans

An Exposition of Chapter 8: 17–39
The Final Perseverance of the Saints

D. M. Lloyd-Jones

ZONDERVAN
PUBLISHING HOUSE
OF THE ZONDERVAN CORPORATION | GRAND RAPIDS, MICHIGAN 49506

ROMANS: THE FINAL PERSEVERANCE OF THE SAINTS

© D. M. Lloyd-Jones 1975
First published 1975
First Zondervan printing 1976

Sixth printing 1981

Library of Congress Cataloging in Publication Data

Lloyd-Jones, David Martyn.
    Romans: an exposition of chapter 8:17-39.
    Sermons delivered on Friday nights in Westminster
Chapel, May 1961–May 1962.
    Includes text of Romans VIII, 17-39.
    1.   Bible. N. T.   Romans VIII, 17-39—Sermons.
2.   Sermons, English.   I.   Bible. N. T.   Romans VIII,
17-39.   English.   1976.   II.   Title.
BS2665.4.L59   1976   227'.1'06   76-2574

British ISBN 0-85181-231-3
ISBN 0-310-27930-5

Printed in the United States of America

To the faithful and enthusiastic Friday-nighters at Westminster Chapel 1955-68

Contents

[vii]

Contents

Contents

[ix]

Contents

[x]

Preface

Little needs to be said by way of introduction to this volume. The verses considered in it are generally agreed to be one of the sublimest portions of scripture.

In it the Apostle brings his argument concerning assurance of salvation to a grand climax. The way in which he advances surely from argument to argument, piling one upon another, is astonishing, and constitutes the supreme example of inspired logic. In doing so he brings us face to face with the fundamental theme of the Bible – God's plan and purpose of redemption conceived before time and the foundation of the world, and spanning the whole of human history from the original creation to the final glory.

What is perhaps most astonishing of all is that all this was done out of a primary pastoral concern, the Apostle's main object being to comfort and to help those early Christians in Rome who were enduring what he calls 'the sufferings of this present time'.

As is characteristic of all Paul's letters, doctrine and practical application are intertwined, reminding us that doctrine and theology should never be treated in isolation or regarded as an academic subject. The only comfort and consolation the Apostle has to offer his readers is based on doctrine. Every step and detail matters, and is of crucial importance in the development of the grand argument. To set the details and the broad principles in opposition is a sign of failure to understand the Apostle's method.

It is only as we follow him 'with the eyes of our own understanding being enlightened' that we shall be able to understand, and to be 'more than conquerors' face to face with the sufferings of our own times. God grant that these expositions may help many in that respect!

Preface

I can imagine no greater privilege than that of attempting to expound these profound truths week by week to a congregation of eager and expectant Christians; and I can wish nothing better for those who read than that they may know something of the joy and exhilaration it was my privilege to experience in the preparation and the delivery of these messages.

They were delivered on Friday nights in Westminster Chapel during the period May 1961–May 1962.

Once more I am happy to record and to express my great and ever-increasing gratitude to Mrs E. Burney, Mr S. M. Houghton and my wife for their endless help and encouragement.

London 1975   D. M. LLOYD-JONES

One

*

And if children, then heirs; heirs of God, and joint-heirs with Christ; if so be that we suffer with him, that we may be also glorified together.

For I reckon that the sufferings of this present time are not worthy to be compared with the glory which shall be revealed in us.

Romans 8: 17, 18

The purpose of the whole of this 8th chapter of the Epistle to the Romans, as we have seen in previous studies, is to show Christian people the way to a full assurance of their salvation. They have a new spirit within them working for righteousness, a spirit which also guarantees their ultimate glorification, including even their bodies. Moreover they are 'sons of God' and should have within them the 'spirit of adoption whereby we cry, Abba, Father'. Over and above all this it is possible for them to experience the Spirit Himself bearing witness with their spirit that they are the 'children of God, and if children, then heirs; heirs of God and joint-heirs with Christ'.

This knowledge, in particular, helps us to understand why we should be subject to trials and sufferings. Such experiences, far from shaking our faith, should strengthen it, and be a further proof to us of our ultimate salvation. They prove that we are united to Him, and that as He suffered in this world so we suffer also. So when we find ourselves suffering as Christians we should deduce from that the fact that we are Christian people. 'It is the way the Master went, should not the servant tread it still?' He was a 'Man of sorrows, and acquainted with grief'. We have also seen that the Apostle uses our sufferings a and trials in second way to prove that we are children of God, namely, that the sufferings are a proof that we are being prepared for the glory to which we are being taken. Many scriptures teach clearly that it is 'through much tribulation that we must enter into the kingdom of God' (Acts 14: 22). 'Whom the Lord loveth he chasteneth, and scourgeth every son whom he receiveth' (Heb. 12: 6). This is a great mystery, yet there can be no question but that suffering is one of the means used by God to prepare us for the glory that awaits us. We therefore translate the second part of the 17th verse thus: 'Since we suffer with him, in order that we may be also glorified together.' We suffer 'in order that' we may be prepared for that glory. This throws great light upon the terrible, devastating power of sin which makes it necessary that suffering should have to be used in this way in order to prepare for the glory. You would have thought that the simple positive presentation of the truth would be sufficient in itself; but it is not.

That is the point at which we arrived at the end of the previous volume. The Apostle is concerned to emphasize that the ultimate end and object of salvation is our glorification; and that is the point which he is now going to work out. He states it in these terms – that we shall be glorified 'together' with Him. Everything that happens to us is 'in Christ', and because we are united to the Lord Jesus Christ. We must constantly remind ourselves of the profound argument which the Apostle has been working out from the beginning of the 5th chapter of this Epistle where he introduces this great theme of certainty and assurance, and indeed of glorification. 'Being justified by faith, we have peace with God through our Lord Jesus Christ.' Not only that, 'by him also we have access by faith into this grace wherein we stand, and rejoice in hope of the glory of God'. This is what should always be uppermost in the minds of Christian people. Glorification is the ultimate end and goal of salvation; and we must never stop short of it. We must never think of our Christian position as merely one of being forgiven. That is but the beginning of it, it is not the end. Even sanctification is not the end. The end is glorification; and this is the great theme to which the Apostle is now about to introduce us.

What does 'glorification' mean? What does the Apostle mean when he says that we shall be 'glorified together'? Glorification means full and entire deliverance from sin and evil in all their effects and in every respect – body, soul, and spirit. The whole man will be completely and entirely delivered from every harmful effect of sin, every tarnishing, polluting effect of sin. Not only so, we

[2]

shall become like the Lord Jesus Christ, perfect men, glorified men. *He* is already glorified, and we shall be glorified; and our glorification, like everything else that happens to us in the Christian life, is the result of our being joined to Him.

Let us remind ourselves again of the crucial importance of chapter 5 of this Epistle to the Romans. The Apostle introduces this theme in the 10th verse of that chapter: 'For if, when we were enemies, we were reconciled to God by the death of his Son, much more, being reconciled, we shall be saved by his life' (A.V.). But we saw that it should really be translated, 'we shall be saved in his life'. We are 'in Christ', we are *in* the life of Christ. Then the Apostle elaborates this great doctrine of our union with Christ in that same chapter from verse 12 to verse 21. Never forget that section, it is absolutely essential. We were in Adam, we are now 'in Christ'. This 8th chapter is just a working out of that doctrine. We derived from Adam all the painful effects of the Fall. 'As by one man sin entered into the world, and death by sin; and so death passed upon all men, for that all have sinned.' Because of our connection with Adam we have reaped all the terrible consequences of his sinful act; but on the other side 'grace has much more abounded'. Because we are 'in Christ' we receive all the benefits of the things which are true of Him. So 'where sin abounded, grace did much more abound'.

The Apostle works it out still further in chapter 6 which also speaks about our union with Christ. 'Know ye not, that so many of us as were baptized into Jesus Christ were baptized into his death. Therefore we are buried with him by baptism into death: that like as Christ was raised up from the dead by the glory of the Father, even so we also should walk in newness of life. For if we have been planted together in the likeness of his death, we shall be also in the likeness of his resurrection.' And here in chapter 8, verse 17 and onwards, Paul is still dealing with it; and his point is that because we are 'in Christ', and therefore joined to Him, we are 'children of God', and if we are suffering now with Him and as He suffered, we shall also be 'glorified together with him'.

It is vital and essential that we should be clear about this doctrine of glorification, for it is the ultimate end of our salvation. God forbid that any of us should stop short at forgiveness, or look at salvation negatively as merely being saved from hell. I do not want to minimize the value of that aspect of salvation; we can never thank God sufficiently for delivering us from death and hell and everlasting punishment. But that, according to the teaching of the Scripture, is only the first step, the mere beginning. The end is glorification.

The scriptural way of presenting this doctrine is along the following lines. God made man in his own 'image' and 'likeness'. That is what we are told in the book of Genesis, and it is the teaching of the Bible in all its parts. God said, 'Let us make man in our image, after our likeness'. We must always remember that man at the beginning had a kind of glory. He was made the lord of creation; he was over all the animal creation, indeed over the whole of creation. Everything was there for man's sake, and man, having this image of God upon him, was its lord. Now all that suggests something of the glory that belongs to God Himself. He gave something of this to man; He put this special dignity upon him.

Such was man as God made him. But unfortunately man listened to the temptation of the devil, and he sinned and fell. The terrible result of that fall was that man lost the original position which he had. The Apostle has already stated that in the 3rd chapter of this Epistle in the 23rd verse: 'All have sinned and come short of the glory of God.' We were never meant to 'come short of the glory of God', but it has happened to us as the result of sin. Such is the truth about all of us born into this world. Man is not what he was meant to be. This is basic biblical teaching. Man has lost the glory that he originally possessed, and tends to demonstrate his loss in every aspect of his behaviour. This is the essential tragedy of man; this is the real problem of mankind. It is the only way of truly understanding man, the only way of understanding the world as it is today. Man still has a kind of memory and recollection of what he once was, and he is always trying to return to it and to persuade himself that he is succeeding. But failure dogs his steps. Hence his frustration. Now that is the key to the understanding of the whole of human history, the explanation of all the intense effort which man puts forth as he seeks the glory which he feels belongs to him. But he can never get it, he cannot find it.

Here we find the explanation of man's restlessness and unhappiness. There is nothing more characteristic of sinful man than restlessness. Isaiah puts it thus: 'The wicked are like the troubled sea when it cannot rest' (57: 20). We see that in the world round about us. What causes this restlessness? The fact is that no one is satisfied with what he has. The world is full of ambition, rivalry, jealousy and pride. Why? It is just this matter of trying to be what we feel deep within us we were meant to be, and ought to be. Our Lord put the matter on one occasion very plainly and clearly to the Jews who so persistently argued with Him. I refer to what is found in the 5th chapter of the Gospel according to John, verse 41 and following: 'I receive not honour from men. But I know you, that ye have not the love of God in you. I am come in my Father's name, and ye receive me not: if another shall come in his own name, him ye will receive. How can ye believe, which receive honour one of another, and seek not the honour that cometh from God only?' The word 'honour', as found here, could be translated as 'glory'. 'How can ye believe, which receive glory one of another, and seek not the glory that cometh from God only?' Man is always seeking glory, always trying to rise superior to his fellows. He wants to be on top, to be praised, to obtain honour. All are seeking for honour. The sinful world craves for position, for elevation, for lordship. In other words, man is seeking for glory. And the explanation of this is that man has the feeling within him that he is meant for it, that he ought to have it, but that he has not got it. This inward urge makes him restless; and that largely accounts for the trials, the troubles, and the tribulations and unhappiness of life.

What a tragic creature fallen man is! He is a mass of contradictions. He does not understand himself; he cannot explain his restlessness, this feeling that he was meant for something better. He has no idea how to account for it; hence he so constantly believes that he can achieve it by his own efforts. But he cannot do so. Throughout the long centuries he has been labouring hard at the task, but he has met with failure all along the line.

Then look at man in his relationship to the world. He is clearly not 'lord of creation'. All his wonderful technological achievements do not prove that he is lord of creation. He is but touching a small part of the hem of the great cosmos. The fact of the matter is that man is afraid of creation. The discoveries of scientists are terrifying in the extreme. Far from being the lord of creation man is mastered by it. The things that he is discovering may prove to lead to his own destruction. He is not master. He finds out many things, but his discoveries do not give him control. Creation is too vast, too big for him; and man has become the victim of the creation of which he was originally appointed lord and controller. That is a part of this glory which man has lost as the result of sin.

Indeed, we can even see this in the matter of the human body. Man's body was not at the beginning what it is now. It did not suffer from diseases, it did not know pain, it was not a frail body, it was not what the Apostle calls 'the body of our humiliation' (Philippians 3: 21). Our bodies at best are very poor, there is an element of decay in them. Physically, man is in disgrace; but he was not created so. There was originally a beauty, a perfection, a kind of glory even about the very body of man. But when man fell he fell in every respect; the primeval glory departed from every part of him – his spirit, his soul, his body. The entire man is no longer what he was meant to be.

It is only as we understand that, that we can realize two things. The first is related to the state and condition of man and his world today. Because man lacks understanding of this truth he is always bringing forward schemes, always making his proposals, always confident and assured, always believing that he is about to arrive. Suddenly everything crashes again; and he is back where he was before, or even further back. The history of mankind illustrates this principle of cycles. There is no steady advance; for a while we seem to be progressing well; then suddenly we begin to experience set-backs. Events, we find, proceed in cycles, civilizations rise and fall after the same manner. But, rise or fall, man retains the feeling that he is meant for glory.

The second lesson we learn from all this is that you can only understand the Christian salvation fully as you grasp these considerations, and as you realize their truth. What is offered us in Christ is nothing less than glorification. And, of course, in the light of what I have just been saying, that is absolutely essential. If man were merely forgiven but left unchanged, it would mean that the devil was victorious and that God had failed. Salvation is not salvation unless at the very least it puts man back where he was before. Consider man as God made him – perfect! The devil comes in, and mars the work and defaces it. What is salvation? The restoration, the bringing back of what was lost!

You see, immediately, that salvation cannot stop at any point short of this entire perfection, not only with regard to the spirit, but with regard to the soul and body also. Such is the meaning of this term glorification.

Here, then, is the theme the Apostle is introducing at this point: man is going to be completely and entirely restored in the Lord Jesus Christ, and as the result of his union with Him. Here we have to emphasize an additional point, namely, that according to this teaching man is not only restored to what he was in Adam, he is taken beyond that. The minimum, I am arguing, is to be restored to the condition of unfallen Adam; but it is certainly not the maximum. Adam was perfect as man but his perfection fell short of glorification. There was room for development, and it is clear that glorification was the ultimate that was intended for man. As man he was perfect; there was no blemish in him, there was no sin in him, there was no fault in him. He was in a state of innocence, but innocence falls short of glorification. But what is held before us and offered to us in Christ, and promised us in Him, is nothing less than glorification. The thing to which man, if he had continued to keep God's commandments, would have arrived, and which would have been given to him as a reward for his obedience, is the thing that is now freely given us in and through our Lord and Saviour Jesus Christ. So I quote again two lines of Isaac Watts which for some strange reason are omitted from most of the hymn-books:

> *In Him the tribes of Adam boast*
> *More blessings than their father lost.*

That is a clear statement of the truth. Not merely are we restored to where Adam was, we are taken beyond it to the place at which Adam would have arrived had he continued in a state of innocence and of obedience. Adam sinned and failed, and thereby lost even what he already had. He could not recover it. The cherubim and the flaming sword were set at the eastern end of the Garden of Eden, prohibiting man's return. Man has been trying to get past that obstacle ever since. He is for ever trying to recapture the glory that he has lost. He cannot do so. But here, in Christ, this very thing that was impossible to Adam after the Fall, and to the whole progeny of Adam ever since, is given to us freely as the gift of God. And so, as we think about glorification, it must be in this way; that man is not only delivered from all the effects of the Fall, and the sin and the transgression of Adam, but granted a far superior blessing, and given something of the glory of the Lord Jesus Christ Himself. And this is what the Apostle is saying in the words found at the end of verse 17: 'If so be that we suffer with Him, that we may be also glorified together.'

We shall have occasion to consider the matter in greater detail as the Apostle develops his theme. But let me sum up his argument to the end of verse 17. What is the position of man 'in Christ' therefore up to this point? We are already delivered from the tyranny and the dominion of sin, we have 'died with Christ', we are 'dead to sin', we are 'dead to the law'. We are no longer under the dominion of sin. We have been told in chapter 6 verse 11, 'Reckon ye also yourselves to be dead indeed unto sin, but alive unto God through Jesus Christ our Lord'. In spirit we are already in Christ, and safe. We died with Him, we have been buried with Him, we have risen with Him, we are 'seated with him in the heavenly places' at this very moment. There is no question about that; it is certain, it is absolutely sure. We are saved, we are secure, but we are not yet glorified. What, then, is our relationship to glorification? We have glimpses of it, we have intimations of it. We are given the privilege of tasting something of its first-fruits, we are given a foretaste of it. Not yet glorified, but knowing about it; seeing it afar off, being prepared for it. In a glorious statement at the end of the third chapter of the Second Epistle to the Corinthians, verse 18, the Apostle puts it thus: 'We all, with open face beholding as in a glass the glory of the Lord, are being changed into the same image from glory to glory, even as by the Spirit of the Lord.' That is our present position. The glorification itself is yet to come. We are justified, we are being sanctified, we are going to be glorified. That is the way to look at the matter. And therefore 'we rejoice in hope of the glory of God'. We know enough about it to look forward to it, to rejoice in it, to anticipate it. We do not understand it fully, we shall not even be given a full description of it in this passage that is before us. However, the Apostle tells us enough for us to realize that it is something that really baffles description. 'We rejoice in hope of the glory of God.' Sin remains in the body, this mortal body of ours, and we have to mortify the deeds of the body, as we have been reminded already in verse 13 of this chapter. 'If ye through the Spirit do mortify the deeds of the body, ye shall live.' There is still a fight, there is still a struggle, and the body itself is decaying and dying. This is not glorification; this is the process of sanctification preparatory to the entry into the state of eternal glorification. Such is the present position of the Christian.

What, then, has the Apostle proved as we arrive at the end of verse 17? He has demonstrated that there are certain proofs of the fact that we are the children of God, and that we are being prepared for glory. These are the proofs: in verse 14, the fact that we are being 'led by the Spirit of God'. That is a proof that we are 'the sons of God'. If you can give proof that you are being led and directed and guided by the Spirit of God you can be certain that you are a child of God. If you are deriving real enjoyment from a consideration of these things you can be sure that you are a child of God. But if it all appears to be some sort of gibberish to you, you had better examine yourself very seriously and carefully. Consider the words found in 1 Peter 2: 2: 'Desire the sincere milk of the word, that ye may grow thereby.' That is an exhortation addressed to children, and if you have that desire it is a proof that you are born again. The natural man has not got that desire; he sees nothing in it, it is all nonsense to him, he is not interested. If you really have a love for this Word and want to know more about it, it is a proof that you are a child of God, that you are led by the Spirit. It is He alone who leads to this.

The second proof, found in verse 15, is that we have lost 'the spirit of bondage' and that we have within us 'the Spirit of adoption, whereby we cry, Abba, Father'. If you have got that Spirit within you, if there is something welling up within you crying out to God, 'Abba, Father!' you must be a child of God. It is beyond dispute. But beyond that, as we have seen in verse 16, 'The Spirit itself beareth witness with our spirit, that we are the children of God'. Have you known the witness of the Spirit? If so, you can be certain that you are a child of God. The Spirit only witnesses in that way to the children. I am not saying, let me remind you, that if you lack these things you are not a Christian. You must have something of the leading of the Spirit, but you may not have the Spirit of adoption, you may never have known the testimony of the Spirit. You must continue to seek that blessing until you get it. But if you have got it, it is an absolute proof that you are a child of God.

And, lastly, we have seen that the Apostle even uses suffering: 'Since we suffer with him.' If you are really suffering as a Christian it is a proof that you are a Christian, that you are a child of God. The thing is inevitable. We must suffer if we are Christians. This is an absolute rule. As He suffered, so shall we. So if we are suffering because of our relationship to Him, and as Christians, it is an absolute proof of our relationship to Him.

There, then, is the Apostle's argument in the short paragraph from verse 14 to the end of verse 17. As we leave it I must emphasize one point. Have you ever noticed that this Apostle, and indeed all the other Apostles, never mention glory without immediately mentioning at the same time suffering? It is a very odd juxtaposition, is it not? The moment they begin to talk about this glory they always go on to speak about suffering. Our Lord Himself did so, as we find recorded in the Gospel according to St John, chapters 15 and 16. And we have already found the theme of suffering in chapter 5 of this Epistle. 'We rejoice in hope of the glory of God. And not only so, but we glory in tribulation.' Paul cannot mention glory without immediately being made to think of this element of suffering. We find it again in this eighth chapter, and in many other places in the Apostle's teaching. Take, for example, the Second Epistle to the Corinthians, chapter 4, verses 17 and 18: 'Our light affliction, which is but for a moment, worketh for us a far more exceeding and eternal weight of glory.' Suffering and glory – glory and suffering; always the same! In the fifth chapter of that same Epistle to the Corinthians we find: 'We know that if our earthly house of this tabernacle were dissolved, we have a building of God, an house not made with hands, eternal in the heavens.' That is the glory. 'In this we groan, earnestly desiring to be clothed upon with our house which is from heaven: if so be that being clothed we shall not be found naked. For we that are in this tabernacle do groan, being burdened: not for that we would be unclothed, but clothed upon, that mortality might be swallowed up of life.' Glory and suffering! They are always put together. And indeed we find the same in the Epistle to the Colossians, the first chapter, verses 24 to 27. The Apostle says: 'Who now rejoice in my sufferings for you, and fill up that which is behind of the afflictions of Christ in my flesh for his body's sake, which is the church.' Then he goes on to talk about 'The mystery which hath been hid from ages and from generations, but now is made manifest to his saints: to whom God would make known what is the riches of the glory of this mystery among the Gentiles; which is Christ in you, the hope of glory.' Sufferings and glory brought together once more! Then finally, in the Second Epistle to Timothy, chapter 2 verse 12, we find, 'If we suffer, we shall also reign with him'.

Now this is remarkable, is it not? And yet it has been one of the greatest stumbling-blocks to Christian people throughout the centuries in spite of this plain and clear teaching. Most believers still seem to assume that the moment people become Christians they never have any more troubles and trials; and if they do experience them they say, 'I thought I would never have trouble any longer, that bodily illnesses would all be cured and disappear, problems would vanish, and everything would be absolutely perfect' – in spite of this teaching! It has always been a stumbling-block. Doubtless that is why, in the teaching of the New Testament, we always find these two things mentioned together. Whenever the Word talks about the glory it immediately talks about the suffering, in order that unenlightened Christian people might be put right on this matter, and therefore might never become such easy prey to the devil and all his wiles and subtleties.

That is exactly what the Apostle is doing in this 8th chapter of Romans. Because you are suffering with Him, he says to Christians, you are certain to be glorified with Him. It is in order that you might be glorified that you are suffering. And then he seems to say, 'Is anyone troubled about this? is anyone unhappy about this suffering? is anyone failing to understand this suffering? Very well,' says the Apostle, 'I will tell you about it.' So at the beginning of verse 18 he really takes up this subject of suffering in the light of the glory that is to come.

Here, we really are starting with what constitutes a new section in the Epistle. It starts at the beginning of verse 18 and goes on to the end of verse 25. We have finished with the particular matter of sonship which was dealt with from verse 14 to verse 17; but here there is a new paragraph, and the connection with the previous one is quite clear. Do you notice the Apostle's method? Are you fascinated by it? He has been working out this great idea of sonship, and shown that sonship leads to glorification. But he chose to put it in this way: 'If so be that we suffer with him, that we may be also glorified together.' That, then, is the introduction to the theme of this next paragraph – the theme of suffering, and glorification in the light of suffering. I confess that to me this is very wonderful. Observe this perfect architecture as it were, the design, the great scheme being unfolded, as Paul proceeds to work out his plan.

This section, therefore, is not to be regarded as a digression; the Apostle is not merely turning aside to deal with the problem of suffering. He does so because he was a pastor and had a pastoral heart. He was not a lecturer, he was always a preacher, he was always a pastor. He could not just leave the question of glorification and suffering as it were in the air. He wants to help these Christians, so he gives them a word of explanation. But more than that, he introduces a new and a wonderful conception; he shows us that our glorification is only a part of a still more sublime and greater glorification which will include the whole cosmos. He has not touched upon that so far, but here he is going to deal with it. And as he does so he provides us with yet another proof of the absolute certainty and assurance of our individual salvation. If he can prove to us that it is God's purpose that the whole cosmos should be glorified in Christ, and as the result of His work, then all of us who belong to Christ are destined to share in it. This is the very thing Paul does. So in this paragraph at one and the same time we are given a further proof of the absolute certainty and assurance and finality of our ultimate and entire deliverance and glorification. But at the same time we are given an understanding as to the nature of our Christian life in this world, and especially in the light of the suffering that we are inevitably called to endure because we are the children of God.

Such, then, is the theme that is facing us as we look at this new paragraph which begins at verse 18 and goes on to verse 25. But it goes on beyond verse 25; it is indeed the theme right through to the very end of the chapter. It is a most glorious vista that is opening out before us. The Apostle wants us to be sure and certain that our glorification is coming; he wants us to look forward to it with a sense of thrill and with ecstasy. He wants us to be able to answer every argument that the devil will hurl at us, and especially when he says, 'Look at your suffering. Can you be a child of God? Is this what God is doing?' Paul gives us the answer, and makes us doubly certain and assured. It is essential for our well-being as Christians, for our happiness as Christians, and above all, for our testimony as Christians in the world as it is today, to have a clear understanding of this teaching concerning the association of present suffering and future glory 'together with Christ'.

We are now in a position to enter into a consideration of this great new theme beginning at verse 18.

Two

*

For I reckon that the sufferings of this present time are not worthy
to be compared with the glory which shall be revealed in us.

Romans 8: 18

The Apostle having shown that because we are children of God,
and joint-heirs with Christ, we share now in His suffering and shall
share in His future glory, now takes up this whole question of
suffering in the life of the Christian and sets it in the light of that
glory which is to come. This paragraph, from verse 18 to verse
25, is the classic statement on the question of suffering. It is not
the only one, of course, but in many ways it is the most profound
statement on the suffering of the Christian in this present life.

No subject is more urgently important for Christian people
at the present time. With the world as it is today, and with the
possibilities which are becoming increasingly clear, surely nothing
is more important for us than to know how exactly we are to react
to the troubles and the trials, the tribulations and the suffering
which we have to endure as we live our lives in this world.

As we come to examine the statement we can best subdivide
it in the following way. First, let us take a glance at some of the
negative characteristics of this teaching. How should the Christian
react to this fact of suffering? The first answer is that he should not
be surprised at it, never be taken by surprise. Why not? Mainly
for the reasons we have already been considering. We have seen
quite clearly that we cannot be united to the Lord Jesus Christ
without in some shape or form knowing something of 'the
fellowship of His sufferings'. It is something that is inevitable in
the life of the Christian. Therefore, putting it at its very lowest,
we should not be surprised at this. It is quite clear, however,
that many of these early Christians were surprised at it, and were

very upset by it. But that is altogether wrong, as the Apostle shows here, and as the New Testament everywhere shows.

So I move on to a second point. Not only should we not be surprised by suffering, still less should we be shaken by it, or cast down by it. It is just here that this whole matter becomes so urgently important. If we as Christian people are cast down by our suffering, if we are shaken by it, then the effect upon others who are watching us may very well be quite devastating. We make certain claims for the Christian faith, and others test the value of our faith and testimony by watching us and observing us when we are undergoing trial and suffering; so if we fail we shall be doing great harm to the gospel. It is a simple fact of history that there was nothing which was more potent in bringing people to conviction and conversion in the early days of the Church than the observation of the way in which these Christian people endured suffering. When believers were put on trial they were not confounded. Even when they were condemned, and thrown to the lions in the arena, far from grumbling and complaining, they were to be found thanking God that at last they had been counted worthy to suffer shame for His Name. The final crown of glory in this world, they used to say, was martyrdom, and 'the blood of the martyrs is the seed of the Church'. That is the great testimony of history. Nothing has so much shaken the unbelievers and made them feel that there is something in Christianity after all, as the way they have observed that the Christian has some secret, mysterious power and capacity to endure suffering even joyfully, to rejoice in tribulations. The opposite therefore is true, that we are not to be shaken by suffering, we are not to be cast down by it. In other words we should never be caused to doubt the truth of salvation itself because we suffer.

Examples can be quoted of godly people who have been guilty of failure at this point. There is a case of it in the seventy-third Psalm. We see there a man who was in trouble, and he says, Why is this happening to me? I am in trouble but these ungodly people are flourishing, 'their eyes stand out with fatness'. 'There are no bands in their death' – they are having a marvellous time, and here am I living a good life but I am in trouble. 'Verily I have cleansed my heart in vain.' Is there anything in this godly life after all? Now when a Christian behaves in that way he is denying the faith, as the man in the seventy-third Psalm also realized. He tells us that, when he thought thus, he went into the house of God and saw that he would be offending against the generation of God's people. He could not understand it, he was bewildered; but fortunately he met with the explanation in the house of God, and all was well. But he should never have been in that trouble, he should have done his thinking first before he allowed these thoughts to rise up within him, and before he harboured them. It is quite clear also that the people to whom the Epistle to the Hebrews was written were in a like case and condition. That is why the author writes to them. They were tending to say: Well now, if the gospel that we have heard preached and which we have believed is true, why is all this trouble happening to us? They were shaken by their suffering and their trials and tribulations. Some of them were being caused even to begin to query the truth of the Christian gospel.

The purpose of the paragraph we are now considering is to show us how terribly wrong this reaction is. The Christian must never be taken by surprise by suffering and led to query and to question the truth of salvation itself because he is suffering. There is something wrong with his view of salvation if he does so. He may have heard some superficial type of evangelism which gave him the impression that if he only said that he believed in the Lord Jesus Christ he would never have any problems, there would never be any more difficulty, the whole of life would be continuous sunshine and he would never have to suffer. Of course, if that is his idea of salvation, it is inevitable that he is soon going to be disillusioned. But this should not be true of the Christian.

Still less should Christians in trouble or suffering be led to doubt God's love. 'Where is God's love?' they say. And their unbelieving friends encourage them in that, saying, 'If God is a God of love, why does he allow this to happen to you?' This is a thought which the Christian should never allow to cross his mind. If the devil hurls it at you you must answer it at once. Whatever is happening, never doubt the love of God. This whole paragraph is meant to show us why that is wrong.

Others doubt the power of God. 'Ah,' they say, 'the love of God we do not deny, but he hasn't the power. If God has the power to prevent his people suffering why does he not use it, why does he not bring it into exercise? Has he got the power?'

The devil will be ready to suggest that question, but it must be rejected in the light of the Apostle's teaching.

Or perhaps the doubt will come in the form of a suggestion that perhaps we are not Christians at all. The argument may run like this: God's people are obviously those who are going to be kept; Christ said that 'the very hairs of your head are all numbered', that nothing can happen to His disciples apart from God. But look at what is happening to me! It is obvious that I am not a Christian at all. The devil will say that to you, he will come and insinuate that thought. The object of Paul's teaching here is to put you into a position in which you can reject these thoughts the moment they come. They must never be allowed to have an entry into the mind. If the devil throws them at you they should be immediately quenched by the shield of faith.

Finally, the Christian should never be so shaken by suffering and trials and tribulations as to feel a sense of grudge against God, or ever to grumble at his lot. For a Christian to grumble or to have a sense of grudge against God is a terrible thing. Whatever the suffering, however great, however intense, the Christian, if he understands this teaching, will never feel a sense of grudge against God, or a sense of complaint. He will never grumble at his lot, he will never say, Why is this happening to me, why should I be asked to endure this? Such a thought must never be allowed to enter into the mind and the heart of the Christian believer.

But turn now to another negative. There is no promise given, or expectation held out, of any relief or any improvement in our lot. Now this is obviously most important. The Apostle is writing to Christians who are suffering and in trouble, but there is not a suspicion of a suggestion from the Apostle that things are soon going to be better, that they can look forward to relief before long, that it cannot possibly continue like this. No such suggestion is made; neither here nor anywhere else in the whole of the New Testament. To some people this is a very alarming thought, and many are offended at it. But let us be clear about it; it is a part of our Lord's teaching. You remember how a certain man came to Him one day. He wanted to follow Him and said, 'Master, I will follow thee whithersoever thou goest'. Our Lord, recognizing the mentality and the condition of the man, said to him, 'Foxes have holes, and birds of the air have nests;

but the Son of man hath not where to lay his head'. He was challenging the man and showing him that he must be prepared for many trials and sufferings if he proposed truly to follow Him. The Lord has never promised His people an easy time. The teaching of the Bible never offers a general kind of comfort.

One reason I am emphasizing this is that Christianity has been described as 'the opiate of the people', a kind of drug, and there are many who come to the Church of God to be made to feel a little happier and to forget their troubles. But neither the Bible nor the Apostle deal with troubles in that way. The Bible does not tell us that in a year or two things are going to be better; it says, rather, 'there will be wars, and rumours of wars'. The Bible has never promised that under the influence of Christian teaching men are going to banish war, and that the world is gradually going to become perfect. On the contrary, it says that 'evil men shall wax worse and worse' (2 Tim. 3: 13). It does not promise that people are going to become so nice and kind, as civilization and education advance, that there will be no more persecutions, difficulties and troubles, that the whole of life for the Christian is going to be easier. Not at all! Indeed, you have but to read the 24th chapter of the Gospel according to St Matthew, where our Lord gives a preview of history, and you will see that He warned His followers then, and, through them, all of us and all Christians at all times, that we have nothing to anticipate in this world but sufferings and trials in various shapes and forms. You find the same in the Second Epistle to Timothy in the third chapter: 'This know also, that in the last days perilous times shall come. For men shall be lovers of their own selves, covetous, boasters, proud, blasphemers, disobedient to parents, unthankful, unholy, without natural affection, trucebreakers, false accusers, incontinent, fierce, despisers of those that are good, traitors, heady, high-minded, lovers of pleasures more than lovers of God' (vv. 1-4).

What an accurate description of life today! And that is what the Bible teaches! Not that the world is going to get better and better, but that it is going to be a place of sin and trouble and strife and evil. The Book of Revelation in particular emphasizes this teaching. It is a book which has been speaking to Christian people from the very beginning of our era, teaching every generation of Christians that we are set in a world where we are surrounded by powerful enemies which are compared to various beasts. Their activities are not confined to the future, they have already begun. They may come in still worse forms, but they have always been here. Christian people have suffered at the hands of the State, they have been caused to suffer by certain travesties of the Church, where the Church has formed an alliance with the State and has become worldly. All these powers have been manifest throughout the running centuries. This Book of Revelation is a book that speaks to every generation of Christians and will go on doing so right until the end. In other words, there is no false optimism here, there is no teaching here of some kind of evolution or gradual progress, a gradual improvement in the state and condition of the world. That is not the comfort that is given to us. It has often been given (has it not?) in the name of the Church and of Christianity; a kind of false optimism has been preached. But it is not found in the Book of Revelation; it is not found in Romans; or anywhere else in the parallel statements in Scripture.

So we move on to a further negative. There is no call here to Christians to try to change the conditions or to improve them. This is another very important point; and it is a crucial issue at the present time. The Apostle says that there is suffering in this life for the Christian, but he does not therefore exhort the Christians to band themselves together, and to rise up and try to do something to lessen the sufferings. Read the paragraph carefully, and you will not find a word to that effect; nor will you find it anywhere else in the New Testament. I would emphasize this. What the Bible teaches on the matter is found in the 13th chapter of this Epistle where Paul puts it thus: 'Let every soul be subject unto the higher powers. For there is no power but of God: the powers that be are ordained of God. Whosoever therefore resisteth the power, resisteth the ordinance of God: and they that resist shall receive to themselves damnation. For rulers are not a terror to good works, but to the evil. Wilt thou then not be afraid of the power? Do that which is good, and thou shalt have praise of the same: For he is the minister of God to thee for good. But if thou do that which is evil, be afraid; for he beareth not the sword in vain: for he is the minister of God, a revenger to execute wrath upon him that doeth evil. Wherefore ye must needs be subject, not only for wrath, but also for conscience sake.'

In other words it comes to this. The Christian is to be law-abiding. As a citizen he is to play his part, not only in keeping and observing the laws and the rules and regulations, but even in formulating them and in bringing them into being. But what I am anxious to emphasize is that he must not believe that by means of legislation, or by any similar kind of activity, he can get rid of the causes of suffering.

This is a crucial issue, it seems to me, at the present time. There are many good Christian people who seem to fall into error at this point. They say that Christianity is the only hope of the world in the sense that it alone can lead the nations to reform the world and life in general. Some of them believe that Christian witness and testimony, for example, can persuade governments to abolish the making of bombs. Some teach that, if one nation can be persuaded to act in that way, all the others will be so astonished at this moral gesture that they will proceed to destroy their bombs also, and so the world will be rid of bombs and perhaps rid of war altogether. But that is not only not Christian teaching, it is a blank denial of Christian teaching. The matter is perfectly clear.

There are others who express themselves in the following way. They say that the business of Christianity is to have a moral influence upon the rulers of the world, and that if we but exercise that influence in the right way, and organize accordingly, we can persuade people to put an end to the causes of our sufferings. I say once more that there is no such teaching in Scripture. The Apostle does not exhort Christians to band themselves together, to send a petition to the Roman Emperor, or to the seat of power anywhere else, in order to try to influence the factors that produce the suffering. Christian teaching never speaks thus; there is nothing of that kind in the whole of the Bible. We are to be law-abiding, but if we believe that the function of Christianity is to abolish the causes of suffering, then I say we are actually denying the very teaching that is before us. It is not here at all. Christianity is not a movement for world reform. The Bible is quite explicit about this. As I have already quoted, 'there will be wars, and rumours of wars'. 'Evil men will wax worse and worse.' The time of the end is going to be so terrible that our Lord asked the question, 'When the Son of man cometh, shall he find the faith on the earth?' (Luke 18: 8). And yet, in the

[20]

name of Christianity some people say that the chief business of Christianity is to do away with all trouble, and that if we but band ourselves together we can achieve success. But this involves a denial of the whole programme of God, as we shall see.

We move on to the fifth and last negative. What, then, are we exhorted to do in the light of all that I have said? The answer is not merely resignation. Many have deduced that, but it is a false deduction. They say: Ah well, in view of the picture you are painting of world history, and of the relationship of Christianity to it, we suppose your teaching is that we have nothing to do but just to put up with things; we have to resign ourselves to our fate; we have to say that in a world like this there must be suffering, that there is no purpose in making a fuss about it, or in trying to do anything about it; we have just to put up with things and get on as best we can. I answer, that such an attitude is not at all the teaching which we find here. You cannot fit resignation into the Apostle's words: 'I reckon that the sufferings of this present time are not worthy to be compared with the glory which shall be revealed in us.' That is not resignation! There is something here which makes us, as he puts it in verse 37, 'more than conquerors'. The idea of mere resignation has often entered into the thinking of the Church. People have reacted in that way. But the Apostle is positive. He is not merely advocating that we should 'put up with it'; he is not saying, as they used to say here in London during the Second World War, 'London can take it'. No, it is positive, it is triumphant, it is glorious. 'Not worthy to be compared with the glory which shall be revealed in us.' It is important, then, that we should grasp the negative characteristics of this teaching, and of the Christian's attitude towards suffering in this life.

Having dealt with the negatives I move on to consider the positive characteristics of Paul's teaching. We must be clear about the principles before we come to the details. The general positive characteristics of the teaching are clear. The first is that it is utterly and absolutely unique. It is the only teaching in the world that faces the problem in this particular way and manner. There is literally no other teaching that faces it as this does. Think of the teaching of Stoicism which was so popular when the Apostle was writing his Epistle. Stoicism is entirely negative, it is a resignation without hope; whereas this is positive, triumphant, glorious. Not only is Paul's teaching not Stoicism, it is not Buddhism. Buddhism is becoming popular; it is increasing in this country, and increasing by leaps and bounds in parts of India. It is the official religion in Ceylon; it is increasing in many parts of the world: people are turning to Buddhism. Why? Because of the state of the world! The suffering and the tribulations that abound make people turn to it. But what does Buddhism teach? Ultimately it is nothing but escapism. It also is entirely negative. It is without hope; it is thoroughly pessimistic. We shall have to be careful to draw the distinction between the element of pessimism in the Christian teaching and the complete and unmixed pessimism in Stoicism and in Buddhism, and Hinduism, any one of the so-called great religions of the world. Every one of them is hope-less. They think that matter is evil, and our only hope, therefore, is that we escape from matter. Some of them tell us that it may involve a number of reincarnations; that we purge a certain amount of evil away each time we reappear and at last we become merged and lost into the Absolute in a kind of Nirvana. But that is the most hopeless, pessimistic and discouraging view imaginable. It is the opposite of Paul's teaching.

The same is the case with other forms of teaching. Some people are just sheer fatalists. Some will recall how that was expressed during the last war – 'If your name is written on that bomb, it's for you.' There it is, don't think about it, don't bother about it, don't worry: if it is 'for you', you will 'get it'. Fatalism! That is not the teaching that Paul gives us; he speaks far otherwise. Again, consider the so-called great philosophies of today. Ask those who follow the late Bertrand Russell what hope they have to give you. He taught that there is really no case at all for hope; all he hoped is that the evils to come could be postponed for a while. He thought that mankind is mad, that the world is mad. He hoped that we can make it a little more tolerable for the time being. But if we fail to persuade governments to stop doing certain things then there is no hope at all, and when we die, of course it is the end. No hope whatsoever! And the same is true of others, whether they be pure philosophers, as Bertrand Russell was, or are scientific philosophers and humanists, as others of them are; they have no hope to give us, none at all.

All we can do, they say, is to try to stave evil off, and if we do not succeed there is nothing left. The cults, of course, have no hope at all; they just deliberately teach you to fool yourself, to make yourself persuade yourself that you are happy in spite of what is happening – a philosophy of 'pull down the blinds, forget about it all'. The pity is that there are so many Christian people who do something of this kind. They regard their church as simply a place into which you escape to forget your troubles for a little while. But that is not what Paul teaches in this 8th chapter of Romans. His is unique teaching; nothing else in the world puts before us the teaching we find here.

The second general point is that Paul's unique teaching is something that is deduced from the whole of Christian teaching. This is the significant and the interesting and differentiating aspect of it. The teaching of the Apostle with regard to suffering is a deduction from everything that he has been saying prior to this in this great Epistle. He states it plainly in the words, 'For I reckon'. Take note of his word – 'reckon'. It is important that we should give it its true meaning, for we use this word very often in a wrong way. A man says, 'You know I reckon that So-and-so . . .' He means, 'I am of the opinion'. That is not what the Apostle means by 'reckon'. We must return to the older meaning. The word 'reckon' means that you arrive at a conclusion, at a deduction, by a process of logical thinking and reasoning. We have already met with the word in chapter 6 verse 11, and we then emphasized it. 'Likewise reckon ye also yourselves to be dead indeed unto sin, but alive unto God through Jesus Christ our Lord.' We emphasized that it does not mean that you persuade yourself of something that is not true. It means, rather, realize that if you are 'in Christ', then when He died you died, when He rose you rose. To reckon means to reason a thing out, and in the light of all that has been said, to arrive at a deduction and conclusion. So Paul says, 'I reckon'.

The importance of this should be obvious. If a Christian is suffering, Paul's teaching does not merely administer to him a general word of comfort and of good cheer, telling him that all is well, that things are not as bad as he thinks the yare, and that they must get better after a while, that the clouds cannot persist for ever, and there is always a silver lining! That kind of teaching is often presented in the name of Christianity, a mixture of psychology and suggestion treatment. But it is not Christianity at all! 'I reckon', says the Apostle; I am drawing this deduction; this is the inevitable logical conclusion that I come to as the result of working my way through all the great doctrines of the Faith. And if we are to know truly Christian comfort in our suffering we must do exactly the same. In other words, we are entitled to say that any Christian who is unhappy because of suffering, or who is guilty of any of the things I have mentioned under my negative headings, is found in such a condition for one reason only, namely, that he has not been thinking clearly. The business of preaching is not merely to make the hearer feel a little happier while he is listening or while he is singing particular hymns; it is not meant to be a way of producing an atmosphere of comfort. If I do that I am a quack, and am a very false friend indeed. No, the business of preaching is to teach you to think. We may have to be severe, to chastise you, and to show you that your thinking has been altogether wrong. And not only so, but also to show you that you have not grasped the doctrines, because the comfort that is given by them is a deduction drawn as the result of working them out for yourselves.

The next point is that the teaching is obviously only for Christian people. Here again is a most important proposition. The Apostle says, 'I reckon that the sufferings of this present time are not worthy to be compared with the glory which shall be revealed in us.' Who are included in the 'us'? Everyone in the world? It is only Christian people; the Apostle and other Christians. This matter is entirely confined to 'I' and 'us', to Christian people. It has nothing whatever to say to people who are not Christian. There surely should be no difficulty about this, for it is a matter of reckoning and of deducing on the part of believers. If I, a believer, arrive at my comfort, at that which enables me to go on in spite of my suffering, as the result of this logical process of working out the doctrine, obviously the man who does not believe the doctrine cannot do the reckoning. That is plain matter of fact. The Bible has no comfort whatsoever to give to people who are not Christians – none at all; indeed the exact opposite. The Bible has nothing to say to such people except to warn them to flee from 'the wrath to come'. It tells them that the sufferings of this present hour are not worthy to be compared with the sufferings they are going to endure, that these are but a foretaste of what is coming to them, that the account of the Flood, the destruction of Sodom and Gomorrah, and all similar calamities are but faint pictures of the suffering that is going to come to those who do not belong to the Lord Jesus Christ. There is no comfort here for an unbeliever – none at all! Before a man can get this comfort he has to be a believer; necessarily so, because, as I say, it is a matter of 'reckoning'.

In other words, if we are not clear about the doctrine that we have been considering so far in this Epistle to the Romans we shall not be able to follow the Apostle when he says 'For I reckon'. This is how I face it, he says, this is my way of approaching it. He links up the problem of suffering with all that has gone before from the very first verse in the Epistle. This means that we have to be clear about the whole doctrine of God and the whole purpose of God in and through our blessed Lord and Saviour Jesus Christ. If we do not believe all that is written, there is no comfort for us. And the Apostle, of course, has been working it out for us. He started doing so at the very beginning. The Epistle to the Romans was written to believers: 'Paul, a servant of Jesus Christ, called to be an apostle, separated unto the gospel of God, which he had promised afore by his prophets in the holy scriptures, concerning his Son Jesus Christ our Lord, which was made of the seed of David according to the flesh; and declared to be the Son of God with power, according to the spirit of holiness, by the resurrection from the dead.' If a man does not believe that in chapter 1, this passage in chapter 8 has nothing to say to him. There is no comfort for him at all; it will be nonsense to him. The Epistle speaks only to Christians. It speaks to those who, believing in God, have accepted the revelation which we have in the Bible of God's purpose with regard to this world and all who are in it. It assumes a basic acceptance of the revelation that God had a plan 'before the foundation of the world' with respect to this world and its peoples. In the Old Testament you find God doing two things. He begins to put the plan into operation and into practice, and also gives promises, prophecies and indications of still greater things that He intends to do. The Old Testament is the account of God calling a people unto Himself, making a people, adding to the people. Then, too, there are wonderful prophecies of the Messiah, the Deliverer who was to come, through whom God should do the greatest thing of all. When you turn to the New Testament you read: 'When the fulness·of the time was come, God sent forth his Son, made of a woman, made under the law, to redeem them that were under the law.' Such is the doctrine, and such is what we have been considering in this Epistle: 'Jesus Christ, the Son of God, made of the seed of David according to the flesh, and declared to be the Son of God with power, according to the spirit of holiness, by the resurrection from the dead.' The gospel includes all He did, all He taught, but supremely His death. 'God hath set him forth as a propitiation through faith in his blood' (Rom. 3: 25). That is God's way of righteousness.

It is only people who believe these truths who can derive the promised comfort from them. Failure to see and to realize this causes endless confusion. People in trouble try this philosophy and that cult but are still miserable. Then they say, 'I wonder whether the Christian church can help me?' And they come to the church; all they want is a ministry of comfort, a pleasing, soothing atmosphere. They want a bright service, a spice of entertainment, something to help them, something to soothe and comfort them. Suddenly they are confronted by a man standing in a pulpit who preaches about a holy God who hates sin and who is full of wrath against sin. And they say; 'Things were bad enough already; this is but making it worse. I wanted some comfort.' But that is the answer of the gospel; there is no comfort except to those who are in Christ Jesus. There is no comfort except to those who believe that Jesus is the Son of God, that He died to make atonement for our sins, that He was buried, that He literally rose triumphant o'er the grave, having conquered the last enemy, and that He has ascended through the heavens. If you do not believe that, this passage has nothing to say to you. 'I reckon' – I deduce logically from all that has gone before. This is the only conclusion at which I can arrive in the light of the doctrines I have been laying before you. That is what the Apostle is really saying.

This at once introduces us to the whole method of living the Christian life. It is not something that suddenly comes to you, it is not merely a feeling, it is not something you 'catch' as it were. Christianity is not 'a spirit that you catch'. Christianity is a faith which you believe and experience; and which you then reason out. You 'reckon', you deduce logically. And if you fail to do so, you have got something else. Is this principle clear? It is the most important characteristic of this teaching. This is the introduction to the details to which we shall come. What the Apostle is saying in effect is: In the light of the doctrine, the propositions we have already agreed upon, I deduce the following points: one, two, three and four. But it is no use looking at 'one, two, three and four' unless we realize what we are doing. This can be emphasized in the form of a question. How do you react to suffering? How have you done so in the past? What do you do with yourself when you are suffering, and when the devil comes and – coward as he is – takes advantage of you when you are ill or suffering in some other form? How do you deal with him when he hurls various insinuations at you? Do you just try to shake him off, or do you take up a book and read, or play the piano, or sing – is that your method? Up to a point there may be some value in such things, but that is not the truly Christian method. The way to deal with him is to think, to reason, to argue logically, to work out the doctrines you believe, and then you say 'I reckon'. 'This is a conclusion I arrive at.' That is the way to deal with the devil. It is the only way. It is the only way, likewise, to deal with sufferings and trials and tribulations. Here, then, we have a teaching which is unique, which is only for Christian believers, and which is always the result of belief in and certainty concerning the great fundamental doctrines of the Christian Faith.

Three

*

For I reckon that the sufferings of this present time are not worthy to be compared with the glory which shall be revealed in us.

Romans 8: 18

We come now to the outworking of the Apostle's argument concerning suffering; that is to say, we are going to watch him as he moves from step to step, and from point to point, in order that he may arrive at the conclusion which he states in this verse. It is interesting, once more, to notice his style. He very often states the conclusion first, and then tells us how he arrives at it. All his arguments and his reasons in detail are to be found in this particular paragraph. I repeat that there is surely nothing more important for us as Christian people at this present time than this very teaching. With the world as it is, and all the possibilities that are confronting us, what can be more important for us than to know exactly how to face the trials and troubles, tribulations and sufferings that are the lot of God's people while in this life?

I would remind you again that these sufferings, some of them at least, are peculiar to Christians. In certain respects only a Christian can suffer. For instance, no one is ever going to suffer persecution for Christ's sake if he is not a Christian. But there are other and larger forms of suffering which the Christian shares with all others. The Apostle in verse 17 is, I believe, dealing with the peculiar sufferings of the Christian, but I think that later on we shall find that he has other kinds of suffering also in mind. Here, then, are the propositions, the statements of the doctrine from which the Apostle is able to arrive at his conclusion.

Let us look at it in this way. What is it that enables a man in the midst of sufferings and trials, tribulations and disappointments, and everything that a Christian is liable to experience in a world like this, that enables him to say in the midst of it all, and while it is all taking place, 'I reckon that the sufferings of this present time are not worthy to be compared with the glory which shall be revealed in us'? What gives him this note of triumph? What is it that enables him – to use the language of the Apostle later in verse 37 – to be 'more than conquerors [in all these things] through him that loved us'?

The first answer is that the Apostle has a correct view of time and of his life in this world. Notice that he says: 'I reckon that the sufferings of this *present time* are not worthy to be compared with the glory which *shall be* revealed.' Here are the two points which enable us to understand the Christian view of time. The whole trouble with the man who is not a Christian, that is, the worldly man, is that to him this present life and this world are the only life and the only world. He knows nothing except what can be called chronological time, time as measured by the clock or by the calendar. His whole outlook is circumscribed entirely by the temporal, by the present, by the seen, and by the visible; and to him there is no division of time at all. His view is that you come into this world, you live in it, and you go out of it. That is all he knows about time. But that is not the view of the Christian; and it is because of this that the Christian is able to face suffering in a way that no one else can. It is good to put it in terms of the contrast between the Christian and the non-Christian. When things go wrong with the non-Christian he has nothing to fall back upon; he has no comfort and no consolation; and he has nothing to look forward to. All he can do is to hope that these things will improve while he is still here; but if they do not seem to be doing so then he is entirely without comfort. As the Apostle puts it in writing to the Ephesians in the 2nd chapter, verse 12, 'That at that time ye were without hope' – without hope! – 'and without God in the world'. The non-Christian has nothing to comfort him now, he has nothing to look forward to. That is, very largely, because he is ignorant of this Christian teaching with respect to time.

What is that teaching? The Christian is aware of a division of time. That is not strictly accurate, as we shall see in a moment, and yet it is a good way of looking at it at first. The Christian talks about 'this present time' and then something which lies beyond it. We shall see that what does lie beyond it does not belong to time at all; but the point is that the Christian recognizes a division which the non-Christian does not.

Take the term 'present time'. It is important for us to realize that it does not mean 'for the time being'. You must not translate this verse as follows: 'For I reckon that the sufferings that I am enduring for the time being are not worthy to be compared with the glory which shall be revealed in us.' It does not mean 'the time being' only. What then does it mean? It really means 'this present age', 'this whole age in which we live', 'this present existence'. We talk about 'the time being'. We say 'things are not too well with me for the time being', by which we mean, 'I hope that tomorrow or some time later they will be better'. It is a little division which we make in time. That is not what we have here at all. The division here is made by the end of time. 'The present time' is this age, in which we are now living, between the resurrection of the Lord Jesus Christ and His coming again. 'This present time' here means 'this present age'. The Apostle is not thinking of his death only, he is not just saying, 'the sufferings that I am enduring while I am still alive and which will go on until I die are not worthy to be compared with the glory which shall be revealed'. That is not it at all. The 'present time' does not end at death; the present time ends when 'the age to come' shall come in.

Those who are truly familiar with their Bible will recognize at once that here is a principle of division and of teaching that is found running right through the Bible. It is found in the Old Testament as well as in the New. In the Old Testament they very largely lived in the hope of that age that was coming when the Messiah would appear. They regarded their own age as a preparatory period, and looked forward to another age that was to come. The Lord Jesus Christ came, and His people then knew that that age to come to which the Old Testament people were looking forward, had already come. But they, in turn, were looking forward to something even beyond this. That is what the Apostle has in his mind. You will find this almost everywhere in the Bible, and I must emphasize it, because if we are not right on this time factor we shall never know the particular comfort and consolation of the Scriptures. We are living in this 'present age' but as Christian people we know that it is not the only age. We know of something beyond time, we have something to look forward to; and it is only in the light of this teaching that we are able to rejoice in trials and sufferings.

This can be stated also in the form of a second principle. The Christian not only has a correct view of time, and of life in this world, he has grasped and knows something about the teaching of the Scripture with regard to that coming age. This is introduced to us by the Apostle in the phrase 'shall be revealed'. Our entire thinking must be governed by those two points. One focus is this 'present time'; the other is 'shall be revealed'. 'The sufferings of this present time are not worthy to be compared with the glory which shall be revealed in us.'

Let us examine this. The very word 'revealed' really explains what the Apostle has in mind. This is the apocalypse. This is a reference to that which is to come. It is the beginning of the age which is to come. This is the great event to which the whole of the Bible looks forward. It does so, as the Apostle goes on to explain to us, because of what happened to the world and to man as the result of the Fall, because of the misery, failure, sin and shame that came in. God's first promise to mankind after the Fall was that there should be an ultimate restoration. 'The seed of the woman shall bruise the serpent's head' (Genesis 3: 15). That is the great promise, and the whole of the Bible, Old Testament and New Testament, looks forward to its fulfilment, introduced as it will be by the Second Coming of our Lord and Saviour Jesus Christ. That is the event of all events. Anyone who is a Christian should be looking forward to it. It is the great theme that runs through the Bible from beginning to end. It is interesting to note that this is the first time it has been mentioned in this particular Epistle. The Apostle gave us a hint of it in the second verse of chapter 5 where he says, 'We rejoice in hope of the glory of God'. But it was no more than a hint; it was not stated explicitly. But here he puts it plainly and clearly before us. In the remainder of this chapter it is his major theme, and he will work it out and develop it. He does the same thing at the end of chapter 11 where he says it once more. And again at the end of chapter 13 where he says, 'Our salvation is nearer than when we believed. The night is far spent, the day is at hand.' That is what is meant by 'the glory which shall be revealed in us'.

This is such an important part of New Testament teaching,

and such a vital, essential part of the comfort and consolation that the Christian alone can know and experience and enjoy, that I must turn aside for a moment to show how constantly the Scriptures emphasize this very thing. Let us look at some examples. Take the teaching of our Lord Himself in chapter 19 of the Gospel according to St Matthew, verses 27 and 28: 'Then answered Peter and said unto him, Behold, we have forsaken all, and followed thee; what shall we have therefore? And Jesus said unto them, Verily I say unto you, That ye which have followed me, in the regeneration when the Son of man shall sit in the throne of his glory, ye also shall sit upon twelve thrones, judging the twelve tribes of Israel.' He talks about this 'regeneration' when the Son of man shall come, when everything will be renovated and renewed. That is 'the glory that is to be revealed'. Then you find the Lord expressing the same idea in the whole of the 24th and 25th chapters of the Gospel according to Matthew and the parallel passages in Mark 13 and Luke 21. In all these discourses our Lord was preparing His people. He has told them that in the world they 'shall have tribulation'; He has warned them not to expect an easy time in this life. What He does hold before them is this glory which is coming; and He keeps on holding it before them. Take John 14: 1: 'Let not your heart be troubled: ye believe in God, believe also in me. In my Father's house are many mansions: if it were not so, I would have told you. I go to prepare a place for you. And if I go and prepare a place for you, I will come again, and receive you unto myself; that where I am, there ye may be also.'

But this theme is not confined to the Gospels. It is found in the Acts of the Apostles chapter 1, verse 11. Two men stood by the Apostles, who were looking at our Lord ascending to heaven, and said, 'Ye men of Galilee, why stand ye gazing up into heaven? this same Jesus, which is taken up from you into heaven, shall so come in like manner as ye have seen him go into heaven.' He will come again, they said, so do not stand here disconsolate and amazed; go about your work. Another striking statement of it is found in the 3rd chapter of Acts where the Apostle Peter is preaching after the man at the Beautiful Gate of the temple had been healed. In applying his message Peter says in verse 19: 'Repent ye, therefore, and be converted, that your sins may be blotted out, when the times of refreshing shall come from the presence of the Lord: and he shall send Jesus Christ, which before was preached unto you: whom the heaven must receive until the times of restitution of all things, which God hath spoken by the mouth of all his holy prophets since the world began.' It has been said by the prophets from the beginning, says Peter. There is to be this great time, this great event of the 'restitution of all things'. The whole creation is moving towards this, and, as we shall see, is looking and waiting for it. The Apostle Paul preaches the same message in Athens, as the account in the 17th chapter of Acts shews. He warns them that 'a day is coming', this 'day of Christ', this 'day of the Lord', this 'day of judgment'. His words refer to 'the glory which shall be revealed'.

Look at the same matter in the First Epistle to the Corinthians. The Apostle mentions it at the very beginning because it is such a vital doctrine. In chapter 1 verse 7 we read: 'Ye come behind in no gift; waiting for the coming of our Lord Jesus Christ: who shall also confirm you unto the end, that ye may be blameless in the day of our Lord Jesus Christ.' In connection with the Communion Service he teaches those Christians that they are to partake of the bread and the wine regularly because in doing so 'you declare the Lord's death until he come' (1 Corinthians 11: 26). They are to go on doing that in this 'present time', in this 'present age', 'until he come'. The 15th chapter of First Corinthians is obviously devoted entirely to this selfsame thing: 'The trumpet shall sound, and the dead shall be raised', and He shall appear. It is the one theme. We find another notable example in 1 Corinthians 16, verse 22: 'If any man love not the Lord Jesus Christ, let him be Anathema, Maranatha.' Those early Christians were enduring terrible persecution, they had bitter enemies, many of them were being put to death; their houses were being destroyed, they were being robbed of their goods, but the word that they uttered as they met one another was 'Maranatha', 'The Lord cometh'. All that was happening to them was always regarded in the light of that event: the end of this present time, the coming age when the Lord has come! 'Maranatha!' In the Second Epistle to the Corinthians, chapters 4 and 5, there is precisely the same teaching.

In the Epistle to the Ephesians, in the 10th verse of chapter 1, Paul says that the ultimate object of God's plan is, 'that in the dispensation of the fulness of the times, he might gather together in one all things in Christ, both which are in heaven and which are on earth; even in him'. This 'gathering together' really means 'head up together'. Everything in heaven and in earth is going to be 'headed up together' in Him in this great future age. All that God has purposed leads to that ultimate conclusion. We are not to stop with forgiveness and justification, nor even with sanctification. We are to look forward to this glory which is yet to be revealed. We find exactly the same teaching in the 14th verse of this same chapter where Paul teaches that the Holy Spirit is not only the seal of the promise, but also 'the earnest of our inheritance until the redemption of the purchased possession'. The 'purchased possession' will be redeemed when He comes. We now have 'the earnest of the Spirit' to uphold us until then; we are given a foretaste of the first-fruits of our great inheritance. Again, look at Philippians 1: 6: 'Being confident of this very thing, that he which hath begun a good work in you will perform it until the day of Jesus Christ.' Paul does not say 'as long as you live in this world' but 'until the day of Jesus Christ'. He says it again in Philippians 3, verses 20 and 21: 'Our conversation is in heaven; from whence also we look for the Saviour, the Lord Jesus Christ.'

In the Epistle to the Colossians, 1st chapter, verses 21 and 22, we read: 'You . . . hath he reconciled in the body of his flesh through death, to present you holy and unblameable and unreproveable in his sight.' Then later the Apostle goes on to say: 'To whom God would make known what is the riches of the glory of this mystery among the Gentiles; which is Christ in you, the hope of glory.' Then in Colossians 3: 4: 'When Christ, who is our life, shall appear, then shall ye also appear with him in glory.' In the First Epistle to the Thessalonians, chapter 1 verse 10, we read: 'And to wait for his Son from heaven, even Jesus whom he raised from the dead.' Again, the 4th and 5th chapters of that Epistle are mainly devoted to that theme. The 1st and 2nd chapters of 2 Thessalonians are still concerned with this 'day of the Lord Jesus Christ', this 'day of the Lord'. Some of the early Christians were confused about this, so he desires to put them right, because this is the one thing which enables a Christian to rejoice even in the midst of his tribulations.

The same teaching is found in the Pastoral Epistles. In 1 Timothy 6: 14: 'That thou keep this commandment without spot, unrebukable, until the appearing of our Lord Jesus Christ, which in his times he shall show, who is the blessed and only Potentate, the King of kings, and Lord of lords.' Again in the 19th verse of that chapter, in telling rich men how to behave themselves Paul says, 'Laying up in store for themselves a good foundation against the time to come, that they may lay hold on eternal life'. In the Second Epistle to Timothy, chapter 1 verse 12, he writes: 'For the which cause I also suffer these things; nevertheless I am not ashamed: for I know whom I have believed, and am persuaded that he is able to keep that which I have committed unto him against that day.' It is always 'that day'. In the last verse of that same chapter: 'The Lord grant unto him [Onesiphorus] that he may find mercy of the Lord in that day.' This man had been kind to Paul in prison and he can wish him nothing better than that. Again in the 4th chapter of Paul's last Epistle, the Second Epistle to Timothy, he writes: 'I charge thee therefore before God, and the Lord Jesus Christ, who shall judge the quick and the dead at his appearing and his kingdom' (v. 1). Everything is to be done in the light of this great 'day'. It encourages us, it warns us. The Apostle says precisely the same thing to Titus in the 1st chapter, verse 2: 'In hope of eternal life, which God, that cannot lie, promised before the world began, but hath in due times manifested his word through preaching, which is committed unto me according to the commandment of God our Saviour.' In the 2nd chapter of that Epistle, beginning at verse 11, we find: 'For the grace of God that bringeth salvation hath appeared to all men, teaching us that, denying ungodliness and worldly lusts, we should live soberly, righteously, and godly, in this present world: looking for that blessed hope and the appearing of the glory of the great God and our Saviour Jesus Christ; who gave himself for us.' We are to live in this present life, this present world, looking for 'the glorious appearing' or 'the appearing of the glory' of our Lord and Saviour Jesus Christ.

This teaching, however, is not confined to the writings of the Apostle Paul. In Hebrews 9: 28: 'So Christ was once offered to bear the sins of many; and unto them that look for him shall he appear the second time apart from sin unto salvation.' 'Salvation', there, means this glory, this glorification which is to come. James, in chapter 1 verse 12 of his Epistle, writes: 'Blessed is the man that endureth temptation: for when he is tried, he shall receive the crown of life, which the Lord hath promised to them that love him.' Notice also chapter 5 verse 7, where he is offering comfort to Christians who were suffering, and says: 'Be patient, therefore, brethren, unto the coming of the Lord. Behold, the husbandman waiteth for the precious fruit of the earth, and hath long patience for it, until he receive the early and latter rain. Be ye also patient; stablish your hearts: for the coming of the Lord draweth nigh.' In the Epistles of Peter you will find that it is his great theme in many ways. 1 Peter 1: 3–5 says: 'Blessed be the God and Father of our Lord Jesus Christ, which according to his abundant mercy hath begotten us again unto a lively hope by the resurrection of Jesus Christ from the dead, to an inheritance incorruptible, and undefiled, and that fadeth not away, reserved in heaven for you, who are kept by the power of God through faith unto salvation ready to be revealed at the last time.' He continues, 'Wherein ye greatly rejoice, though now for a season, if need be, ye are in heaviness through manifold temptations: That the trial of your faith, being much more precious than of gold that perisheth, though it be tried with fire, might be found unto praise and honour and glory at the appearing of Jesus Christ'. Verse 13 continues the theme: 'Wherefore gird up the loins of your mind, be sober, and hope to the end for the grace that is to be brought unto you at the revelation of Jesus Christ.' In the 4th chapter of that First Epistle, verse 7, Peter writes: 'The end of all things is at hand: be ye therefore sober, and watch unto prayer.' Verse 13: 'Rejoice, inasmuch as you are partakers of Christ's sufferings; that, when his glory shall be revealed, ye may be glad also with exceeding joy.' All these Apostles say the same thing. They keep on repeating it, and they all say it in almost identical language. Peter, again, in chapter 5 of that First Epistle says in verse 1: 'The elders which are among you I exhort, who am also an elder, and a witness of the sufferings of Christ, and also a partaker of the glory that shall be revealed'; and in verse 4: 'When the chief Shepherd shall appear, ye shall receive a crown of glory that fadeth not away'; and again in verse 10: 'But the God of all grace, who hath called us unto his eternal glory by Christ Jesus, after that ye have suffered a while, make you perfect, stablish, strengthen, settle you.' The Second Epistle of Peter is largely devoted to this theme, and especially the 3rd chapter which goes into it in detail.

You find the same theme also in the First Epistle of John, chapter 2, verse 28. Also in chapter 3 verses 1-3: 'Beloved, now are we the sons of God, and it doth not yet appear what we shall be: but we know that when he shall appear, we shall be like him; for we shall see him as he is.' See it there in all its glory once more. And obviously the Book of Revelation, the last book in the Bible, is devoted entirely to it. The cry at the end is this, 'Even so, come, Lord Jesus'. Christians are crying out for Him, they are looking forward to His coming, and with great longing they cry out 'Even so, come, Lord Jesus'.

It is clear that this 'glory which shall be revealed in us' will be ushered in by the Second Coming, the reappearance and manifestation of our Lord and Saviour Jesus Christ. The angels said to the disciples on Mount Olivet: 'Even as he has gone he will come back again.' He will come back bodily, He will come back visibly. He will not come back merely as an appearance; He will come back in His glorified body, and 'every eye shall see him'. He will be visible, openly visible. The Word implies the personal, visible, bodily return of our Lord and Saviour Jesus Christ. What will that usher in? It will be the end of 'this present time', this present age. Only a Christian can truly understand history. All others seem to think that history is endless, they think that it has always been, and that it will go on for ever. But that is not the teaching of the Bible which tells us that God made the world and that He started the time process. He created this present world. But, alas, the Fall took place. From the moment of the Fall you have 'this present world'. But the Bible teaches that there will be an end to that, and that the day which is coming, 'the day of the Lord', will be the end of time. Time will be finished, 'time will be no more'; the present age, the present time will have come to an end, and eternity will be ushered in, this endless glorious age which is to come.

The Apostle says, 'I reckon that the sufferings of this present time are not worthy to be compared with the glory which shall be revealed in us'. He is saying that in a sense the glory is already there. It is not something that is to be made, it is already in existence. He is saying that when this great day comes the glory that is already there will be revealed. To use an obvious comparison, it is exactly as if you were sitting in a theatre and you see nothing but curtains. You have no idea as to what is behind the curtains. But there is something there; and suddenly the curtain goes up, or is drawn aside, and you find yourself looking at a great sight. That is the idea. It is not to be created, it is not something that is yet to be produced; the glory is there. What will happen is that this glory will be 'revealed', it will be 'made manifest', it will be 'shown'. Our Lord Himself taught this very thing in Matthew 25, verse 34: 'Then shall the King say unto them on his right hand, Come, ye blessed of my Father, inherit the kingdom prepared for you from the foundation of the world.' The Kingdom is already there, it has been prepared for us from the foundation of the world. The 'new Jerusalem' is there, and it will come down, it will 'descend out of heaven'. So it is not something that is going to be created, it is something that is already in existence. It will be revealed.

The world, of course, knows nothing about this. It does not believe it, it ridicules it. 'Ah,' it says, 'you Christians believe in some "pie-in-the-sky". It is the dope of the people.' This teaching is ridiculed, is hated, is dismissed; the world knows nothing at all about it. What is the position of the Christian? We do not know much about it, but we believe and must believe in it. It is an essential part of our gospel. This, as our abundant quotations have shown, is what the early Christians were looking forward to.

The Apostle Paul was certainly in a privileged position with respect to this matter. It is not surprising that he talks about the glory that is going to be revealed to us. He had had glimpses of that glory. Remember what happened to him on the road to Damascus. He saw the risen Lord in His glory! He saw Him as He is now! He saw the glory of the Lord! And he never forgot it. That was the one thing to which he looked forward. To see Him again, and to see Him permanently! He had had a glimpse of the glory. He tells us in 2 Corinthians 12 of a similar kind of experience he had had later: 'I knew a man in Christ above fourteen years ago, (whether in the body, I cannot tell; or whether out of the body, I cannot tell: God knoweth;) such an one caught up to the third heaven. And I knew such a man, (whether in the body, or out of the body, I cannot tell: God knoweth;) how that he was caught up into paradise, and heard unspeakable words, which it is not lawful for a man to utter. Of such an one will I glory'. In other words he had been given a preview of this glory, so he knows that it is there, and so he says that it will in due time be revealed. The curtains will be drawn back and then we shall see it. Having had these experiences he passes on the knowledge to us; and we, knowing that these are authentic experiences, and that he is a divinely inspired apostle, believe the message. And we do so by faith! 'We walk by faith, not by sight.' We have not yet seen, but, thank God, we not only believe this, but God in His grace gives us intimations of it through the medium of 'the witness of the Spirit', and the filial spirit within us. These are intimations of the glory, and they are enough to make us certain and sure. The Holy Spirit 'witnesses' this to us; the Holy Spirit 'seals' it to us; the Holy Spirit is the 'earnest' of it, He is the first instalment of the glory itself. So we know something about this glory which is coming. That, says the Apostle, is what you must bear in mind as you suffer in 'this present time'.

I close by emphasizing something which one can so easily miss in this same verse. 'I reckon', he says, 'that the sufferings of this present time are not worthy to be compared with the glory which shall be revealed in us.' This old Authorized Version translation is quite good here but one of the new translations is actually better. Instead of 'revealed in us' it has, 'which is in store for us'. We must not think that we are merely to be spectators of this glory. We shall not merely have the privilege of being 'lookers on'. We are going to be partakers and sharers in it, and to be involved in it. It is going to happen to us, it is 'in us', 'the glory which shall be revealed in us', revealed 'to us-ward'. It is a glory which will be bestowed upon us and we shall actually be partakers in it. The Apostle has already told us so in verse 17: 'Heirs of God, and joint-heirs with Christ; if so be that we suffer with him, that we may be also glorified together.' Of course we shall be looking at His glory, but we shall also be partakers of it; we shall 'see him as he is', and be 'like him'.

The Apostle Peter states this perfectly in 1 Peter 5: 1 which I have already quoted: 'The elders which are among you I exhort, who am also an elder, and a witness of the sufferings of Christ, and also a partaker of the glory that shall be revealed.' By 'partaker' he means 'sharer'. 'I', says Peter, 'am not only a man who was an eye-witness of the sufferings of Christ, I am also to be a sharer of the glory that is going to be revealed.' And this is true of all of us who are Christians. It is a glory which is to be revealed 'in us'. In other words, a part of the glory which is going to be revealed to the whole cosmos is what happens to us. We shall be a part of the glory, of His glory. His people are His glory. And what He will do to us will make us a part of this mighty demonstration of His own glory when 'this present time' is finished and He, by His coming, ushers in this 'age to come' with all its indescribable glory.

Those, then, are the first postulates which the Apostle lays down, and that is where we must start. How wonderful it is! Is anything so difficult as the problem of time? Look at it in the following way. Imagine a father and mother who lost their only son in the last war. This is what they often say to each other: 'How can we go on enduring it? it seems so impossible to go on living year after year, decade after decade, time seems so long.' All they have lived for has gone, they have lost their treasure, how can they live? Time! What a burden time is when you are looking forward to something! how it seems to drag! If you are not a Christian you have no answer to that problem; you have just to resign yourself to your fate, and 'go on with it'. But that is not how the Christian looks at time. The Christian has a view which enables him to handle time as it ought to be handled. He says, 'Yes, here I am in this world. I may have to live another ten, twenty, thirty, forty, fifty, sixty, even seventy years. I look at it as a man, and in earthly terms, and it seems a terribly long time. But when I think of eternity, when I think of the glory that is coming in eternity, everything changes.' Eternity! There is no end to it! Can you think of a million years? Well, multiply that by a million, and multiply that by a million, and go on and on for ever and for ever, and there is still no end. Eternity! When you think of it, what is this life of ours? 'Brief life is here our portion' we sing in our hymn; and it is indeed so. 'What is your life?' asks James. 'It is but a vapour.' It is just like a breath, an exhalation. It is nothing in comparison with eternity. And that is how Christian teaching helps us, whatever the suffering, whatever the enduring. 'Our light affliction', says the Apostle, 'which is but for a moment.' It is but a flash as it were; we are here today and gone tomorrow. But 'The glory that shall be revealed'.

Today and tomorrow are only 'this present time', this present age, this present passing world. The great reality is the glory that is coming, the end of time, the eternal state to which we are going, the glory which 'shall be revealed', the coming age. Hold on to this idea, that we do not really belong to this present age, that 'our citizenship is in heaven'. This present world is passing, transient, temporary. 'The world to come' is the real, the permanent world. That is the one that has substance and which will endure for ever. And it is coming for certain: nothing can stop it.

Thus, then, have we looked at the first step of the argument which enables a Christian, whatever is happening to him, to say, 'I reckon that the sufferings of this present time are not worthy to be compared with the glory which shall be revealed in us'.

Four

*

For I reckon that the sufferings of this present time are not worthy to be compared with the glory which shall be revealed in us.

For the earnest expectation of the creature waiteth for the manifestation of the sons of God.

For the creature was made subject to vanity, not willingly, but by reason of him who hath subjected the same in hope.

Because the creature itself also shall be delivered from the bondage of corruption into the glorious liberty of the children of God.

For we know that the whole creation groaneth and travaileth in pain together until now.

And not only they, but ourselves also, which have the firstfruits of the Spirit, even we ourselves groan within ourselves, waiting for the adoption, to wit, the redemption of our body.

Romans 8 : 18–23

We are studying and analysing this process of 'reckoning' which the Apostle tells us he engages in as a Christian. He is able to deal with the sufferings, his trials and troubles and tribulations, indeed to be 'more than conqueror' in spite of them because he 'reckons' certain things. We are analysing his manner and method of reckoning, and what it is that he reckons. We are looking at the doctrines which, he tells us, particularly help him to endure.

The first was, as we have already seen, the Christian doctrine of time, which he divides up into this 'present time' and an age yet to come, which is 'to be revealed'. The Apostle is not simply saying that he knows that the sufferings of this present time will cease when we die. He is contrasting life in this age and life as it will be in a future age. That led us to a second doctrine concerning the glory that is to be revealed at the Second Coming and appearing of our Lord and Saviour Jesus Christ. We ended by emphasizing that the Apostle says that Christian people are not merely going to be spectators of this. It is a glory which is to be revealed 'in us', we are a part of it.

Christian faith, he tells us, takes hold of its present troubles and sufferings and problems and looks at them in the light of this glorious state of things which is to be revealed to the whole world at the Second Coming of our Lord and Saviour Jesus Christ.

Such, then, is the Apostle's method, and it is very important that we should understand it. Christianity never provides a ready-made comfort. You only enjoy the Christian comfort and consolation as you put into practice this process of 'reckoning'. It is not something that is done to you. Christianity is not like a drug which acts on you; it is not like the Roman Catholic view of the sacraments which, they say, act *ex opere operato*, which means that they act in and of themselves without your doing anything at all. Not so! It is nothing mechanical. You only get the comfort of the Christian message as you do what it tells you to do. The Apostle says, therefore, that, when he suffers, he views his sufferings in the light of this glorious event which is yet to be. The immediate result of this, he tells us, is that he finds that 'the sufferings of this present time are not worthy to be compared with the glory which shall be revealed in us'.

Let us look at his phrase, 'not worthy to be compared with'. It carries two meanings. It is a term which refers to price or value. You may have an object which you think is very valuable; but then you are shown a similar object, and the moment you see it you realize that what you already possess is comparatively worthless. I may think that my watch is very valuable; but I am shown the gold watch of another, and I realize that mine is of little value. That is part of the meaning of 'not worthy to be compared with'. It has no value at all. It may have appeared to have had some intrinsic value, but the moment you put it up against this standard it is nothing, it is valueless. You simply write off the thing which you thought before was so valuable.

But the phrase has another meaning which refers to the question of weight. One thing has no weight when you compare it with another. The Apostle uses the same idea in 2 Corinthians 4: 17: 'Our light affliction' (he means 'light in weight') 'which is but for a moment, worketh for us a far more exceeding and eternal *weight* of glory.' In other words he is saying: However heavy the load of suffering you may be carrying now, it becomes nothing when you compare it with the weight of glory that is to be yours.

This is typical of the Christian method, and at the same time it helps to bring out the very striking and remarkable contrast between the Christian method of administering comfort to sufferers and all the other agencies in the world that are trying to do the same thing. What does the world do to you when you are suffering? You have a terrible problem, you have a great weight, a great load, upon you; you are carrying a burden, you are suffering and it is most oppressive. What does the world do? It tends to say, 'Cheer up, don't be depressed; things will soon be better'. But that really does not help. It actually tends to make us feel all the worse. You say to yourself, 'It's all very well for him to say that. There is nothing wrong with him at the moment, so he dismisses my trouble lightly. If only he knew the load I am carrying he would not speak like that.'

That also is the method of the cults. They act like a drug. They endeavour to make this 'weight' appear to be lighter than it really is. They do something to your faculties, and make you less sensitive to what is happening. That is always the effect of a drug. A man who is troubled begins to drink, and as he goes on drinking the alcohol he begins to feel brighter and happier, and is no longer depressed. So the poor fellow keeps on drinking. The alcohol does not change the problem in any way, it but changes his appreciation of the facts, his reaction to the facts. He is drugging himself, he is damaging himself, and is in a kind of fool's paradise, as we call it.

But this is never the method of the Christian faith. I know that the charge often brought against it is that it is the 'dope of the people', or the 'opiate of the people', but that is a totally false charge. I admit that there have been representations of Christianity that have justified such a charge, and I accept, too, that certain people use Christianity as an opiate. But what they present is a mere travesty of Christianity. They are utterly unlike the Apostle who here teaches the genuine Christianity. Notice how he does it. He does not make light of the weight of the problem. He grants to the full that the suffering is very intense. This Apostle, of all men, does that time and again. I have already referred to 2 Corinthians chapter 4. Read what he says there about his sufferings. Start at verse 7 and go through to the end of the chapter; and you will find that he does not minimize or in any way subtract from the terrible sufferings that he had been or was enduring. He has similar lists in the 11th and 12th chapters of that same Second Epistle to the Corinthians, and in other places. He does not in any way try to minimize the actual nature, the concrete character of the sufferings. Instead we find him saying that, terrible though the sufferings are, they are nothing when viewed in the light of the glory which is yet to come.

A simple illustration will help at this point. Think of a man sitting at a table with a pair of scales before him. On one of the scales are his sufferings. The man looks at them and sees that they are very heavy. But then he puts on the other scale the very heavy weight of the glory yet to be, and what seemed so heavy before appears now to be as light as a feather. It is not that it is light in and of itself; it only becomes light in contrast with the far greater weight in the other scale pan. That is exactly what the Apostle is saying here, and it is also his teaching about this matter in all his other writings. Do not make light of sufferings. Sufferings are very real, and he is a false comforter who just says, 'Cheer up, it is soon going to be all right with you'. There is no value in such words; and we know it. Still less turn to drugs in any shape or form. Here is the answer. Be realistic, face the trouble as it is, and at its worst. Then, when you feel that you are so borne down that you cannot stand any longer, look at the other side, look at the glory that is to be revealed. And, says the Apostle, if you have a true sight of it you will come to one conclusion only, that whatever your sufferings are at this present time, they are not worthy to be compared with the glory which shall be revealed in us. That is the essence of the Christian method of administering comfort.

You will find this method in use everywhere in the Bible. Consider the argument of Hebrews chapter 11. What was the secret of a man like Abraham who had to suffer greatly? It was that he was 'looking for a city which hath foundations, whose builder and maker is God'. Look at Moses and all he had to endure. What was his secret? Was it not this, that he had his eye on 'the recompense of the reward, esteeming it better to suffer affliction with the children of God, than to enjoy the pleasures of sin for a season'? 'The recompense of the reward' which was coming! Go to the supreme example in Hebrews 12, verse 2: 'Looking unto Jesus the author and finisher of our faith; who for the joy that was set before him endured the cross, despising the shame.' It was 'the joy that was set before him' that enabled our Lord Himself to go through Gethsemane, and the agony and the shame and the suffering of the cross. He knew where He was going, and in the light of that He was able to endure. This, too, is the very way, says the Apostle here, that you as Christian people should go through life also.

It surely needs no further demonstration that what we have to be sure of, and to concentrate on as Christian people, is that we know something about the greatness of the glory that is coming. This is vital doctrine. It is the only way to be 'more than conquerors' in a life such as this. Notice that Paul takes it up with the word 'For' – 'For I reckon that the sufferings of this present time are not worthy to be compared with the glory which shall be revealed in us. *For* the earnest expectation of the creature . . . ' He is about to demonstrate to us the greatness of this coming glory. That is the purpose of the connecting word 'For'; it is an amplification of what he has said, a demonstration of the greatness of the glory which is coming. If we have but a glimpse of it, it will make us regard everything we are suffering now as not worthy to be compared with it. The greatness of the coming glory is the theme. Not only its certainty, not only its futurity, but its greatness, its magnitude, its vastness! And it is this, of course, that draws out all the great reserves of this mighty man of God and makes him surpass himself in eloquence and in the daring character of his statement.

Paul demonstrates the greatness of the glory in a most extraordinary, and what is to us a most unexpected manner. He does so by introducing his third doctrine. We have already had the Christian doctrine of Time; we have also looked at the Christian doctrine of the Last Things, of the Second Coming and the glory which it will bring. The third major doctrine is the explanation of the present state of the universe. At this present time in particular, when we consider the great tensions that are in the world as between the two sides of the 'Iron Curtain', when we view the sufferings of great communities and contemplate the whole uncertainty and precarious character of life, there is nothing more important for us than that we should be clear in our thinking as to why things are as they are. I cannot imagine anyone really having any final comfort who does not understand why the world is as it is. The most depressed people in the world today are the philosophers, because they had been so confident, and especially at the end of the last century, that the world was advancing and developing. They indulged in talk about evolution and the golden age when everything would indeed be marvellous. 'Let knowledge grow from more to more' sang Tennyson, who also saw the coming of 'The Parliament of man, the Federation of the world'. There were to be no more wars, swords were to be turned into ploughshares, and spears into pruning-hooks. And then came the 20th century and all we have experienced. It is not surprising that our philosophers are in the depth of depression. They do not understand what is happening. They have no explanation to offer. Everything has gone against what they had said, and what they had thought, and what they had hoped for. So they are left without any hope at all, because they have no explanation.

But there is an explanation; and the Apostle gives it here. He does so by making two main statements. The first is that the 'creature', the 'creation', the whole of the creation, is looking forward to this glory that is coming. The second statement tells us why the whole of creation is looking forward in that way. And in his second point he introduces to us a most remarkable doctrine, namely, the relationship between man and the whole of creation. He works that out along two lines. He says that, because of its present condition, the whole of creation is looking forward to this coming glory; and further, that in the coming glory the entire creation is destined to share.

We must examine this doctrine in detail concerning as it does the present state of the world. It is introduced as the result of Paul's saying that the world as it is now is looking forward to the glory. Then he explains why it is doing so. So let us look at the first statement of verse 19: 'The earnest expectation of the creature waiteth for the manifestation of the sons of God.' What is here meant by 'creature'? It is generally agreed that a better translation would have been 'creation' – 'The earnest expectation of the creation'. Indeed in verse 22 it is so translated: 'We know that the whole creation.' 'The earnest expectation of the whole creation waiteth for the manifestation of the sons of God.' But, here, at once a question arises. What is included in 'the whole creation'? It sounds at first as if it is a comprehensive term excluding nothing and comprising everything that God has ever

[47]

created. But that cannot possibly be the meaning, as is made clear when we note the Apostle's other expression: 'The earnest expectation of the creation.'

'Earnest expectation' is a most picturesque term. If you are interested in diction, poetic diction, poetic imagery, you will never get a more thrilling statement than this. The word the Apostle used suggests, 'An uplifted head stretching forth'. In other words it is a picture of creation stretching up its neck, lifting its head, doing its utmost to see, to have a peep of something. Then follows the word 'waiteth'. 'The earnest expectation of the creature *waiteth* for the manifestation of the sons of God.' This again is a very strong term. It means 'to wait with eager expectation'. The Apostle would not be a popular writer today! The modern pedants and purists do not like writers who throw adjectives about freely! Ah, the style must be chaste! But the Apostle did not write in that way. He is so full of his subject, and so carried away by the splendour of it all! He marvels at it all, so he talks about 'earnest expectation' and then of 'waiting with eager expectation' on top of it. He wants to express himself as vividly as he can, and language seems to fail him.

All that helps us to see what he means by 'creation'. It is 'the creation' that is anticipating the coming glory with this eagerness, and waiting and craning its neck. The expression obviously cannot include angels. It cannot include the good angels because they have not been made 'subject to vanity' as has the creation, neither are they 'groaning' as Paul says the whole creation is groaning; 'the whole creation groaneth and travaileth in pain'. That is not true of the holy angels, so they are obviously not included in the whole creation. Neither can it include the fallen angels, for they most certainly are not looking forward to this coming glory because they know what is to happen to them in the day of judgment. Jude and Peter tell us in their Epistles that they are 'reserved in chains under darkness' for the time being, until the final verdict is passed upon them and they enter upon their final punishment. They are certainly not earnestly waiting for this coming glory. So they are excluded.

What of men? God created man; so are men included in the Apostle's expression? Clearly Christian men cannot be included. Verse 23 makes that quite clear. 'Not only they, but ourselves also, which have the first-fruits of the Spirit.' Here 'they' and 'ourselves' are set in contrast. 'Not only they' – what he is saying about creation – but we who are Christians also. So that Christians are clearly not included in this use of the term 'creation'. But what about those who are not Christians? Obviously, again, they are not included. The natural man, the godless irreligious man, is most certainly not looking forward to this coming glory. He does not believe in it; and if he were to believe in it, it would be something that he would not desire, but rather avoid. The natural man does not like the thought of dying. He does not know the reason, but an instinct in him makes him afraid of death. He has an idea within him that there is a judgment, that he is responsible, and therefore he is afraid of it. He most certainly is not looking forward to the manifestation of the sons of God.

So we exclude angels, and we exclude men of every description. What remains? This is the extraordinary situation: we are left with the irrational creation, with the material creation, animate and inanimate, organic and inorganic. What does this mean? It means the animals; it means vegetation, flowers, grass; it means the rivers and the streams, the mountains and the hills; it means the earth itself; it means the visible heavens. The Apostle is saying that this part of the creation of God is earnestly expecting and waiting for this manifestation of the sons of God. In other words the Apostle is personalizing this irrational part of creation. And in doing so he is doing something that one finds very frequently in the Bible.

Hear the Prophet Isaiah in chapter 35 for instance: 'The wilderness and the solitary places shall be glad.' How can a wilderness be glad? He personifies it. 'The wilderness and the solitary places shall be glad for them; and the desert shall rejoice, and blossom as the rose.' Or take again what he says in chapter 55 verse 12 in poetic imagination: 'The mountains and the hills shall break forth before you into singing, and all the trees of the field shall clap their hands.' That is just a personification of creation, a specimen of something that one finds very frequently in the Scriptures. The poets, the writers of many hymns, following the scriptural method, often express themselves in the same way.

What is creation waiting for? The answer is that it 'waiteth for the manifestation of the sons of God'. Hence we were right when we emphasized the expression 'revealed in us' at the end

[49]

of verse 18. 'The sufferings of this present time are not worthy to be compared with the glory which shall be revealed in us.' And Paul virtually repeats himself as he tells us that creation is waiting for 'the manifestation of the sons of God'. He means that the sons of God will be 'put on exhibition'. God will show what He has done in salvation in and through us. We shall be show-pieces, when we are revealed in *our* glory with Him. The whole creation is waiting for this great event. This particular aspect of the coming glory was clearly central in the Apostle's mind. The argument began half way through verse 17: 'if so be that we suffer with him, that we may also be glorified together'. Our glorification is in the forefront of his mind. But as we shall see later, our glorification is but the central feature of this greater glorification which Paul will describe later.

The creation is craning its neck, stretching its head, eagerly expecting and waiting for this manifestation of the sons of God. The Apostle is describing the world that we are living in now; and he is talking about our troubles and sufferings and trials. This is not a fairy-tale. I have not suddenly become a poet. This is sheer fact. The Apostle is describing something that is actually true now, in this material world that we are in at this moment. His concern is to show the greatness of this glory, a glory so great that the whole creation is craning its neck, longing for it, waiting for it to appear.

But why is the creation looking forward to it in this way? Here we come to this further remarkable doctrine. It is because the fate of creation is indissolubly linked with that of man. This is most remarkable teaching. It is found only in the Bible. The fate of man, and the fate of the whole cosmos, are inextricably linked; and the one follows the other. Now let us observe how Paul works the matter out. The first argument is that man's sin has produced the present condition of creation; and the Apostle is referring to the animals, the birds, the flowers, the grass, everything that we know about in the visible creation. Creation is as it is because of the fall of man. Verse 20 says that 'the creation was made subject to vanity'. 'Vanity' is a very interesting term. It means, in a sense, 'futile'. Or perhaps, more particularly, it means 'something which is not fulfilling its function', something which does not measure up to that for which it was intended. It carries also the obvious further meaning that there is in it a tendency to deterioration and to dissolution. 'Vanity!' 'Vain!' 'Empty!' Paul is referring to the whole of creation, and he says that it has been made subject to that kind of vanity. It is not fulfilling the function for which it was originally intended. It does not 'measure up to' that which it was meant to be. There is in it something which seems to be destructive and which reduces everything in the end to that which is null and void – 'Vanity'.

The Apostle helps us to understand matters still further when in verse 21 he says, 'The creature itself also shall be delivered from the bondage of corruption'. Creation is in a state of corruption. By corruption is meant 'physical corruption', 'putrefaction', 'death and destruction'. It is like a piece of meat which has decayed, become polluted, and which will gradually disintegrate. It is offensive. Similarly creation now is in this state of physical corruption. It is putrefying and it is subject to death and to destruction.

But Paul says also that creation is 'in bondage' to this corruption, and that is a most important addition. He means that it cannot free itself from its corruption, try as it will. The creation cannot get rid of this element of decay and of corruption that is in it, and that renders it ultimately vain and utterly futile.

Here we have one of these dividing points as between the Christian and the non-Christian. The non-Christian looks out upon life, and taking his superficial view he says, 'Isn't life wonderful?' The Christian looks out at the same world as he says, 'Change and decay in all around I see.' The Christian takes a deeper view than the non-Christian. The latter becomes excited and says, 'There is something starting there. You should not be a pessimist, life is starting there and advancing.' 'I know,' says the Christian; 'but I also know this, that because life has started it is already moving on to its termination.' 'Every man who lives is born to die,' says the poet. 'Ah,' says the non-Christian, 'you mustn't say that about a new-born babe. A babe was born five minutes ago, surely there is someone starting to live.' I agree. But it is also equally true to say 'There is someone who is starting to die.' The moment you come into this world you begin to go out of it; your first breath is linked with your last. 'What is your life? It is but a vapour.' 'Change and decay in all around I see.' Everything is decaying, there is no question about that. 'Bondage of corruption.' There is a principle of corruption in the whole creation, and it is evident everywhere. Do what we will we cannot get rid of it.

What is the cause of this? The Apostle's explanation is a vital piece of teaching. 'The creation', he says, 'was made subject to vanity and to the bondage of corruption.' 'Was made subject' could be better translated by 'was subjected to'. The tense used is the aorist tense, which means that it happened in the past once and for ever. A single act, definite, concrete, not repeated. 'It was subjected' at a given point. Previously it was different; it was not vain, it was not empty, it was not corrupt, it was not in bondage. But at a given point 'it was subjected to'. Note the passive. Note the additional emphasis also in the words 'not willingly': 'The creation was subjected to vanity, not willingly'; an expression that means that it did not happen to it as the result of its own volition; it did not desire to be like that. Neither did it happen to it as the result of anything that it had done 'willingly' or voluntarily. The whole creation has not become vain and empty and corrupt and in bondage as the result of anything that itself has done. How did this happen to it, and why did it happen to it?

Put the question to an unbeliever, to a man who is not a Christian. Ask him why the world is as it is. Why this element of decay, disruption, disintegration, pollution, putrefaction? Why is it that these beautiful flowers which we see budding and then blooming, blossoming so marvellously, end on the manure heap quite soon? Why is decay true of everything, our own bodies included?

The Apostle's answer is this: 'The creature was made subject to vanity, not willingly, but by reason of him who hath subjected the same in hope.' What does this mean? There is an alternative translation in a footnote in the so-called New English Bible: 'because God subjected it'. This is actually the rendering in some of the older versions. But the better translation is, 'The creature was made subject to vanity, not willingly, but on account of [or in accordance with] the will of him who subjected it to it.' Who is it that has subjected the whole of creation to this vanity and to this bondage of corruption? Patently it is not man. He has been trying to do the very opposite to creation throughout the centuries. He has been trying to get rid of the putrefaction, he has been inventing chemicals and producing disinfectants; but he cannot get rid of the corruption. No, it is not man!

Who then is it, the devil? No, it is not the devil. There is no indication that he ever had, or ever will have such power. The answer is provided in the 3rd chapter of the Book of Genesis, verses 14–19. The crucial statement is in verses 17–19: 'And unto Adam he said, Because thou hast hearkened unto the voice of thy wife, and hast eaten of the tree, of which I commanded thee, saying, Thou shalt not eat of it: cursed is the ground for thy sake; in sorrow shalt thou eat of it all the days of thy life. Thorns also and thistles shall it bring forth to thee; and thou shalt eat of the herb of the field. In the sweat of thy face shalt thou eat bread, till thou return unto the ground; for out of it wast thou taken: for dust thou art, and unto dust shalt thou return.' That is the Bible's explanation of why creation is as it is, and it is the only adequate explanation. The earth, the creation, was cursed because of the sin of man. This is of vast importance. You do not understand the world in which you live if you do not grasp this, and if you do not believe it. We have never seen this world, this creation, as God made it. 'Ah, but', you say, 'I think creation is very wonderful.' I agree with you. Indeed it is wonderful that, having been cursed because of man's sin, it is as wonderful as we see it today. Does not that help us to see what it was like before it was cursed? There was never meant to be any element of vanity, any bondage, any corruption about creation. There were never meant to be any thorns or briars. Nature was not meant to be 'red in tooth and claw', as a poet puts it. It was never meant to produce weeds. One of man's greatest struggles is against weeds. Leave the ground alone for a while and it will produce weeds. Man is for ever fighting, the wilderness always tends to come back. We see that in the bombed sites of London without going any further. Why does all this happen? It is a part of the curse. We are not seeing creation as it was, nor as it was meant to be.

All this, says the Apostle, has come upon creation involuntarily as the result of the voluntary sin and rebellion and fall of man. The creation has done nothing to produce this. It is man who did the something that has produced it. 'Unwillingly' is true of creation; it is not true of man. Man sinned voluntarily, willingly, deliberately, knowing what he was doing; and he is bearing the sufferings of his voluntary action.

So the Apostle opens our eyes to this extraordinary doctrine

[53]

of the intimate connection between man and creation. It is not surprising that this should have happened to creation, because God, when He made man in His own image, made him 'the lord of creation', and when 'the lord of creation fell', a part of his punishment was that that over which he was lord should be turned to vanity and made subject to the bondage of corruption. Man because of his sin was not allowed to enjoy the paradise into which God had placed him. When he fell all that was under him fell with him, and became a creation which is 'subject to vanity' and which is 'in the bondage of corruption'.

We see then the unity between man and his surroundings, the creation. What happens to man happens to it. The negative has already happened; but what the Apostle is about to say is that the positive is also in the plan of God. That is why the whole creation is 'earnestly expecting', craning its neck, waiting with eager expectation for the manifestation of the sons of God.

Five

*

For I reckon that the sufferings of this present time are not worthy to be compared with the glory which shall be revealed in us.

For the earnest expectation of the creature waiteth for the manifestation of the sons of God.

For the creature was made subject to vanity, not willingly, but by reason of him who hath subjected the same in hope.

Because the creature itself also shall be delivered from the bondage of corruption into the glorious liberty of the children of God.

For we know that the whole creation groaneth and travaileth in pain together until now.

And not only they, but ourselves also, which have the firstfruits of the Spirit, even we ourselves groan within ourselves, waiting for the adoption, to wit, the redemption of our body.

Romans 8: 18–23

Before we proceed further with our exposition of the Apostle's teaching we must pause for a moment to draw certain very important deductions from what we have seen hitherto. The first is that the state of the world is not to be explained, and cannot be explained, by the theory of Evolution. According to that theory everything is progressing and developing and advancing. Those who hold that theory would have us believe that the present state of affairs as regards man, and indeed the whole of life, is only an intermediate one, and that things are as they are because we have only advanced to this particular stage of development. But the Apostle's teaching is the exact opposite of that theory; and is that the present calamitous condition of the world is the result of the Fall. We are not at a particular stage in an upward trend, but everything has been reduced from an original state of perfection to its present state and condition. So the explanation of the state of the whole of creation is not incomplete development, but the result of the cursing which God has meted out as a part of the punishment of man for the folly of his rebellion and his sin. God will not allow man to enjoy the benefits of his position as lord of creation when, as the result of his sin, he has forfeited it. Creation is as it is, and is suffering, not because of anything that it has done but because of what man has done. That throws very important light, therefore, on the belief in Evolution which has captured the public imagination for a hundred years and is perhaps the greatest controlling influence on the thought of mankind in practically every realm of life and of living. The Apostle's teaching is the exact negation of such a belief.

But that leads to a second deduction, namely, the all-importance for the Christian of the early chapters of the Book of Genesis. There is a tendency on the part of many today to say that you can be a Christian, and hold the doctrines of the Christian faith, and at the same time ride very loosely to the early chapters of Genesis; that it does not matter whether they are historically true or not; that you hold on to the doctrines of salvation whether the early chapters of Genesis are literal history or whether they are a collection of myths. But in the light of the Apostle's teaching here in this section of his Epistle that cannot be the case. We have already dealt with the same matter in the 5th chapter, verses 12–21, where the Apostle bases a central and vital argument on the historicity of Adam. Here he does the same thing. You cannot really hold the biblical doctrine of salvation without accepting its history, and part of that history is, as this passage shows so plainly, that creation is as it is because at a given point in history, as Genesis 3 tells us, God cursed the earth. So a man is in a totally unsatisfactory position when he imagines that he can hold on to the doctrines of the Christian Faith and yet reject the factual, the historical element.

Our third deduction is that there is no hope for man or creation or the cosmos in terms of Evolution. This passage, of course, again gives the lie direct to any such idea. The Bible holds out no hope whatsoever for the idea that as the centuries pass things will get better, that man and his environment will improve, and that at last he will arrive at a state of perfection. Here we are told that the exact opposite is the case, and that you find nothing in creation itself but 'vanity'. There is nothing in creation that leads to an optimistic view of the future either of man or of creation itself. Indeed, science in a sense confirms this. It talks about the second law of thermodynamics, which teaches that the whole universe is running down; and that does not fit in with the theory of Evolution. And as for Scripture, the optimistic idea that things are going to advance and develop is quite foreign to its teaching. It teaches, rather, that there is to be a crisis, a judgment, an end to the world as it is, and that something new and different is to be introduced. So from a variety of standpoints the teaching here is diametrically opposed to what is so commonly and currently held at the present time.

My fourth and last deduction is that there is only one hope, and that is rooted in the character and purpose of God Himself. The only hope for the creation, for the whole universe as well as man, is in the character of God, and in the following way. God's glory and God's honour prohibit His leaving the world as it is. If God is God, the great Creator, and if God is all-powerful with all rule and authority at His command, then the very character of God makes it quite impossible that He should leave creation as it is at the present time. He cannot leave it in this condition of vanity, in this condition of 'groaning' and 'travailing'. It is inconsistent with the character of God that this should be the permanent state of affairs; and of course that is precisely what the Bible tells us. So in a very odd way the actual condition of creation gives us an insight into what the Apostle is saying here. Looking at creation we see the imperfections, the vanity and corruption, and we are led to argue that the very fact that it is in such a state is proof positive that it will not be left ever to continue so. Because God is God He cannot leave it like that, He must do something about it. And that is the very thing we are told He is going to do.

We can now proceed further. The Apostle, as we have already seen, tells us that the creation is actually looking forward to the glory that is to come because it will itself share in it. On what grounds is that statement made? Here is the answer as the Apostle himself puts it before us. 'The creature', he says in verse 20, 'was made subject to vanity, not willingly, but by reason of him who hath subjected the same in hope.' I did not quote those last two words in our previous study because there I was only concerned to show that the creation is as it is as a consequence of man's sin; it was made subject to vanity, though 'not willingly' so. But the statement does not stop at that; the creation has been subjected to the same 'in hope'. To what does the Apostle refer? Surely to the fact that at the selfsame time that God cursed the earth He also gave it a hope of deliverance. That is what makes Genesis 3 so important, and that is why its history is so essential to the understanding of the biblical doctrine of salvation. Man sinned, and God came down to the Garden of Eden and told man what was going to happen to him as the result of his sin. He told him that He was going to curse the earth, that henceforth he would not just pick the fruit and eat it, but that he would have to work and eat by the sweat of his face, he would have to struggle against nature, he would have to keep down the thorns and the briars. Nature, creation, would be cursed. But God did not stop at that. He said that there would be enmity between the seed of the serpent and the seed of the woman, but He went on to promise victory, for, said He, 'the seed of the woman shall bruise the serpent's head'. That is the hope. We have already seen that creation is inevitably and always tied to man. So if there is a promise of a hope of deliverance for man it includes the promise of the hope of the deliverance of the creation also.

We thus learn the meaning of 'by reason of him who hath subjected the same in hope'. God gave a promise and a hope to the creation at the very moment when He originally cursed it. As if God were saying to creation, I am cursing you because of the sin of man, but this is not always to be your condition. It is to be your condition until I deliver man, and then your deliverance will come also. We see here the complete difference between the biblical teaching and everything that man himself has ever thought or suggested. This is teaching that you only find in Scripture and, as I am emphasizing, it is the exact opposite of all the hopeful idealistic optimism that characterizes those who believe in the theory of Evolution.

There is another interesting and important phrase in verse 22: 'We know that the whole creation groaneth and travaileth in pain together until now.' The Apostle says that we know this, we are aware of this. What does he mean by saying that the whole creation is 'groaning and travailing in pain together'? There has often been confusion about the word 'together'. Does it mean together with Christians? It is simply another way of saying 'every part' of creation, the whole of it together, every part and portion, every aspect is involved in this 'groaning and travailing in pain'. But how are we to understand 'groaning and travailing'? Some have thought that this merely means the kind of agony that we see in nature in the predatory character of certain animals that live on others. When you look carefully into nature you find that there is much suffering, in the animal realm and in every other realm. So some tell us that all this expression means is that nature, creation, when you really look into it, is full of pain and suffering and death. But that is not what the Apostle is saying. If he meant that, he would be contradicting the expression 'in hope' that he has just used. Indeed, he would be contradicting what he says in verse 21: 'The creature itself also shall be delivered from the bondage of corruption into the glorious liberty of the children of God.'

What then does Paul mean? At this point the New English Bible translation is of help. It says that 'the whole created universe groans in all its parts as if in the pangs of child-birth'. That is undoubtedly what the Apostle means. The word 'travail' generally has the connotation of child-birth. Paul uses precisely the same expression in writing to the Galatians in chapter 4, verse 19: 'My little children, of whom I travail in birth again until Christ be formed in you'; and here in Romans he is saying that the whole of creation is in process of trying to give birth to something better. It is a painful process, and a kind of agony is involved. That, he says, is the condition of the whole of creation at the present time; it is experiencing, as it were, the pangs of child-birth in an attempt to produce the better thing that it knows is coming to it.

Here again we have one of these wonderful personifications of Nature which the Apostle uses from time to time. But someone may very rightly ask whether this just pure imagination on the part of the great Apostle. On what grounds does he make such a statement? We do not know exactly, but I can suggest certain answers, one of which is mere speculation. I wonder whether the phenomenon of the Spring supplies us with a part answer. Nature every year, as it were, makes an effort to renew itself, to produce something permanent; it has come out of the death and the darkness of all that is so true of the Winter. In the Spring it seems to be trying to produce a perfect creation, to be going through some kind of birth-pangs year by year. But unfortunately it does not succeed, for Spring leads only to Summer, whereas Summer leads to Autumn, and Autumn to Winter. Poor old Nature tries every year to defeat the 'vanity', the principle of death and decay and disintegration that is in it. But it cannot do so. It fails every time. It still goes on trying, as if it feels things should be different and better; but it never succeeds. So it goes on 'groaning and travailing in pain together until now'. It has been doing so for a very long time – the Apostle wrote his Epistle nearly two thousand years ago – but Nature still repeats the effort annually.

We must not misinterpret this statement as they do who always preach on the Resurrection in that way. They say that the message of the Resurrection is a general spirit of hopefulness, that though death comes there is always a new beginning. The Resurrection, they say, is like the Spring after the death of Winter – a burst of life! So they exhort us not to be pessimistic, and assure us that all is going to be right in the end. Though there is a struggle going on, eventually out of it all will come this Resurrection life. But this is not in any sense what the Apostle is teaching and asserting. He does not say that this groaning and travailing of nature is eventually going to produce the perfect state. He is saying the exact opposite, namely, that all the struggle and the agony and the birth-pangs never bring anything to birth.

That, of course, is not only true of the whole of creation, it is true of man himself. Man is a born optimist, he is always going to make a perfect world. He has been saying that ever since he fell, but he has never succeeded. There have been periods when he thinks he has triumphed and the world seems to be advancing and developing. But the cycle of change brings him back again to some dark era and to a sense of hopelessness. The Apostle does not give us any grounds whatsoever for a false, idealistic optimism. What he is saying is that there is no hope whatsoever in creation in and of itself – none at all! But he certainly tells us that there is a kind of consciousness in creation that it was meant for something better. Nature does every Spring what men tend to do on the 1st January every year in their New Year resolutions, but nothing comes of it – a lot of agony and sweat and proposal, but back you go to Winter again. There is no hope for man or creation apart from God's purpose of salvation as taught in the

Bible and suggested here by the expression 'in hope'. We shall look into this in greater detail. There are promises in the Old and New Testaments alike that there will ultimately be a different state of creation. It is nothing that creation itself can produce; it is something that is going to be 'done' to creation by God Himself. As He cursed it, He is going to restore it.

Another ground for this optimism is the connection between man and creation. We have already considered it negatively. Because creation is tied to man, when man fell creation was cursed. But that is only one side. Look at the other side. As it is certain and sure that man is to be delivered – I mean by 'man' those who are believers, those who are in Christ, those who are saved, those who belong to Him – so it is equally certain that they shall have a creation in which to live which corresponds to their restored condition. So all the promises of man's final deliverance are proof positive at the same time that there is going to be this deliverance for the whole of creation. As creation is tied to man, that which happens to man is inevitably bound to happen to creation.

We have been working through the argument in order that we may proceed to take a positive view of the glory which is coming, and to which the whole of creation is looking forward. 'We ourselves', says the Apostle, are looking forward to it: 'even we ourselves groan within ourselves, waiting for the adoption'. The redeemed are looking forward, and the creature, the creation, is also looking forward. Why? Because the prospect is so glorious. We can divide what Paul says about this glory in the following manner. The greatness of the glory which is to come is seen first of all in our blessed Lord and Saviour Himself; it will be His glory. Then secondly, it will be seen in us, the redeemed. Thirdly, it will be seen in creation itself. Christian people, he says, who are suffering together with Him, if they but understood God's plan and purpose would soon see that 'the sufferings of this present time are not worthy to be compared with the glory which shall be revealed in us'. Nature, inanimate nature, has some awareness of this, so how much more should we have it!

Look at the glory first in Christ; it will be His glory. 'If we suffer with Him, that we may be also glorified together.' He is already glorified. We start with Him always. Nothing happens to us apart from Him. What is this glory that belongs to Him? We are told something about it in the Scriptures. We are given a glimpse of it in the event which took place on the Mount of Transfiguration. Our Lord took Peter and James and John with Him up the Mount of Transfiguration. I take the account of it from Matthew 17, commencing in verse 2: 'He was transfigured before them and his face did shine as the sun, and his raiment was white as the light.' That is a glimpse of the glory which is to be manifested when He comes again, the manifestation of the Son of God, the Lord of glory. The Apostle Peter who was there, and was an eye-witness, never forgot this, and in comforting Christian people who were going through a time of trial and suffering, he says to them: 'I will endeavour that ye may after my decease have these things always in remembrance. For we have not followed cunningly devised fables, when we made known unto you the power and coming of our Lord Jesus Christ, but were eye-witnesses of his majesty. For he received from God the Father honour and glory when there came such a voice to him from the excellent glory, This is my beloved Son, in whom I am well pleased. And this voice which came from heaven we heard, when we were with him in the holy mount' (2 Peter 1: 15–18). There, they had a glimpse of it. The Apostles who were with Him there had been with Him for some time, listening to Him and seeing His miracles. But suddenly on that mount they saw the transfiguration, this shining of the glory, this bright light which is ever the characteristic of holiness and of the glory of God. This glory will be fully revealed in Him when He comes again.

There is another glimpse of His glory in Matthew 24, verses 29–31: 'Immediately after the tribulation of those days shall the sun be darkened, and the moon shall not give her light, and the stars shall fall from heaven, and the powers of the heavens shall be shaken: and then shall appear the sign of the Son of man in heaven; and then shall all the tribes of the earth mourn, and they shall see the Son of man coming in the clouds of heaven with power and great glory.' And yet again, the martyred Stephen was given a glimpse of this same glory, as recorded in Acts 7, verses 55 and 56: 'But he [Stephen] being full of the holy Ghost, looked up steadfastly into heaven, and saw the glory of God, and

Jesus standing on the right hand of God, and said, Behold, I see the heavens opened, and the Son of man standing on the right hand of God.' The glory passes description, of course, but these men were given glimpses of it, and we have the accounts of what they saw.

The Apostle Paul knew something about the glory. The 9th chapter of Acts gives an account of Saul of Tarsus going from Jerusalem to Damascus, 'And as he journeyed, he came near Damascus: and suddenly there shined round about him a light from heaven: And he fell to the earth, and heard a voice saying unto him, Saul, Saul, why persecutest thou me? And he said, Who art thou, Lord?' He saw the risen, glorified Lord. But what he first saw was this bright light from heaven, this dazzling effulgence. That is a part of the glory of the Lord Jesus Christ; that is what is going to be revealed. He will come as He is now in glory. The Apostle had a glimpse of it and it threw him to the ground, blinding him. It is not surprising that he writes as he does here in Romans 8. He tells us more about this elsewhere. Take the statement in the Second Epistle to the Thessalonians where he writes about 'the brightness of the coming of the Lord Jesus Christ'. He says, 'To you who are troubled (there will be) rest with us, when the Lord Jesus shall be revealed from heaven with his mighty angels, in flaming fire taking vengeance on them that know not God . . . when he shall come to be glorified in his saints, and to be admired in all them that believe'. Then in the 2nd chapter, verse 8: 'Then shall that Wicked be revealed, whom the Lord shall consume with the spirit of his mouth, and shall destroy with the brightness of his coming.' These are the terms that are always used – light, brightness, shining. In exactly the same way Paul exhorts Titus and all others to look for that 'blessed hope and the glorious appearing', or 'the appearing of the glory of our great God and Saviour Jesus Christ' (Titus 2: 13). It is always in terms of this great glory and brightness.

The Book of Revelation is particularly concerned with this glory, so you find it even in the 1st chapter in verse 7: 'Behold, he cometh with clouds; and every eye shall see him, and they also which pierced him: and all kindreds of the earth shall wail because of him.' But look at the detailed description which begins in verse 12: 'And I turned to see the voice that spake with me. And being turned, I saw seven golden candlesticks; and in the midst of the seven candlesticks one like unto the Son of man, clothed with a garment down to the foot, and girt about the paps with a golden girdle. His head and his hairs were white like wool, as white as snow; and his eyes were as a flame of fire; and his feet like unto fine brass, as if they burned in a furnace; and his voice as the sound of many waters.' This is imagery, of course. But it is all designed to give us the impression of His glory. 'He had in his right hand seven stars: and out of his mouth went a sharp two-edged sword: and his countenance was as the sun shineth in his strength. And when I saw him, I fell at his feet as dead.' It is not surprising that the persecuting Saul on the road to Damascus should have fallen to the ground, as John the apostle does here. When he gets this glimpse he falls at His feet 'as one dead' because of the shining of the glory of the countenance that was bright as 'the sun that shineth in his strength'. I cannot imagine anything more glorious than that.

There is another description of Christ in chapter 5, verses 6–8: 'And I beheld, and lo, in the midst of the throne and of the four beasts, and in the midst of the elders, stood a Lamb as it had been slain, having seven horns and seven eyes' – 'seven' is the number of perfection – 'which are the seven Spirits of God sent forth into all the earth'. Strength and meekness, the glory of a Conqueror, and yet the tenderness of the Lamb of God! Take again chapter 17 of that Book of Revelation, verse 14: 'These shall make war with the Lamb, and the Lamb shall overcome them: for he is Lord of lords, and King of kings: and they that are with him are called, and chosen, and faithful.' Next turn to the 19th chapter for a great and a noble description, beginning at verse 11: 'And I saw heaven opened, and behold a white horse; and he that sat upon him was called Faithful and True, and in righteousness he doth judge and make war. His eyes were as a flame of fire, and on his head were many crowns; and he had a name written, that no man knew but he himself. And he was clothed with a vesture dipped in blood: and his name is called The Word of God. And the armies which were in heaven followed him upon white horses, clothed in fine linen, white and clean. And out of his mouth goeth a sharp sword, that with it he should smite the nations: and he shall rule them with a rod of iron: and he treadeth the winepress of the fierceness and wrath of Almighty God. And he hath on his vesture and on his thigh a name written, King of kings and Lord of lords' – supreme above all others! Yes, 'At the name of Jesus every knee shall bow, of things in heaven, and things in earth, and things under the earth; and every tongue shall confess that Jesus Christ is Lord, to the glory of God the Father' (Philippians 2: 10, 11).

These passages give some idea of what the Scriptures have to say concerning the glory of His coming when He shall appear. It is a glory which is to be revealed. Who is to see it? 'Every eye shall see him.' The whole cosmos shall see Him. There is no one that shall not see Him. This is the teaching of the Bible. He shall be seen as He is in this character of 'King of kings and Lord of lords'. He is to be 'admired' in us, according to that passage in 2 Thessalonians chapter 1: 'Admired in them that believe' (v. 10). But as for others, His coming is to be feared. 'Every eye shall see him, and they also which pierced him': and they shall wail and lament. Here is the description given at the end of the 6th chapter of the Book of Revelation, verse 15 to the end: 'The kings of the earth, and the great men, and the rich men, and the chief captains, and the mighty men, and every bondman, and every free man, hid themselves in the dens and in the rocks of the mountains: and said to the mountains and rocks, Fall on us, and hide us from the face of him that sitteth on the throne, and from the wrath of the Lamb: For the great day of his wrath is come; and who shall be able to stand?' That is the day to which the whole creation is looking forward. That is the glory as it will appear in Him when He comes again in God's appointed time.

But, secondly, on the great day which is coming there is to be not only a manifestation of His glory but of ours also. 'If we suffer with him (we shall also) be glorified together.' 'The sufferings of this present time are not worthy to be compared with the glory which shall be revealed in us.' Part of the glory is to be revealed in us and through us. Paul says clearly that 'The earnest expectation of the creature waiteth for the manifestation of the sons of God.' Creation is waiting for this glory which is to be shown, in part, in us. To whom are we to be shown in glory? We have seen that the Lord is to be shown to 'every eye'. To whom are we to be shown? The same is more or less true of us also, for we shall be with Him. Not only so, but we are a part of His glory. We find such teaching in Ephesians 3: 10: 'To the intent that now unto the principalities and powers in heavenly places might be known by [or through] the Church the manifold wisdom of God.' Similarly Hebrews 2:13, quoting from the Old Testament, says that our Lord will say, 'Behold I and the children which God hath given me.' We shall be 'on show' as it were; we are the proof of the manifold wisdom of God. We shall also be shown to the devil and all his angels and followers, and to all who are opponents of the Lord. This will be the final triumph of God over the devil; and it will be 'in us'. We shall be shown in our glory, showing what man has become as the result of the action of God in Christ. This is what the Son will have made of the ruin and the havoc wrought by the devil, who was so pleased with himself and proud of himself because he had persuaded man to disobey God, and had brought this 'vanity' into the very warp and woof of creation. This is the answer of God.

And the glory will be shown also to the whole of creation. There is a wonderful statement about us and our future glory in the 13th chapter of Matthew's Gospel, verses 41–43: 'The Son of man shall send forth his angels, and they shall gather out of his kingdom all things that offend, and them which do iniquity; and shall cast them into a furnace of fire: there shall be wailing and gnashing of teeth. Then shall the righteous shine forth as the sun in the kingdom of their Father. Who hath ears to hear, let him hear.' Did you notice that it says, 'Then shall the righteous shine forth as the sun'? These are the very words used about Him, as we have already seen. That is what you see – this shining, this brightness, this light of the sun – when you look into the face of the glorified Lord. But that is to become true of us also. 'Then shall the *righteous* shine forth as the sun in the kingdom of their Father'; and the whole of creation will be looking not only at Him but also at us, He shining as the sun, we shining as the sun in His righteousness, in His glory.

We have not yet finished with the part we shall play in this great glory, for we must go on to consider what we shall be like then. We must also go on to consider what we shall be enjoying then; and we must also consider what we shall be doing then. All we have seen so far is that in that great day we shall be 'shining as the sun' as He is. The Apostle John expresses it thus: 'We shall see him as he is, and we shall be like him' (1 John 3:1 and 2). Do you live by these things? Are you having a hard time? Are you suffering? Have you trials and troubles and tribulations? Have you had a very unhappy and miserable week? Have you been listening to the devil, and are you downcast and discouraged and disconsolate? If so, shame on you! It matters not what our condition may be; we must take it and place it in the light of this glory which is coming. Christian, whatever you are, however humble and lowly, however ignorant and fallible, however suffering, you are to be manifested in that great day, and you will 'shine as the brightness of the sun'. That is the Apostolic teaching. Whatever your state or condition or circumstances, remember that 'The sufferings of this present time are not worthy to be compared . . . ' How ridiculous we are, and what fools, if we listen to the devil and allow him to depress us! By the grace of God we are destined to shine like the sun in glory in that 'great day'.

Six

*

For I reckon that the sufferings of this present time are not worthy to be compared with the glory which shall be revealed in us.

For the earnest expectation of the creature waiteth for the manifestation of the sons of God.

For the creature was made subject to vanity, not willingly, but by reason of him who hath subjected the same in hope.

Because the creature itself also shall be delivered from the bondage of corruption into the glorious liberty of the children of God.

For we know that the whole creation groaneth and travaileth in pain together until now.

And not only they, but ourselves also, which have the firstfruits of the Spirit, even we ourselves groan within ourselves, waiting for the adoption, to wit, the redemption of our body.   Romans 8: 18–23

We now turn to look at our part in the coming glory. We have seen something of it in the Lord Himself; but we are to partake of this glory with Him – 'if so be that we suffer with him, that we may be also glorified together'. What is this? It is what the Apostle calls in the 23rd verse 'the adoption'. 'Not only they, but ourselves also, which have the first-fruits of the Spirit, even we ourselves groan within ourselves, waiting for *the adoption.*' The adoption means 'the placing as sons'. We are already children of God; Paul has reminded us of that. 'The Spirit itself beareth witness with our spirit, that we are the children of God' (verse 16). Yes, but though we are children we have not yet entered into the inheritance: 'If children, then heirs; heirs of God, and joint-heirs with Christ.' So while we are in this world we are indistinguishable as regards external appearance and circumstances from those who are not the children of God. 'The adoption' means 'the entering into the estate', 'the full status and position' of the children, the sons of God. The way the Apostle puts it is very interesting. He says, 'The earnest expectation of the creature waiteth for the manifestation of the sons of God'. We are the 'sons of God' now. That is so, but we have not yet been 'manifested' as such. An obvious comparison may help here. The Lord Jesus Christ when He was in this world was the eternal Son of God, but He was not obviously manifest as such, except occasionally. People looked at Him and saw a man, a carpenter. The glory was hidden, was veiled. But there is a day coming when it will be revealed. As regards our Lord, those who had eyes to see could see something of it even when He was here. John says in his Prologue, 'We beheld his glory, the glory as of the only begotten of the Father, full of grace and truth.' John and Peter and James certainly saw more of it on the Mount of Transfiguration. There the glory was manifest; as it were, the veil was drawn back for a moment, and the glory shone out. But while He was here in the flesh, speaking generally, the glory was veiled. He came 'in the likeness of sinful flesh', the glory was not manifested openly. But when He comes again it will be visible to all. The same applies to us. The creation is 'waiting for the manifestation', the revealing, the unveiling of the sons of God.

What shall we be like in that day? We are dealing with what you and I as children of God, as those who are believers in the Lord Jesus Christ, will be like. How wonderful it is that here in the midst of life with all its problems and difficulties we can consider what we are going to be! That is what the Apostle invites us to do. The answer is found in many places in the Scriptures. Take, for instance, what we read in the great 15th chapter of the First Epistle to the Corinthians. There we have a very wonderful account of it from verse 39 to verse 54. 'The corruptible' is going to be put aside and we shall be 'incorruptible'. All that is but 'natural' will no longer be natural, it will become spiritual. That is what Paul emphasizes in that chapter, which we normally think of – and rightly so – as a chapter concerning the resurrection. But we must not stop at the resurrection, we must include the glorification as well as the resurrection. The body is not only to be raised; it is to be changed and glorified. That is the argument. His emphasis is upon the changing, the glorification, and all that is involved in it. 'As we have borne the image of the earthy, we shall also bear the image of the heavenly.' 'For this corruptible must put on incorruption, and this mortal must put on immortality.'

[69]

You find the same teaching in its essence in the Second Epistle to the Corinthians, chapter 3, verse 18: 'We all, with open face beholding as in a glass the glory of the Lord, are changed into the same image from glory to glory, even as by the Spirit of the Lord.' In other words we are being prepared for something of this even at this present moment. But still more definitely in 2 Corinthians chapter 5, beginning at the 1st verse: 'For we know that if our earthly house of this tabernacle were dissolved, we have a building of God, an house not made with hands, eternal in the heavens.' The Apostle says that if this body, which is but a tent or 'tabernacle', should die and disintegrate and dissolve, we have an house not made with hands, eternal in the heavens. 'For in this we groan, earnestly desiring to be clothed upon with our house which is from heaven: if so be that being clothed we shall not be found naked. For we that are in this tabernacle do groan, being burdened: not for that we would be unclothed . . . ' The Christian does not merely desire to get out of the body. That is Hinduism, that is false religion. The Christian does not merely want to die and get out of the body so that he may get away from his troubles – 'not for that we would be unclothed, but unclothed upon'. This is positive – 'clothed upon, that mortality might be swallowed up of life'. The Christian desires to be clothed with this house which is from heaven, this glorious body that is coming. 'Now he that hath wrought us for the selfsame thing is God, who also hath given unto us the earnest of the Spirit.'

Another notable statement is found in Philippians chapter 3, verses 20 and 21: 'For our conversation is in heaven' – that is where we belong, that is where our citizenship is – 'from whence also we look for the Saviour, the Lord Jesus Christ, who shall change our vile body [this body of our humiliation] that it may be fashioned like unto his glorious body [the body of his glorification] according to the working whereby he is able even to subdue all things unto himself.' This body is the body of my humiliation; this is the body in which sin still dwells, and which is decaying. This is the body which has resulted from the Fall. But then it will be entirely different; it will be the body of my glorification, 'like unto the body of his glorification', similar to what the Apostle saw when he was on the road to Damascus.

Let us continue to look at the evidence. We can never know too much about it. Christian people are as they are because they are not aware of this great truth. The Church is as she is because very largely she does not even believe it. But this is the scriptural teaching; this is the teaching of the Lord Himself and of the inspired apostles. So turn to 1 Thessalonians 4, verses 16 and 17: 'For the Lord himself shall descend from heaven with a shout, with the voice of the archangel, and with the trump of God: and the dead in Christ shall rise first. Then we which are alive and remain shall be caught up together with them in the clouds, to meet the Lord in the air: and so shall we ever be with the Lord. Wherefore comfort one another with these words.' And what a comfort it is !

We go for our last description to a verse in the First Epistle of John, chapter 3, verses 1 and 2: 'Behold, what manner of love the Father hath bestowed upon us, that we should be called the sons of God: therefore the world knoweth us not, because it knew him not.' Do not be worried, do not be troubled if the world does not recognize you; do not be troubled if the world regards you as a fool. That was their attitude towards Him; and we shall experience similar treatment because we are children of God. 'Beloved, now are we the sons of God' – we are already the sons of God, even at this moment – 'and it doth not yet appear what we shall be: but we know that when he shall appear, we shall be like him; for we shall see him as he is'. What a wonderful statement! We do not know all about it, indeed we do not know much about it; but we do know this, that we 'shall be like him, for we shall see him as he is'. Here on earth, as 1 Corinthians 13: 12 reminds us, we 'behold as in a glass, darkly'. We look at Him as reflected in a mirror, but even thus we 'are changed into the same image, from glory to glory' (2 Cor. 3: 18). But then, seeing Him 'full disclosed' as He is, we shall be like Him, our bodies and everything pertaining to us glorified.

Notice that in all these passages the emphasis is upon the glorification of the body, the physical body, the material body; and this is very important for us to grasp. There are many today who regard themselves as Christians who do not believe in the resurrection and glorification of the body. They believe that when the Christian dies he goes to be with Christ; and they seem to think of that as some vague, nebulous, indefinite spiritual state and condition. But that is not the teaching of the Scripture.

The Scripture teaches the resurrection of the body as an essential part of our salvation. And, as we shall see, we shall dwell in these glorified bodies on the glorified earth. This is one of the great Christian doctrines that has been almost entirely forgotten and ignored. Unfortunately the Christian Church – I speak generally – does not believe this, and therefore does not teach it. It has lost its hope, and this explains why it spends most of its time in trying to improve life in this world, in preaching politics, in protesting against war and bombs, and in urging disarmament. Alas, it knows nothing of, and does not believe in, the scriptural teaching concerning this glorification of the body which is to come. The body will then be perfect, without blemish, without weakness, free from disease; it will be 'without spot or wrinkle, or any such thing'.

The Apostle tells us elsewhere that there are two ways in which believers will enter into that state of the glorified body. Those who have died will come to it through a 'resurrection'; those who are still on earth when our Lord returns will be changed immediately. We shall experience the one or the other. But, says the Apostle, it does not matter which; the important thing is that it is going to happen. It will happen for certain to all who are the children of God. They will have a glorified body. It will not be the body as it now is; it will then be a glorified body. It will not be a body of flesh and blood – 'Flesh and blood cannot inherit the kingdom of God'. It will be a 'spiritual body', but it will be a true body, even as our Lord's glorified body in resurrection was a true body also. Our Lord did not appear as a phantom to the disciples.

Note the emphasis which is given to this point in Luke 24: 38–43. There are those who teach that the resurrection is but some kind of spiritualistic phenomenon and that our Lord's appearances were similar to the so-called 'materializations' of spirits. That is a denial of the resurrection. The biblical teaching is that the resurrection body is a true body, a glorified body, a spiritual body. Whether we get it in one way or the other the important thing is that we shall have it.

That, then, is the first thing we have to realize about ourselves; our very bodies will be absolutely perfect, glorious bodies like the body of our risen Lord Himself. But we shall be spiritually perfect also at the same time. Indeed we shall be perfect in every respect. Let us look at the Apostle Paul's description of spiritual perfection in Ephesians 5: 26 and 27. He is comparing the relationship of husbands and wives to that of Christ and the Church. 'Christ also loved the church, and gave himself for it; that he might sanctify and cleanse it with the washing of water by the word, that he might present it to himself a glorious church, not having spot, or wrinkle, or any such thing; but that it should be holy and without blemish.' That is a description of what you and I as members of the Church and as children of God are yet to be. There is another description of it in Colossians 1: 28: 'Whom we preach, warning every man, and teaching every man in all wisdom; that [in order that] we may present every man perfect in Christ Jesus.' Then there are descriptions of the change in the Book of Revelation. Here, for instance, in the 7th chapter, beginning at verse 13, we read: 'One of the elders answered, saying unto me, What are these which are arrayed in white robes? and whence came they? And I said unto him, Sir, thou knowest. And he said to me, These are they which came out of great tribulation, and have washed their robes, and made them white in the blood of the Lamb. Therefore are they before the throne of God, and serve him day and night in his temple: and he that sitteth on the throne shall dwell among them. They shall hunger no more; neither thirst any more; neither shall the sun light on them, nor any heat. For the Lamb which is in the midst of the throne shall feed them, and shall lead them unto living fountains of waters: and God shall wipe away all tears from their eyes.' These words describe what we shall be like: no more sorrow, no more sighing, no more sin. Christian people, this is what is promised you. Again, look at the matter in Revelation 21, verses 2–4: 'And I John saw the holy city, new Jerusalem, coming down from God out of heaven, prepared as a bride adorned for her husband. And I heard a great voice out of heaven saying, Behold, the tabernacle of God is with men, and he will dwell with them, and they shall be his people, and God himself shall be with them, and be their God. And God shall wipe away all tears from their eyes; and there shall be no more death, neither sorrow, nor crying, neither shall there be any more pain: for the former things are passed away.' We cannot imagine anything that excels that! In other words we shall be perfect and entire in every respect, spiritually, morally, physically, bodily. Not only so, we shall be enjoying complete satisfaction – every need will be fully satisfied, and we shall be delivered for

ever from all the things that have ever caused us misery or
unhappiness or pain or sorrow. That is our destiny. It is with this
that we have to compare our present sufferings; and it is only as
we understand this that we shall be able to say that 'the sufferings
of this present time are not worthy to be compared with the
glory which shall be revealed in us'.

But let us go on. So far we have seen what we are going to be
like; but what are we going to inherit? The Apostle's argument
runs: 'if children, then heirs; heirs of God, and joint-heirs with
Christ'. He tells us in 2 Timothy 4: 8 that we shall inherit 'a
crown of righteousness'. 'Henceforth there is laid up for me a
crown of righteousness, which the Lord, the righteous Judge,
shall give me at that day: and not to me only, but unto all them
also that love his appearing.' A kind of garland – 'a crown of righteousness'! But in addition to that we shall receive a kingdom.
Our Lord so taught in the 25th chapter of the Gospel according
to St Matthew in the third and last parable where He contrasts
those who have believed in Him with those who have not believed.
He says to those who have believed in Him (verse 34): 'Then shall
the King say unto them on his right hand, Come, ye blessed of
my Father, inherit the kingdom prepared for you from the
foundation of the world.'

What is this kingdom? There is an interesting sidelight on this
in the 2nd chapter of the Epistle to the Hebrews. Here again is
something which is much neglected. Beginning at verse 5 we
read: 'For unto the angels hath he not put in subjection the
world to come, whereof we speak.' Or, to put it in plainer
English, 'He has not put the world to come, of which I am
speaking, in subjection unto angels'. To whom, then, is it put
in subjection? Read on: 'But one in a certain place testified,
saying, What is man, that thou art mindful of him? or the son
of man, that thou visitest him? Thou madest him a little lower
than the angels; thou crownedst him with glory and honour,
and didst set him over the works of thy hands: thou hast put
all things in subjection under his feet. For in that he put all in
subjection under him, he left nothing that is not put under him.
But now we see not yet all things put under him. But we see
Jesus.' He says that 'the world to come' of which he has been
speaking has not been put aside, or prepared, for angels but for
us who are the children of God. 'The world to come' there can

be explained by what the Apostle Peter writes in his First Epistle. In the 1st chapter, beginning at verse 3 we read: 'Blessed be the God and Father of our Lord Jesus Christ, which according to his abundant mercy hath begotten us again unto a lively hope by the resurrection of Jesus Christ from the dead.' To what? 'To an inheritance incorruptible, undefiled, and that fadeth not away, reserved in heaven for you, who are kept by the power of God through faith unto salvation ready to be revealed in the last time. Wherein ye greatly rejoice, though now for a season, if need be, ye are in heaviness through manifold temptations.'

The apostles all preach the same doctrine. Each one of them has the same association of coming glory and present suffering. In the passage I have quoted the Apostle Peter gives us a picture of our inheritance. It is incorruptible, it is undefiled, and it will never fade away. Let evil men let off all their bombs together, it will not touch this inheritance. And it is reserved for us. Man with all his folly and malignity can never touch it; God Himself is reserving it for us.

Again, in the 21st chapter of the Book of Revelation, beginning at verse 9 we find an extraordinary description of the inheritance. It is in symbolic form, of course. The Apostle John supplies us with pictures of the inheritance we are going to enter into, of the world that we are going to live in when we have our glorified bodies, when we shall be like our Lord and Saviour. The New Testament writers call upon all their powers of expression, and use many remarkable images in order to give us some notion of it.

I proceed to my next question. What shall we be doing there? how shall we occupy ourselves in that state? We have already had a part of the answer in the 7th chapter of the Book of Revelation, verse 15: 'Therefore are they before the throne of God, and serve him day and night in his temple: and he that sitteth on the throne shall dwell among them.' But something still more remarkable is going to be true of us according to the Apostle Paul in 1 Corinthians 6, in the first three verses: 'Dare any of you, having a matter against another, go to law before the unjust, and not before the saints? Do ye not know that the saints shall judge [govern or rule] the world, and if the world shall be judged by you, are ye unworthy to judge the smallest matters? Know ye not that we shall judge angels?' We are destined to rule, with Christ, over the world and over the ministering angels of God. We are glorified together with Him, everything will be subject to Him, and 'with Him' everything will be subject to us. So we shall judge the world and we shall judge the angels.

This is Christianity. This is the truth by which the New Testament Christians lived. It was because of this that they were not afraid of their persecutors. They would not say 'Caesar is Lord' to save their lives. No, they knew that this glory was coming. This was the secret of their endurance, their patience, and their triumphing over everything that was set against them.

Thus have we seen something of the glory of the Lord Jesus Christ Himself, we have also seen it as it shall be revealed and manifested in us and through us. But we have not finished. The whole creation is going to participate in this also, as we learn from verse 21 of our chapter: 'For [because] the creature [the creation] itself also shall be delivered from the bondage of corruption into the glorious liberty of the children of God.' This explains why the creation is looking forward to it. It has this sense, this feeling, it has been given this promise, that it is going to share in the glory, or, as a better translation reads, in 'the liberty of the glory of the children of God'. This means that creation is going to be set free from the bondage of corruption. We have already considered the matter. It is only then that creation will really be free to develop as it was meant to do, as God created it to do. It is only then that it will be entirely delivered from every element of disintegration. We saw that, at the present time, it is 'subject to vanity', that there is a kind of futility about it, that there is this element of decay and putrefaction in it. Then, it will be free from everything of that nature. There will be no more strife, no more discord, no more disease, no more weeds, no more fungi, no more abnormal growths. At present nature is full of that sort of thing, but then it will be entirely different. It will then be Paradise regained! We have already considered Paradise lost. But Paradise is to be regained. This is a part of the great salvation, and the whole creation is involved. It is not just that believers are forgiven and that they go to heaven in a spiritual form. No, Paradise is to be regained. When man was created, he was put in Paradise; but on account of his sin he was driven out of it, and he has been trying to get back ever since. But he cannot do so because the Flaming Sword and the Cherubim are there to stop him. But Paradise is to be regained for those who are the children of God!

This regained Paradise that is to come is something of which the prophets of the Old Testament spoke. Read the prophet Isaiah, chapter 11, verses 6-9: 'The wolf shall also dwell with the lamb, and the leopard shall lie down with the kid; and the calf and the young lion and the fatling together; and a little child shall lead them. And the cow and the bear shall feed; their young ones shall lie down together: and the lion shall eat straw like the ox.' The lion is carnivorous now, but he will not be so then. 'And the sucking child shall play on the hole of the asp, and the weaned child shall put his hand on the cockatrice' den. They shall not hurt nor destroy in all my holy mountain: for the earth shall be full of the knowledge of the Lord, as the waters cover the sea.' Such is Isaiah's prophecy of this condition in which the whole creation shall be delivered from the bondage of corruption. 'Nature red in tooth and claw' will no longer exist, parasites will have gone, all that makes life difficult will have disappeared, and there will be this amazing, incredible harmony even among the animals and the beasts of the field.

Isaiah has another description of it in the 35th chapter of his prophecy beginning with the words, 'The wilderness and the solitary place shall be glad for them; and the desert shall rejoice, and blossom as the rose. It shall blossom abundantly, and rejoice even with joy and singing: the glory of Lebanon shall be given unto it, the excellency of Carmel and Sharon, they shall see the glory of the Lord and the excellency of our God.' It ends with the words, 'No lion shall be there, nor any ravenous beast shall go up thereon, it shall not be found there; but the redeemed shall walk there. And the ransomed of the Lord shall return, and come to Zion with songs and everlasting joy upon their heads; they shall obtain joy and gladness, and sorrow and sighing shall flee away.' There is something similar in the 55th chapter of that great prophecy. Look at the last verse, the 13th: 'Instead of the thorn shall come up the fir tree, and instead of the brier shall come up the myrtle tree: and it shall be to the Lord for a name, for an everlasting sign that shall not be cut off.' Then a final quotation from Isaiah 66, verses 22-24: 'For as the new heavens and the new earth, which I will make, shall remain before me, saith the Lord, so shall your seed and your name remain. And it shall come to pass, that from one new moon to another, and from one sabbath to another, shall all flesh come to worship before me, saith the Lord. And they shall go forth, and look upon the carcases of the men that have transgressed against me: for their worm shall not die, neither shall their fire be quenched; and they shall be an abhorring unto all flesh.'

I have already quoted from our Lord's teaching concerning this matter in His prophecy recorded in the 19th chapter of Matthew, verses 27-29: 'Then answered Peter and said unto him, Behold, we have forsaken all, and followed thee; what shall we have therefore? And Jesus said unto them, Verily I say unto you, That ye which have followed me, in the regeneration when the Son of man shall sit in the throne of his glory, ye shall also sit upon twelve thrones, judging the twelve tribes of Israel.' In this 'regeneration' all things are made new; that is to be the condition. We have already quoted Acts 3 where you have the same prophecy made by the Apostle Peter. There, Peter says that God, from the beginning, through the mouth of his prophets has been talking about this time of the 'restitution of all things'. Do you believe this? Why is this not being preached? And why is it being denied? It is an essential part of the teaching. 'All the prophets' have spoken about it.

Then there is the Apostle Paul's own description of it in 1 Corinthians 15, verses 24-28: 'Then cometh the end, when he [Christ] shall have delivered up the kingdom to God, even the Father; when he shall have put down all rule and all authority and power. For he must reign, till he hath put all enemies under his feet. The last enemy that shall be destroyed is death. For he hath put all things under his feet. But when he saith, all things are put under him, it is manifest that he is excepted, which did put all things under him. And when all things shall be subdued under him, then shall the Son also himself be subject unto him that put all things under him, that God may be all in all.' That refers to the Son handing back this perfected kingdom to His heavenly Father who had entrusted it to Him. But that, says the Apostle in Ephesians 1: 10, is the ultimate purpose of salvation: 'That in the dispensation of the fulness of times he [God] might gather together in one all things in Christ, both which are in heaven, and which are on earth; even in him.' Again, Hebrews 12 gives a description of it in verses 26 to 28: 'Whose voice then shook the earth: but now he hath promised, saying, Yet once more I shake not the earth only, but also heaven. And this word, Yet once more, signifieth the removing of those things that are shaken, as of things that are made, that those things which cannot be shaken may remain. Wherefore we receiving a kingdom which cannot be moved, let us have grace, whereby we may serve God acceptably with reverence and godly fear.'

We have a more detailed description in the Second Epistle of Peter, chapter 3, verse 7. 'The heavens and the earth, which are now', says Peter, will not be destroyed by a flood as formerly, but by the same word they are kept in store, 'reserved unto fire against the day of judgment and perdition of ungodly men'. Then follows a detailed description beginning at verse 10: 'But the day of the Lord will come as a thief in the night; in the which the heavens shall pass away with a great noise, and the elements shall melt with fervent heat, the earth also and the works that are therein shall be burned up. Seeing then that all these things shall be dissolved, what manner of persons ought ye to be in all holy conversation and godliness, looking for and hasting unto the coming of the day of God, wherein the heavens being on fire shall be dissolved, and the elements shall melt with fervent heat? Nevertheless we, according to his promise, look for new heavens and a new earth, wherein dwelleth righteousness. Wherefore, beloved, seeing that ye look for such things, be diligent that ye may be found of him in peace, without spot, and blameless.' There is yet to be a great cleansing of this old universe. Every vestige of sin and evil will be burned out, will be purged out of it, and there will be a 'new heavens and a new earth, wherein dwelleth righteousness'. Look further at Revelation 20 where there is a very striking statement in verse 11: 'And I saw a great white throne, and him that sat on it, from whose face the earth and the heaven fled away; and there was found no place for them.' And in verses 14 and 15 we read: 'And death and hell were cast into the lake of fire. This is the second death. And whosoever was not found written in the book of life was cast into the lake of fire.'

This is a very important statement because it reminds us again that death is going to be destroyed – 'death and Hades' are to be 'cast into the lake of fire'. In other words, as a result of this renovation there will be no more death. Death came in as the result of man's sin. In this restitution, re-constitution in the glory, death will have no place at all. All that belongs to the realm of evil – men and women, the devil and his angels, and all others – will be cast into that state of everlasting destruction. There will be no place for them in God's perfect universe.

Such, then, is the description given in the Scriptures of the wonderful renovation that is to take place even in the creation: 'The creation itself also shall be delivered from the bondage of corruption into the liberty of the glory of the children of God.' We are told that you and I who are children of God are destined to dwell in that kind of world, under those new heavens and on this new earth, while the animals that have been such bitter enemies, attacking and destroying and eating one another, will now eat and lie down peaceably together, and a little child shall lead them. There will be nothing whatsoever to harm us in any way. This is inconceivable, of course; but that is exactly what we are told is coming.

All this is a fulfilment of what is prophesied in Psalm 8. Read there the description given by the Psalmist, inspired by the Spirit of God. 'O Lord our Lord, how excellent is thy name in all the earth! Who hast set thy glory above the heavens. Our of the mouth of babes and sucklings hast thou ordained strength because of thine enemies, that thou mightest still the enemy and the avenger. When I consider thy heavens, the work of thy fingers, the moon and the stars, which thou hast ordained, what is man, that thou art mindful of him? and the son of man, that thou visitest him? For thou hast made him a little lower than the angels, and hast crowned him with glory and honour. Thou madest him to have dominion over the works of thy hands; thou hast put all things under his feet: all sheep and oxen, yea, and the beasts of the field, the fowl of the air, and the fish of the sea, and whatsoever passeth through the paths of the seas. O Lord our Lord, how excellent is thy name in all the earth!' Yes, says the author of the Epistle to the Hebrews again, in chapter 2, verse 8; that is very wonderful poetry, but it is not yet fulfilled, for 'We see not yet all things put under him'. Quite so, says that author, I agree that creation is not under man now. What hope have I then, what comfort have I? The answer is given in verse 9: 'We see not yet all things put under him, but we see Jesus, who was made a little lower than the angels for the suffering of death, crowned with glory and honour.' He is there in the glory already. And because He is there, we shall also be there. And when that day arrives Psalm 8 will be true of us. We shall be the 'lords of creation' again. Paradise will have been regained. Adam in Paradise was the lord of creation; he lost that position as the result of sin. Man is not lord of creation now; but the believer will regain Paradise. 'We see Jesus.' And we are going to be like Jesus; we shall be glorified, and we shall be the lords of creation.

That is the great promise that is held before us; and it is in the light of this that we are to draw the deduction that 'the sufferings of this present time are not worthy to be compared with the glory which shall be revealed in us'. In some senses our Lord's miracles were a foreshadowing of the day of glory. He could banish diseases, He could control the raging of the sea, He could stop the wind, He could control everything. All this was a clear indication of the glory which is coming. Our Lord's nature miracles, I believe, are a foreshadowing of something of this glory that will be His, and which we shall share with Him because we are God's children, and therefore joint-heirs with Him. Read these things for yourselves. It is not surprising that the whole creation is looking forward to that day of days, stretching out its neck 'waiting for the manifestation of the children of God' – waiting to see it, to see Him, to see us; yes, and waiting for what is going to happen to itself – 'delivered from the bondage of corruption into the liberty of the glory of the children of God'.

It is because we do not know about all this that we are as we are, and are so often defeated and dispirited and discouraged. But this is literally what is going to be true of all of us who are the children of God. Can we ever again allow anything to get us down in this world? Will you ever grumble and complain again? Will it worry you very much what man may do to you? You are being prepared for this indescribable glory which is awaiting the children of God. It is to be manifested and revealed. Lift up your heads, lift up your hearts, by faith keep your eye on the coming glory. 'Set your affection on things above, not on things on the earth.' All here is passing and temporary; but we belong to the kingdom which cannot be moved, the kingdom which God has prepared for His people, His children, 'before the foundation of the world'.

Seven

*

For I reckon that the sufferings of this present time are not worthy to be compared with the glory which shall be revealed in us.

For the earnest expectation of the creature waiteth for the manifestation of the sons of God.

For the creature was made subject to vanity, not willingly, but by reason of him who hath subjected the same in hope.

Because the creature itself also shall be delivered from the bondage of corruption into the glorious liberty of the children of God.

For we know that the whole creation groaneth and travaileth in pain together until now.

And not only they, but ourselves also, which have the firstfruits of the Spirit, even we ourselves groan within ourselves, waiting for the adoption, to wit, the redemption of our body.

Romans 8: 18–23

We have been looking at the way in which the Scriptures describe the glory that awaits us, and tell us something of its character and its nature. Doubtless there is a question in the minds of many as to when this is to be, and as to what exactly it refers. We have seen from our exposition that that question should not arise at all. But it does arise in people's minds; and very largely so because of a teaching which has been very popular for the last hundred years or more with regard to the millennium. Is all we have been describing a description of the millennium, or is it not? In order to clarify the position it may be wise to advert to this matter briefly before we proceed further.

As we approach this problem it is essential that we should bear in mind that the description which is given here of what is to happen to the children of God and to the whole creation in a coming day, refers to something final and permanent. What is described is the entire deliverance of the whole creation from the bondage of corruption; not a temporary deliverance, but a final, permanent and complete deliverance. There is no suggestion whatsoever of a temporary state in the account which is given here of the glory that is awaiting both the sons of God and the whole of creation. This is the basic consideration which should help to clear up any misunderstanding that may arise in people's minds with regard to this question.

Therefore I do not hesitate to assert that these verses have nothing whatsoever to do with any supposed millennium. Those who believe in a literal, physical, material millennium here upon earth emphasize that that will be a temporary condition; it will only last a thousand years and it will be followed by a state of conflict and of sin and confusion when the devil will be released again. But there is nothing of a temporary nature about the glory which the Apostle is describing in these verses. That alone, I repeat, is sufficient to establish once and for ever that this has nothing to do with an earthly millennium.

It is important to remember that there is no reference anywhere in the Bible to a period of a thousand years except in the 20th chapter of the Book of Revelation. The statement in 2 Peter, chapter 3, does not refer to any period. All that it says is that 'with God a thousand years are as one day, and one day as a thousand years'. The sole passage on which the case for a millennium is based is the 20th chapter of Revelation. Now it is interesting to note that in that 20th chapter of Revelation there is no reference whatsoever to the condition of creation. It does not tell us anything about the state of the earth or the animals or anything else. That confirms what we have already discovered from these verses, that they have nothing whatsoever to do with a millennium. What we have been considering refers to what is described and dealt with at the end of that 20th chapter of Revelation, where the devil is finally cast into the lake of fire, where death and Hades are cast in after him, and evil is finally dealt with once and for ever.

The Book of Revelation is a book which is full of symbols, pictures and images. It describes conditions in terms of 'beasts' and it uses 'numbers'. It is generally agreed that the numbers are clearly symbolic, but when they come to the 20th chapter the millennialists hold that it must be a literal thousand years. It is generally agreed that the figure 10 is used symbolically of completeness: therefore when you have 10 multiplied by 10 and again by 10 it clearly represents a long period of time. But they persist in materializing the symbol and insist that it must be taken literally without realizing the difficulties in which they become involved. All that the passage in Revelation 20 says is that for a long period of time our Lord will reign and those who suffer for His Name's sake will be reigning with Him.

But someone will say, 'What about the Old Testament teaching, and passages such as that from the 11th chapter of Isaiah which you have quoted? Do they not point to the millennium?' Actually they do not mention a millennium at all. What happens is that people who take the reference to a thousand years in Revelation 20 literally, and who form their theory on the basis of that passage, and that alone, then try to argue that all these other passages refer to the same thing. But that is no proof at all; it is mere assertion. There is no reference to a limited period of a thousand years in any of the other passages; it is found only in Revelation 20.

But look at another fact. Nowhere in the whole of the Bible are believers exhorted to look forward to a coming millennium. Christians are exhorted everywhere to look forward to the coming of the Lord and the glory which shall be revealed. There is no injunction or exhortation anywhere to us to look forward to a coming literal thousand years of reign by the Lord and His saints here upon the earth. All we are told even in Revelation 20 is that over a given period, a long period, our Lord and the saints will be reigning; but nowhere are we exhorted to look forward to a literal, material, earthly millennium.

Then consider this striking fact. If there is to be such a thing as a literal millennium, surely this passage in Romans 8 of all places is where we would expect to find a reference to it. In Romans 8: 17 and following, the Apostle is comforting afflicted and suffering saints. Why did he not say to them in effect: Do not be downcast; do you not realize that ere long the Lord will come and will set up His earthly kingdom for a thousand years, and then, at the end of that period, Satan will be let loose again and there will be trouble, but then after that Christ will come again and there will be the final judgment? But Paul does not write in this fashion. Surely we are entitled to argue that if there is to be a literal thousand years' reign on earth, with its various accompaniments, then Romans 8, of all places, is the one place where we are entitled to expect some reference to it. But there is none. Nor is there any reference to such an event in any of the epistles of the Apostle Paul, or of the other Apostles. Moreover our Lord Himself never referred to it.

All the confusion and trouble is the result of taking one statement only in the Scripture – and that in a book which is full of symbols and pictures – and literalizing and materializing it. I am referring to this, not only because it creates confusion, but because it militates against a true understanding of this glorious teaching we are examining, teaching that the whole of the Bible, as we have already seen, emphasizes and declares. This is to be no temporary condition; this is permanent and final.

In other words what we have described here is what is called 'the eternal state and condition of the redeemed'. It will be ushered in by our Lord's Second Coming, by the Last Judgment, by the casting to final perdition of everything that belongs to sin and evil, and by the introduction of 'the new heavens and the new earth wherein dwelleth righteousness'. It cannot have any other meaning. The whole creation is going to be delivered, not temporarily, but absolutely, from the bondage of corruption into 'the liberty of the glory of the children of God'.

Let me emphasize again that this is not a reference to what happens when we die. It is a reference to that which is to happen at the end of the world, at the end of time, following the final judgment at the return of the Lord Jesus Christ. When we die, according to the teaching of the Scripture, we go to be 'with Christ'. Take, for instance, the teaching of Paul in the 1st chapter of the Epistle to the Philippians. He says in verses 21 to 24: 'For to me to live is Christ, and to die is gain. But if I live in the flesh, this is the fruit of my labour: yet what I shall choose I wot not. For I am in a strait betwixt two, having a desire to depart, and to be with Christ; which is far better. Nevertheless to abide in the flesh is more needful for you.' When the Christian believer dies he goes in spirit to be with Christ. That is perfectly clear. As I understand the teaching of Revelation 20 the unbeliever does not experience that, he has no part in that; he has no part in 'the first resurrection'. That expression refers to regeneration and to the fact that the spirit of the believing person at death goes immediately to be 'with Christ'. This is only true of the believer. But obviously that is not what we are dealing with here in

Romans 8: 18–23. Here the great emphasis is on the fact that the body is included and so it must not be thought of in terms of what happens to us when we die. This is something which is reserved until the end of time when the body itself is going to be delivered from all the corruption that still belongs to it. We are 'waiting for the adoption', to wit, 'the redemption of our body'.

In other words, what we have here in this passage demands and insists upon the full, the final, and the complete redemption of man – body, soul and spirit – and also the full redemption of creation. It demands the final, ultimate defeat of Satan and all who belong to him, the perfect salvation of the redeemed, and the restoration of the whole creation not only to what it was before, but to something yet more glorious. That is not temporary, it is final, it is full, it is permanent. Let us be clear in our minds, then, that this is not an exhortation to the Christian to hold on, and to continue, in spite of his suffering, because when he dies he will immediately be 'with Christ, which is far better'. That is true, but that is not what the Apostle teaches here. He teaches it in Philippians, chapter 1, but here he says something further.

But, again, someone may ask, and rightly so, 'Well then, what do you mean by heaven, and what is the relationship of what we have here to heaven?' This, I have to admit, is a difficult subject, and yet it seems to me increasingly that we should not be in difficulties about it. As I understand it, what is commonly described as 'heaven' in the Scripture is what we should regard as the intermediate state, not the final state, not the eternal state. I mean that what is generally described as 'heaven' in the Scripture is the condition described by Paul in Philippians 1: 23, where he talks about being 'with Christ, which is far better'. That is the intermediate state for this good reason, that in the eternal and final state, the body is involved. But when he talks about 'being with Christ, which is far better', the body is not involved. The body may be in a grave, it may be in the depths of the sea somewhere, it may have been blown to atoms. He is not referring there to the body. That is the intermediate state, the state and condition of the redeemed while they are waiting for the resurrection of the body and its final glorification.

It is indeed most significant to notice – and yet it is frequently missed – that in the famous passage in Revelation 20 the writer goes out of his way to tell us that he is only referring to certain 'souls'. Starting at verse 4 we read: 'And I saw thrones, and they sat upon them, and judgment was given unto them; and I saw the souls of them that were beheaded for the witness of Jesus, and for the word of God, and which had not worshipped the beast, neither his image, neither had received his mark upon their foreheads, or in their hands; and they lived and reigned with Christ a thousand years. But the rest of the dead lived not again until the thousand years were finished.' Note he says 'the souls', and that is the correct translation. The bodies are not involved, they are not included. In other words Revelation 20: 4 itself seems to give a complete refutation of the theory of a literal earthly thousand years. It is 'souls', not bodies. In other words, Revelation 20 describes the condition of all believers who have died and who have gone to be 'with Christ, which is far better'. That is exactly what happens to their 'souls'; they are there with Him now, and are reigning with Him now. Christ is reigning now; let us never forget that! He is seated at the right hand of God, He is reigning and waiting until His enemies be made His footstool. And all believers who have ever died since He came to complete the work of redemption are with Him. They are 'with Christ', and they are reigning with Him now. That state lasts a very long time; it has already lasted nearly two thousand years. Revelation 20, verse 6, does not mean a literal 'thousand', it means a very long time. It is already more than a literal thousand years, and we do not know how long it will yet be. But what I am establishing and emphasizing is that that is the intermediate state; it is a state of the 'soul', it does not include the condition of the body.

Various statements which we find in the Scriptures deal with these matters. We have seen some in 1 Corinthians 15; and you find others in the well-known passage in 1 Thessalonians 4 about those who 'sleep'. Verse 15 reads thus: 'For this we say unto you by the word of the Lord, that we which are alive and remain unto the coming of the Lord shall not prevent (precede) them which are asleep.' 'Asleep' refers to Christians who have already died. Again, verse 13: 'But I would not have you to be ignorant, brethren, concerning them which are asleep, that ye sorrow not, even as others which have no hope.' Then in 1 Corinthians 15 we read: 'We shall not all sleep, but we shall all be changed.'

There are some who teach that the 'sleep' here means a 'sleep of the soul', and that believers when they die are in a state of unconsciousness, and will remain in that condition until the resurrection. But that seems impossible in the light of Philippians 1: 23. Paul is not looking forward to a 'sleep of the soul', he is looking forward to 'being with Christ, which is far better'; and that agrees with what we are told everywhere else. Why then are the Christian dead referred to as being asleep? I answer that it is a term which is used to describe an incomplete condition, an intermediate state. At the final 'glorification', when the resurrection of the body takes place and man is fully saved in every respect, it will no longer be incomplete but full and complete. There is a sense in which that cannot happen until the glorification of the body. The body at death as it were 'falls on sleep', it is not yet revived and alive and active. So I take it that 'sleep' refers mainly to the condition of the body. The body is asleep, waiting. It is no longer active, as it will be in the state of glorification; there is an intermediate condition.

So we have accounted for the soul – it is 'with Christ, which is far better'. And we have also accounted for the condition of the body as 'asleep'. The point we are concerned to emphasize is that what we have in Romans 8: 18-23 does not refer to these matters at all. It deals with the final, the eternal state; not the intermediate, the temporary state. We must realize that in our eternal and everlasting state we shall not be disembodied spirits. When you think of heaven, when you think of your eternal future, how do you think of yourself? Probably most of us have always thought of ourselves as being in a kind of disembodied spiritual condition. But that is quite wrong; that is only the intermediate state, and even there we have a 'spiritual' body. In the final, the everlasting state, we shall not be disembodied souls, we shall be living in our glorified bodies. That is the point the Apostle is establishing. The body is to be redeemed; the 'adoption' is 'the redemption of our body'.

That in turn means that there must be a glorified earth in which we are to live in our glorified bodies. Our eternal state is not going to be lived in the heavens, in the air, in some vague, nebulous spiritual condition. We are taught here that we shall spend our eternity on the glorified earth under the new heavens – 'the new heavens, and the new earth, wherein dwelleth righteousness'. In other words, we can say that heaven in an eternal sense is going to be 'heaven on earth'. Heaven on earth – that is where we shall spend our eternity, and not as disembodied spirits, for the whole man will be redeemed, the body included. A concrete body must have a concrete world in which to live; and we are told that that will be the case. The whole creation is going to be delivered. All that we know now of the evil in creation will be done away with when the 'elements will melt with fervent heat', and the heavens will be on fire. That will mean the dissolution of the present, and the exclusion from the cosmos of all evil and sin. You and I, the redeemed, will dwell in our glorified bodies on a glorified earth under the glorified heavens.

That is all we know! We do not know, and I cannot give details about the relationship between that glorified earth and the heavens; but we are given a suggestion in Revelation 21 and 22 that this 'new Jerusalem' will come down from heaven to earth. So we must not think of our eternal state and future in terms of some spirit condition. Spiritism has affected the teaching of the Christian Church more than is often realized. Most people in the Christian Church today do not seem to believe truly in the resurrection of the body. All they believe is that we shall continue to live in some other realm. That is not the biblical teaching, which is, that we shall live in the body on this renewed, renovated, regenerated earth.

Why am I insisting on this? Because if this is not true then God has not really defeated Satan. When God made man, He first of all made a world for him to live in. Man was not made as a spirit; from the beginning he was made body, soul and spirit, and God made him to live in a physical universe. My argument is that, if God is to defeat Satan finally and completely, He must restore everything to its original condition. So if heaven just means that those of us who are believers are finally going to get rid of this old body and dwell in a spiritual realm in a purely spiritual condition, then redemption and salvation are not complete. God's plan of redemption is not complete until there is an earth for man to live in and on, in the body. Paradise regained cannot be anything less than that. Thank God, that is the very thing Scripture teaches. We are not to look forward merely to a vague, indefinite, nebulous spiritual state. No, we shall be in the body, and we shall be on a new earth, under new heavens, wherein dwelleth righteousness. That, and nothing short of that, will establish God's glory and His final triumph over the devil and all who belong to him. That is why in the last book of the Bible we find the figure of the 'new Jerusalem'. It is a figure, a symbol. I do not intend to press the details about the number of gates and about the gold; that is all picture, symbolical language to describe a very glorious universe. The Book of Revelation tells us that it is a book of symbols, so we must regard it as such.

But, in conclusion, and in the light of all that I have been saying, what should be our outlook? How should we live in this world? What should be our state and condition now? First of all, we should never be surprised at anything that happens to us in this world. Do not be surprised if you are persecuted because you are a Christian; do not be surprised if you are laughed at, if people think you are a fool, if they show malignity towards you. That, according to the Apostle, is what you must expect in this world. That is how they treated your Lord. You are 'in Him' and they will do the same to you. You are 'suffering with Him'. Do not be surprised also if things go terribly wrong in this world instead of getting better; it is what is to be expected. The whole creation is subject to 'vanity', so do not expect it to be any different. Many people get into trouble in their spiritual lives and experiences because they thought that once they believed and became Christian they would have no more trouble, but that is not Christianity. It is the kind of teaching given by the cults. Christianity teaches that 'through much tribulation we must enter into the kingdom of God' (Acts 14: 22), so you must expect this. 'In the world ye shall have tribulation' (John 16: 33). That is our Lord's own teaching, as it is the teaching of the Apostles.

A second conclusion is that as a Christian you must never pin your faith or your hope to anything that man can do to improve worldly conditions. There will be no lasting improvement. There may appear to be improvements now and again; there will be no radical improvement. This world will never be put right by man. It cannot be; at its centre there is this principle of disintegration, this vanity, this corruption. So a Christian must not get excited about reform, and feel that by Acts of Parliament men will bring in the new Jerusalem. I am old enough to remember that type of preaching. It was common in the Church until the First

World War. Men really thought that they were going to usher in a new Jerusalem by legislation. What utter nonsense! Do not hope for anything in this world, nor from it; then you will not be disappointed. But if you do hope for much from it you will certainly be disappointed. There is no hope held out for the world as it is, and as it is organized. It is doomed, it is under the wrath of God, it will be destroyed. Let men do their utmost – and I do not say they should not, nor that we should not have politics and statesmen – let them keep evil within bounds as much as they can, but let us not believe that they will ever succeed in making a perfect world. We must believe that 'the powers that be', magistrates and others, have been ordained by God and given the power of the sword to keep order and to prevent utter chaos, but ultimately it is only a negative and a restraining influence.

Thirdly, we must always realize that our salvation in the 'here and now' is always incomplete. Ever since we began our study of chapter 6, we have been noting that the position of the Christian in regard to salvation in the present is that in the realm of his spirit he is already saved, and as much saved as he ever will be. He is no longer in Adam, he is 'in Christ'; and he is safe there. 'More happy, but not more secure, the glorified spirits in heaven.' In regard to his spirit he is already redeemed. Not only so, as the Apostle tells us in chapter 8, verse 23, 'We have the firstfruits of the Spirit'. In other words, as believers, the Holy Spirit is in us; and the Spirit gives us a foretaste of the glory which is coming. His presence in us does that as well as His work of sanctification in us.

In Ephesians 1, verses 13 and 14 the Apostle puts it in the same way: 'In whom, having believed, ye were sealed with that Holy Spirit of promise, which is the earnest of our inheritance until the redemption of the purchased possession.' Such is our position. I am 'saved' now, I am a 'child of God', I am 'regenerate', I am a 'partaker of the divine nature', I am 'in Christ'. I have died with Him, I have risen with Him, I am seated with Him in the heavenly places – that is absolute! But my body is not saved; sin remains in the body. This mortal body has not yet been delivered. Hence the Apostle says that he is looking forward to 'the redemption of the body'. The body is not yet redeemed, it is a body of sin, and sin takes its opportunity there. Many times we have seen that truth in chapters 6, 7 and 8. In chapter 8, verse 10, we read: 'If Christ be in you, the body is dead because of sin; but the Spirit is life because of righteousness.' Such is the position of the believer. He is saved, and safe ultimately, but his body is not yet redeemed.

What then is the result of this? The result is, says the Apostle, that at the present time we 'groan within ourselves'. He says 'the whole creation groaneth and travaileth in pain together until now. And not only they, but ourselves also, which have the firstfruits of the Spirit, even we ourselves groan within ourselves, waiting for the adoption, to wit, the redemption of our body.' The Christian in a world like this, and still having an unredeemed body, is a man who is groaning within himself. Why does he groan? Because he knows the condition of his body and of the world. The body is his problem, and he knows that while he is in this life it will continue to be so. He is not promised anywhere in Scripture that the body will be redeemed in this life. He knows that, and that leads to a conflict. The devil takes advantage of this situation; that is why the Apostle exhorts us in chapter 6, verse 12: 'Let not sin therefore reign in your mortal body.' He had just said: 'Reckon ye yourselves also to be dead indeed unto sin, but alive unto God', and then at once he adds: 'Let not sin therefore reign in your mortal body.' Sin will always be trying to reign, but do not let it succeed: it means a fight, a conflict. We have already considered the matter many times over.

But it is part of the explanation of the fact that the Christian groans within himself. Yet it is not the main reason for his groaning. He groans chiefly because he has got 'the first-fruits of the Spirit' in him. Paul says: 'We ourselves also, which have the first-fruits of the Spirit, even we ourselves groan within ourselves.' We groan not only because we see what we are now, but also because we know what is coming. The extent to which you know what is coming is the extent to which you will be groaning at the present time. Let me use a simple illustration. Do you remember yourself as a child looking forward to a holiday or something equally pleasurable? Do you remember the groan – 'another six weeks to go'? But that was because you knew it was coming. If you had not known it was coming you would not have groaned. The more you know of the wonderful thing that is coming, the more difficult it is to wait until it comes! Spiritually speaking, the unregenerate do not 'groan within themselves'; and there are many Christians who do not seem to groan within themselves. It is because they do not know about the glory; they have never grasped this teaching. If they but grasped this teaching they would soon begin to groan.

But let us be quite sure and clear in our minds that the groaning of Romans 8: 23 has nothing to do with the 'wretched man' of Romans 7: 24. I repeat the emphasis I formerly gave. The trouble with the man in Romans 7: 24 is that he is not clear about his salvation. He knows nothing about the glory which is coming. Hence he is a 'wretched man' and cries out 'Who shall deliver me?' But the man in Romans 8: 23 is groaning because he knows about the deliverance, he has tasted of the 'first-fruits of the Spirit' and he is anxiously longing to get to glory. Not only is the creation stretching out its neck, this man is also doing so because he has the 'first-fruits of the Spirit'. So there is nothing in common between the groaning of Romans 8: 23 and that of the wretched, miserable man of Romans 7: 24. It is an entirely different matter. This groaning is the result of certainty; that 'wretchedness' was the result of the uncertainty which cries out 'Who shall deliver me?'

Here then is the Christian; and he is groaning. But that in turn leads to the waiting for the glory that is coming, which includes even his body. This is a picture of the Christian groaning but 'waiting for the adoption', not of the Christian wasting his time in anxiously trying to determine 'the times and seasons'; and fix everything he reads of in the morning newspaper with a 'prophetic clock'. How sad it is that so many Christian people are busying themselves making prophecies, and fixing exact dates for the Second Coming, and then becoming bewildered and unhappy when they are proved to be wrong! That is not the groaning to which the Apostle refers.

Wait for this glory, this 'adoption' which is coming. This is the exhortation of the Scripture, 'waiting for the adoption'. Or in Titus 2: 13: 'Looking for that blessed hope, and the glorious appearing of the great God and our Saviour Jesus Christ.' Again, in 2 Peter 3: 12: 'Looking for and hasting unto the coming of the day of God.' Such is the New Testament teaching.

There should be no confusion of mind about these matters, or about such sterile, futile refinements as, 'Is there to be a preliminary rapture of the saints?' There are people who are made unhappy and perplexed as the result of the prophetic teaching which began to be popular from about 1831 onwards. But there is none of that in the Scriptures. The Scripture holds before us this great, central, glorious fact, not some temporary condition which will ultimately end with the devil again having great sway. Instead, it presents the blessed appearing of the Son of God, and the manifestation of believers as the sons of God, the children of God with Him. This is the final redemption, the body included, with the whole creation delivered from 'the bondage of corruption into the liberty of the glory of the children of God'.

I leave the theme with a test and with a practical experimental question. Do you know anything about this groaning? Can you say honestly, 'I myself groan within myself, waiting for the adoption, to wit, the redemption of my body?' It should be true of all Christians. Do not waste your time in trying to fit communism into the biblical scheme, or Russia, or anything else. The teaching of Romans 8 is given to comfort us, to strengthen us, to enable us to endure suffering; not to confuse us with all the detailed minutiae of so-called prophetic systems and schemes. The Apostle's teaching is concerned about the glory of the blessed hope. It is taught everywhere in the Bible from beginning to end. God began teaching it in the Garden of Eden, as we have seen, in Genesis 3:15, and it goes right on to the end. That is why the final cry at the end of the Book of Revelation is this: 'Even so, come, Lord Jesus.' And when He comes we shall see the new heavens and the new earth, the new Jerusalem that has come down from heaven, all evil excluded for ever and ever and finally destroyed. And you and I, and all who have believed on the Lord, will be fully glorified, entirely redeemed, and we shall dwell in the sunshine of His face on that new earth under the new heavens, wherein dwelleth righteousness for ever and for ever.

To overcome suffering, and to be 'more than conquerors', we must be certain about this glory which is coming to us. Let us be practical, therefore, and test our interpretation of the Scripture by its practical effect upon our experience and upon our daily life in this present world. Can you say, quite honestly, 'I reckon that the sufferings of this present time are not worthy to be compared with the glory which shall be revealed in us'?

Eight

*

For we are saved by hope: but hope that is seen is not hope: for what a man seeth, why doth he yet hope for?

But if we hope for that we see not, then do we with patience wait for it.   Romans 8: 24, 25

In these verses the Apostle completes the argument of verses 18–23. He has finished with the details of his argument as such, and, as is his custom, having worked it out in detail he sums it up and states it again clearly. 'For', he says, 'we are saved by hope: but hope that is seen is not hope: for what a man seeth, why doth he yet hope for? But if we hope for that we see not, then do we with patience wait for it.' It is a reaffirmation, and a setting forth of the doctrine as something which is quite inevitable once we really have a grasp of God's plan and method of salvation. The very first word of verse 24, 'For', clearly links up with what has gone before. The Apostle always reasons an argument right through. He does not throw out a number of disjointed statements; he is always working out a theme. That is why in his epistles it is impossible to understand the parts unless we have some grasp of the whole.

The continuing argument in these two verses is essential in order that we may have a true understanding of the nature of the life of the Christian in this present world. And surely this was never more essential, more important, than at this present time. We are all involved in a world of trouble, and there are many who are really perplexed about what they see and hear. They are bewildered in their minds and do not understand what is happening. They ask such questions as 'Why does God allow this?' 'If God be God, then why?' The only way to find an answer to such questions is to follow and to understand the

Apostle's teaching. He has been saying in verse 23, 'Not only they' (namely the animals and inanimate creation) 'but ourselves also, which have the first-fruits of the Spirit, even we ourselves groan within ourselves, waiting for the adoption, to wit, the redemption of our body.' The Apostle's teaching here alone enables us to understand why the Christian groans within himself while he is still in this world of time and sin and shame. It is the Christian alone who really can and should understand contemporary history. No one else understands it. As Christians we should not be confused in our minds by what is happening in the world. If we are in trouble about it, it is because we have probably some vague, optimistic teaching which the world believes but which we should never have believed. Indeed, what is happening in the world today is but a confirmation of what the Apostle teaches us here. Far from being confused, then, and in wonderment as to what is happening, as Christians we should feel that the world today provides a most perfect proof of the whole teaching of the Bible, and that should lead us to rejoice. We are given an insight, an understanding which no one else can possibly have, and which no one else certainly does have.

An understanding of this teaching is really essential to our happiness in the Christian life. I must emphasize that again. We are meant to enjoy the Christian life. 'Ah, but', you say, 'does not the Apostle say that we who have the firstfruits of the Spirit groan within ourselves?' That is so, but it is not incompatible with the rejoicing; because we 'rejoice in hope of the glory of God'. Indeed, as we have seen, the more you rejoice in hope of the glory of God the more you will groan within yourself while you are still left here in this world. Far from being incompatible, these two things go together; and the one is the measure of the other. It is the man who knows something about the hope and the glory who, when he looks at this life and this world, groans, even as our Lord Himself groaned at the grave of Lazarus before He raised him: He groaned and He 'wept'. Why? It was not human sympathy alone; He groaned because of what sin had introduced into this world, including death, and because He knew the contrast between God's original creation and what God intended on the one hand, and what man had made of it on the other. So groaning and rejoicing go together. And therefore I say that if we really are to rejoice in our salvation, if we are to pay heed to this same Apostle's exhortation to the Philippians to 'Rejoice in the Lord always: and again I say, Rejoice', we must realize that we are to be rejoicing now, despite what the world is at the present time, and despite what may be happening to ourselves individually and personally. We are still to go on rejoicing in the Lord, and we can only do so as we understand the teaching which we are given here so succinctly and so clearly.

'For', says the Apostle, 'we are saved by hope.' That is his way of explaining and expounding what he has just been saying. He says that we should not be troubled and in difficulties about life's problems, for, 'after all' – that is what 'for' means – we are 'saved by hope'. Then he goes on to ridicule the Christian who is not rejoicing, and who is in trouble because of what is happening in the world. Is it not obvious, he says, that 'hope that is seen is not hope; for what a man seeth why doth he yet hope for?' It should be quite obvious to us that our salvation is in these terms. But we must be careful about our translation at this point. It is generally agreed that the rendering of the Authorized Version is not as good as it might be. It is the word 'by' that is misleading. A better translation is, 'For we were saved in hope'. Paul uses the past tense, 'we *were* saved'. It is certainly true to say that because we were saved we are saved; but you can say that 'we are saved' and mean that it is a process, that the salvation is still going on. But Paul says 'we were saved', it is something in the past, it has already happened. And furthermore, 'we were saved', but '*in* hope', not '*by* hope'. There is a danger that if you adhere to the translation, 'we are saved by hope', some might very well run away with the idea that hope is the instrument which leads to our salvation. But all who know this Epistle, and the entire teaching of the Bible know that 'we are saved by faith' not by 'hope'. So to say that we are saved by hope is a misleading translation.

But what does the Apostle mean by this statement that 'we were saved in hope?' The term 'hope' is used here by the Apostle himself in different senses, as is also the case in other places in the Scripture. Hope can mean, of course, a spiritual grace. Faith, hope, love are three spiritual graces. Indeed in the two verses we are considering, hope appears as a spiritual grace. 'What a man seeth, why doth he yet hope for?' Then Paul proceeds to say, 'But if we hope for that we see not . . .' Here again hope is a spiritual grace. So that is one possible meaning for it in its first use in verse 24. But does hope mean a spiritual grace when Paul says, 'We were saved in hope'? Let us look at its second meaning, which carries the idea not so much of a grace that is in us, as of the thing that is hoped for. There are many instances in the Scripture of this usage. We read about 'the hope of the gospel'; and here in verse 24, where we read, 'Hope that is seen is not hope' the reference is not to a spiritual grace. You cannot 'see' a spiritual grace in that sense. Here, obviously, 'hope' points to something objective. It has reference to that which is 'hoped for' rather than to the 'hoping' itself.

As the word 'hope' is used in the Scriptures to convey these two distinct meanings, we must be careful to distinguish between them as we consider verses 24 and 25. In the phrase, 'hope that is seen is not hope' there is clearly a reference to the great Christian hope, to the day of glory that is coming, the event to which the whole creation is looking forward, and is 'groaning and travailing in pain' as it does so. It is the event to which 'we ourselves also, which have the firstfruits of the Spirit' are also looking forward. It is the 'blessed hope' of which the Bible speaks; it is the 'hope of our calling' referred to in Ephesians 1: 18: 'The eyes of your understanding being enlightened; that ye may know what is the hope of his calling.' It means the objective hope. He is not referring to the grace of hope in their hearts as believers, but he desires them to know exactly what it is that God has prepared for them.

As for the spiritual grace which is called 'hope', we find it here in the expression, 'for what a man seeth, why doth he yet hope for?' The reference here is to a grace in the believer. 'But if we hope' (the grace again!) 'for that we see not, then do we with patience wait for it.'

The question is, What is the meaning of 'hope' in the first statement, 'We were saved in hope'? Here the commentators disagree. Some say it is subjective, some objective. But it seems to me that we are compelled to say that it is both; and that you cannot make it mean either the grace of hope or the thing itself hoped for exclusively. Neither of the alternatives is adequate in and of itself. What the Apostle is really saying is, 'We were saved in the sphere of hope', 'in the realm of hope'; or again, 'We were saved in expectation', 'We were saved into expectation'. In my view the two elements are included because Paul is talking about our salvation. The man who is saved has this grace of hope within him, but it is a hope with respect to something objective outside himself. As Christians that is our position; we were saved in the sphere and realm of hope.

As we analyse the Apostle's words we must consider what we may call the 'tenses' of salvation, or the 'stages' in our salvation, for inattention to this matter is a frequent cause of confusion. 'We were saved.' Paul is looking back. It is essential for us to realize that salvation can be viewed as belonging to the past, the present and the future. It is a much greater matter than we customarily think, and we only come to a knowledge of its greatness when we realize that it can be looked upon in these three aspects.

First, look at it in the past – 'We were saved'. The Christian is a man who should be able to say 'I am saved', 'I was saved'. He can look back at something that has happened. He should know that he has been saved already from the guilt and from the punishment of sin. 'There is therefore now no condemnation to them that are in Christ Jesus.' That is finished with; it has happened in the past. That is why I have been constantly emphasizing Paul's frequent use of the aorist tense which brings out the notion of something done in the past and done once and for ever. The Christian should not continue to be troubled about the guilt of his sin. He should rejoice with Philip Doddridge when he writes, 'Tis done, the great transaction's done'. This matter was emphasized in the crucial 6th verse of chapter 6, 'Knowing this' – we know this as Christians – 'that our old man was crucified with him'. We should all, as Christians, be clear that our past has been dealt with, that the 'old man' is dead. It means that we are completely forgiven, are justified by faith, and reconciled to God. It means that we have got nothing more to do with the law: 'Reckon ye also yourselves to be dead indeed unto sin, but alive unto God through Jesus Christ our Lord' (Romans 6: 11). Remember also Romans 7: 4: 'Wherefore, my brethren, you also are become dead to the law by the body of Christ; that you should be married to another, even to him who is raised from the dead, that we should bring forth fruit unto God.' We must never think of ourselves again as 'under law'. And again in verse 6 of the same chapter: 'We are delivered from the law, that being dead wherein we were held; that we should serve in newness of spirit, and not in the oldness of the letter.'

If you are not clear about these things you cannot follow the rest of the argument. It amounts to this, that you cannot be saved several times – only once; and to this, that you were crucified with Christ and are now in union with Him. When He died you died. That is the end of the 'old man'. Do not go back to the question of your forgiveness; do not let the devil trap you at that point. When you fall into sin do not raise the whole question of your justification again. If you do, it means that you do not understand the teaching of this Epistle. 'There is therefore now no condemnation to them which are in Christ Jesus.' We are no longer under the wrath of God. Even when you sin you must not feel that you are back again under the wrath of God. The devil will do his utmost to make you feel that you are; but you must not allow him to do so. When we sin we should not feel that we are back under the wrath of God, but that we have hurt a loving Father. What a difference! 'There is no condemnation', but we have wounded and hurt a loving Father. So we go back to Him as the prodigal son did, and find that all is well. That is the past aspect or tense of salvation.

But look next at the present tense. The past is absolutely final and finished with, but when you come to this present tense of salvation you are looking at something that is continuing. We are being saved from the power of sin, and also from the pollution of sin. We must not say that we have been delivered in that sense. If you say that you have been delivered from the power of sin it means that you will never sin again, and that you are perfect. The same is the case with respect to pollution. And we know that the claim does not ring true. No, this aspect of salvation is present and continuous; it is a process, an on-going process. We are being saved from the power of sin and from the pollution and the vileness of sin; we are being prepared for that which awaits us. And while being prepared, the Christian does his utmost to prepare himself. 'He that hath this hope in him, purifieth himself, even as he is pure.' In this way salvation is a continuing process; it is salvation in the present tense.

But there is also a future tense to salvation. There is all that which awaits us with God – our final glorification, the glory which is coming when even the body will have been delivered and will be glorified. The whole man, body, soul and spirit, will be entirely delivered, fully glorified in every respect. But this is something which is still in the future. We are not there yet. So we look in this way at the tenses of our salvation; and it is essential that we should do so. Thus far we have received the 'first-fruits', as verse 23 assures us: 'ourselves also, which have the first-fruits of the Spirit'. But what we have had is the 'first-fruits' only; there is a great fulness yet to come.

This is, perhaps, from the standpoint of the enjoyment of the Christian life, the most important portion of doctrine we can ever grasp. There are two dangers always confronting us as Christians. The first is that we claim too little, and the second, as usual, is the exact opposite, that we claim too much. Whichever of the two errors we fall into is bound to lead to trouble and to unhappiness. The first danger is that we claim too little. There are many Christian people who say, 'Knowing myself as I do, knowing my failure, and seeing what is happening in the world and my reaction to it, I cannot say that I am saved; it would be presumption for me to say that I am saved.' You ask such a person, 'What is your position then?' 'My position', he replies, 'is that I am hoping to be saved.' You then say, 'What are your grounds for saying so?' 'Well,' he replies, 'Romans 8: 24 says "We are saved by hope".' The *New English Bible*, so-called, does not actually say that, but it comes very near to doing so. It says, 'We have been saved, though only in hope'. But there is no 'though' in the original; the translators have introduced it. It is an equivocal statement, and read superficially it tends to support the idea that we must not say that we are saved, but only that we are hoping to be saved – 'saved, though only in hope'. This is not a true translation, it is interpretation, and it is misleading.

But there are many Christian people in this position. They say, 'I am hoping that I shall one day be saved.' But this is completely to misunderstand the meaning of the term 'hope'. To begin with, the past tense that the Apostle uses proves that this view is wrong. He says 'We were saved in hope', or in 'the realm of hope'. It has already happened. So it sets aside that interpretation automatically. It is not a mark of spirituality to say, 'Ah well, of course I know certain glib people who say "I am saved", but I would not dare say that because I am aware of my deficiencies.' To speak in that way is to fail to understand the Scriptures. The Apostle says that you should know that you were saved, and you should have absolute certainty and assurance concerning it. The

[101]

whole argument of this chapter is designed to give us this absolute certainty and assurance. We should be crying 'Abba, Father'! We should know 'the witness of the Spirit with our spirit that we are', not that we are hoping to be, but that we are 'the children of God, and joint-heirs with Christ'.

On the other hand there is the danger of claiming too much. This is the position of those who say that they already have everything. They claim that they have a 'full salvation' here and now. They claim it for their spirits, and some even claim it for their bodies. Some claim 'entire sanctification' now; they assert that they are entirely delivered from sin, and are filled with perfect love. Their sanctification, they claim, has happened in a second experience. The Apostle does not say so; indeed he says the exact opposite. But some of them also claim it for the body. These are the friends who say that a Christian should never be ill, that sickness and illness are the result of the Fall and that the Atonement has dealt with the Fall in every respect. They teach that healing is in the Atonement and that you can and should claim it with the consequence that the Christian should never be ill. The Apostle's answer is, 'We groan being burdened, waiting for the adoption, to wit, the redemption of our body'. The body is not fully and finally redeemed here in this life; and to say that it is, is to claim far too much. That is why the Apostle introduces this category of 'hope'. We have not yet arrived, he says, 'we were saved in the realm of hope', but we are not yet in the realm of full achievement, of final completeness. So it is important to get tenses clear in order that we may know what we must claim, and what we must not claim. We must not abuse the term 'hope' and claim too little; on the other hand we must not claim too much.

And so we arrive at our last question. What exactly does this 'hope' mean as introduced here by the Apostle? It does not merely mean that the Christian is a man who wishes, or desires or has longings for certain things. It includes such longings, but very much more besides. This 'hope' is described in 1 Thessalonians 5 : 8 as a helmet: 'And for an helmet, the hope of salvation.' It is not merely some vague longing or desire, it is something you can put on your head to protect it against all the wiles of the Evil One, and the world, and the flesh. Again, in Hebrews 6 : 19 we read: 'Which hope we have as an anchor of the soul, both sure and steadfast, and which entereth into that within the veil.'

You cannot talk about vague longings and desires as an 'anchor of the soul'. But the writer of the Epistle to the Hebrews speaks of hope in that way. He does so because hope is strong and steadfast, it is something that is going to 'hold', it is 'an anchor of the soul'. Indeed we have already seen in Romans 5 : 5 that the Apostle says, 'Hope maketh not ashamed'.

What then is hope? The best answer is to look at it in its various relationships, and especially in its relationship to faith. For example, in 1 Corinthians 13 : 23 we read: 'And now abideth faith, hope, love, these three; but the greatest of these is love'. Or again, take Hebrews 11 : 1: 'Faith is the substance of things hoped for, the evidence of things not seen.' Here we see the relationship of hope to faith. That means that faith provides the grounds or reasons of our belief in those things that are coming to us; it is the substantiating of them. They would mean nothing at all to us if we had not faith. Faith gives us an assurance that God has done certain things for us once and forever in Christ Jesus, and that He will do yet more. In that sense we are saved 'by faith'. Faith represents the reality of our salvation.

But hope goes further still. Many go wrong at this point, and tend to think of hope as something we fall back on when our faith becomes weak. 'Ah,' says a man, 'normally I live a life of faith, but sometimes my faith is so shaken that I cannot say that I am certain any longer, or that I believe; all I can do now is just to hope.' In other words he thinks of hope as 'hopefulness', and hopefulness is weaker than faith. 'Hope', says the poet, 'springs eternal in the human breast.' Perhaps it does, and I am ready to agree that that is a good psychological statement. But it has nothing whatsoever to do with the term 'hope' as it is used throughout the Bible. Hope is strong, not something vague and indefinite. Faith comes first, hope goes beyond it; faith leads to hope. What is it then? It is, as a familiar hymn says, 'The earnest looking forward'. Faith gives us a certainty about these things, hope makes us stand on tiptoe to have a look at them. It is stronger than faith, it takes us a step further.

To put it in yet another way, faith looks back to the finished work of Christ, and gives us certainty concerning the things He has purchased for us. That is why it is the substantiating of which Hebrews 11 : 1 speaks. Hope looks forward with eager expectation to the things which Christ has thus purchased for me.

[103]

That is how hope takes us a stage higher. It is something which is so certain of the blessings that are believed and accepted by faith that it really lives for and is always looking forward to them.

Hope is the measure of true Christianity, which is through and through other-worldly. Pseudo-Christianity always looks chiefly at this world. Popular Christianity is entirely this-worldly and is not interested in the other world. But true Christianity has its eye mainly on the world which is to come. It is not primarily concerned even with deliverance from hell, and punishment, and all the things that trouble us and weary us. That really belongs to the past. True Christianity 'sets its affection on things which are above, not on things which are on the earth'. It is that which says, 'We look not at the things which are seen, but at the things which are not seen: for the things which are seen are temporal, but the things which are not seen are eternal' (2 Corinthians 4: 17 and 18).

'We were saved in hope.' Faith brings us into the realm of the things hoped for. I have the first-fruits of them now, but I have not the reality yet. I have a first instalment of it, I have an earnest of it, but I have no more now. So while I thank God for what I have, and rejoice in it, and can look back with absolute assurance to what has been done once and for ever, and will never be repeated because it does not need to be repeated, it nevertheless makes me look all the more, and with the more 'earnest looking forward', to that which is yet to come. You should not be in any trouble about this, says the Apostle, your salvation has brought you into this kind of position. Do not be disappointed because things go against you; do not feel that God has let you down; do not turn and say, 'But when I believed the gospel I thought I would never have another problem, that the story would be "They all lived happy ever after".' You should never think and speak in that way, says Paul, because you have been 'saved in the realm of hope', you have been saved absolutely in certain respects, but still the greater part of salvation is yet to come. What you have already received is but a very small percentage of the whole, it is merely a foretaste. So, he says, do not be stumbled by this; always remember that 'you were saved in hope'.

As long as you remember the Apostle's teaching you will be able to say, 'I reckon that the sufferings of this present time are not worthy to be compared with the glory which shall be revealed

in us'. Christian people, hold on to this, and especially in these
dark and difficult and uncertain days. This is not our world. 'I am
a stranger here, heaven is my home.' 'Our citizenship is in heaven',
not here. Such is the Christian position, such is the Christian
attitude. The world will call it escapism. Let it call it what it
chooses; its language but reminds us of its blindness and darkness.
The Scriptures place before us the truly Christian position. The
way in which the Apostle himself lived was 'in a strait betwixt
two'; whether to remain in this world to help the Philippians
and others, or to depart to be with Christ, 'which is far better',
and beyond that to 'the blessed hope' of His appearing. We are
saved into this realm of hope. Christian, do not claim too little,
do not claim too much; but understand your present position
as it is taught in this great passage.

Nine

*

For we are saved by hope: but hope that is seen is not hope: for what a man seeth, why doth he yet hope for?

But if we hope for that we see not, then do we with patience wait for it. Romans 8: 24, 25

We have seen that, according to the Apostle's teaching, what we have received of the Christian salvation, or ever can receive in this world, is but a very small instalment or foretaste of that which we are ultimately going to receive in the glory. That is the main argument which the Apostle has been developing from verse 18 in this chapter to the end of verse 23. In verses 24 and 25 he sums it all up, and at the same time applies it. We can now go on to the application of this argument.

He goes on to say, 'But hope that is seen is not hope: for what a man seeth, why doth he yet hope for? But if we hope for that we see not, then do we with patience wait for it.' In his application of the argument, the Apostle makes two main statements, one negative, and one positive. First of all there is the negative argument which he states as a general principle in the words, 'Hope that is seen is not hope: for what a man seeth, why doth he yet hope for?' In other words, he is setting aside the idea that you can really 'see' or 'have received fully' that which, by definition, is mainly a matter of hope. He lays that down as something which is universally true. Your hoping to meet a person comes to an end when you actually meet that person. When you are standing face to face with a person you are not hoping to see him, you are seeing him. This argument is an example of *reductio ad absurdum*. The application is, that if we can see that in ordinary everyday terms, then we should realize that the same is true in this matter of our salvation. Possibly some of the Christians at Rome were not realizing it; hence he writes in this way.

Many portions of the New Testament were written to comfort and to console people who were stumbling over this matter. The Apostle here shows them that their attitude was ridiculous. They were expecting to hold in their hands something that belongs mainly to the future and is to be hoped for. As you were saved in hope it is ridiculous to expect that you can see now what is promised at a future date. If you could see it, it would no longer be a matter of hope – 'hope that is seen is not hope; for what a man seeth, why doth he yet hope for?'

This sounds very obvious when put in a general way; but it is very difficult to realize it in practice. The devil comes in and makes us exaggerate what is possible to the Christian in this life. Sometimes the desire for results on the part of preachers and evangelists tends to increase that tendency. But if we are always Scriptural then we will avoid much trouble in that respect. 'We were saved in hope', or as Paul puts it in the Second Epistle to the Corinthians, chapter 5, verse 7: 'We walk by faith, not by sight.' We do not see these things yet; they are afar off. We see them only by faith.

If we truly grasp this principle we shall never be surprised by anything that may happen to us in this world. We do not live in some magic or charmed circle because we are Christians. We are never promised exemption from the troubles that flesh and blood are heir to in a fallen, sinful world such as this. So we must not be surprised when 'evils' befall us; we must not be disappointed and become dejected. Still less must we begin to query the truth of the Christian gospel. The devil will tempt us to do so. 'Ah,' he says, 'you believed in Christ, and you thought everything was going to be trouble-free; but look at your position. Your gospel is not true.' The best reply to such a challenge is to understand and grasp this argument that 'hope that is seen is not hope; for what a man seeth, why doth he yet hope for?' We are now living by faith and in hope. So get hold of this negative argument and it will save you from ever being surprised or disappointed, and ultimately from being dejected.

The positive argument is stated in verse 25. 'But if we hope for that we see not, then do we with patience wait for it.' Here again is a statement which is true more or less in every realm. It is true as a general proposition. When we realize that something is only in the realm of promise at the moment, we are prepared to wait until it comes. For instance, you have to wait for your holidays to come. Or if you have an inheritance coming to you in a Will you have to wait until probate has been granted. You do not have it immediately, and you realize that you cannot have it immediately. So if you have common sense, if you use your reason, if you are in control of yourself, you discipline yourself, you say, 'Well, I see that I cannot get it until a certain date, so I must reconcile myself to that fact and go on living patiently until it arrives.' That is true, I say, as a universal principle.

But here the Apostle is concerned to apply the universal principle in the special sense in which it is true of the Christian, and to his position and condition while he remains in this evil and sinful world. It is in reality an exhortation. He says, If you grasp this principle that you 'were saved in hope', that you are hoping for something you do not see at the present time, then wait for it with patience. This statement therefore comes to us not only as instruction but also as a challenge, and at the same time as a source of great comfort and encouragement. What are we to do as Christians at this present time in this evil world? The injunction is that we must 'hope for that we see not'. This is a positive exhortation, not merely a matter of negative resignation. There is always the danger of falling into the state of mere negative resignation. We are awakened to the sad state of this world, we see evil increasing, and we know that man can do nothing about it in an ultimate sense. Sin cannot be eliminated by Acts of Parliament; an immensely greater power is needed; and at times the temptation that comes to the Christian is to wish to be out of such a world. I have heard Christian people, particularly the older ones, saying occasionally, 'I wish I were dead, and out of this old sinful world. Why doesn't God take me home?' They want to be out of it, to get away from it because it is what it is, because as Christians they have come to see its true character. But that is not what is meant by 'hoping for that which we see not', because it is an entirely negative attitude.

The Apostle is concerned about this, not only here in this Epistle but wherever he deals with this particular aspect of

Christian teaching. Another instance of it, and one which is very illuminating as a commentary upon this passage, is in 2 Corinthians 5, verses 2–4: 'In this tabernacle we groan, earnestly desiring to be clothed upon with our house which is from heaven: if so be that being clothed we shall not be found naked. For we that are in this tabernacle do groan, being burdened.' Then, significantly, 'not for that we would be unclothed'. That is not what I desire, he says. He was not in the negative condition of the Stoic who merely wants to get out of it all, or in that of the eastern religions which display the same attitude. They are always longing to get out of the body because they believe that the body is entirely evil. But Paul says, 'Not for that we would be unclothed', which means that his teaching is not merely negative, the expression of a desire to get out of this life by some kind of release and escape. That is not the Christian attitude. The Christian attitude is essentially positive. So the Apostle says, 'Not for that we would be unclothed, but clothed upon'. What we should be longing for is not the 'unclothing', but the new clothing. The Christian is not primarily concerned to get rid of this present 'clothing', this body and all its encumbrances, and to be naked, as it were. What he desires is to be 'clothed upon'. He has a positive outlook, and is looking forward to the glory. 'Not for that we would be unclothed, but clothed upon, that mortality might be swallowed up of life.' Or, as Paul puts it later in 2 Corinthians 5: 8, his desire is not so much to be 'absent from the body' as to be 'present with the Lord'.

This is a most vital distinction. There are many who, having looked at life, and having suffered a great deal, simply long to get out of it. But that is never the Christian position. The Christian is always positive. He wants to be 'with the Lord', he wants to be 'clothed upon, that mortality might be swallowed up of life'. This Apostle teaches that everywhere. Take, as another instance, the moving passage in Philippians 3, from verse 10 onwards. His desire is, 'That I may know him, and the power of his resurrection . . . if by any means I might attain unto the resurrection of the dead'. That is his real desire; it is essentially positive. He was having a very difficult time in this world, but he does not merely desire to be out of it. He says, 'Not as though I had already attained, either were already perfect'. No, he is not perfect, he is saved 'in hope'. 'But I follow after, if that I may apprehend that for which also I am apprehended of Christ Jesus. Brethren, I count not myself to have apprehended.' He has not received all, though he had received a great deal, and probably more than anyone has ever had since, but he says, 'I count not myself to have apprehended: but this one thing I do, forgetting those things which are behind, and reaching forth unto those things which are before, I press toward the mark for the prize of the high calling of God in Christ Jesus. That is the truly Christian attitude, and you find it taught everywhere in the New Testament.

This teaching is not confined to the writings of Paul; the Apostle Peter in his First Epistle, chapter 1, verse 13, says exactly the same thing: 'Wherefore gird up the loins of your mind, be sober, and hope to the end for the grace that is to be brought unto you at the revelation of Jesus Christ.' Salvation includes a looking forward, a hoping for that which is to come, the thing which we do not yet see. 'Gird up the loins of your mind', do not allow circumstances to control you, do not allow your feelings to control you, pull yourself together, 'be sober, and hope to the end'. Go on!

The same teaching is found in the First Epistle of John, chapter 3, and the whole object of the Book of Revelation is really designed to teach precisely this same truth. Is this our condition as Christian people? Are we all obeying the exhortations? Are we hoping for that which we do not see? This is Christianity. This is what I would venture to call the *differentia* of Christianity, the thing that marks it off from every other teaching or creed. The Christian is one who is hoping for the things he does not yet see.

How are we to do so? We can subdivide the Apostle's answer into two main sub-divisions. 'If we hope for that we see not, then do we wait for it with patience.' There are two elements here – the 'waiting', and the 'patience'. Here, once again, we must be clear about the meaning of the terms. What is desirable in a translation of the Bible is not only simple words, as the advocates of the New English Bible urge, but the true meaning accurately expressed. This New English Bible translates it thus: 'But if we hope for something we do not yet see, then, in waiting for it, we show our endurance.' The whole emphasis there is upon ourselves, and our wonderful endurance. But that is not the Apostle's intention at all. His emphasis is on that for which we are waiting; not on our endurance but on the glory of this event for which we are waiting. So we must reject that translation. Not only is it bad translation but it misses the whole point and purpose of the Apostle's teaching. A better translation, I suggest, would be,' If we hope for that we do not see, then, through patience, we eagerly wait for it'. The emphasis is to fall upon the 'it' – this great event for which we are waiting, and which we are earnestly expecting.

Look next at the phrase, 'Wait for it'. The Authorized Version translation itself is not adequate; it just says, 'then do we with patience wait for it'. It is correct, it points in the right direction, unlike the New English Bible translation; but it does not bring out the full meaning of the word 'wait'. The true meaning is 'eager waiting'. There are many kinds of waiting. The Apostle's concern is that we should be 'eagerly waiting'. It even includes the notion of being joyful. I have consulted the best and latest lexicon on this matter – that by Arndt and Gingrich – and they give 'eager waiting' as the meaning of the Apostle's word. The whole context makes it inevitable that that should be the translation. The Apostle has told us in verse 19, 'The earnest expectation of the creature waiteth for the manifestation of the sons of God'. If the creation has an 'earnest expectation', surely the Christian believer, a son of God, should have nothing less than that! If the whole of the inanimate and brute creation is 'eagerly' expecting, 'earnestly' looking forward to this, this should be much more true in the case of the believer.

But for another reason also we must adopt the translation 'eager waiting'. It is the only way of bringing the waiting into line with what Paul has already told us in chapter 5, verse 2, where he says, 'We rejoice in hope'. We are not just 'waiting'. You can wait and look very dull, and be dull, and feel dull; but that is not the Apostle's idea of waiting. 'We rejoice in hope'; there is the joyful element. The joyful eagerness is an essential part of this exhortation. The manner in which we wait proclaims what kind of Christians we are. 'Eager expectation.'

In other words it is not just a passive waiting. When you really want something, passivity is not much in evidence. When you are looking forward to something, and longing for it, you are more like a dog on the leash. The waiting is not relaxed and passive. You are straining for it, 'stretching out your neck', as we translated the 19th verse. The whole of inanimate creation is doing that, and so should we be on tiptoe, stretching out our necks. Let me expound Scripture by Scripture, which is the best way of expounding it. We have here what the Psalmist has in mind in the 130th Psalm, verse 5: 'I wait for the Lord, my soul doth wait, and in his word do I hope. My soul waiteth for the Lord more than they that watch for the morning: I say, more than they that watch for the morning.' Note the repetition. His picture is that of people who, having to do duty right through the night, are waiting for the morning to come so that they may go and rest. Or, it may be the case of people besieged and beleaguered, and they know that in the morning help is due to arrive; so they wait for the morning, they know that when the dawn comes there will be relief. But, says the Psalmist, 'My soul waiteth for the Lord *more* than they that watch for the morning'. And then, 'I say, *more* than they that watch for the morning'. He thus expresses the intensity of his eager waiting for the Lord, his watching for Him, and his hoping for His appearance for his relief.

Again, we find this intensity of hope in Philippians 3. The Apostle is waiting, but he emphasizes the character of the waiting. 'I count not myself to have apprehended: but this one thing I do, forgetting those things that are behind, and reaching forth unto those things which are before, I press toward the mark for the prize of the high calling of God in Christ Jesus.' Note the kind of waiting that he is talking about: 'pressing toward the mark', straining to reach it; it is not merely some passive resignation and waiting. The Apostle says a similar thing in writing to Titus, in the 13th verse of the 2nd chapter: 'Looking for that blessed hope, and the glorious appearing of the great God and our Saviour Jesus Christ.' Similarly the Apostle Peter, in his Second Epistle, chapter 3, verse 12 says: 'Looking for and hasting unto the coming of the day of God.'

There is no purpose in our looking at great phrases such as these unless we allow them to search us and to examine us. The Word is always to be preached, and also to be applied; so I ask a question. Can we say that we are eagerly waiting for and anticipating this great glory? Let every man examine himself. 'The world is too much with us', so the question is: Are we 'eagerly awaiting', 'looking for', longing for the glory?

Furthermore, the Apostle says that we are to be 'eagerly waiting' 'with patience'; at least, that is the translation in the Authorized Version. Again, it is correct, but it is not sufficiently clear. At this point 'with' really means 'through'. Dr E. W. Bullinger, whose teaching on many matters I do not accept, although on the meaning of words I find him helpful, defines this word as indicating 'the cause by means of which an action passes to its accomplishment'. So we are eagerly to await the coming of this hope 'by means of' or 'through' patience.

It is also important that we should give the word 'patience' its full and rich meaning. It means 'patient endurance'. I grant that in this verse the New English Bible has the word 'endurance'. It is right at that point, but it has missed the full meaning. 'Endurance', 'patient endurance', includes constancy, and also the notion of firmness. Another good way of expressing it is by the word 'unwearying'. You are not to get tired, you must not become weary. 'Unwearying endurance, and patience and continuance.'

Here again it is important to avoid the negative. We often tend to think of patience as passive; but it is a very active virtue. Certain people have a reputation for being patient, but sometimes the real truth about them is that they are just dull. They are not sensitive, they do not react, and are more or less stupid. That is not patience. Patience is an active virtue, for which reason we are so constantly exhorted to it. It is a virtue which has to be developed, so that it becomes strong and firm. Actually the Apostle here is giving us a fuller exposition of what he said in a few phrases in chapter 5. I have quoted already the end of verse 2 in that chapter, '. . . and rejoice in hope of the glory of God'. But he continues, 'And not only so but we glory in tribulations also: knowing that tribulation worketh patience; and patience, experience; and experience, hope.' So I emphasize this particular aspect of 'patience'. It is a virtue strong and active; it grows and develops as the result of the tribulations we are called to endure.

In his 5th chapter the Apostle says specifically that trials and troubles and tribulations actually lead to patience and strengthen it, and that as it produces experience it eventually increases the hope with which we began. I quoted the remark of a Puritan about this whole matter at that point. He says, 'Hope is at one and the same time the mother and the daughter of patience.' You start with hope, and you end with hope. You travel from hope to patience, and patience to experience, and then back again to hope. And what produces these steps, he says, is the effect of tribulations upon the Christian.

The Christian starts with 'hope'. You could not be patient if you did not have the hope. If you have nothing to hope for how can you be patient? That is the tragedy of the man who is not a Christian; he has nothing to hope for, nothing to look forward to; so how can he be patient with things as they are? But the man who possesses the Christian hope has got patience, because patience is the daughter of hope. But as we exercise patience we develop experience, and experience in turn leads back again to hope. And in that way patience seems to be the mother of the hope. The truth is that each leads to the other. Christian truth is a circle. If you start at any one particular point and proceed from it you will come back eventually to the same point. All these truths work together. 'All things work together for good to them that love God.' That is the kind of argument the Apostle puts before us at this point.

The Apostle is still expounding his original statement, 'I reckon that the sufferings of this present time are not worthy to be compared with the glory which shall be revealed in us', and he bids us to wait eagerly for the great coming event in an unruffled, undisturbed and steadfast manner. We must not be surprised at anything that happens to us. Indeed, we are to be like the good man who is described in Psalm 112, verses 6–8: 'Surely he shall not be moved for ever: the righteous shall be in everlasting remembrance. He shall not be afraid of evil tidings: his heart is fixed, trusting in the Lord. His heart is established, he shall not be afraid.' The Christian is not afraid of evil tidings, he is ready for anything that comes. 'His heart is fixed, trusting in the Lord.' He is like a rock, he is solid. He has this quality of patient endurance, and it does not matter what comes. 'His heart is established, he shall not be afraid.' Why? Because of this hope that he has! This too is the position of the Christian: he 'hopes for that which he sees not', and therefore through patient endurance he eagerly expects it and waits for it.

Now notice the remarkable way in which the Apostle states this truth. First of all, note the wonderful picture we have here of the Christian man and his character. Here is a man who can combine eagerness and patience together at one and the same time. What a perfect balance! Eager people, in a natural sense, are generally not very patient. A man, we say, is either mercurial, impulsive, and eager, or else he is the calm, quiet, phlegmatic, patient type. But the Christian, as Paul depicts him, is a man who is at once both eager and patient. In the Scripture we are shown the perfect balance that should characterize the Christian character. The Christian is eager, but he is never excitable. What an important distinction! It illustrates the difference between the natural and the spiritual man.

But, again, because of this patient endurance the Christian is not a man who sees things in spasms and behaves in an erratic manner. He is constant, reliable, dependable. He is not a variable man, sometimes praising the Lord excitedly, at other times looking dejected and unhappy and wondering whether he will continue in the Christian life. That is the very antithesis of what we have here. Paul depicts a man of wonderful balance. He is not merely a negative and a passive man; he is a lively man, a living man. But he is not a boisterous man, for that is not compatible with patient endurance. One aspect balances the other. This is what the Spirit produces in a man who is truly in the Christian position. He is other-worldly, but yet he is a very practical man. He is not an idle visionary. He is not a man who spends his time sitting and doing nothing because of the Christian hope.

There were people of the unbalanced type in the early Church. Hence Paul says to the Thessalonians 'that if any would not work, neither should he eat' (2 Thessalonians 3 : 10). He was not merely rebuking laziness, he was dealing with people who thought that they were ultra-spiritual, and who claimed to be marvellously clear about the Second Coming of our Lord. They were so confident of its imminence that they spent the whole of their time looking up, so to speak, into the heavens, and abstaining from earning a living. But the glory of the truly Christian man is that his head, as it were, is in heaven, but his feet are solidly on the earth. He has this perfect balance – eagerness and patient endurance!

The Apostle Peter expresses this point in his characteristic phrase, 'a lively hope' or 'a living hope'. Hope is not a mere whim, a mere fancy, a mere passing feeling. That is why, as we have seen, Peter is so practical and exhorts us to gird up the loins of our mind, and not to live merely in the realm of feelings.

Secondly, note the nature of the longing, the eager expectation. It is not something theoretical and academic. 'If we hope for that we see not, then do we through patience eagerly await it.' Paul does not mean that we have a mere abstract, theoretical interest in the details of prophetic teaching. It is not just something bookish and academic. He does not mean that we become involved in the vagaries of a dispensationalism, and that we spend all our time in trying to fix dates and in manipulating figures. The hope is something practical which affects a man's life and manner of living. It is not that you spend the whole of your time intellectually trying to unravel mysteries and to work out schemes. The element of patient endurance means that the feelings are also involved.

The important question, therefore, is not what prophetic theory you may chance to hold, but whether you are really longing for this glory? Is this in your heart as well as in your head? It was so in the case of the Apostle. His desire was, 'That I may know him, and the power of his resurrection, and the fellowship of his sufferings, being made conformable unto his death; if by any means I might attain unto the resurrection of the dead' (Philippians 3: 10 and 11). That was his longing and yearning! Is it ours? Let us be careful that the devil does not side-track us, by persuading us to substitute for this glorious 'hope' a mere theoretical, mechanical interest in what the future holds for us. If you cannot say from your heart that you are longing for the coming glory and living for it, then any other 'prophetic' interest is of very little value to you. The Apostle could say, 'To me to live is Christ, and to die is gain'. He had a longing to be with Christ, 'which is far better', and beyond that he looked for 'the glorious appearing of the great God and our Saviour Jesus Christ', and 'the manifestation of the sons of God'. If our study and our interest in these things does not bring us to that same longing we should set about the work of self-examination without delay.

I close with a very practical point. How can we attain to this condition? How can we through patience eagerly await it? First and foremost, if you want to know what it is to be eagerly awaiting for those things, realize the exact truth about this present world. 'The world is too much with us.' We must examine the world, and see it for what it is. Do not be misled by the world, do not be captivated by it. See the rottenness, the ugliness, the foulness; and do not allow it to monopolize your time and your attention. You must see through it. Then, having seen through it, keep yourself from it. 'Mortify therefore your members that are on the earth; fornication, uncleanness, inordinate affection, evil concupiscence, covetousness.' Get rid of them, finish with them.

The next step is to remind yourself of who you are and what you are. 'If ye be risen with Christ' – and you are risen if you are a Christian – well, remind yourself that you are risen. Such is the teaching that we have met with everywhere in this Epistle. We have been crucified with Christ, we have died with Him, we have been buried with Him, we have risen with Him. We have finished with the Law, we are dead to sin, we are new men, we are alive unto God. Remind yourselves of these things. It takes time to do so; but we must do so. The Apostles did so, the saints of the centuries have done so. Then there is the exhortation, 'Set your affection on things above, not on things on the earth'. We have to 'set' our affection, not simply wait for something to be worked up in us; we must dwell on these things and meditate upon them. Do not just say, 'Ah yes, I have read my daily portion of Scripture. I have read about a patient waiting for the coming glory, and the commentary I study has explained the meaning of the words.' Do not stop at that, but say, 'Is this true of me? Is this happening to me?' Dwell on it, think about it, meditate about it. Pray for light upon it until it becomes real to you. We must seek the Lord Himself. That is the secret of it all – to know the Lord! 'That I might know him!' Then having got to know Him, think of the things He is preparing for us. He has gone to prepare a place for us. 'Eye hath not seen, nor ear heard, neither have entered into the heart of man, the things which God hath prepared for them that love him' (1 Corinthians 2: 9). Think of the realm to which you are going. How long are we to be in this world? The shorter it seems to be, think the more of the world to which you are going, set your affection there. Think of it all, try to conjure it up from what you read in the Scriptures. That is what is meant by, 'Set your affection'. Keep on doing so, contemplate what is coming to you. 'Beloved,' says John, 'now are we the sons of God, and it doth not yet appear what we shall be: but we know that, when he shall appear, we shall be like him; for we shall see him as he is' (1 John 3: 2). How often do we dwell on such words? How often do we think about them, and meditate upon them? This is Christianity. This is how the first Christians lived; it explains why they shook everyone and 'turned the world upside down'. It was because they were people who had their affection on things above, not on things on the earth.

Keep on dwelling upon these things until they all become real to you. How real to you is this other realm? How real is this 'blessed hope'? Make it real by reading, meditating, praying, asking the Lord to make it clear. The Spirit has been sent in order to do such a work. Keep on doing all these things until you are so 'conscious' of that other realm that it becomes the greatest thing in your lives.

I read a remarkable statement this very week as I was preparing these matters. I was reading an extract from an autobiography of an old Welsh preacher whom I had the privilege of knowing. He died in 1929. He says that after his mother died he was looking through her papers and various belongings. In a very old book he came across a little sheet of paper on which he found that one of his sisters had written certain words. She was then quite young, I suppose somewhere between ten and twelve years old. Her father had died, and evidently, on the day of his death, the little girl had written these words on the piece of paper, and had put it in the old book. This is what she had written: 'Today Dada has left us. He has gone into the glorious liberty of the children of God.' A little girl of ten or twelve, in the 'sixties of the last century could write in that way. Why? Because those were the terms in which she thought, the climate in which her family lived. How many of us think in that way? How many of us could write like that? Is that our view of our own ultimate departure? Do we think instinctively in that way when our loved ones who are Christians leave us and go to be with Christ? This is true Christianity. I ask again, what is the value of all our head knowledge if it does not bring us to this? This is triumphing. It transforms everything. Life, death, and everything else becomes different. 'If we hope for that we see not, then through patience do we with eager expectation wait for it.' What a poor generation of Christians we are! What has gone wrong, I wonder, during the last hundred years or so? The answer, I fear, is that we are all so subjective, always looking at ourselves and our happiness, instead of thinking and meditating on the truth of the Scriptures and setting our affection on things above. Look at Christ, consider Him and what He is preparing for us. It transforms everything. That is the way in which, it seems to me, we 'through patience should eagerly wait for' this blessed hope that is set before us.

Ten

*

Likewise the Spirit also helpeth our infirmities: for we know not what we should pray for as we ought: but the Spirit itself maketh intercession for us with groanings which cannot be uttered.

And he that searcheth the hearts knoweth what is the mind of the Spirit, because he maketh intercession for the saints according to the will of God. Romans 8: 26, 27

Here we come to a fresh statement. Nevertheless, the word 'likewise' at the beginning of verse 26 reminds us that the Apostle is going to add something to what he has just been saying about the place of tribulations and trials in the life of the Christian, and how he should overcome them.

Our first business is to discover what exactly is the connection introduced by the word 'likewise'. Two suggestions which must arise in the mind of any thoughtful, careful student of the Scripture have been put forward by various commentators. The first and more popular explanation is that the Apostle is still continuing with the same theme. He has been pointing out, they say, that Christians are to face their trials and tribulations by means of hope, that it is hope which comforts us and sustains us and enables us to go on. As we have seen, that explanation is right and true. It is this 'hope' that 'revives our courage by the way' as a hymn reminds us. But at this point, they say, the Apostle adds that not only does 'hope' help us to face trials but the Holy Spirit also is at work to help us and aid us, especially in prayer. In this pilgrimage of life, in the fight of faith, and amidst persecutions, disappointments, and trials of various description, we are driven to prayer.

But how are we to pray? According to this interpretation of the 'likewise' it is in verses 26 and 27 that the Apostle gives his answer. The Spirit gives us this additional aid. So we are not left merely with faith, which leads to 'the hope' and to assurance; we have this further aid which is provided by the operation of the Spirit in connection with our prayer life. And that is certainly true.

But there is a second way in which we can interpret the exact connotation of this connecting link. The suggestion is that the Apostle is not continuing with what he has just been saying and giving Christians additional consolation, but rather continuing with the series of statements he has made about the Holy Spirit Himself. So in one sense he is taking up a new subject here. Not that it is altogether new, of course, for all parts of the Christian life are intimately related, but broadly speaking, he is taking up another facet of the Christian's assurance and certainty of salvation. In other words he is reverting to the theme of verse 17. The connection therefore would be this. In verse 16 Paul says, 'The Spirit itself beareth witness with our spirit, that we are the children of God.' Then in verse 17, 'And if children, then heirs; heirs of God, and joint-heirs with Christ', and 'if so be that we suffer with him, that we may be also glorified together'. His reference to suffering leads to a digression on the whole question of suffering, which he deals with, as we have seen, from the beginning of verse 18 to the end of verse 25. But having finished with this theme, he goes back to that which he had left off half way through verse 17. That is, he returns to the work of the Holy Spirit in assurance.

I regard this second possibility as the better one, for the reason that I have been emphasizing throughout, namely, that the central and continuing theme of this 8th chapter is assurance of salvation. It is a continuing exposition of the theme announced in verse 1, 'There is therefore now no condemnation to them that are in Christ Jesus'; there is none now, and there never will be. The whole object of the chapter is to show that our final glorification is absolutely guaranteed from the moment of our justification; a theme which the Apostle emphasizes, as we have been seeing, in a variety of ways.

Now the controlling factor in all these different aspects of assurance has been the work of the Holy Spirit. For instance, in verse 2, the first ground of assurance, we are told, is that 'The law of the Spirit of life in Christ Jesus hath made me free from the law of sin and death'. In verse 4 Paul tells us that the object of our salvation in Christ is 'that the righteousness of the law might be fulfilled in us'; and that all true Christians 'walk not after the flesh, but after the Spirit'. That truth is then elaborated until the end of verse 10. Because we are now living this new life in the Spirit, we see everything from the standpoint of the Spirit. We no longer have the mind of the flesh, we have the mind of the Spirit. We no longer have the carnal mind, we are spiritually minded, and this is a guarantee of our ultimate salvation. The moment a man is justified, the Spirit of God enters into him; and the Spirit works this work of sanctification. The Spirit enlightens the mind and leads us on, gives us a delight in the Law, and thus prepares us for ultimate glorification. It is absolutely guaranteed. God puts the Spirit in us in order to prepare us for the glory that lies ahead.

Then in verse 11 the Apostle puts the matter in terms of the resurrection of the body. 'If the Spirit of him that raised up Jesus from the dead dwell in you, he that raised up Christ from the dead shall also quicken your mortal bodies by His Spirit that dwelleth in you.' Then in verse 13, on a very practical level, he says, 'If ye live after the flesh, ye shall die: but if ye through the Spirit do mortify the deeds of the body, ye shall live'. It is 'through the Spirit' we are enabled to mortify the deeds of the body.

Then in verse 14, he reminds us of one of the most glorious proofs of our ultimate glorification and full salvation, 'As many as are led by the Spirit of God, they are the sons of God'. The Spirit gives us the 'Spirit of adoption'; but over and above that, 'The Spirit himself beareth witness with our spirit, that we are the children of God'. This, as we have seen, is the highest and most glorious form of assurance a believer can ever have. It is the peculiar witness of the Spirit with our spirits that we are the children of God. In all these ways the Spirit is the guarantee of our ultimate glorification, and gives us an assurance of it even while we are in this world of time.

In verse 23 we have, 'Not only they, but ourselves also, which have the first-fruits of the Spirit, even we ourselves groan within ourselves, waiting for the adoption, to wit, the redemption of our body.' The Spirit gives us a foretaste of that glory, He gives us the 'first-fruits'. That is a guarantee of our ultimate complete salvation, because it means that as God has given us a first instalment of it, God's character is involved in that pledge.

So having told us of the series of things the Spirit does in this connection the Apostle now says, 'Likewise . . .' There is something further that the Spirit does. 'The Spirit also helpeth our infirmities', and especially in connection with prayer. I do not assert that the first suggestion that the Apostle is continuing directly with the theme of suffering is not present at all, because obviously the Spirit does help us to pray in our difficulties; but I feel that the main thrust and the main emphasis is still upon our ultimate glorification. When we come to verse 28 we shall find that Paul takes up yet another aspect of that theme, 'We know that all things work together for good to them that love God, to them who are the called according to his purpose'.

This point is important because it will help to bring out the richness of the teaching which the Apostle gives in these two verses. While we are travelling through this world as pilgrims, what is more important for us than that we should know how to keep in touch with God our heavenly Father? What is more vital to us than to know how we can receive God's blessings? This whole question of prayer is a great problem to many people; indeed it is a problem to all of us. In many ways prayer is one of the greatest problems in our lives. Some teach that prayer is quite a simple matter, and that all you have to do is to start praying, no problem being involved. But that is not what we find in the Scriptures; and the moment we really examine our personal experiences we shall find that prayer in certain aspects can be the greatest problem of all. The Apostle's teaching is that there is a great message of comfort and consolation with regard to prayer as there is with regard to everything else.

The problem of prayer, Paul tells us, arises primarily from our infirmities: 'Likewise the Spirit also helpeth our infirmities.' It is probably right to say that the Apostle put this in the singular, not in the plural – 'Likewise the Spirit also helpeth our infirmity'. In other words he is concerned not so much about the varied manifestations of our infirmity as with the infirmity itself which gives rise to the particular infirmities. He is referring to our general state and condition, which is one of infirmity. Light is thrown on this in Hebrews 5: 2, where the author is describing the qualities necessary in a high priest. He says that he must be one 'who can have compassion on the ignorant, and on them that are out of the way; for that he himself also is compassed with infirmity'. It is the same word exactly as we have here.

Infirmity means primarily weakness, lack of strength. It is not sinful in and of itself. There is a difference between infirmities and sins. Our infirmities may lead us to sin, but our infirmities in and of themselves are not sinful. They are undoubtedly the result and the consequence of the original Fall of man, because there were no infirmities in man as God made him. God made him perfect. But one of the tragedies of the Fall is that everyone born into the world after the Fall of man is 'compassed by infirmities'. There are certain weaknesses, lack of powers, certain disabilities and inabilities that result from the Fall. That is what is primarily meant by 'infirmity'.

Again, we must not think of this only in a physical sense. We cannot exclude the physical, but it is not essentially physical; rather is it spiritual. It really means the various limitations from which we suffer as the result of the Fall. It includes many things, the most important of which is ignorance and inability to understand. These infirmities of ours lead to a great deal of suffering in this life even in the Christian. Although we are saved, and although our salvation is absolutely certain and sure, although we are 'dead to sin', 'dead to the law', dead to any possible condemnation, we are still not perfect, we are still 'compassed with infirmity'. And in consequence, as Paul says in verse 23, 'even we ourselves groan within ourselves, waiting for the adoption, to wit, the redemption of our body'.

These infirmities may arise from the body; they may arise from weakness, tiredness, illness or disease. And because of the intimate relationship between the mind and the soul and the spirit of man, nothing can happen to the one part without a variety of repercussions on the other parts; hence we often find ourselves waking up in the morning in a dull condition – dull in doing our ordinary work, still more dull when we try to read the Bible or to pray. Such dullness is an infirmity. It is not that we have committed some particular sin; we wake up in that condition, and we have no control over it. The various conditions of the body in this way affect our functioning. Not only so, but outside happenings affect us as well; other people behave towards us in ways we do not like; circumstances seem so to conspire against us as to become a discouragement to us. We become perplexed, we do not know what to do, or where to turn. The result is that, because of our lack of understanding and of knowledge, we tend to become depressed, and thus we 'groan within ourselves', even we 'who have the firstfruits of the Spirit'. We long for 'the day' which is coming, the glorious day when we shall be delivered even from this infirmity, these infirmities, as well as from every other manifestation of sin in the whole creation. In other words, various trials come to us because of our infirmities.

An interesting point arises here as to what was true of our Lord Himself. Verse 3 of this chapter tells us, 'For what the law could not do, in that it was weak through the flesh, God sending his own Son in the likeness of sinful flesh'. I emphasized that the Apostle does not say 'in the likeness of flesh' but 'in the likeness of sinful flesh'. He deliberately wrote in this way, I believe, in order to include this very notion of infirmities. Our Lord was entirely free from sin, but He experienced some of these infirmities to which we are subject, and to which we are heir. This was essential in His work as our great High Priest and Representative, as Hebrews 5 reminds us. It should help us to realize the importance of the statement that infirmities are not in themselves sinful.

The Apostle takes up a very special manifestation of the infirmity, and indicates the way in which it tends to show itself most acutely and perhaps most frequently, namely, in the realm of prayer – 'we know not what we should pray for as we ought'. It is a crucial matter because there is nothing more important than our relationship with God, our ability to speak to God and to listen to God; all that is subsumed under the category of prayer. This particular manifestation of infirmity leads perhaps to the greatest perplexity of all to most of us, and is our greatest trial, 'We know not what we should pray for as we ought'.

I have given the translation of the Authorized Version. The Revised Version reads, 'We know not how to pray as we ought'; the New English Bible has, 'We do not even know how we ought to pray'. The Revised Standard Version is virtually the same as the Revised Version, and many others have followed the Revised Version in exactly the same way – 'We know not how to pray as we ought'. But these modern translations make the point much too general. The Authorized Version seems to me to give the translation that brings out the real point that is being made by the Apostle. Our trouble is not that we do not know how we ought to pray – it is not a question of prayer in general – but what to pray for in particular, and in certain given circumstances.

The Apostle's actual phraseology in the original compels me to say this. Take the word 'what'. You will find in the Greek that it is preceded by the definite article. It is 'the what'. 'We know not the what we ought to pray for as we ought.' Surely the Apostle is directing attention to something particular. This phrase 'as we ought' also substantiates and helps to prove what I am suggesting. 'As we ought' means 'what is necessary in the nature of the case', this particular case. That is one possible translation. Another is, 'We know not the what to pray for according to [or in proportion to] our need.' The late A. T. Robertson, a Greek scholar in America, suggests it should be, 'We know not the what to pray for as it is necessary'. J. N. Darby is still better when he puts it thus: 'As is fitting.' A. S. Way who, while he gives a paraphrase rather than a translation, I believe has the spirit of the Apostle's meaning almost perfectly. He translates, 'We are not even sure what boons should rightly be the object of our prayers.' We do not know exactly what we ought to pray for in this particular state or condition. Hence the perplexity.

The Apostle is not concerned to tell us here about the one and only way whereby we have access into the presence of God, namely 'by the blood of Jesus' and by the Holy Spirit. The problem he is handling turns upon the question, What, in my peculiar circumstances, am I to pray for? That is peculiarly the problem when you are enduring trials and troubles and tribulations, and everything seems to be against you. You know how to approach God in prayer, but your difficulty is what exactly to pray for 'as is fitting', as is necessary at a particular time. In this way our infirmity is responsible for one of the most perplexing of the problems that so often face us in the Christian life.

Why should this problem concerning 'the what' be such a difficult matter? One reason is that we do not understand, we do not always know what is best for us, what is right for us, and we may pray for the wrong thing. Greater men than any of us have done so. Take one obvious example. We read about Moses in Deuteronomy 3, verses 23–26: 'And I besought the Lord at that time, saying, O Lord God, thou hast begun to show thy servant thy greatness, and thy mighty hand: for what God is there in heaven or in earth, that can do according to thy works, and according to thy might? I pray thee, let me go over, and see the good land that is beyond Jordan, that goodly mountain, and Lebanon.' Such was Moses' prayer. He was admiring the works of God, and appreciative of God's dealing with him; so he makes his petition. But we read, 'But the Lord was wroth with me for your sakes, and would not hear me: and the Lord said unto me, Let it suffice thee; speak no more unto me of this matter.' That is a strong and a stern rebuke. God silenced Moses and prohibited him from offering that petition any more. Moses had offered a petition which he should not have offered.

In many ways, perhaps, the classic example of this very matter with which we are dealing is found in 2 Corinthians chapter 12, verses 1–10. 'It is not expedient for me doubtless to glory. I will come to visions and revelations of the Lord.' Then Paul proceeds to talk about 'a man in Christ fourteen years ago' who had had wonderful revelations. 'Of such an one will I glory; yet of myself I will not glory, but in mine infirmities. For though I would desire to glory, I shall not be a fool; for I will say the truth: but now I forbear, lest any man should think of me above that which he seeth me to be, or that he heareth of me. And lest I should be exalted above measure through the abundance of the revelations, there was given to me a thorn in the flesh, the messenger of Satan to buffet me, lest I should be exalted above measure. For this thing I besought the Lord thrice, that it might depart from me. And he said unto me, My grace is sufficient for thee: for my strength is made perfect in weakness. Most gladly therefore will I rather glory in my infirmities, that the power of Christ may rest upon me. Therefore I take pleasure in infirmities, in reproaches, in necessities, in persecutions, in distresses for Christ's sake: for when I am weak, then am I strong.'

That is a perfect commentary on the verses we are considering here in Romans 8. The Apostle was in trouble because of the thorn in the flesh; and he acts in a very natural way in terms of human reason. He felt that this was going to cripple his work, to put a limit upon his efficiency; it was obviously wrong. So he prays the Lord to remove it; and he does so three times. But he is told that he must stop offering that prayer; deliverance will not be granted; the thorn in the flesh is to remain. Then he begins to look at his situation in a more spiritual manner; he sees that the Lord's way is right, and that the Lord can perhaps accomplish more through his weakness than He could through his strength. He understands the matter, and so he begins to glory in that which formerly he had been praying to God to remove from him.

Here, then, lies our difficulty; what are we to pray for? Because of our infirmity we do not always know what is best for us. Who would have imagined that the thorn in the flesh was a good thing for the Apostle Paul? But it was! It was necessary at that time. That is why it was sent to him; and that is why it was allowed to remain in him. So we have to be very careful. This is not an easy matter; it is not sufficient merely to say glibly, 'Pray about it', or 'Let us have a word of prayer about it.'

Having seen the real danger of offering the wrong petition in our ignorance and weakness, we do well, with the Apostle, to recognize our infirmity. In doing so we find ourselves also in the company of the writer of the 77th Psalm. He was beginning to complain in his sufferings, and he cries out: 'Hath God forgotten to be gracious? Hath he in anger shut up his tender mercies?' Circumstances were against him, and against the children of Israel. Others were enjoying prosperity, so he begins to think unworthy thoughts of God and to give utterance to them. Then he pulls himself up with a jerk: 'And I said, This is my infirmity', meaning, 'I should not be saying such things; I am speaking foolishly, it is all due to my infirmity; I do not understand.' So instead of continuing to harbour such thoughts he says, 'I will remember the years of the right hand of the Most High'. In other words, he begins to speak and to preach to himself, and so restores himself to a true understanding and confidence. That is the kind of problem the Apostle has in mind here. So before we rush thoughtlessly into prayer let us talk to ourselves about the possibility of our infirmity misleading us. Better still, let us acknowledge our perplexity. In other words, if you are in doubt, and uncertainty, and if you do not know 'the what' to pray for as you ought, do not be afraid or ashamed to admit it, and to confess it, and to do so quite openly.

We have an example of the Apostle doing that very thing when he is writing to the Philippians. In chapter 1, verse 23, he says to them: 'For I am in a strait betwixt two, having a desire to depart, and to be with Christ; which is far better: nevertheless to abide in the flesh is more needful for you. And having this confidence, I know that I shall abide and continue with you all for your furtherance and joy of faith; that your rejoicing may be more abundant in Jesus Christ for me by my coming to you again.' At first he is in difficulties as to what to pray for. He was in prison, possibly suffering ill-health, and had become old before his time. What shall he pray for? Shall he pray to the Lord to take him out of it all, to be with Christ, which is far better? So much seemed to argue in that direction. But then he remembers that it would be better for the Philippians that he should remain alive, that he might still teach and guide and help them. He is in a 'strait betwixt two'; he does not know exactly what to hope for, what to pray for. In such a case it is better that we should acknowledge the perplexity and take it to God, tell Him that we do not know, and leave it entirely in His hands. That is far wiser than forcing ourselves to a decision, or rushing to offer a petition that seems to us to be natural.

Is it going too far to suggest that we see something of this even in our Lord Himself during His days in the flesh here in this world? How do we interpret John's Gospel, chapter 12, verse 27? 'Now is my soul troubled; and what shall I say? Father, save me from this hour?' He Himself answers, 'But for this cause came I unto this hour. Father, glorify thy name.' His soul was troubled. He was facing the supreme crisis, and His soul was troubled: 'What shall I say?' He says, 'What shall I pray?' Shall I ask the Father to save me from this hour?' And He adds in effect, 'No, I cannot do so, because I came into the world in order to come to this hour.' Even the eternal Son of God as Son of man knew something of this perplexity.

The same perplexity appears in the accounts of the happenings in the Garden of Gethsemane. The Lord was in an agony, sweating great drops of blood, and His prayer is, 'Father, if it be possible, let this cup pass from me; nevertheless, not my will but thine be done'. Again, we observe, He is in an agony of soul at a moment of crisis: what shall He pray? The author of the Epistle to the Hebrews deals with the matter in his 5th chapter, where he writes about the qualifications of the high priest. In verses 5 to 8 he writes: 'So also Christ glorified not himself to be made an high priest; but he that said unto him, Thou art my Son, today have I begotten thee. As he saith also in another place, Thou art a priest for ever after the order of Melchisedec. Who in the days of his flesh, when he had offered up prayers and supplications with strong crying and tears unto him that was able to save him from death, and was heard in that he feared; though he were a Son, yet learned he obedience by the things which he suffered.' That is a most important statement. 'Though he were a Son, yet learned he obedience by the things which he suffered.' And in that position He 'offered up prayers and supplications with strong crying and tears'; and as the result of that experience He became the better qualified to act as our High Priest.

We can be encouraged by the thought that 'He learned obedience'. On that account He is able to help and to succour us when we find ourselves in moments of crisis and perplexity. We know how to pray; that is not our problem. We know that there is always a way open to us to go into the presence of God.

> *When all things seem against me*
> *To drive me to despair,*
> *I know one gate is open,*
> *One ear will hear my prayer.*

That is not the problem. I know that I can 'go into the Holiest of all by the blood of Jesus' with 'full assurance of faith', with 'full assurance of hope', and with a holy boldness. That is not my problem. My problem is what exactly to pray for, what blessing to ask for. What I think may be good may be for my harm. I may ask for this or that, but God may say, 'Speak no more to me about it', 'My grace is sufficient for thee'.

Have we any experience of that difficulty, that perplexity? The Apostle raises it in order to tell us that there is a glorious answer to it. It is that 'the Spirit himself maketh intercession for us with groanings which cannot be uttered'. What He does for us is known to God; indeed it is originated by God Himself as a part of the process of our ultimate glorification.

Eleven

*

Likewise the Spirit also helpeth our infirmities: for we know not what we should pray for as we ought: but the Spirit itself maketh intercession for us with groanings which cannot be uttered.

And he that searcheth the hearts knoweth what is the mind of the Spirit, because he maketh intercession for the saints according to the will of God.   Romans 8: 26, 27

We have seen the need for caution, for carefulness in connection with prayer; we have also noted the folly of rushing thoughtlessly into the presence of God, and the advisability of being ready to admit that, at times, we are in a condition of perplexity. We now begin to look at the comfort and consolation offered to us in that condition. In considering the argument of the Apostle in these two verses, I start by asserting that we should not be discouraged by the difficulties which arise out of our infirmity. In the first place, I remind you that the infirmity is not something sinful in and of itself. It results, as we saw, from our sinful state and condition, being one of the consequences of the Fall of man at the beginning. In this fact we may take comfort. We should not feel that we have committed an act of sin because we do not know at any given moment what to pray for.

Again, the mere fact that you sometimes find yourself in a situation in which you do not quite know what to pray for as you ought is not a sign that you are not one of God's children. The devil will come and suggest the contrary immediately. He will say, 'Ah, you do not know what to pray for. You must not call yourself a child of God, for if you were a child of God you would not be in this kind of difficulty. As a child with its father you would always know what to ask for; but you do not know, you are ignorant, you are in perplexity. The fact is that you are not a child of God at all.' The Apostle's teaching gives the lie

[131]

to the devil's charge, and is calculated to preserve to us the joy of the Christian life and experience.

Thirdly, we can say that this kind of infirmity which renders us incapable of knowing exactly what we should pray for as we ought, far from proving that we are not God's children, can indeed, if we but listen to the apostolic teaching, lead to a most wonderful proof of the fact that we are God's children. It is the very thing that the Apostle is emphasizing at this point. This infirmity, if we regard it properly, will turn out in the end to be an additional proof of the fact that we are the children of God and that our ultimate salvation is assured.

How does this work out? The first thing is that we are reminded that the Spirit Himself helps us. 'The Spirit Himself', and not, as in the Authorized Version, 'The Spirit itself'. We have dealt previously with this point, and it certainly does not make any difference to our interpretation of the teaching. Here, then, is an immediate source of comfort. In this situation of perplexity that results from our infirmity, the Holy Spirit of God Himself does something to help us. This is a further action of the Spirit. 'Likewise the Spirit also . . .' In addition to the other things He does, He in the same way does this particular thing.

What the Spirit does in this situation is expressed by the word 'helpeth'. In the Greek, 'helpeth' is a word of rich and wonderful meaning. It is made up of three words, and each one of the three is important for our understanding of the teaching. The first word means 'together'; it occurs in the first part of the English word symphony. The second word means 'over against'. And the third word means 'to take'. The idea is that of two people taking something over against one another. It means that one person gives a helping hand to another by taking hold 'over against that person' of the load that he is carrying. Think of a man struggling to carry some heavy load and almost at the point of collapsing. Suddenly someone comes along and says, 'Let me get hold of the other end of your load'. So that instead of the man having to carry the whole burden himself, the other who comes along takes hold of the other end, and now they together proceed to carry this load that was too much for the one man acting alone. That is the picture. And such is the meaning of the word which the Apostle uses here. He tells us that the Spirit of God comes to our aid in the way I have described.

The exact meaning of this word is illustrated in a familiar incident in the Gospels, that concerning Mary and Martha recorded at the end of the 10th chapter of Luke's Gospel. 'It came to pass, as they went, that he entered into a certain village: and a certain woman named Martha received him into her house. And she had a sister called Mary, which also sat at Jesus' feet, and heard his word. But Martha was cumbered about much serving, and came to him, and said, Lord, dost thou not care that my sister hath left me to serve alone? bid her therefore that she help me.' There you have the same word. What she said was, 'Bid my sister that she give me a helping hand in this matter. She is leaving me to do everything; she is sitting there listening to you. I have to do the cooking and the carrying of the food from the kitchen into this room. I need her aid. Why do you not tell my sister to give me a helping hand, to share this burden with me? Why do you not tell her to take part with me so that the two of us can face the work together?' It is the precise word that we are dealing with here in verse 26, and it brings out something of the rich meaning of the word that Paul uses. He means that Christians are carrying heavy burdens, and experiencing perplexity in prayer. But the Spirit comes and gives them a helping hand; He takes hold of the burden with them in order to help them to know what to pray for.

Another illustration of the same idea is found in our Lord's gracious invitation recorded at the end of the 11th chapter of the Gospel according to St Matthew: 'Come unto me, all ye that labour and are heavy laden, and I will give you rest. Take my yoke upon you, and learn of me; for I am meek and lowly in heart: for my yoke is easy, and my burden is light.' The picture here is of two oxen yoked together, pulling a load together in order to do so more easily. Our Lord is saying in effect to His disciples: You are weary, you are heavy laden, and you are labouring because the load is too much for you. What I am offering is that you be yoked to Me; and as you are yoked to Me we will perform this labour together. Then you will find that it is easy, and that the load which was so heavy becomes light. It is the same idea as we are taught here about the work of the Spirit in 'helping our infirmity'.

Note, in passing, that we are not told that the Spirit intends to do everything for us, and that we have nothing to do. The

Spirit *helps* us. He does not take the whole of the burden from us. What He does is to take up the other end of it. Think of a man carrying a log or a plank which is so heavy that it proves too much for him. Another man comes along and takes hold of the other end of the plank or the log, and so they carry it together. The second man does not do all the work, he helps. The Apostle is not teaching a doctrine of passivity. The Spirit 'helpeth' our infirmity, comes to our aid, gives us a helping hand, comes up over against us, takes hold together with us; and so, together, the problem is solved.

The way in which the Spirit thus helps us is that He 'maketh intercession for us'. Here again is another most interesting word – 'maketh intercession'. The original meaning is defined as 'to be rescued by one who happens on one who is in trouble and who acts in his behalf'. Think of a man walking along a road who suddenly comes upon a poor man in terrible trouble; he is being charged with an offence and is in great difficulties trying to defend himself. The man who arrives on the scene now begins to plead on behalf of the troubled man, either to his master, who may be beating him, or to the magistrate, or to the king, or to whomsoever it was that had brought the charge against the poor man. In other words, he makes intercession for him.

How does the Holy Spirit act in a similar way? Before we can answer that question we must deal with the expression translated 'with groanings which cannot be uttered'. There is no difficulty about the 'groanings', but what of 'which cannot be uttered'? The phrase means 'without words', 'not formulated in words'. It is a groaning or a sighing which is not given expression or form in words. I maintain that it means nothing more than that, but many of the commentators read much more than that into it. They maintain that these 'groanings, these sighs, are so deep, so profound, so moving, that they defy expression'. The groanings within us are so profound in their depth that no words can possibly describe them. I contend that that is forcing a meaning.

The argument used in its favour is that the kind of word that is used here is used elsewhere in the Scriptures to signify the inexpressible. Take, for instance, 2 Corinthians 9: 15: 'Thanks be unto God for his *unspeakable* gift.' Here 'unspeakable' refers to the Lord Jesus Christ, and is used in the sense that no words can ever describe Him adequately, our vocabulary is entirely exhausted.

He is the 'unspeakable gift'. Or take the example found in
2 Corinthians 12: 4. The Apostle is describing his experience of
fourteen years earlier and he writes: 'I knew a man (whether in
the body or out of the body, I cannot tell: God knoweth) such
an one caught up to the third heaven, to Paradise, and heard
unspeakable words, which it is not lawful for a man to utter.' Again
there is no difficulty. Paul had a glimpse of heaven, and he heard
something of the conversation, the language, the music of heaven,
of the glory. There is only one thing to say about that, it is
'unspeakable'. Human language is totally inadequate to describe
happenings in heaven. That is why we are told so little about
heaven in the Bible. People often ask, 'Why are we not told more
about heaven?' That is the answer. All language known to man,
even the best, the most exalted and eloquent, would detract from
the glory of heaven; it is so glorious that it is 'unspeakable',
and to attempt to describe it would be to detract from it.

The Apostle Peter provides another illustration in his First
Epistle chapter 1, verse 8: 'Whom having not seen, ye love; in
whom, though now ye see him not, yet believing, ye rejoice with
joy *unspeakable* and full of glory.' The Christian may know the
Lord Jesus Christ in such a manner that he cannot find words to
describe the joy that fills his heart. We should all be in that
position. It is something so great, so profound, that words are
inadequate to express it.

But I maintain that this is not the meaning of the word as
found in Romans 8: 26. I am supported in this by the very word
the Apostle used. He did not use the word which he uses in
those other cases. He used a word here which simply means 'not
expressed in words', 'wordless' – 'with groanings which are
wordless', or 'with wordless groanings'. He is not saying that the
feelings which we have are so profound and so deep that we
cannot give expression to them, but simply that we are in such
perplexity that we cannot express ourselves and our desires; we
do not know. It is just 'wordless'; and I argue that we are not
entitled to read any deeper meaning into it.

But the question arises, Who does the groaning? 'Ah,' says
someone, 'that is obvious, the Spirit Himself does so, "The Spirit
maketh intercession for us with groanings which cannot be
uttered".' There seems to be no difficulty. But that surely cannot
be the case. The Holy Spirit is one of the three Persons in the

blessed Holy Trinity. He never groans, He never sighs; that is inconceivable. 'But,' you reply, 'did not our Lord groan?' The answer is that He groaned as a man, when He was in His condition of humiliation. The Godhead does not groan; it is inconceivable for every reason. There is no lack of knowledge in the Holy Spirit; He knows all things as the Third Person in the blessed Holy Trinity, and therefore there is no cause for groaning. So I say that it is utterly inconceivable that it is the Holy Spirit Himself who does the groaning.

The groaning is in ourselves, it is we who do the groaning in this wordless manner; it is we who fail to find the words to express what is happening within us. Let me demonstrate my contention and interpretation. Take a very good parallel in this respect in Galatians 4: 6. The Apostle says there, 'And because ye are sons, God hath sent forth the Spirit of his Son into your hearts, crying, Abba, Father'. At first sight you might conclude that the Apostle is saying that it is the Spirit who cries 'Abba, Father'; but that is impossible. The Spirit is not the Son of the Father and therefore does not Himself cry 'Abba, Father'. What happens is that God sends forth the Spirit of His Son into our hearts with the result that He causes us to cry 'Abba, Father'. We have already read in the 15th verse of this 8th chapter of Romans: 'Ye have not received the spirit of bondage again to fear; but ye have received the Spirit of adoption, whereby *we* cry, Abba, Father.' There it is quite plain. But we have seen that Romans 8: 15 corresponds to Galatians 4: 6, where Paul expresses himself in words that might lead us to think that it is the Spirit who cries 'Abba, Father'. It is the Spirit who leads us so to cry; but the cry, the elemental cry 'Abba, Father' is uttered by us. That is why we were at such pains to show the difference between verses 15 and 16. In verse 15 it is 'our' spirit that cries 'Abba, Father', as the result, of course, of the operation of the Spirit. But in verse 16 it is the Spirit Himself who is 'bearing witness with our spirits that we are the children of God'.

So we begin to see what the Apostle means when he says that the Spirit 'maketh intercession for us with groanings which cannot be uttered'. It happens in the following way. The Spirit, as it were, finds us in our trouble. Because of our infirmity, circumstances are such that we do not know what to pray for. We are afraid of praying for the wrong blessing, we do not want to put up the wrong petition, so we do not know what to do, and are in perplexity. The Spirit comes to us in that situation – comes upon us as the word itself suggests – comes to us as an Advocate, and begins to tell us what to pray for. That is always one of the functions of an advocate. When a man who is in trouble facing a trial goes to his solicitor, what does the advocate do? He tells the man what answers he should give. He says, The Magistrate will ask you this question and that question; this is what you must say to him in reply. He prepares his case for him. The poor man does not know what to say; all he knows is that he has had the summons to appear in court, and that he does not know how to answer. The business of an advocate is to put words into the man's mouth, to tell him what to say. And the Spirit does this with us; He formulates petitions for us. We do not know; He knows; so He instructs us and guides us.

There are two kinds of advocacy from which we benefit as Christian people. We know that the Lord Jesus Christ is our Advocate with the Father; He is there in Person pleading for us. We are not there; He is doing it for us. But this advocacy of the Spirit is within us. He does not do it instead of us, but He tells us what to say. Both are advocates but in a different manner. The parallel is quite perfect. The solicitor I am using as an illustration does the two things; he not only tells us what to say, he can also address the court himself. When he is addressing the court the picture is that of our Lord's advocacy for us with the Father. But when the solicitor preparing the case tells us in his office what to say, and puts words into our mouth, he is acting as the Spirit does in this matter of prayer.

The ideas, the thoughts, the suggestions and the petitions come from the Spirit. It is He who knows what is best for us in each and every condition; we do not. We do not know 'the what' to pray for as we ought; but the Spirit does. There is a mystery about this; but it is a very real part of Christian experience. When we are in trouble and find ourselves only capable of groaning and sighing, it is often a sign that the Spirit has been working in us in this way as our Advocate.

Another similar statement in Philippians 2 : 12 and 13 will help to explain the matter: 'Work out your own salvation with fear and trembling, for it is God which worketh in you both to will and to do.' We have to work out our own salvation with fear and trembling. But what makes you do that particular thing? what makes you desire to do what you are doing? It is God. It is God through the Spirit who works in us. We utter these groans and sighs, but it is the Spirit who has 'worked' them up in us. But even now we are not quite clear as to what we are saying. All we know is that we are thus moved, we are conscious of something within us, but we cannot express it perfectly. It is the Spirit who has produced this feeling, and He has done so by working in us these petitions that, because of our infirmity, we can only express in our sighing and in our groaning.

This is a very special action of the Holy Spirit. We could not pray at all were it not for the Holy Spirit. The Holy Spirit is always working in us, and all we do is the result of the operation of the Holy Spirit in us. But what the Apostle is dealing with here is no longer the ordinary, regular, general work of the Spirit; it is the special work that He does when we are in the midst of trials and troubles. Like the man in the illustration which I have used in explaining the word 'intercession', the Spirit comes along, as it were, sees us in difficulty, and tells us what to say. We attempt to say it but we can produce nothing but a sigh or a groan. This is a distinct, a special and a separate work which the Spirit does within us. There is a sense, therefore, in which we must say that it is the Spirit Himself who makes intercession. There would be nothing said at all, there would not be even a groan or a sigh, if the Spirit did not come and take up this burden of ours and help us and act as our advocate and give us these petitions. It is the Spirit Himself, ultimately, who is making the intercession; but because it is done through us, it is 'with groanings which are wordless' and which are in that sense speechless. To understand this special work of the Spirit we must go back, as I have suggested, to the difference between verses 15 and 16. Paul is speaking of our spirit in verse 15, but of the Holy Spirit Himself in verse 16. Ordinary prayer comes from our spirit. We can formulate the words; we speak to God and make our requests known unto Him. That is the result of the work of the Spirit. But here we have a very special type of praying in which we do not know what to pray for.

In the next place I ask: Is there any value in these groanings? The Apostle's first answer is, that God hears them. 'He that searcheth the hearts . . .' Why does he describe God in that way at this point? Why does he not say, 'The Spirit himself maketh intercession for us with groanings which cannot be uttered. And God knoweth what is the mind of the Spirit, because he maketh intercession for the saints according to the will of God'? Why does he refer to God as 'He that searcheth the hearts'? I suggest that he does so in order to bring out the element of comfort and consolation. God is the only one who can search our hearts. A certain proverb tells us that 'The heart knoweth its own bitterness' (Proverbs 14: 10). No one else knows it. We cannot read one another's hearts. There are things inside our hearts that no one else knows. But God knows all about our hearts. The Scriptures teach us that constantly. 'All things are naked and opened unto the eyes of him with whom we have to do' (Hebrews 4: 13). 'The heart', says Jeremiah, 'is desperately wicked: who can know it?' 'I the Lord search the heart' (17: 9, 10). Because he is God he knows all that goes on in our hearts, in the very deepest recesses of our being. There are ideas in our hearts, there are wishes, there are aspirations, there are groanings, there are sighings the world knows nothing about; but God knows them. Because He is God He knows everything.

So words are not always necessary. When you are dealing with God you can, if necessary, do without words, because God knows our hearts. So when we are in such trouble that we cannot find words, and cannot express our feelings except in wordless groanings, God knows exactly what is happening. He knows all about our feelings, all about our desires. I know of nothing which gives greater comfort and consolation than this realization. The faintest whisper in the heart of man is known to God. Even if it should be so faint a sigh that you are not even aware of it yourself, He has heard it. There is nothing which He does not hear, nothing is too faint for Him. The words of a hymn remind us:

> *To Him commend thy cause, His ear*
> *Attends the softest prayer.*

He does not depend upon sounds, upon formulated words. The slightest movement registered in the heart is heard by Him. Listen to Paul Gerhardt, a German saint of the 17th century; he wrote a hymn which is translated thus by John Wesley:

> *God hears thy sighs and counts thy tears,*
> *God shall lift up thy head.*

He says again:

Thou seest our weakness, Lord;
Our hearts are known to Thee;
O lift Thou up the sinking hand,
Confirm the feeble knee!

This is a wonderful expression of the real meaning of the words we are examining.

But God not only hears our groanings, He understands them. How difficult it is to interpret a groan or a sigh in another! You hear a person groaning but cannot always tell whether he is in terrible trouble or whether he has had some profound experience. But God can interpret our sighs and our groans; He understands them; 'He that searcheth the hearts knoweth what is the mind of the Spirit.' It is the Spirit who has created what is expressed in the groaning, and God knows the mind of the Spirit.

We should be in no trouble concerning the meaning of the word 'mind' as we have met it many times already. For instance in the 5th verse of this chapter, 'They that are after the flesh do mind the things of the flesh'. It means 'thought', 'ideas', 'interests', all that leads to a course of action and a way of living. There is a very good illustration of its meaning in Philippians 3: 19, where the Apostle warns the church against certain false believers and teachers of whom he says, 'Whose God is their belly, who *mind* earthly things'. The things that are on their minds are of this world; that is the realm in which they live. God knows what the Spirit is thinking about; He knows what the Spirit has said to us; He knows the meaning of what the Spirit has put into our hearts as petitions. Though we do not understand and cannot express it, God knows; He understands the way in which the Spirit's mind works, and the thoughts that the Spirit has put into us. God knows the meaning behind the groans, He knows the cause of them.

But God not only understands, He approves of the ideas, He welcomes them, He likes them. We do not understand them, but God does. Is there any greater comfort than this? When you are in this condition of perplexity, and you cannot find words, and the devil says 'What is the value of your groaning? You do not know what you are saying, you are not even offering a petition to God', you can answer him by saying, 'God understands groans, God knows the meaning of sighs. The Spirit has put these into me. I agree that I do not quite know, but God knows, and that is what matters.' God understands, 'He knoweth the mind of the Spirit'.

But we can go even further than that, yet more wonderfully. 'He that searcheth the hearts knoweth what is the mind of the Spirit, because he [the Spirit] maketh intercession for the saints according to the will of God.' Paul does not mean solely that the petitions which the Spirit gives us are petitions with which God agrees. That thought is included, but the Apostle would not have troubled to tell us so, because it is quite obvious. As the Spirit is the Third Person of the blessed Holy Trinity anything He does is obviously certain to be in agreement with the mind of the Father. No, the Apostle is saying something much more striking and wonderful. He is assuring us that the Spirit comes alongside us, takes up our burden and begins to act as our advocate within us, because it is God who has sent Him to do so. He is doing this 'according to the will of God'; it is a part of God's plan, a part of God's way of saving His people.

The whole of salvation is God's plan, and this is a part of it. It is a part of our sanctification, a part of God's way of sustaining us and enabling us to persevere while we are in this evil world. God sends the Spirit, and as the Spirit performs this work He accomplishes a part of God's plan for us as His children.

God allows us to be tried, He allows things to go against us, and we become perplexed because of our infirmity. But He also sends the Spirit, and what the Spirit does is to carry out the will of God with regard to His poor children as they are passing through this world of time. We are not yet fully saved, for 'we are saved by hope', we have merely received the first-fruits, the foretaste. 'We that are in this tabernacle do groan, being burdened'; we who have received the first-fruits 'groan within ourselves, waiting for the adoption'. And while we are in that condition He sends the Spirit to do this special work for us.

Once more a parallel will help us to understand. Turn again to Philippians 2: 13: 'Work out your own salvation with fear and trembling, for it is God which worketh in you both to will and to do of his good pleasure.' This does not mean that He causes us to will and to do what is His good pleasure; but that it is His good pleasure that we both will and do these things and that we work out our salvation in this way. It is God's pleasure hat this should happen to us, and so it happens to us.

This brings us to the climax of the argument. It is God who sends the Spirit to us to do this work within us and to produce these groanings which God interprets and understands. But we are told that He does this in the saints alone – 'because he maketh intercession for the *saints*'. I shall shortly deal with this at greater length. I simply want to complete the argument at this point. God does not do this for all men, or for those who are not Christians. It is God who determines who are the saints – that is God's good pleasure, that is the will of God. He only sends His Spirit to the saints, to the believers, to those who are His sons. So the final argument is this. If, therefore, you find yourself giving vent to these groanings which you cannot express, it is proof positive that you are a saint, which means that you are a son of God, a child of God, and therefore an heir of God and a joint-heir with Christ. No one else sighs in this way, no one else knows anything about this groaning. And the Spirit produces the groanings in the saints alone, in those who are the children of God. The groanings, therefore, are a guarantee as well as an absolute proof of your final, ultimate, complete salvation.

What a wonderful argument it is! You started with your perplexity and inability to know what to pray for as you ought, you found yourself groaning and sighing, and the devil suggested to you that you are not a Christian at all and have never been one. But you are now able to turn on him and cause him to flee. You can say to him, 'You are making a great mistake. My groanings are the finest proof I have to date of the fact that I am a child of God. It is only the children of God who groan in this way because the Spirit does this work in none but the children of God.' So, far from being depressed and discouraged by your wordless groanings, lift up your head, it is an absolute proof that you are a child of God.

So what appears at first sight to be altogether discouraging and depressing ends as one of the strongest proofs of our true relationship to God. What a glorious salvation! Rejoice in it. Rise up out of your depression and misery, and praise God even for your groanings and sighings, and remember that every one of them is known to God. It is He who has sent His Spirit into you to lead you along this way, in order that eventually you may be perfect and spotless, glorified in His glorious presence.

[142]

Twelve

*

Likewise the Spirit also helpeth our infirmities: for we know not what we should pray for as we ought: but the Spirit itself maketh intercession with us with groanings which cannot be uttered.

And he that searcheth the hearts knoweth what is the mind of the Spirit, because he maketh intercession for the saints according to the will of God.   Romans 8: 26, 27

While we have really finished our exposition of these two verses as such, we cannot leave it at that. The statement is a practical one so we must draw certain lessons and deductions from it. The whole question of prayer is often to many people a difficult one which causes them to be troubled, so we must now proceed to draw certain lessons from the Apostle's teaching given in these verses.

Let us start by looking at what we may call the 'mystery' of prayer, by which people are often puzzled. It arises because a seeming contradiction is involved. We are told to pray; and yet we are told at the same time that our prayers are prompted by the Holy Spirit, and this prompting is done 'according to the will of God'. The question that arises, therefore, in the minds of many is this: If that is so why pray at all? It seems to them to be a kind of circle. We pray to God, and yet it is God Himself who tells us what to pray for through the Spirit. Not only so, we are told everywhere in the Scripture that God knows all things. He knows what we stand in need of before we even ask Him; therefore what point is there, what purpose is there in praying? Many therefore have come to the conclusion that all you need do is to go on trusting God, and that there is no need to pray at all. But this is an obvious fallacy. Some have fallen into the same error with regard to Philippians 2: 13: 'Work out your own salvation with fear and trembling. For it is God that worketh in you both to will and to do of his good pleasure.' The argument is, that because it is all originated by God, there is no need for us to do anything at all.

The first answer to this problem is that we are clearly commanded to pray. It is always good to start with a clear commandment. Whether we do or do not understand prayer and its meaning, when we have a clear commandment to pray it is our business to pray. We should never argue with a commandment. This can be illustrated in the following way. Some people misunderstand the doctrine of election. They say, 'If God elects people to salvation, He knows who they are, and therefore their salvation is inevitable. What, then, is the point of preaching? If their salvation is to be, it will be.' The answer to that, of course, is that it is God who commands preaching, it is God who sends out preachers, it is God who gives them the ability to preach, and it is God who 'commands all men everywhere to repent'. These are clear statements of the Scripture; and we must never allow any kind of logic, or what we may regard as logic, to carry us to a point at which we find ourselves contradicting either plain commandments, instructions, or any type of teaching found in Scripture.

Such a consideration is really a sufficient answer to the problem of prayer in and of itself. We are not only commanded to pray, we are often taught how to pray; and our Lord Himself gave that instruction. But we can supplement this answer with various other answers. God not only ordains the end but also the means to that end. God is not concerned only about the ultimate result, He is equally concerned as to how that result is to be brought about. There is an obvious illustration of this in nature. We know that ultimately it is God who is responsible for all the crops that are reaped and harvested in late summer and autumn. It is God who by sending the sun and the rain produces all these results. But we know equally well that God has ordained that the farmer should plough and harrow and break up the ground, and sow the seed and roll the ground, and do many other things to it. God ordains not only the ends but the means to the ends. We do not know why; that is a part of the great mystery of the will of God. God has wonderfully arranged that many results should be produced through secondary causes; He works through means, and He is as responsible for the means as He is for the ends.

Now here it is clear that prayer is one of God's own appointed and chosen means of bringing us to the ultimate glory that awaits us. He could have brought us to that end without our praying, but He has chosen to do it in this way. That is how God teaches us and trains us; it is the way in which He brings us to a greater knowledge of Himself. When we are in situations in which we do not quite know what to do, we turn to God, and it is often in such crises that we get to know Him in a manner that would have been impossible otherwise. So He has appointed prayer as one of the ways in which He gives us an increasing revelation and knowledge of Himself. He trains us and perfects us, He tries us and tests us in order that ultimately we may come to 'the measure of the stature of the fulness of Christ'.

All this is seen most perfectly in the case of our blessed Lord and Saviour Jesus Christ Himself. He, the second Person in the blessed Holy Trinity, spent much of His time on earth praying to His Father. If He prayed, and had to pray – if it was a part of His being made perfect as the Captain of our salvation (Hebrews 5: 7-9) – how much more necessary is it in our case. So the fact that the Spirit Himself indites these prayers, and acts as an intercessor within us in this way, far from being an argument against prayer, is a great argument for prayer.

Unhappily it is often the case that those who understand the doctrines of grace most clearly are the very persons who are most guilty of misunderstanding them to this extent, that they cease to pray. Some who are accounted highly orthodox do not have prayer-meetings in their churches, and they spend very little time in prayer in their own personal lives. They have reached the point at which they have left the doctrine and are merely following their own logic and intellectual formulations. But a right understanding of apostolic teaching leads a person to pray more than ever, not less. The Apostle Paul was a great man of prayer; and teachers of his type have been men of prayer throughout the centuries.

The second point I would raise is to query the rightness of advising all and sundry to pray. The Spirit, we are told, 'maketh intercession for the saints'. The Spirit does not put these prayers into the minds and hearts of any but 'the saints'. There is no teaching anywhere in the Bible that the Spirit helps unbelievers in this matter of prayer. The blind man referred to in the 9th chapter of John's Gospel made a very profound statement, 'God heareth not sinners.' This man had been healed by our Lord, and the authorities were consequently criticizing our Lord and denouncing Him as a blasphemer. The man, who was so ignorant, answers them by saying in effect, 'God heareth not sinners; but He has evidently heard this man, therefore this man cannot be a sinner'. His proposition is true – 'God heareth not sinners'. There is an idea current today that we should always tell people to start praying immediately. In times of crisis the whole country is called upon to pray. During the last war we had a so-called national day of prayer. People were invited to crowd into places of worship to pray to God. Similar suggestions have been made since at times of particular difficulty and crisis.

Surely this should be examined in the light of the teaching found in the Bible concerning prayer. We certainly need to instruct people as to how to pray; and we must show them that any man at any moment is not in a position to pray to God. It is not enough to tell people to pray; we must teach them how to pray. The disciples living in the presence of the Lord Jesus Christ realized the need of such teaching. They watched Him praying and they began to feel that they knew very little about prayer. One of them said to Him, 'Lord, teach us to pray, as John also taught his disciples' (Luke 11: 1). Anyone who has never felt the need of being taught how to pray is really telling us that he never has prayed, and that he does not know what prayer means. Owing to our unworthy and imperfect ideas of God we think we can turn to God whenever we like. But the Bible teaches us very plainly that that is not the case, and that we need much instruction with regard to this whole question of prayer.

The first question to be asked is, How do we obtain an entrance into the presence of God? If you have never asked that question you have never prayed. Consider an obvious human analogy. If you want an audience with the Queen in Buckingham Palace the first thing to do is to find out how you can get into the palace, what you have to do, how to obtain an introduction, how to conduct yourself, how to dress and to comport yourself – what your whole approach should be. Multiply this by infinity and you have a soul seeking God. If you do not stop to ask how to get into the presence of God, you cannot possibly be praying to God. We have to realize something of the truth about

God Himself. The moment we do so we realize that certain things are absolutely essential before we can ever pray acceptably to Him.

We obviously cannot pray as we are because we have no standing before Him. The moment we begin to realize who God is we begin to feel with Job the need of some 'daysman betwixt us, that might lay his hand upon us both' (Job 9: 33). The moment we begin to realize something about the being of God we realize how lost and helpless and hopeless we are, and we feel the need of someone, something, to bring us into the presence of God. And that, of course, is the whole message of the gospel. To tell people to start praying as they are is virtually to deny the whole of the Christian gospel. The gospel's first message is to tell us that there is only one way into God's presence, and that the Lord Jesus Christ came into the world, and lived and died to this end, 'that he might bring us to God'. And for this reason He said, 'I am the way, the truth, and the life: no man cometh unto the Father but by me'.

The Apostle Paul teaches the same truth in his Epistle to the Ephesians, 'For through him', he says, referring to our Lord, 'we both (Jew and Gentile) have access by one Spirit unto the Father' (Ephesians 2: 18). And it is the only way. There is no entry into the presence of God, there is no true prayer, except through the Lord Jesus Christ by the influence and the power of the Holy Spirit. This is the only way, and for us to forget it for a moment is not only to deny the gospel, but it means that we do not pray.

Again, take the statement found in the Epistle to the Hebrews, chapter 10, verses 19–22: 'Having therefore, brethren, boldness to enter into the holiest by the blood of Jesus, by a new and living way which he hath consecrated for us, through the veil, that is to say, his flesh; and having an high priest over the house of God; let us draw near with a true heart, in full assurance of faith, having our hearts sprinkled from an evil conscience, and our bodies washed with pure water.' This is the way to pray, the only way, and simply to tell all and sundry, when they are in difficulties, to start praying immediately and to keep on doing so, is a denial of the New Testament gospel. It makes the Cross of Christ unnecessary, and it is ultimately to 'do despite' to the very blood of the Cross itself.

Certain teachers who achieve a measure of popularity at the

present time say to their hearers, 'Those preachers who emphasize the importance of theology and doctrine are but complicating the situation; all you need to do is to turn to God and pray.' They overlook the fact that men cannot pray without doctrine; they cannot go into the presence of God except 'by the blood of Jesus'. There is no other way of getting there, there is no entry into 'the Holiest of all' without this particular offering. The teaching of the Old Testament was preparatory and temporary, but the Jews under the old dispensation at least realized that they needed an offering; so they killed their animals and took and presented the blood. That was but the shadow; the truth to which all the Old Testament sacrifices pointed is this one offering of Christ 'once and for ever' by which, and by which alone, is there any access into the presence of God in prayer. 'The Spirit maketh intercession for the saints', and for no others; and it is our duty to warn people that they may be deluding themselves and merely treating themselves psychologically by imagining that they are praying, when in reality they are but talking to themselves. They say they feel greatly helped by it; and I grant that in certain ways psychology can help. By talking to yourself you can help yourself a great deal; by uttering beautiful thoughts you can make yourself feel much happier and better; but it is not the same thing as believing prayer. The Spirit helps the saints because they are the only people who have any standing in the presence of God, and as a consequence have any access into His holy presence.

Let us now turn to consider what may be termed 'types of prayer'. Some of the commentators draw the deduction from this statement which we are examining that the finest and highest type of prayer is just groaning. They say, 'There are many people who are very voluble in prayer and offer long prayers, but true praying is that prayer in which you cannot say anything but just groan.' But this is a completely false deduction. The devil often provides it as a wonderful excuse for people who have never taken part in a prayer-meeting. He suggests that the most spiritual people are not those who can pray in words, but those who only groan. Such a thought is entirely contrary to Scriptural teaching.

Take, for example, Hosea, chapter 14, verses 1–3: The prophet exhorted the children of Israel: 'O Israel, return unto the Lord

[148]

thy God; for thou hast fallen by thine iniquity. Take with you words, and turn to the Lord; say unto him, Take away all iniquity, and receive us graciously: so will we render the calves of our lips. Asshur shall not save us.' The prophet was writing under the inspiration of the Spirit. The same Spirit who at times deals with us in such a way that we can but groan, at other times tells us to 'take words', and gives us the words, instructs us exactly as to what we are to say. The Hosea passage is surely sufficient in and of itself to refute the false teaching. But the Bible has much similar teaching.

Consider the many prayers recorded in the Scriptures, some of them very great and wonderful. In one sense, most of the Psalms are prayers, but they are 'in words', very wonderful, very eloquent, very beautiful words; not just groaning, but statements, words. Think of the prayers of Daniel that are recorded for us; consider the prayer of Hezekiah. Recall how once Hezekiah took a letter, spread it before the Lord, and then pleaded with Him to deal with the writer of the letter. Again, we find some remarkable instances of prophets of God, mighty, holy men of God, not only praying in words but pleading with God, reasoning with Him, using arguments with Him. One of the best illustrations of this is to be found in the book of the prophet Isaiah, particularly in chapters 63 and 64. He literally pleads with God. In chapter 63, verse 15, we read, 'Look down from heaven and behold from the habitation of thy holiness and of thy glory: where is thy zeal and thy strength, the sounding of thy bowels and of thy mercies toward me? are they restrained? Doubtless thou art our father, though Abraham be ignorant of us, and Israel acknowledge us not: thou, O Lord, art our father, our redeemer; thy name is from everlasting. O Lord, why hast thou made us to err from thy ways, and hardened our hearts from thy fear? Return for thy servants' sake.' Then in chapter 64: 'Oh that thou wouldest rend the heavens, that thou wouldest come down, that the mountains might flow down at thy presence.' The praying prophet not only uses words, but ventures to reason with God, to argue with God and to plead with God, to remind God of His own character and His own promises.

So it is an entirely false deduction to say that the highest form of prayer is just a groan or a sigh. Such is not the Apostle's teaching. He is saying that there are times when, in exceptionally difficult circumstances, amidst trials and tribulations – 'the sufferings of this present time' – we really are in such perplexity that we do not know what to pray for. This is unusual; this is not common; this is not the general condition of the child of God. This is a very special case; and in respect of it we can do nothing but 'groan' or sigh. But this is not to be the norm of the Christian life. As a child of God the Christian is to talk to his Father, to commune with his Father, to speak with Him and to listen to Him; that is prayer, that is true worship. Even as our Lord Himself did, so are we meant to do.

Therefore let us beware lest the devil trap us at this point and make us feel that the fact that we cannot pray and have never known any liberty in prayer is a sign of great spirituality. The exact reverse is the truth. The more spiritual a man is the more he will pray, and the greater freedom will he know in prayer, the greater liberty, the greater enjoyment. Let us then examine ourselves very carefully at that point. But let me add this, that if we have never known what it is to groan in this way, or to sigh, it is again indicative of something wrong with us. For the Christian does know this state, it is an experience that the Christian should know; and the more we realize the true character of our spiritual warfare, the more we shall know something about this groaning and sighing. It does not take the place of prayer, but is the occasional experience of one who has entered to such an extent into the 'fellowship of Christ's sufferings' that he knows just a little of what it is to groan as our Lord Himself groaned at the grave of Lazarus and on other occasions.

Let us now consider certain general rules concerning prayer in the light of all this. The text itself indicates that we all stand in need of such rules – 'We know not what to pray for as we ought'. Thank God, we are given this great comfort, that the Spirit is interceding within us the whole time; but elsewhere in Scripture we find very practical advice and help given to us. The intercession of the Spirit is a kind of final comfort when we are 'in extremis'. You do not start with it; it becomes your comfort when you really can do nothing. When you find yourself in difficulties, you must not just sit back and groan and say, 'I do not understand'. Do everything you can before you come to that!

To start with, realize what you are doing when you pray. Whatever your circumstances, start with the realization of who and what God is; and that you are in relationship with God. Whenever you find that you do not know what to pray for as you ought, you can always worship God; you can always adore Him; you can always praise Him. 'Ah, but', you say, 'I am in terrible difficulties'; to which I reply, that although you may be in perplexity about your situation, you should not be in any difficulty with regard to God. If you cannot talk to Him about your particular problem, and do not know what to say to Him about it, talk to Him about something that you do know.

The classic Scripture passage concerning this is found in Acts 4, verses 23 to 31. The background to the story is as follows: Peter and John had been on trial because of the healing of the lame man at the Beautiful Gate of the temple. They had been set at liberty but with a very severe warning. They were told that if they continued to preach or teach in the name of this Jesus, certain things would happen to them. They had been 'straitly threatened', which undoubtedly means, not only that further preaching on their part would lead to further imprisonment, but that they would face certain death. We are told that Peter and John, being thus reprieved, went back to their own company, that is, to the Church, and reported the threats. What they said, of course, was that the authorities were determined to put an end to Christianity, to exterminate the Church. In fact, the Christians seemed face to face with 'the end of all things'. In these circumstances we are told that 'They lifted up their hearts to God with one accord and said . . .' They prayed. What did they say? One amazing fact in that recorded prayer is that, unlike us, they did not start with themselves and their problem; they started with God! Though they are in desperate circumstances this is how they pray, 'Lord, thou art God, which hast made heaven, and earth, and the sea, and all that in them is'. They did not know what to do, so in their uncertainty, perplexity and bewilderment, they do not talk about their uncertainties; they talk about what they are sure of, they talk about God Himself to God: 'Lord, thou art God, which hast made heaven, and earth, and the sea, and all that in them is.' They start by praising God.

We can always do the same thing, and it is always a safe course to take. Whatever your perplexity, whatever your problem, when you do not know what to pray for as you ought, praise

God, worship God, adore God, remind yourself of who God is, and ascribe unto Him all praise and honour and glory. That is the teaching of Scripture from beginning to end.

Paul in his Epistle to the Philippians, chapter 4, verse 6, has precisely the same teaching. 'In nothing be anxious; but in all things by prayer and supplication with thanksgiving' – notice what he puts first – 'let your requests be made known unto God'. Do not immediately become speechless because of your perplexity; start by doing what you can do, what you know; in other words, worship and adore and praise God. That is something we can always do.

A second principle is that spiritual requests are always right, because they are always in accordance with God's will. Spiritual requests! I mean, for instance, that prayer for the success of God's work and God's Kingdom is always right, so you can always pray for that. Our trouble usually is, that we are so deeply concerned about our little problem, and our particular difficulty, that we forget everything else, as if our problem was the one thing that mattered in the whole universe. Pray for the success of God's Kingdom, for the spread of His Kingdom, for the success of His work. It is always safe to pray for a greater knowledge of God, a greater knowledge of His love, a greater knowledge of the Lord Jesus Christ, and a greater understanding of His love towards you. You need never hesitate about offering such prayers; they are always acceptable to God, they are always well-pleasing in His sight. He delights in them, and the more we pray in that way the more God will be pleased with us. Prayer for greater holiness, greater sanctification, greater strength and help in the battle against sin, is always right. Spiritual prayers, as we may so term them, are always right and you need never be in any hesitation at all concerning them.

Thirdly, it is always right to plead the promises of God. I have already given examples of such pleading, and I would universalize that as a principle and say that whenever you have a clear promise of God, plead it. The promises of God are meant to be used. And, similarly, quote Scripture. Notice how the early Church in Acts 4 quoted the 2nd Psalm to God Himself. You may say, 'What is the point of that? as God is the Author of Scripture through the Spirit, what is the point of quoting His own Psalm to God? Is not that a waste of breath and of energy?' Far from being so, it is true prayer. Analogies are never perfect, but look at the position in this way, as our Lord Himself suggested more than once. Does a father ever object to a little child quoting his own words to him, reminding him of something that he has said or promised? Of course not; he likes it, he enjoys it. He is always pleased when his own child or grandchild quotes his own words to him against himself, as it were, in order to get something from him. Well, God is our Father, and you are always right when you quote the promises of God, or when you quote God's own word to God. No need to hesitate there!

Let us now turn to a second group of instructions which in reality are cautions. We have already seen in our exposition that they are necessary. I would lay it down as a general principle that we should exercise great care and caution concerning purely personal requests. So far I have been dealing with, and indeed urging personal spiritual requests for growth, for a knowledge of God, for greater love, and so on; but now I am concerned about requests for ourselves other than these spiritual desires and spiritual requests. Here, I repeat, we have to be very cautious, and especially so when we come to the matter of details. Otherwise we may well find ourselves praying for something against the will of God, as we have seen earlier in the case of Moses, and in the case of the Apostle Paul with the thorn in his flesh. If we are too urgent and insistent concerning particular requests with regard to personal matters we may bring upon ourselves most undesirable results. Consider the terrible warning in Psalm 106, verse 15: 'And he gave them their request; but sent leanness into their soul.' This is a reference to the children of Israel when they 'lusted exceedingly' in the wilderness and 'tempted God in the desert'. They kept on pleading with Him for flesh and other items of food. 'They lusted exceedingly in the wilderness, and tempted God in the desert. And he gave them their request; but sent leanness into their soul.' If you bombard God with certain particular, personal, material requests, there is the possibility that He will let you have them; and you will bitterly regret it. He may grant you your request; but because it was not a true request, nor in your best interests, and because you would not listen to Him and His discouragements, He will let you have your request but you will find leanness in your soul. The day will come when you will bitterly regret that you ever made that request, and you will almost upbraid God for having answered you. But if you see the folly and repent, God will graciously forgive you again; and you will probably learn one of the greatest lessons of your spiritual and Christian life. Let us be extremely careful when we come to these personal requests.

Again, where God's will is not certainly known, exercise great care and caution. In such a situation I suggest that, first of all, you must submit yourself entirely to God and His will. Tell Him that your one desire is not so much to do this, or to do that, but to do His will; that to know His will in the matter is your supreme desire. Go further; tell Him that you are ready to do His will, and to be content with it, whichever course it takes, though you may personally prefer one course rather than the other. 'Only to do thy will, my will shall be.' That is something of which we are always capable. 'We do not know what to pray for as we ought.' If that is the case, do not pray for anything in particular but start by telling God that you are absolutely submitted to Him, and that you desire nothing but the knowledge of His will in order that you may do it. Having done that, let your requests be made known unto Him. 'In all things, by prayer and supplication with thanksgiving, let your requests be made known unto God.' That is what we can always do. Tell Him what your request is, but only and always after first of all putting yourself entirely into His hands.

Then, having made your requests known to God, make absolutely certain that you have within you 'the peace of God which passeth all understanding'. I put it in that way because of the nature of the statement made by the Apostle in Philippians 4: 6 and 7: 'In nothing be anxious, but in all things by prayer and supplication with thanksgiving let your requests be made known unto God.' Do that, 'And the peace of God, which passeth all understanding, shall keep your hearts and minds through Christ Jesus.' If you are not enjoying this peace, it is because you have not surrendered yourself and your whole case fully to God; you are holding on to something, you are not really willing for God to have His way with you. Make certain therefore that you are enjoying, 'the peace of God, which passeth all understanding'. You still do not know what is happening to you, you still do not know which is right, you still do not know what to pray for as you ought; but you should always be enjoying 'the peace of God, which passeth all understanding' in your mind and in your heart. God's promise is absolute, so we should always make sure that we are enjoying His peace.

My next and third caution is that we should never demand anything of God, never claim anything of God. Unhappily there is much teaching along that line today. When you realize who God is, you do not claim, you 'make your requests known'. People claim healing and many other things; they get some kind of answer to their request, but it is often in the way the children of Israel experienced. Do not claim anything, do not demand; realize who God is! God allows you to come as a child with the sweet and engaging reasoning and pleading which we saw in Isaiah 63 and 64. But this is very different from claiming, demanding, almost telling God that He has to do what you require. We must approach God with 'reverence and godly fear'. 'Our God is a consuming fire.' The children of Israel demanded certain things in the wilderness, and they got their requests, but it was accompanied by leanness in the soul. Be careful then not to demand physical healing. Indeed, I would add, do not even demand the salvation of someone who is very dear to you. Pray for it, but do not demand it, do not claim it.

The Bible has clear teaching about this matter. No saint has a right to argue that all his children must be saved. It is not true to Scriptural teaching; nor is it true in the history of the Christian Church. Do not claim, do not demand, let your requests be made known, let them come from your heart. God will understand. We have no right to demand even revival. Some Christians are tending to do so at the present time. Pray urgently, plead, use all the arguments, use all the promises; but do not demand, do not claim. Never put yourself into the position of saying, 'If we but do *this*, then *that* must happen'. God is a sovereign Lord, and these things are beyond our understanding. Never let the terminology of claiming or of demanding be used.

Finally, it is in no sense wrong, but essentially right, to tell God when we are in a perplexing position that we do not know 'the what' to pray for 'as we ought'. At that point there is nothing wrong in groaning or in sighing. 'God knows our sighs, he counts our tears.' 'He that searcheth the hearts' knows all about us and it. Do not feel that you are failing, still less must you feel that the man who claims and demands things is a man of greater faith than yourself. No, he is a man of very small faith, even if he is not actually sinning at that point. God prefers the sighs of the humble sinner who does not know, but who leaves it to Him, and who rejoices in the fact of the intercession of the Spirit within him.

I must add this final word in order to make the doctrine complete. 'Are you not leading us to the point', says someone, 'that we can therefore never be certain as to what to pray for?' Far from it, I am still dealing with these exceptional circumstances. I have shown many respects in which you can always pray freely. 'But', asks someone, what is 'the prayer of faith'? James refers to it and says "The prayer of faith shall save the sick" (James 5:15). What does Mark 11:24 mean – "What things soever ye desire, when ye pray, believe that ye receive them, and ye shall have them". How do we do that? How can we offer the prayer of faith?'

There are those who teach that 'the prayer of faith' means that you say to yourself, 'I believe it'. You try to work yourself up into saying, 'Yes, I do believe it; it is the Word of God, I do believe it'. But it means no such thing; indeed it means almost the exact opposite! That is to be frantic, that is to be desperate; that is a kind of 'whistling to keep up your courage in the dark'; that is an attempt to persuade yourself. But it is not 'the prayer of faith', it is not 'believing that you receive them'. What is described there is surely the absolute certainty that is given to us occasionally by the Holy Spirit Himself. He puts a prayer into our mind and into our heart; He gives us a prayer and He tells us as He gives it that it is going to be answered. It is not a very common experience; but it does sometimes happen. It ought to happen to us more and more frequently, and as we grow in the school of prayer it will do so.

There is such a thing as an absolute certainty. There is an illustration of this in the incident which I have already mentioned, the healing of the man at the Beautiful Gate of the temple. The man asked Peter and John for alms. But they had not anything to give him. Then, we are told, Peter 'fastening his eyes upon him with John said' – do not forget the 'fastening his eyes' – 'Look on us; silver and gold have I none; but such as I have give I thee. In the name of Jesus Christ of Nazareth rise up and walk' (Acts 3:4–6). What was happening there? Peter was not trying an experiment, he was not trying to work up a great faith, and wondering at the same time whether the desired result would follow. No! Peter was given a commission; he knew that the man would be enabled to rise up. There was no uncertainty at all. He was absolutely certain as he spoke the word that his commission would be fulfilled. The same is true of Paul in the case of the lame man at Lystra (Acts 14). Beholding that this man had faith to believe, Paul spoke, and the miracle happened. Of course! In such matters there were no failures in the case of the Apostles in the Book of Acts.

Two things concerning the work of the Apostles differentiate them from many who claim great faith today, and the ability to perform striking works by the prayer of faith. The Apostles never announced beforehand that they were going to work miracles! They did not say, 'Next Wednesday there will be miracles of healing', and for this reason, that they did not know beforehand, they never knew until the commission was given. But once it was given they were absolutely certain. Secondly, there were no failures. There were failures before Pentecost, never afterwards. The commission was given by the Spirit, and it never failed.

I use this matter by way of analogy. There is a prayer given sometimes by the Spirit concerning which He tells you that it is going to be answered. That is 'the prayer of faith'. It is not an experiment, it is not a trying to persuade yourself, or to 'work yourself up'. It is an absolute certainty that is given by the Spirit, and you know, therefore, when you are praying and making your requests, that your prayer is answered. And it happens because the prayer was given, and the assurance of it was given, by the blessed Holy Spirit Himself.

May God grant us understanding in this vital and important matter of prayer! Thank God, we always have the ultimate consolation that when 'we know not what to pray for as we ought, the Spirit Himself maketh intercession for us with groanings which cannot be uttered'. 'And he that searcheth the hearts knoweth what is the mind of the Spirit, for he maketh intercession for the saints according to the will of God.'

Thirteen

*

> *And we know that all things work together for good to them that love God, to them who are the called according to his purpose.*
>
> *For whom he did foreknow, he also did predestinate to be conformed to the image of his Son, that he might be the firstborn among many brethren.*
>
> *Moreover whom he did predestinate, them he also called: and whom he called, them he also justified: and whom he justified, them he also glorified.* Romans 8: 28–30

We come here to another sub-section in this marvellous progression of arguments which the great Apostle works out in order to provide us with a full assurance, an absolute certainty of our ultimate, final, complete salvation and deliverance from everything that sin has ever done to us.

The indication that we are moving on to a further link in the chain is supplied by the word 'And' which here serves two main functions. First of all it forms the link with the main argument of the whole chapter. It is another proof of the certainty of our final and ultimate salvation. That is probably the main connection. But there is also a subsidiary connection, a secondary connection in the sense that it is a continuation of what Paul has just been saying in the immediately preceding section about the Spirit helping our infirmities and making intercession for us with groanings which cannot be uttered. This new statement certainly has that in mind, but I maintain that the fundamental connection is with the series of arguments he has been developing and deploying throughout the chapter.

I make this point because we find that such a distinguished commentator as Dr Charles Hodge links this 28th verse solely with the previous paragraph. He includes this verse with those other verses in his sub-division of this chapter. One should always hesitate to disagree with him, but I feel compelled to do so and to emphasize the larger connection. The very last phrase in this 28th verse suggests something altogether greater and higher – 'them who are the called according to his purpose'. So I argue that we must regard this as essentially a new sub-section though it is connected with what Paul has just been saying. As I have repeatedly emphasized, the Apostle's style can be compared with that of a great symphony in which a central theme is worked out in a number of subsidiary themes. Each one is taken up in turn, and at the end of each a hint is thrown out of the one that is to come; then that is taken up and worked out and ends with a hint of the following one until you arrive at the grand finale where the central theme is again asserted. That is precisely what the Apostle does in this chapter. There is a connection between each of the parts and yet each is a distinct part in the whole theme of assurance.

The new section can be analysed thus. In verse 28 the Apostle lays down a proposition, makes an assertion. Then in verses 29 and 30 he proves and demonstrates his assertion. Or, to state it in another way – having made a comprehensive statement in verse 28, in verses 29 and 30 Paul elaborates the last statement in verse 28 – 'the called according to his purpose'. As we have seen so frequently, this is his method; he makes a statement, and throws out an assertion; but he never leaves it at that, he always argues it out and gives us his reasons for making it. That was the peculiar quality of his mind. Our view of inspiration must allow for such variations in the styles of the different writers, otherwise it would be mechanical dictation. We believe in the absolute control of the Spirit over the minds and thinking and style and everything else of the writers. He so controlled them that they were kept from error, but the Holy Spirit did not dictate to them mechanically, otherwise there would be no variation in the style. Incidentally, in connection with this matter, any translation of the Bible that does away with the variations in the styles of the authors is a bad translation. There are several such at the present time.

We are considering here one of the most remarkable statements that even this Apostle ever made. It is also one of the most comforting statements in the whole range of Scripture. We are surely entitled to say that in respect of the statement of exalted doctrine there is really nothing higher than this. Here is ultimate doctrine. There is no greater privilege on earth than to be allowed to examine a statement such as this, realizing as we do so that we are not, as it were, students of philosophy or art or literature, but men and women considering doctrine concerning ourselves. These things – even this exalted doctrine – are written for our consolation, as well as for our edification.

First, we must look at the statement itself; then, having done so, we shall proceed to consider how we know that it is true. The statement asserts, 'We know that all things work together for good to them that love God, to them who are the called according to his purpose.' We note immediately that there is a limitation in the statement; Paul does not say that 'all things work together for good' for everyone. All things work together for good only to the people specified in the statement, not to anyone else. In the original Greek this comes out much more clearly than it does in our translations. It should be, 'And we know that to the ones loving God all things work together for good'. By putting 'the ones loving God' at the beginning there can be no mistake about the nature of the statement. It is to 'the ones loving God' that all things work together for good.

We are reminded here of something which is emphasized everywhere in the Bible. There is only one real division of the human race ultimately. We are on one side or the other of this dividing line, and all other divisions and distinctions are finally irrelevant. This statement is true only of those 'who love God and are the called according to his purpose'. As for all others the Scripture tells us quite plainly that all things do not work together for good to them. They, we are told, are 'under the wrath of God'. The Apostle has already told us in the 18th verse of the 1st chapter of this Epistle that 'The wrath of God is revealed from heaven against all ungodliness and unrighteousness of men who hold down the truth in unrighteousness'. Such is their position. Whatever may be true of them at the moment, however prosperous and happy they may be, however much the sun may seem to be shining upon them, the terrible fact about them is that they are under the wrath of God. Appearances may seem to belie that fact, but, they will ultimately discover that that is their position and state.

Never was this truth more important perhaps than at a time such as this. None but Christian people have any consolation in the world as it is at the present time. There is no consolation for anyone else, as they are beginning to realize. Here, then, is our opportunity to tell the world that the only way to experience the consolation is to believe the gospel, to conform to God's way and manner of life and of living. The promises of the Word are only for such people.

It is important for all Christians to grasp this truth, for sometimes people in an expansive mood are tempted to say in general, 'All things work together for good; isn't it marvellous how everything seems to be conspiring together for our well-being!' But that is not what the Apostle says. The poets sometimes state it in that way. Take Browning for instance:

> *The year's at the spring,*
> *And day's at the morn;*
> *Morning's at seven;*
> *The hill-side's dew-pearled;*
> *The lark's on the wing;*
> *The snail's on the thorn;*
> *God's in His heaven –*
> *All's right with the world!*

That is typical of the philosophy of the Victorian era. There had been the long peace – the 'Pax Britannica'. No war of great importance had taken place since the Napoleonic period. Everything seemed to be developing and advancing in those halcyon days of Queen Victoria's reign. So they sang 'All's right with the world!' That is the kind of thing the poets sometimes sing. They do not always express themselves with such optimism. The poet has to be in a given mood before he can so write. The muse has to be stimulated by pleasing happenings before they make these wonderful assertions. But they are not true! Read accounts of the private lives of many of these people and you will find that it was not true in their own lives, and it is most certainly not true of the world. No one believes Browning's words today. 'All's right with the world', yes, so long as you are but looking at the dewdrops and the hillside and the lark and the snail. But look at the hydrogen bomb, look at the rockets, look at the building up of armed forces! Is all 'right with the world'?

There is a vast difference between the false optimism of the world, the generalities in which worldly people delight, and the particular statements of the Scripture. All is not right with the world; all is wrong with the world. That is why the Christian salvation ever became necessary. That old false optimism, thank God, has gone. I prefer to see people believing nothing, and feeling utterly hopeless and bereft, rather than lulling themselves to sleep with a false kind of optimism that does not stand up to the test of truth and the facts of life. Browning's verse is very good poetry, I agree, but it belongs to the realm of fantasy and lacks the realism which always characterizes the true Christian. There is then a limitation in the apostolic statement which we must be careful to observe.

As we turn to the assertion itself we see immediately why the limitation is inevitable. 'All things work together for good.' Some of the manuscripts, as the commentators point out, very rightly, have an additional statement here. In them the verse reads, 'We know that God works together all things for good to them that love God'. It is God who works all things together. In the Authorized Version, based on the particular text which lies behind it, we are not told that it is God who does the 'working together'. Ultimately of course the variation in translation makes not the slightest difference, because we know that it is God who works all things. 'All things' do not 'work' in and of themselves; there is no impersonal principle in working life. It is God who acts everywhere. God not only has made everything; it is God who sustains everything, it is God who controls everything. The universe does not work automatically, it is still under the control of God through the Lord Jesus Christ – 'by Him all things consist'. They have not only come into being, they also subsist in that way. So we must not say, we cannot say, that all things work together automatically.

In any case, it is quite obvious, even if you adopted the other view, that 'all things' would not differentiate between 'those who love God' and all others. If you confine your view to the universe and its working you are not able to detect any difference between the godly and the ungodly. Indeed, sometimes you might come to the conclusion that the ungodly are the favourites, and that all things seem to be working in their favour. The fact is that were the universe working automatically and not under the control of God there would not be the slightest difference between what happens to the Christian and to the non-Christian. They would all be subject in exactly the same way to the things that happen; whereas, here, the whole purpose of the statement is to emphasize that there is this wonderful difference between those who love God and those who do not love God. 'To those who love God all things work together for good.' God is over-ruling all things in such a manner that they turn out for the good and the benefit of His people. That is the fundamental assertion.

But we must analyse the Apostle's statement and see exactly what it means, because it is, as I say, one of the most glorious things we can ever know about ourselves. Do you know that as a Christian all things are working together for good for you? Do you know that God is over-ruling everything in the whole cosmos for your good? If you do know it you cannot be depressed. You cannot know it and be depressed at the same time; for such knowledge and depression are mutually exclusive. In other words there is a very practical aspect to this glorious teaching.

Let us work it out. Paul says 'all things'. Some interpreters say that 'all things' means trials and tribulations only. The great John Calvin, for instance, said that. In other words, he limits the 'all things' by what has been dealt with in the previous verses, namely, all the trials and the troubles and the tribulations with which the Apostle began to deal in verse 17, and with which he continues to deal until the end of verse 27. The interpretation of such commentators is that we know that whatever may happen to us along that line is being made by God to work for our good. But in my view there is no justification for limiting the statement in that way. When the Apostle says 'all things' I believe he means all things literally. He means good things, favourable things; but he also means things that seem to be against us, things that seem to be bad for us, things that are discouraging, disheartening, dispiriting. He includes all. In the end, of course, it amounts to much the same – all things, even those which seem to be most adverse. In a sense the Apostle is but repeating what he has already said in chapter 5: 'We rejoice in hope of the glory of God. And not only so, but we glory in tribulations also: knowing that tribulation worketh patience; and patience, experience; and experience, hope: and hope maketh not ashamed; because the love of God is shed abroad in our hearts by the Holy Ghost which is given unto us'. (vv. 2–5) All his major themes are in that

[163]

5th chapter. He takes them up one by one and works them out; and that is what he is working out here.

We can say, then, that 'all things' are working together for our good – good things, bad things, trials, troubles, tribulations, illnesses, accidents, disappointments, even failure. God can make all, and does make all, work ultimately for our good. This is surely a staggering statement; but it is the statement that is made by the Apostle. It is only in the case of Christians that we can demonstrate exactly how this happens, how all things are made to work together for our good. Trials and tribulations and failures and sin are not good in and of themselves, and it is folly to pretend that they are. They are bad. How then can we justify the statement that all of them 'work together for good'? The answer is that they are so used by God, and so over-ruled by God and employed by God that they turn out for our good.

It is essential that we grasp that the 'all things' are not good in and of themselves. Many have fallen into that trap. In the lives of some of the saints, at least in some of the so-called saints, you can read that many of them fell into error at this point. They believed that there was something inherently good in suffering. When they were not suffering they courted suffering, and sometimes they deliberately brought suffering upon themselves. All tendencies to mutilate the body, to scarify the flesh, are the result of that particular error. Such people worked themselves into the position in which they believed that there was something inherently good in self-inflicted suffering. That is the theory that leads to masochism; and many of the 'saints' have been guilty of that error. But it is a perverted notion, and is quite unlike the teaching which we have here, or anywhere else in Scripture.

If these things were good in and of themselves they would do as much good to the non-Christian as to the Christian; but it is not so. It is what God does with them that turns them into our good. There is no need to spend much time in showing how the good things work for our good; that is obvious. Our problem is to demonstrate that things that seem to be against us work to our good. How can we show that trials, tribulations, persecutions, sickness, or physical weakness, the things which trouble us and get us down so much – how can we demonstrate that these things work together for good to us who are Christians? They start by just arresting and awakening us. That is always good for us.

The most dangerous condition for all of us is that in which everything seems to be going well without much change and without much incident. Many a man has found in his business that in the days when he was struggling and battling against problems and difficulties, and having to pay constant attention to the business, all went well. But when he reached a second stage when everything seemed to be running smoothly and automatically, it turned out to be a condition fraught with danger. He became slack and negligent, and soon things began to go wrong. He was not aware that anything was happening because he was not showing the same keenness as in the first stage.

It is exactly the same in the Christian life. That state in which everything just comes and goes, and the wheels of life are just turning round, or, to use a phrase common among motorists, when life is ticking over, is generally a very dangerous state for the soul to be in. It is the very time when our enemy, our adversary the devil, takes advantage of us; so when something goes wrong, when a trial or a tribulation comes to us, it has the effect of pulling us up and startling us and awakening us. That is always good for us because it makes us think; and anything that sets us thinking is always good for us. The worst state to be in is a state in which we do not think but merely take things for granted and go on with our routine in life. It is good to have the routine of life upset occasionally, no matter what the actual cause of the interruption may be.

The first effect of trials is that we are shocked, we are awakened, we are made to think; and already we are in a better state than before the trial started. We are now ready to pay attention, not only to the problem, but also to ourselves and our condition. A similar thing happens to a man whose health has been deteriorating. He was not aware of it, and just went on, perhaps not feeling as well as he had done, but able to shake off the trouble. Suddenly he feels a severe pain; and this forces him to pay attention to his condition and to visit his doctor. The doctor discovers that the trouble has been growing and developing in the man for quite a long time, and he asks: 'Why didn't you come to me before?' But the man does not go to the doctor until the pain compels him to do so. Similarly tribulations and trials pull us up, they make us pay attention to our lives and to face the position as it is.

When these troubles and tribulations and trials thus come in various ways they reveal to us our own smallness and weakness and frailty. We are not always aware of that, for the devil encourages us to develop a false self-confidence. Although we know that we have been saved by grace, we begin to think that we can live the Christian life ourselves, and before we realize it we begin to develop a carnal confidence. But suddenly we find ourselves overwhelmed by some happening, and we are reminded again of our smallness and, still more, of our lack of understanding. We may have been reading much theology and other books and beginning to think that we were complete authorities on all God's ways. Nothing could ever upset us. Suddenly we are stricken in some way, and we find ourselves as helpless as babes, and completely unable to understand. We suddenly discover that the Christian life is a much greater thing than we imagined. We had reduced it to our system, to our degree of knowledge; but, immediately, we are caused to see our lack of understanding and of knowledge. In turn that leads us to see our sinfulness and our liability to entertain wrong ideas of God.

This experience is described frequently in the Bible, and also in the biographies of God's people, and we have known it ourselves. When things go wrong we tend to complain and to grumble and to wonder why God has allowed the trial to happen to us. 'Why should this happen to me?' Thus we are awakened to our own sinfulness and to our readiness and proneness to harbour unworthy thoughts concerning God who has loved us with an everlasting love. These things arrest and apprehend us, and bring us to a realization of the truth concerning ourselves. In other words they humble us. And there is nothing better for us than that we should be humbled. We are in a dangerous state when we are not humble; and we all need to be humbled. This apostle puts the matter clearly in that classic passage on this whole matter in 2 Corinthians 12: 'Lest I should be exalted above measure through the abundance of the revelations, there was given to me a thorn in the flesh, the messenger of Satan to buffet me, lest I should be exalted above measure.' Because of the amazing experience he had had, a tendency to be puffed-up had entered; and he had to be brought down, 'lest I should be exalted above measure'.

> *He that is down need fear no fall;*
> *He that is low no pride.*

Humility is ever the greatest safeguard in the spiritual life. So when we are brought low and humbled, it is good for us; and anything that does that for us is working for our good. In this condition we begin to see a host of things we had been tending to forget. We see our need of forgiveness again. I have known Christian people who have said quite sincerely that they really did not believe that there was any need for them as Christians to ask to be forgiven. What a terrible state to be in! When the Holy Spirit works in us we soon begin to see the need of forgiveness, were it merely because of our wrong thoughts about God, and our tendency to grumble and to complain. That is a horrible sin, much worse than sins of the flesh, because it involves evil and unworthy thoughts about the God of love who has done so much for us.

We not only see our need of forgiveness; we see also our need of strength and of help. Thus in our utter helplessness we are driven back to God. Anything that drives us back to God is good for us. That is how this principle works out; these things drive us back to God. We admit that in our prayers, 'We know not what to pray for as we ought'; but that makes us pray all the more. We cry out with groanings; and that is a good state to be in because it means that we have been driven back to an utter, entire dependence upon God. And in that condition we begin to discover things about God we never knew before. This is how we 'grow in grace and in the knowledge of God'. If we did know some of these things before, we get to know them with a new depth, with a new meaning, with a new understanding. It has been the universal testimony of the saints of the centuries that it is through this kind of experience they have truly got to know God. The babe in Christ knows very little about God. He knows he is forgiven, but that is the mere beginning, the 'first principles of the gospel of Christ'. There are depths, there are riches that he knows nothing of, and sometimes it is necessary that he should be dealt with through suffering in order to bring him to that knowledge.

It is only in that way that we really get to know the love and grace of God, His kindness, His compassion, His tenderness, His patience, His longsuffering. How little we know of them! But these are some of the greatest characteristics or attributes of God. How much do we know about God's patience, God's solicitude, God's tenderness, God's care for us? It is only in this sort of condition that we begin really to learn about them and His readiness to forgive, His readiness to restore, His readiness to help and to lead us. We can read the parable of the Prodigal Son and accept it theoretically, but have you known God dealing with you in that way? What a wonderful revelation it is of the character of God, of His heart of love! It is only when you have been through this kind of experience that you get to acquire that knowledge. You may know it theoretically, but when you have actually passed through the experience yourself you begin to know it in a much deeper way.

We can sum it up by saying that our greatest trouble is our ignorance of God. We know things about God, but our real trouble is our ignorance of God Himself – what He really is, and what He is to His people. And the way in which He brings us to that knowledge, and reveals Himself to us, is by using the various things that happen to us to draw us to Himself. This is our greatest need, and it is also, at the same time, the best preparation for eternity, and for dwelling everlastingly in the presence of God. That is the explanation, then, of the way in which 'all things' work together for our good. It is tragic that trials and troubles should be necessary; but that is what sin has done to us. We cannot take the truth directly and positively as we ought, so we have to pass through trying experiences in order to bring us to our senses and prepare us for the deeper knowledge.

These things also compel us to realize the nature of life in this world. 'The world is too much with us.' Our business, our profession, our family, our affairs tend to monopolize our time and attention; half our spiritual troubles arise from the fact that we become lost in these things and tend to live for them. These are the things that stand between us and the knowledge of God and of eternity. But trials and tribulations teach us that we have to be more detached from earthly things. It is very difficult to detach yourself from this life and this world when you are well and healthy and strong; but when you are lying on a sick bed it is not quite so difficult. You are then made to think about life and its true nature. You are reminded that you are here but for a little while. That is good for us, because it tends to loosen our attachment to this world. It reminds us that we are but 'pilgrims and strangers'. Or, to put it positively, these things make us think more of the glory to which we are going.

Why do we meditate so little about that glory? We have descriptions in the Scriptures of the amazing glory which is coming and which we have been considering. The whole creation is 'waiting for the manifestation of the sons of God'. Why do we think so little about it? The answer is that we are too pre-occupied with this life, with this world, with the 'things that are seen'; but when we are suddenly deprived of these things, and are shown how tenuous is our hold upon them, we begin to remind ourselves that, after all, we are pilgrims of eternity, that death is not the end, and that the glory is awaiting us.

Anything that makes us think of that glory is good for us. It matters not at all what it may be – an illness, an accident, or a disappointment. As a Christian you should be made to realize by these things that you really are destined for the indescribable glory that is coming, and made to think more of it. To learn this lesson is good for you; the thing that seemed hard and troublesome and almost cruel is being used for your good. And, to use the phrase the Apostle will use later in verse 37, it is thus that 'We are more than conquerors through him that loved us'. As Christians we are meant to be 'more than conquerors'. It is in this way that 'all things work together for good'.

An old preacher who lived about 100. years ago used a very good illustration to explain this matter. He said: 'Here is a statement which appears to be contradictory, "All things work together for good to them that love God". How can that be? The good things, I can see, are working in that direction; but look at those other things – they seem to be working in the opposite direction. How can you say that things which are working in opposite directions are for my good?' The old preacher answered by using the illustration of a watch. He said, 'Take your watch and open it. What do you see? You see that one wheel is turning in an anti-clockwise direction, but it is attached to another wheel that is working in a clockwise direction. You look at this machinery and you say, "This is mad, this is quite ridiculous; here are wheels turning in opposite directions; the man who made the watch must have been a madman." But he wasn't. He has so arranged this watch and put in a main-spring to govern all the wheels, that when it is wound up, though one wheel turns this way, and another that way, they are all working together to move the hands round the face of the watch. They appear to be in contradiction but they are all working together to the same end. Our lives are like that. Look at life, and you ask at first what is happening? I can see that certain things are good for me, but other things seem to be all against me. But think again of the great Watchmaker who has planned it all. Do not jump to conclusions, look for the ultimate purpose, look for the ultimate end. And if you do so with a spiritual eye you will soon begin to see that God knows what He is doing.'

We shall see this truth clearly in the great doctrine which is to follow. It is all God's purpose. Look at life again with spiritual eyes and you will come to the conclusion that 'all things' that are happening to you are 'working together'. God has planned it all, He has wound up the watch of our lives, He keeps it going, and all is working together for our good, our immediate good, but still more for our ultimate and final good.

Fourteen

*

And we know that all things work together for good to them that love God, to them who are the called according to his purpose.

For whom he did foreknow, he also did predestinate to be conformed to the image of his Son, that he might be the firstborn among many brethren.

Moreover whom he did predestinate, them he also called: and whom he called, them he also justified: and whom he justified, them he also glorified.   Romans 8: 28–30

We have emphasized that 'all' means all. It is not confined to trials and troubles and tribulations. It is an all-inclusive term, so we have to say that it includes even our falling into sin and our backsliding. One has to make such a statement very carefully, and here especially we have to emphasize the fact that this does not happen automatically. To fall into sin, to be a backslider, is always bad. And yet I venture to assert that even falling into sin, or backsliding, because of our relationship to God can work for our ultimate good, and help to produce our final glorification.

This is taught in many places in Scripture. In Isaiah 45, verse 7, God says, 'I create evil', which means, partly, that He creates the evil consequences of sin, but also includes this further notion that He controls even evil and can use it to promote His great and grand purpose of bringing His people to their final glory.

It happens in this way. He makes use of sin to show the Christian his weakness, his frailty and his fallibility. Self-confidence is always one of our greatest dangers, as we have seen. But when a man falls into sin his self-confidence is shaken. Let me repeat words I have quoted from John Bunyan, 'He that is down need fear no fall; he that is low no pride'. When things are going well with a man he is in danger of pride, and of being uplifted and high-minded and puffed up. But the moment he falls into sin he is made to realize again what a weak, frail, poor creature he is. This does not mean that to sin is good. The Apostle Paul, as we saw at the beginning of our exposition of chapter 6, was charged with that teaching. His accusers said, 'What shall we say then? Shall we continue in sin, that grace may abound?' 'God forbid', is the Apostle's answer. This teaching is not an enticement to sin; but it is meant to show how God can use even our sin to do us good. Of course, that only happens to the Christian; it does not happen in the case of the unbeliever when he sins. His whole view of sin is entirely different, he does not believe in sin as such at all, so God does not turn it to his advantage.

At the same time, of course, when we truly repent, having seen what evil we have done, God shows us that He is ready to forgive us. The Prodigal Son knew much more about his father after he returned home than he ever knew before he left him. He thought he knew him before he left home, but it was not so. It was when he was received back, when he saw his father running to meet him when he was yet a long way off, and embracing him, that he began to know his father's love truly. He never knew this before. Though he was quite wrong in leaving home, and going to that foreign land, and though what he did there in his riotous living was all wrong, he was nevertheless a very much better man at the end than he was at the beginning. He knew more about sonship, he knew more about his father, he knew more about his father's love. That is the kind of way in which this works out. In other words it brings the Christian to see his constant need of grace, and of watchfulness and care. And all that is very good for us; it is a part of our development, our growth in grace and in the knowledge of the Lord. So we are able to assert that even when the Christian falls into sin or becomes a backslider, when he is restored it all ends up 'for good'.

In this way we have a glimpse into the many-sided grace of God. Even our defeats can be turned to our good. God takes hold even of them and uses them to bring us nearer to Himself, and to give us a knowledge of Himself which otherwise we would never have had. I am simply arguing that this term 'all things' really must be taken in all its fulness, not even excepting sin or our falling into a condition of backsliding.

So far we have been looking at the way in which this works, that is to say, at the mechanics of the matter. But how exactly does God bring this happy result about? One way is that He permits things to happen to us for our good. He could have stopped them, but He does not; He permits them, He allows them to take place. That is an activity on the part of God. God's permissive will is nevertheless an activity of God. It is a negative one, I agree, but it is a part of His activity. Therefore, when sometimes in life we find things happening to us which we cannot understand, we must not always assume that it is God who is doing this to us. We tend to assume that, and ask, 'Why has God done this to me?' But God has not always done it in that positive sense; what has happened is that He has permitted it to happen to us. The classic example of this is the case of Job. God permitted the devil to try and to test His servant Job. It was not God who actually brought about the various things that happened to Job, but He permitted the devil to do so. This is a very important part of our understanding of the life into which God has brought us.

Many analogies help to show how this principle is employed. If you want to train a young man in any business or profession or employment, a time comes when you have to allow certain things to happen to him in order that he may learn. If you continue to do everything for him he will never learn, so you allow things to happen in order that he may learn by experience.

God, however, not only permits things to happen to us, He sometimes does things to us directly and sends things upon us for our good. This is the point at which many people get into trouble. Their idea is, as it is the idea of every child, that a father is nothing but a mass of benevolence who is always smiling, always giving out money, always giving everything we ask for immediately. Children always tend to think in that way, and therefore feel very grieved and hurt when anything is withheld from them, or when punishment is administered to them. The same is true in the spiritual life; God sometimes does things to us for our good. The children of Israel are a classic example of this. God not only permitted many things to happen to them, He raised up enemies against them. He sent 'hornets' to trouble them, and 'pestilences' upon them, quite deliberately. He was doing it for their good because they were His people. 'You only have I known of all the families of the earth: therefore I will punish you' (Amos 3: 2). And He did. These are specific Scriptural terms. He 'raised up enemies against them' to molest them, to attack them and to trouble them. And the enemies were not only human enemies, their trials came in many ways. The clearest statement on all this is in Hebrews 12: verse 6: 'Whom the Lord loveth he chasteneth, and scourgeth every son whom he receiveth.' There is no question about that! There is an interesting statement in the First Epistle to the Corinthians, chapter 11, verse 29: 'He that eateth and drinketh unworthily, eateth and drinketh damnation [that is, judgment] to himself, not discerning the Lord's body. For this cause many are weak and sickly among you, and many sleep.' 'For this cause . . .' They had been guilty of sinful behaviour. That is why they have become ill and weak, and why some of them have even died. It does not mean that they have lost their salvation, but it does mean that their death has been the direct outcome of some particular failure. This is startling doctrine; but it is true. God does this for our good. That is why, sometimes, when a man will not listen to the gospel and be led by God and submit to the direction of the Holy Spirit, God will sometimes send an illness upon him. Do not assume that I am saying that every illness is due to such a cause, but sometimes it is so. My first point was that God permits things to happen to us. But He does not always stop at permitting, He may send them upon us; but it is always for our good.

A third way in which He does this is that He withholds or withdraws blessings from us. This is not the same thing as God permitting something to happen to us, or sending something upon us by way of a trial; it means that God, as it were, averts His face, turns away from us, and we feel that we cannot find Him. This is a method that God often uses for the good of His people. Once more the human analogy is obvious; it is something that has to be done in practice constantly with children and those who are under our care. For their good, at times, you either have to look severely at them, or you refuse to look at them, and turn your face away from them. And in consequence they are troubled. It is a way of convicting them, and of humbling them; it is a way of getting them to repent and to admit that they have been wrong and are sorry, a way to make them ask for forgiveness and for restoration. For this reason sometimes there are periods of dryness and barrenness in the life of the Christian. You find the psalmists asking God when He is going to come back; why He is like a traveller, or a journeyman; why He does not show them His face? 'Show us the brightness of Thy face; look upon us; why art Thou turning away from us?' they ask. This is an experience that the saints throughout the centuries have described. It is one of God's ways of doing us good.

My point is that even such an experience of barrenness and of aridity and dryness of the soul in one's spiritual life can be used to our advantage; it makes us desire Him more; it makes us seek Him more, and long for Him. We have to realize that everything can thus be used by God. Some are tempted to argue, 'What value can there be in a period of dryness and aridity?' My answer is that there is nothing in life which is of greater value than the experience that you have when such a period is suddenly ended, and when God again smiles upon you. This is something which is found universally in the testimony of the saints. God sends a period of 'clear shining' to 'cheer us after rain'. The rain, and the drenching it brings, is a small price to pay for the experience of the period of 'clear shining' that He sends afterwards. When the period of withdrawal ends you enjoy the nearness and the presence of God to a greater degree than you have done before. All these things are to comfort us. 'All things' are made to work together by God. What appears to be so wrong, and so opposed to us, is meant and designed for our ultimate good.

The last thing I would mention is that God grants us spiritual illumination and understanding in order that we may see what is happening to us. Without this we would inevitably be depressed. The devil comes and says, 'See what is happening to you; do you call yourself a Christian?' Or he may say, 'Do you say that God is a God of love? Do you say you are a child of God? Look at what is happening, look at your position.' Thus he tries to create doubt within us, and to make us grumble and complain. But one of God's ways of using every kind of circumstance and condition for our good is that suddenly, by His Spirit, He illumines our understanding as to what is happening to us; and the moment you begin to understand, all is well.

I could easily illustrate what I am saying from my pastoral experience. Let me cite but one instance. I remember the case of a lady who had been passing through one of these periods of dryness and aridity and who was in great trouble. It was partly physical, and many of her friends had gone to her, some of them being ministers of the Word, and they had all spoken in the same way. They were all trying to make her rouse herself, all talking in a theoretical manner to her and saying that feelings do not matter, that indeed nothing matters except the truth of justification by faith. She knew that quite as well as they did, better indeed than many of them, but that did not help her, for her problem was that she did not know the blessedness she once had known. 'Where is the blessedness I knew when first I saw the Lord?' That was her condition, the condition described by the poet William Cowper.

The advice of her friends did not help her, because it never helps such people to tell them to pull themselves together and to rouse themselves. That is just what they cannot do; and they are right in saying that that is not the remedy that should be given at that point. Superficial people who know nothing about the depths of spiritual experience do not understand this. The way to help such a person, the way in which the particular person to whom I am referring was helped, is to say, 'Ah yes, you know, there are periods like that in the lives of the saints. Sometimes God for His own inscrutable reasons withholds His face from us.' She looked at me in amazement saying, 'Is that true?' 'Of course it is true,' I replied; and I proceeded to give her many examples and illustrations of it. At once her problem was solved, because she now had an explanation. The other counsellors were not giving her an explanation, and so she had no reply to give to the devil. But now she could turn to the devil and say, 'Yes, the child of light sometimes has to walk in darkness, and sometimes he does so because he *is* a child of light'. The fact is that God teaches the Christian something as the result of this experience that can only be taught in this way. When he comes out again into the light, he will have learned something in that experience, which nothing else in the world could ever bring him to know. And that proved to be this particular lady's very experience. It is an illustration of how God works by giving us spiritual illumination and understanding to know and to realize what is happening. So you say to yourself, 'I do not understand fully, but, if it is a part of God's treatment of me, I am content.

I am ready to go on even in the dark in this way, as long as I know that it is God who is dealing with me for my good.'

Let us now move on to consider how we may know that the Apostle's statement that 'We know that all things work together for good' is true. He assumes this knowledge in all the saints. We have met previous instances of this assumption of knowledge in Christians. Do *we* know this? The Apostle assumes that it is common knowledge among all Christian people – 'We know that all things work together for good to them that love God'.

But, further, note that Paul says, 'We *know* that all things work together for good', whereas in verse 26 he had been saying, 'We *know not* what we should pray for as we ought.' How can these two statements be reconciled? The answer reminds us of one of the paradoxical truths about the Christian. He is a man who can be certain about the ultimate even when he is most uncertain about the immediate. That is the real secret of this statement, and it is, I would add, the final comfort and consolation of the Christian. The Christian does not know everything, but he does know this one thing. Look at him in trouble with everything apparently going against him, and he is so perplexed that he does not know what to pray for as he ought. All that he can do is to emit the groanings that are produced in him by the Holy Spirit. He is confused and does not understand. Yet even at that very point he can say, 'I do not know which way to turn or to go; I do not understand why these things are happening, and I do not know exactly what to ask for at this moment. But I know this, that in spite of my ignorance, and in spite of everything that is happening to me, this and everything else is working together for my good.' That is the final comfort and consolation of the Christian.

It is essential, however, that we draw this vital distinction. The fact that we do not understand what is happening to us in the present should never be allowed to disturb us about the ultimate. It is just at this point that the devil comes in again. He will take up some detail in your present position and he will say, 'How can you say in the light of this that you are a child of God, that God is a God of love and that He is going to bring you to glory? See what is happening to you.' And the danger is that, because you cannot explain some particular point of detail, you will give in to the devil and doubt your salvation. The way to deal with the devil in such a situation is to allow him to speak, and then say to him, 'I agree and I admit that I cannot understand, I cannot explain this particular incident or detail, but though I cannot do so I am still certain about the end, I am certain about the ultimate. I do not understand the mind of God fully, but I do know the purpose of God with respect to me and that it cannot fail.'

Using a military analogy we can say that you can lose many battles and still win the campaign. It is the ultimate victory that is assured. It is the ultimate outcome of the campaign that is beyond any question or doubt. You may lose many a battle, you may fail in many a detail; but that makes no real difference; it is the ultimate that is guaranteed. That is how to reconcile the 'We know not' of verse 26 with the 'We know' of verse 28. This is a principle that one has constantly to be applying in the Christian walk and warfare in a world like this. Do not allow particulars to interfere with the whole. Or, to use a medical analogy, do not be too upset by the appearance of particular symptoms if you know that the patient as a whole is getting better and making progress. He is a very poor doctor who gets too alarmed and excited about particulars; he must keep his eye on the patient as a whole. The devil will always try to pin us down to little particulars, and so we get excited and alarmed. The way to repulse him is to draw that distinction between symptoms and the case itself. The whole, the ultimate, the end is absolutely certain and guaranteed; so do not allow the devil to upset you about particular temporary things that may or may not be happening to you.

'We know not', 'We know', is a good summary of the Christian life. The end, the ultimate, is guaranteed, but as we are travelling towards it there are many things which we fail to understand, and we shall often be perplexed and in confusion.

> *Oft in danger, oft in woe,*
> *Onward, Christians, onward go.*

You are not promised exemption from troubles and trials. The devil deludes many into thinking that once you become a Christian you never know any more trouble. That is his lie.

'Oft in danger, oft in woe' is to be our lot in this world. But we are to march on and 'face the foe', keeping our eye upon the ultimate. Remember who your Captain is and the absolute certainty of the final outcome. The Apostle's assertion is that 'we know' this with an assured certainty. He could not put it more strongly; it is a categorical statement.

Our next query is as to the basis on which we have this knowledge. Here two separate points need consideration. We must know that this is true in general, but we must also know that it is true of us individually. Let us start with the general truth. How do we know that 'All things work together for good to them that love God, to them who are the called according to his purpose'? The answer is that it is clearly taught in the Scripture, and especially in the promises of the Scripture. Take, for instance, Psalm 91, where, in verse after verse, we find the promises of God to His people, promises both definite and true. One such promise runs, 'He shall give his angels charge over thee, to keep thee in all thy ways'. Can you imagine anything better than that? This is but one of the promises which were given so abundantly to the children of Israel. God tells them that they are like 'the apple of his eye' (Deuteronomy 32: 10; Zechariah 2: 8). The 'apple of the eye' is the most sensitive part of the most sensitive organ in the human body, which we always protect carefully. That is what you are to me, says God to the children of Israel. But all the promises and statements to the children of Israel are equally applicable to us, and even more so.

Again, look at God's dealings with the children of Israel as recorded in the Old Testament. He blessed them freely, but at various times He also withheld His blessings for their good. He raised up enemies against them; then He conquered their enemies and delivered them. All this but shows how God works all things together for good to those that love Him, to those who really are His called people. In many ways it is the central theme of the Old Testament.

The New Testament supplies similar teaching. In the Gospel of Matthew, chapter 6, we read: 'Therefore I say unto you, Take no thought for your life, what ye shall eat, or what ye shall drink; nor yet for your body, what ye shall put on. Is not the life more than meat, and the body than raiment? Behold the fowls of the air: for they sow not, neither do they reap, nor gather into barns; yet your heavenly Father feedeth them. Are ye not much better than they? Which of you by taking thought can add one cubit unto his stature? And why take ye thought for raiment? Consider the lilies of the field, how they grow; they toil not, neither do they spin: and yet I say unto you, that even Solomon in all his glory was not arrayed like one of these. Wherefore, if God so clothe the grass of the field, which today is, and tomorrow is cast into the oven, shall he not much more clothe you, O ye of little faith?' (vv. 25–30). And again, in chapter 10, we read: 'Fear not them which kill the body, but are not able to kill the soul: but rather fear him who is able to destroy both soul and body in hell. Are not two sparrows sold for a farthing? and one of them shall not fall on the ground without your Father. But the very hairs of your head are all numbered. Fear ye not therefore, ye are of more value than many sparrows' (vv. 28–31).

'Count it all joy, my brethren, when ye fall into divers temptations', says James in the first chapter of his Epistle, verse 2. He is referring there to trials and to the various things which come to test us. In verse 12 he puts it thus, 'Blessed is the man that endureth temptation: for when he is tried, he shall receive the crown of life, which the Lord hath promised to them that love him.' Turn also to Hebrews chapter 12, and note especially the emphasis in the 10th verse. He has been reminding the Hebrew Christians that they had had fathers after the flesh who 'verily for a few days chastened us after their own pleasure; but he [God] for our profit, that we might be partakers of his holiness'. Nothing can be more specific! 'Whom the Lord loveth he chasteneth, and scourgeth every son whom he receiveth.' 'If ye be without chastisement, whereof all are partakers, then are ye bastards, and not sons' (vv. 6–8). All this is plain, explicit, teaching in the Scripture showing that God causes all things to work together for good to His people, because they are His people.

Add to that, secondly, the experiences of the saints as they are recorded in the Scriptures. Look at the Book of Job; its message is summarized at the very end. Job was a much better man at the end than he was at the beginning. James in his Epistle takes up that very point in order to apply his message. He says, 'Behold, we count them happy which endure. Ye have heard of the patience of Job, and have seen the end of the Lord; that the Lord is very pitiful, and of tender mercy.' Then he exhorts his readers to be patient in exactly the same way and for the same reason. Always examine the end. Do not form judgments as the process is continuing, consider the end, keep your eye on the end. The explanation of the unbeliever's attitude and conduct is that he never considers the end. He sees the attractions of 'the wide gate' and the 'broad way' – the illuminated signs, the promises of pleasure, the pictures of people cheerful and happy, and apparently enjoying themselves. What a contrast with that other way, the narrow way! But what about the end, to what does it lead? The 'wide gate' and the 'broad way' lead to destruction; the narrow way leads to life.

The same truth is found in the life-story of Jacob. Jacob was so constituted by nature that God had to deal with him in a variety of ways in order to make a man of him, as it were. Look at his sufferings and his trials; but again look at the end. Or take the case of David and his experiences. I ventured to say earlier that even sin and backsliding can be turned to the good of the child of God, and surely that is the message of Psalm 51. It does not excuse David's sin – the adultery and the murder and the rest – but it is clear that David was taught something through it, and his life and experience were enriched. He is a better man at the end than he was at the beginning. These things happened to him as a part of his training for perfection.

Perhaps the clearest statement of this particular truth is found in Psalm 119. Take, for instance, verse 67: 'Before I was afflicted I went astray: but now have I kept thy word.' Verse 71: 'It is good for me that I have been afflicted; that I might learn thy statutes.' Here is a man giving his experience. He adds another word in verse 75: 'I know, O Lord, that thy judgments are right, and that thou in faithfulness hast afflicted me.' This is not theory; it is the picture of a man writing a textbook; it is a man giving his experience. Then to crown it all, the Apostle Paul tells us in 2 Corinthians 12 that after much stumbling and perplexity he was able at last to receive the Lord's word. 'My grace is sufficient for thee', and to say 'When I am weak, then am I strong'. He had not known that before. He had to be struck down, as it were, God allowing the devil to act – 'the messenger of Satan'. But it was all a part of God's purpose.

Finally, add to all this the experience of the saints in the subsequent history of the Christian Church. They are all unanimous in their testimony, saying in their different ways, 'It is good for me that I have been afflicted'. Christian people are generally at their best when they are in the furnace of affliction, and being persecuted and tried. We remember the epic stories of some of the German Christians during the Hitler regime and during the Second World War, and also some of the experiences of the saints in Norway during the time of occupation by the Germans. Go back to the story of the Covenanters 300 years ago in Scotland, and beyond that to the early martyrs and confessors. They all agree in saying that they had never known God as they knew Him when they were in the furnace of affliction. 'Testing times', they say, 'are healing times, they are growing times.' Their trials and tribulations were the means whereby God revealed Himself to them in a newer and a deeper way. So this is not only the clear teaching of the Scripture; it has been supported and confirmed and verified by the experience of the saints of God in the Church through all the running centuries ever since.

Thus we see in general the way in which 'we know' that all things work together for good to them that love God. We shall go on to consider how we may know the same truth individually. But you will never know it in your own case unless you have understood the teaching. We should all be able to say that 'we know' this to be an inviolable principle that 'all things work together for good to them that love God, to them who are the called according to his purpose'. Can we so speak?

Fifteen

*

And we know that all things work together for good to them that love God, to them who are the called according to his purpose.

For whom he did foreknow, he also did predestinate to be conformed to the image of his Son, that he might be the firstborn among many brethren.

Moreover whom he did predestinate, them he also called: and whom he called, them he also justified: and whom he justified, them he also glorified.   Romans 8: 28-30

We come now to the practical question as to how we can know that the Apostle's statement, 'All things work together for good. . .' is true with respect to *us*, as to how I may know that this is true of *me*. Clearly that was the object which the Apostle had in his mind. We must never think of him as a theologian only, writing a treatise on theology or on the Christian life. His interest is always primarily pastoral. He was writing to the Roman Christians in order to help them with their problems and struggles. The Apostle never fell into the error into which many of his followers and even his admirers have so often fallen, that of divorcing theory from practice. He always combines them, he always has a practical intention. Indeed he brings out these great theological statements in order to help people in a practical sense. The Apostle was never guilty of that false dichotomy which divides a man into brain or understanding only, or heart and will only; he always addressed the whole man. And he is doing so here.

The way, therefore, to know whether all this applies to us is to discover whether we conform to the description that is given of the people to whom this does apply, for it applies to certain people only. The first thing we are told about such people is that they 'love God'. 'All things work together for good to them that love God.' Why does Paul describe Christian people in these terms? Why does he not say, 'All things work together for good to them who believe on the Lord Jesus Christ'? That is equally true of Christians. Why does he choose in particular to describe them firstly as people who 'love God'? He does this quite frequently. Take for instance the statement in 1 Corinthians 2: 9: 'Eye hath not seen, nor ear heard, neither have entered into the heart of man, the things which God hath prepared for them that love him.' And there are other examples. Why does he choose this particular description of the Christian here instead of one of many others that he might well have chosen?

He does it, partly, I believe, in order to contrast the Christian with the non-Christian in terms of what he has said about the latter in verse 7 of this chapter, where he says, 'The carnal mind is enmity against God: for it is not subject to the law of God, neither indeed can be.' That emphasizes the striking contrast between the Christian and the unbeliever. We find a similar statement in the Epistle to the Ephesians, chapter 4, verses 17 and 18: he says, 'This I say therefore, and testify in the Lord, that ye henceforth walk not as other Gentiles walk, in the vanity of their mind, having the understanding darkened, being alienated from the life of God through the ignorance that is in them, because of the blindness of their heart'. It is the same contrast. This needs to be borne in mind, especially at the present time, because there are many who describe their relationship to the Christian faith solely in terms of the mind and regard it as being a matter of intellectual acceptance of truth only. But that is not Scriptural. The trouble with the unbeliever, the non-Christian, is that he is a God-hater. It is not only that they do not believe, they hate God. These are the only alternatives in the Scripture; you either love Him or else you hate Him. So the Apostle's expression here helps to bring out the contrast between the natural man who is at 'enmity against God' and the Christian who 'loves God'.

The Apostle is concerned to show that the Christian goes beyond simply believing in God. James in the second chapter of his Epistle tells us that 'The devils also believe, and tremble'. So it is not sufficient simply to ask a man whether he believes in God. You can believe in God and still not be a Christian, and so this great promise is not true of you. Something further is required. It is not just a matter of giving intellectual assent to the truth about God, or certain aspects of the truth concerning

God. A more thorough and searching test is needed. It is one thing to be religious, it is quite another to be Christian. It may sound well to say, 'I have always believed in God' but that belief may be of no value whatsoever; it is not of necessity Christian belief. A man can be a theist without being a Christian. So the test needs to be more thorough. If you merely give an intellectual assent to a body of doctrine you will never know the assurance of which the Apostle is writing. Assurance is deep and it presupposes certain things in us. Our Lord sums up the first and the greatest commandment in these terms, 'Thou shalt love the Lord thy God with all thy heart, and all thy soul, and all thy mind, and all thy strength.' Love is all-inclusive. When you love, every part of you is involved. You cannot love in sections of your personality; love is always totalitarian in its demands and responses. And the same applies to our relationship to God – the heart, the mind, the soul, and the strength are all to be included. So the Apostle's use of the term 'love' here puts the emphasis at the point at which our profession of the Christian faith is tested most thoroughly.

It is essential, however, that we be quite clear in our minds as to what love includes, what it represents. 'All things work together for good to them that love God.' What is meant by loving God? I would emphasize that it is not merely a matter of sentiment or of feeling. There is another snare with which the devil tries to trap us. Some people think they love God because they may be aware of certain emotional feelings, or may undergo some emotional experience in a service. That is not love! Love includes emotion, but it is much greater than emotion, much deeper. You can experience emotion, and believe that you are loving God, and yet show later that you do not love God at all. Our Lord makes this quite clear in many places in His teaching. For example, in John's Gospel, chapter 14, verse 21, we find Him telling His disciples, 'He that hath my commandments and keepeth them, he it is that loveth me'. There is no value in talking about love unless we are keeping the commandments. This is one of the tests of love. There is no such thing as a theoretical love. Love is always practical. To love God includes this, that our true desire is to please God, and to live to His glory, and to keep His commandments, and to be like Him. And this we must never forget when we are considering whether we belong to those who 'love God'. The Apostle, I suggest, chose the term because it is all-inclusive and leaves no uncertainty. He takes us right to the heart of the matter, so that we may be quite sure as to where we stand.

But I believe that Paul had a special reason for using the term 'love' rather than the term 'believing' at this point. One of the best ways whereby we can decide immediately as to whether we love God or not is our reaction to adversity. How do we react to the trials and the troubles of life? There are many people, as our Lord Himself taught in the parable of the sower, who seem at one time to have believed the gospel and to be enjoying the Christian life. But when trials and tribulations arise because of the gospel they give up. They cannot face that test; they feel they have been let down. They entertained the notion that to be a Christian meant that you would never have any troubles and problems, so the moment trials come they say, 'There is nothing in Christianity after all', and turn their backs upon it. They do not love God.

Trials and tribulations will very soon show us whether we love God, if we look at it in terms of whether we are more like Job or more like Job's wife. The devil came before God and said in effect, 'It is all very well for Job to be a good man and to go on serving you. It is simply because he is being blessed. If Job were only to begin to suffer, you would very soon see that he does not believe in you.' So God gave the devil permission to test Job, and he was tested severely. When the first test came we read, 'Job arose, and rent his mantle, and shaved his head, and fell down upon the ground, and worshipped, and said, Naked came I out of my mother's womb, and naked shall I return thither: the Lord gave, and the Lord hath taken away; blessed be the name of the Lord' (Job 1: 20, 21). That is a picture of a man who loves God. He can still speak in that way. 'In all this Job sinned not, nor charged God foolishly.' Then certain further tests came and Job begins to suffer in his own flesh. 'Put forth thine hand now, and touch his bone and his flesh,' says the devil, 'and he will curse thee to thy face. And the Lord said unto Satan, Behold, he is in thine hand; but save his life. So went Satan forth from the presence of the Lord, and smote Job with sore boils from the sole of his foot unto his crown.' At that point Job's wife said to him, 'Dost thou still retain thine integrity?

curse God, and die.' But Job said to her, 'Thou speakest as one of the foolish women speaketh. What? shall we receive good at the hand of God, and shall we not receive evil? In all this did not Job sin with his lips' (2 : 9, 10). That is the test. It is shown still more clearly in the noble statement Job makes later on, 'Though he slay me, yet will I trust in him' (13 : 15). That is the man who loves God. There is no better test than this. When everything is going against you, when you are being tried and tested and disappointed, do you feel like cursing God, and do you grumble and complain? If you do, you have little if any grounds for thinking that you are one who loves God. But if, in spite of it all, you bow your head and say, 'I am in the hands of God and he knows what he is doing; far from cursing Him I say, "Blessed be the name of the Lord. I do not understand, but I know that God is love"', then you have stood the test. And notice that the Apostle introduces it here in the context of trials and troubles and tribulations, when we are in the state and condition in which we 'know not what we should pray for as we ought'. But we do know that 'all things work together for good to them that love God', to those who can go on loving Him when everything seems to be against them, and everything seems to testify against the fact that God loves them. They still love Him.

A final reason for the Apostle's use of this expression is that there is no more absolute proof of God's love to us than the fact that we love Him. That is the argument found in the First Epistle of John, chapter 4, verse 19: 'We love him.' Why? 'Because he first loved us.' We would not love Him if He had not first loved us. So if I find that I love him I have an absolute proof that He loves me. That is the very thing the Apostle is telling the Roman Christians. So it is wise to put it in terms of our love to God. No man would ever have loved God unless God had first of all loved Him. Therefore if we can prove by our love to God that God loves us, we can be absolutely certain that everything will be overruled by God for our good, and for our benefit, and for our ultimate glory. If in the light of these things we can say that we love God, then the promise that 'All things work together for good to them that love God' applies to us.

The second description of these people is that they are 'the called'. Why suddenly introduce this term? Because it is the only explanation of why these people love God. 'The carnal mind is enmity against God; for it is not subject to the law of God, neither indeed can be' (Romans 8: 7). These people love God because they are 'the called according to his purpose'. As this is a crucial word in Scriptural teaching we must examine it carefully. The word 'called' – 'to call' – is used in two main senses in Scripture: the one indicating a 'general call', and the other an 'effectual call'. There is a sense in which everyone hears the call of this gospel; at least, anyone who has ever heard the gospel truly preached has heard 'the call' of the gospel. Our Lord sent out the disciples with this commission, 'Go ye into all the world and preach the gospel to every creature'. He refers to the general call. The gospel is to be preached to everyone. The same applies to Matthew 22: 14: 'Many are called, but few are chosen', and also to what the Apostle Paul says in Acts 17 in Athens, 'God commandeth all men everywhere to repent' (v. 30). This is the general call to every person; there is no exception.

It is important for us to be clear about this matter. There are some who have misunderstood the doctrine of the great reformers and who say this should not be done, that the gospel is only to be offered to those who are chosen and elect. Many in their ignorance regard that as Calvinism. But it is hyper-Calvinism. John Calvin taught that the general call, the offer, should be made to everyone, to all creatures.

It is manifest however that all to whom this call comes do not respond. It is but too easy to think of people sitting in the same seat in the same church building and hearing the same call who nevertheless react quite differently. Some believe while others do not believe. Though they have heard the same general call there is a difference; and this is where the term 'effectual call' comes in. It is obvious that in the case of the one group the call has been effectual. It is equally clear that in the case of the other it has not been effectual or effective and has done nothing. It is obvious that the Apostle is using the term here in the second sense. There are no promises to the effect that all things work together for good to them who do not respond to the call of the gospel; indeed they are threatened with the damnation of hell. God's wrath is upon them. Clearly, therefore, this is the 'effectual call'.

Indeed verse 30 makes this clear beyond any doubt. 'Moreover whom he did predestinate, them he also called: and whom he called, them he also justified: and whom he justified, them he also glorified.' That is not true of an unbeliever. Whenever this term is used as a description of the Christian it always means the effectual call. There is an illustration of this in the first chapter of this Epistle: 'Paul, a servant of Jesus Christ, called to be an Apostle', or 'a called Apostle' (v. 1). It was an effective call, an effectual call. He was not merely given an invitation, he was 'put into the ministry'. That is what he says of himself. He is 'a called Apostle'. Exactly the same thing is found in the 7th verse of that 1st chapter: 'To all that be in Rome, beloved of God, called to be saints', or 'called saints'.

It is to people who have been effectually called in this way, and who are thus 'saints', that this great promise is made. I have already mentioned the distinction found in Matthew 22:14: 'Many are called, but few are chosen', and the preceding parable makes that abundantly clear. It tells us that a general invitation to a feast had been given to certain people, but they made excuses and did not go; then the king's servants went out and took certain other people in more or less forcibly. That is the effectual call – 'Many are called, but few are chosen'. The same truth is found in Paul's Second Epistle to Timothy, chapter 1, verse 9: 'Who hath saved us, and called us with an holy calling, not according to our works, but according to his own purpose and grace, which was given us in Christ Jesus before the world began.' Again in the Epistle to the Ephesians, chapter 4, verse 1, we find: 'I therefore, the prisoner of the Lord, beseech you that ye walk worthy of the vocation wherewith ye are called.' Here Paul is writing to none but Christians, and speaking of this particular effectual call, a call which has been made effectual. The same is found in the 1st verse of the Epistle of Jude: 'Jude, the servant of Jesus Christ, and brother of James, to them that are sanctified by God the Father, and preserved in Jesus Christ, and called.' And there are many other illustrations of the same thing in the New Testament.

The test therefore which each of us must apply to himself is, 'Have I been called?' To begin with, let us deal with this question from the experimental standpoint. We shall deal with it from the standpoint of theology and doctrine when we move on to verse 30.

Here are some of the tests: Can you say honestly 'I am what I am by the grace of God'? Why are you interested in these things? Why are you a member of the Christian Church at all? What has made you what you are? These are fundamental questions. Is it simply that you have decided to do certain things? Or do you say, in one way or another, 'I am what I am by the grace of God'? Are you amazed at yourself? does it astonish you that you are what you are, and live as you do? These are the proofs as to whether you have been called or not. The true Christian is a man who cannot understand himself; he can only say 'I am what I am by the grace of God. I have not done this of myself.' But he knows that something has been done to him. He is amazed at the fact that he loves God. The Christian is a man who is conscious that God has been dealing with him. To be 'called' means that your life has been interrupted and disturbed, that God has done something to you. You do not call yourself, it is God who calls – 'the called according to his purpose'. Are you aware of the fact that God has entered your life and has disturbed your life? Do you know something of the experience of Francis Thompson in *The Hound of Heaven*?

> *I fled Him, down the nights and down the days;*
> *I fled Him, down the arches of the years;*
> *I fled Him, down the labyrinthine ways*
> *Of my own mind; and in the mist of tears*
> *I hid from Him. . . .*

To be called means that you know that God has been concerned about you, that He has done everything to you, has interfered in your life, has irrupted into your life and laid hold upon you. This is entirely different from our deciding to do something, or our 'taking up religion' because we find it interesting. The people to whom 'all things work together for good' are those who feel that the hand of God has come upon them and taken hold of them. They have been 'apprehended' as the Apostle Paul states it in Philippians 3 : 12.

God interferes with our life, and then you find yourself convicted of sin. You do not desire this; it is entirely 'against the grain'. You do not want to be disturbed; your desire was to go on living in the same way, you enjoyed sin and found your happiness in 'the world'. But you are disturbed, you feel condemned, you are convicted of the wrongfulness of it all. You are not doing this to yourself. It is the last thing you would do; but it has been done to you, and in spite of the fact that you did everything you could to resist it, and wished it were not happening to you. As John Bunyan describes it, a voice keeps on coming to you and you try to stop your ears and to run away from it.

But having struggled against it, and fought with it, you begin to have a feeling that this Word of God that disturbs is true. The natural man does not believe that this Word is true; to him the Bible is just a book like any other book. But when a man is really called by God he knows that the Bible is not the mere word of a man. As the Apostle Paul says in 1 Thessalonians 2: 13: 'For this cause also thank we God without ceasing, because, when ye received the word of God which ye heard of us, ye received it not as the word of men, but as it is in truth, the word of God, which effectually worketh also in you that believe.' They felt a persuasion that, though the lips of a man were speaking, and the words were coming out of a man's mouth, it was nevertheless God who was speaking to them. The call of God was coming through this human instrumentality; they knew that the word was the Word of God and not the mere words of a man.

This, in turn, leads to a feeling of our own utter helplessness and need. No 'natural man' ever has, or can ever bring himself to have that feeling. Anyone who tells you that he has 'received' Christ, or 'taken' Christ, who does not at the same time tell you that he was utterly convinced and convicted of sin and that he felt completely helpless, does not conform to the New Testament description, 'I came not to call the righteous, but sinners to repentance'. The Lord calls the sinner to repentance and then displays to him the greatness of His own salvation. Anyone therefore who has this feeling of helplessness has good presumptive evidence of being called. Nothing can produce that feeling in you but the Spirit of God – it is His work to do this calling.

Next we begin to see the fulness and the sufficiency of our blessed Lord and Saviour Jesus Christ and His salvation. We see that He is the Son of God and we believe in Him as such. Only the Christian does so. Even 'the princes of this world' do not know this, for as the Apostle says, 'had they known him they would not have crucified the Lord of glory' (1 Corinthians 2: 8). The religious leaders of the Jews called Him, 'this fellow', this 'carpenter', and cried 'Away with him'. It is the Holy Spirit alone who can convince a man of the truth that Jesus of Nazareth is the Son of God, and of the truth of His Atoning death and its sufficiency, and the glory of His resurrection.

These are the tests. It is only the man who has been 'called' who believes these things. There are many who call themselves Christians who deny much, and at times most, of the apostolic teaching; but they have never been effectually called, and are not Christians. They never have assurance of salvation and do not even believe in assurance; they write and argue against it. They are quite consistent, but they are simply announcing that they have never been called. The man who has been called delights in singing,

> *I hear Thy welcome voice*
> *That calls me, Lord, to Thee,*
> *For cleansing in Thy precious blood*
> *That flowed on Calvary.*

He has heard it, and it is the most blessed voice and call he has ever heard in his life. 'Thy welcome voice'! He responds and says,

> *I am coming, Lord!*
> *Coming now to Thee!*
> *Wash me, cleanse me, in the blood*
> *That flowed on Calvary.*

His greatest desire now is to know the Lord better. He feels a magnetic spiritual attraction. Something is constantly calling him, and he responds to this blessed call of God. Are you aware of this calling of God? 'All things work together for good to them who are *the called* according to his purpose.' Has He laid His hand upon you and arrested you and apprehended you? Has he drawn you with the cords of His love? The inevitable result is amazement at yourself; and you say with Paul, 'I live, yet not I, but Christ liveth in me' (Galatians 2: 20). Paul was amazed at himself. 'Even unto me', he says, 'who am less than the least of all saints, is this grace given' (Ephesians 3: 8). In 1 Timothy, chapter 1, verse 13, he says: 'I was a blasphemer, and a persecutor, and an injurious person. But I obtained mercy.' He never ceased to be amazed at himself as an apostle.

This is always the great characteristic of the man to whom the great promise of this 28th verse is true. Are you surprised at yourself? Are you surprised at the fact that you are reading these words, that you can enjoy them, and do not find them extremely boring? Whether you are or are not a church member, if the truth of the gospel does not ravish your heart, if you do not feel that it is the most glorious thing you have ever heard, you have never been called. 'The called' are the people who desire more and more of this; they cannot help themselves; they are 'newborn babes', and they desire 'the sincere milk of the word that they may grow thereby' (1 Peter 2: 2).

We 'love God', we are 'the called according to his purpose'; and our actual experience in the Christian life tells us that this is true. It adds its 'Amen' to what the Scriptures say; or to use a scriptural expression, 'We set our seal to it that it is true' (John 3: 33). The Scripture pays us the compliment of saying that we can set our seal to it, we can say our 'Amen' to it. The Christian, the man to whom the promise applies, is a man who can say, 'I know in my personal experience that this is true, that "All things work together for good to them that love God" '. It means that you still have the feeling that God is dealing with you; not merely that He brought you into this life, but that He is still dealing with you. Do you continue to feel that God is interfering in your life? Is what is expressed in a well-known hymn true to your experience, 'O Love that wilt not let me go'? There may have been times when, as the result of the devil's temptation and your ignorance and weakness and folly, you wished that He would let you go; you wanted to go to do something, and you were being pressed to do so, but you could not. He who is love would not let you go. His intervention in our life is a continuing process in the Christian's life.

Do you find that you cannot be happy in sin? You may have tried it. Has it proved to be a failure? A child of God cannot be happy in sin. I am not saying that he may not sin, or that he may not continue in sin for some time; that is what is meant by backsliding. But the backslider is never happy; he is the most miserable man in the world. He goes on sinning but he is miserable. It must be so because he has a seed of divine life in him. So failure to be happy in sin is a good proof of the fact that God is still dealing with you.

Again, can you say honestly that in your experience chastisement has always been good for you even when it has hurt you deeply ? Can you thank God for it ? Do you find that when unkind things have been said about you, and men have reviled you, and criticized you wrongly and harshly, that instead of being furious and wanting to strike back, you say to yourself, 'This is good for me; it is better for me than praise. My danger is to be puffed-up, and to think that I am self-sufficient' ? And do you sometimes almost ask Him, 'Keep on doing it, keep me down, keep me humble, keep me in the place where Thou wouldest always have me, keep me in the place where I can always have uninterrupted communion with Thee' ? In other words, can you say from your own experience that even things that appear to be working against you, quite clearly are working for you, and working for your good? Do you bow your head with the Psalmist and thank God for it all, and say, 'It is good for me that I have been afflicted' ? (119: 71). If so, it is a proof that you have been 'called', for non-Christians never speak in this way. They curse God, they hate God, they despise the Christian faith and say it is a fraud. But the Christian can look into the face of God and say,

Let nothing please or pain me,
Apart, O Lord, from Thee.

Those, then, are some of the tests we have to apply to ourselves in order that we may of a surety know that the promise applies to us – 'All things work together for good to them that love God, to them who are the called according to his purpose'.

Sixteen

*

And we know that all things work together for good to them that love God, to them who are the called according to his purpose.

For whom he did foreknow, he also did predestinate to be conformed to the image of his Son, that he might be the firstborn among many brethren.

Moreover whom he did predestinate, them he also called: and whom he called, them he also justified: and whom he justified, them he also glorified.   Romans 8 : 28–30

We return to this statement which is probably more packed with doctrine and comfort than any other in the whole realm of Scripture. We have been looking at the promise itself and have been seeing what it means in actual practice and operation. The Apostle starts with the practical and experimental and from that rises to the doctrinal. We have also considered how we can be sure of this truth in personal experience.

We now turn to consider why it must be true of necessity that God works all things together for good to them who love Him, and who are 'the called'. The answer is provided in the great phrase at the end of the 28th verse – 'according to his purpose'. This promise must be true in the light of God's purpose with respect to His people. In other words, the statement is not that all things work together for good 'as long as we love God'. The statement is true of us because we are 'the called according to his purpose'. This is a most important distinction. Some would interpret the words as saying that as long as I love God, as long as I am in a state of faith, this is true of me; but if I should backslide, then it is no longer true of me. But such an interpretation entirely reverses the Apostle's statement. All things must work together for me because I love God, and I love God because I am 'called' of God, and because I am included in God's purpose of salvation.

At this point we are face to face with what is called the doctrine of the final perseverance of the saints, which first began to be taught at the time of the Protestant Reformation. It had been taught earlier but it was defined and became a famous expression in the Christian Church at the time of the Reformation. It is a part of our great Protestant heritage. The Roman Catholics, as I have had occasion to point out before, do not believe this doctrine; they reject it *in toto*. There would really be no place for their church if they believed it to be true, which explains why they have always fought it with such great zeal. In these verses we have the greatest statement in Scripture of this doctrine. It is stated elsewhere, and it is implicit in many places. But here we have the plainest, clearest, and the most explicit statement of it that can be found anywhere.

The working of all things together for good for true Christians is subsidiary to the great fact of God's purpose for His people. We must never think of it as something in and of itself. It is but a means to an end, and the vital thing is the end. So we are compelled to say that the real object is not even our good; it is God's purpose; and our good, and any good that comes to us, is nothing but a part of the carrying out of that great purpose of God. We find that principle enunciated here. The Apostle has been working up to it. The way in which it is handled matters little. You may start with a great enunciation of the truth as a basic principle, and then work down to its practical consequences. Or you may start from experience and rise from that to the great doctrine itself: it can be deduction or induction. Actually, of course, it is a part of God's great revelation which the Apostle sets before us by the method of induction.

The guarantee that all things will work together for our good, that they always have done so, that they are now doing so and that they will always do so, lies in the fact that it is all a part of God's great purpose with respect to us. We must understand the statement in this way, for it is the ultimate ground of assurance. Upon this every other form and type of assurance is ultimately based. This is what explains every part and detail in our great salvation. There is nothing beyond this; hence it is the ultimate and supreme form of assurance. We have been considering other aspects of assurance. They are all true, but here is the climax of them all. For this reason, in verses 29 and 30 the Apostle works out the steps and stages involved in salvation. He goes on to say, 'For whom he did foreknow, he also did predestinate to be conformed to the image of his Son, that he might be the firstborn among many brethren. Moreover whom he did predestinate, them he also called: and whom he called, them he also justified: and whom he justified, them he also glorified.' He gives a complete summary of salvation from beginning to end in order to show that each step is but a part of the outworking of this original purpose of God. In other words, as I have previously suggested, verses 29 and 30 are an exposition of the great phrase at the end of verse 28: 'according to his purpose'. We are to look at such great doctrines as the foreknowledge of God, God's predestination, God's calling, justification, glorification. They are all particular elements in God's purpose, and show its outworking.

In the first place we must realize the magnitude of the task which we are undertaking. It is of such a nature that, to borrow a phrase from the Epistle to the Hebrews, we must approach it 'with reverence and with godly fear'. This is so because we are dealing with the mind and the will of Almighty God. We are venturing to consider the mind and purpose of God. Man can never engage in any higher occupation. We, pigmy creatures of time, fallible creatures as we are, unworthy and sinful, are now going to look together into this particular revelation that God has been pleased to give of His own mind. There is no activity in which we can ever engage which is more solemn than this, or more holy. It is good at this point to recall what happened to Moses at the burning bush. He suddenly saw a bush aflame and yet the bush was not consumed. He was about to investigate it in a spirit of curiosity, saying 'I will now turn aside and see this great sight, why the bush is not burnt'. But a voice came to him saying, 'Draw not nigh hither; put off thy shoes from off thy feet, for the place whereon thou standest is holy ground' (Exodus 3: 1–5). And as we examine this statement we also stand upon 'holy ground'.

Something similar happened when God gave the Law on Mount Sinai. There were similar rules and regulations. The mount became a 'holy mount' and the people and their beasts were not allowed to come near it or to touch it. If they did so they would be immediately killed, whether man or beast. The people were to survey the scene from a distance. And in this 8th chapter of Romans God is doing something which is even higher: He is giving us a view of, and an insight into, His whole eternal mind and purpose. There is nothing higher than this. So it is of vital importance that our whole spirit should be right as we approach it.

Negatively, we must not approach the theme in a merely intellectual manner, still less in a merely theoretical manner. This is not a problem in philosophy, it is a revelation that God has graciously given us of His own mind and will. Nor are we to come in a controversial or argumentative spirit. To approach these doctrines in that way is totally wrong. Indeed it is sinful. It indicates that a person who does so has never really understood the doctrine, otherwise he could never approach it in that way.

Neither must we come to this great matter with the idea that we can fully understand and comprehend it. This is the mind of God, so if you make your own understanding the basis of your approach you are doomed to failure. It is His purpose, and no finite, human, sinful mind can ever grasp it fully. If we could do so it would mean that our minds are as great as the mind of God, if indeed not greater. We must constantly remind ourselves that we are not engaged here with a matter which is primarily philosophical. But that is far too commonly the way in which people approach it. So often they say, 'But I do not understand this; my idea of love is . . .' The moment you speak in that way you are speaking as a philosopher. Or if you say, 'I cannot possibly see how a God of love can do . . .', that is philosophy once more, and it is entirely inappropriate here. If you approach it in that way you have already gone astray and you cannot possibly have any kind of grasp of the doctrine. Philosophy is the main cause of trouble in this matter. What counts here is not what you can understand. We must start as Moses did, by putting off our shoes from off our feet, as we approach this holy revelation of the mind of God. We must not be at all surprised if we find that there are quite a number of things which we cannot understand or reconcile. The Apostle will emphasize this yet more plainly when he comes to chapter 9. It is not our business finally to understand nor to reconcile all we read in this Epistle. There are ultimate antinomies in connection with divine truth; there always have been, and always will be. So we must approach the teaching in a humble and reverent attitude, which is alone appropriate in the rarefied atmosphere of this 'mount of God'.

Whom does this doctrine concern? Who are the people who should be engaged in any attempt to deal with it? It is quite clear from the whole context that this is a doctrine for believers only. No one else can possibly receive it. Indeed, this entire doctrine is utterly repugnant and even hateful to the natural mind, a fact that is significant in and of itself. You will never find unbelievers, 'natural' men, believing this doctrine. They ridicule it, they hate it, they scout it. They say they could not possibly believe in a God of whom these things are true. The unbeliever reacts always in this way, and it is because he is pitting his own mind against it. I venture to say therefore that it is not a doctrine which should be preached in an evangelistic service. It is not the doctrine that unbelievers need to hear. I know that there have been teachers who have said that this doctrine should be preached in order to humble unbelievers; but I cannot find a single example of that in the Scriptures themselves. But someone may say, 'But I know of a man who was converted through hearing this'. That can happen in spite of the fact that it should not be done. God can even use our mistakes to bring about men's conversion. So we must not generalize from particular incidents. That is to argue from results. We must argue from the Scripture, not from what God in His infinite wisdom may occasionally choose to do. These doctrines were never meant for unbelievers; for if a man does not truly believe in God he cannot possibly receive such teaching. We would expect unbelievers to reject it and to hate it; and that is what they always do.

I come to another matter which is still more practical. This is a subject that you should never argue about or discuss with an unbeliever, and for the same reason. This is often done; I did it myself many years ago. I spent many hours of my life in doing so, but I see now that it was quite wrong. You should tell unbelievers at the outset that, being unbelievers, they cannot possibly hope to receive such truth nor have any kind of understanding of it. Furthermore, if you discuss this with them they are on very happy ground, for while they are arguing about these doctrines they are not facing themselves. Our first duty towards an unbeliever is to make him face himself. He is always ready to argue about election and predestination, of course. He sits back happily; you are on the defensive, and he is attacking. We are to be the attackers, and therefore we must direct these people to face themselves and their lives and their need of the Lord Jesus Christ. Men are not saved by believing the doctrine of election, or by believing in predestination. The way of salvation is to believe on the Lord Jesus Christ.

This is so important that I must adduce some authorities who confirm what I have been saying. I start with Octavius Winslow. Octavius Winslow believed these great doctrines of salvation, the great doctrines that are taught here, as staunchly as any man who lived in the last century; but when he deals with the question of how to handle an unbeliever, whether in preaching or in discussion, he says, 'It is not essential to your salvation that you believe in election, but it is essential to your salvation that you believe on the Lord Jesus Christ'. He says further, 'In your case as an individual debating the momentous question of how a sinner may be justified before God, your first business is with Christ, and with Christ exclusively. You are to feel that you are a lost sinner, not that you are an elect sinner.'

This is of extreme importance, but it is often forgotten. Let me produce a further quotation from Winslow. 'Whence this marvellous revolution, this essential and wonderful change? We answer, It is the Spirit of God moving upon your soul. And what truth, think you, meets the case – predestination? election? Oh no; these are hidden links in the great chain of your salvation upon which in your present state you are not called to lay your hand in grasping that chain. But there are other and intermediate links visible, near, and within your reach; take hold of them and you are saved. "This is a faithful saying, and worthy of all acceptation, that Christ Jesus came into the world to save sinners." "God so loved the world, that he gave his only begotten Son, that whosoever believeth in him should not perish, but have everlasting life." "The blood of Jesus Christ his Son cleanseth us from all sin." ' Winslow adds various other scriptural quotations. Election, predestination, etc., are not truths for the unbeliever; what he needs is repentance, and faith in the Lord Jesus Christ. Never allow him to discuss these deeper doctrines; to do so shows a complete failure to understand their purpose.

Let me give a further quotation from Winslow. He says, 'But we must rise to the fountain by pursuing the stream. Conversion, and not predestination, is the end of the chain we are to grasp.' In other words, he says that you must start with conversion. 'We must ascend from ourselves to God and not descend from God to ourselves in settling this great question. We must judge of God's objective purpose of love concerning us by His subjective work of grace within us. One of the martyr reformers has wisely remarked that we need not go about to trouble ourselves with curious questions of the predestination of God, but let us endeavour ourselves that we may be in Christ. For when we be in Him then are we well, and then we may be sure that we are ordained to everlasting life. When you find these three things in your heart – repentance, faith, and a desire to leave sin, then you may be sure your names are written in the Book, and you may be sure also that you are elected and predestinated to everlasting life.' Again, 'If thou art desiring to know whether thou art chosen to everlasting life thou mayest not begin with God, for God is too high, thou canst not comprehend Him; begin with Christ and learn to know Christ and wherefore He came, namely, that He came to save sinners and made Himself subject to the law and a fulfiller of the law, to deliver us from the wrath and danger thereof. If thou knowest Christ then thou mayest know further of thy election.' Illustrating this idea by his own personal experience Octavius Winslow says, 'If I believe in Christ alone for salvation I am certainly interested in Christ, and interested in Christ I could not be if I were not chosen and elected.' In all those quotations Winslow has been quoting the great English Protestant Father, Hugh Latimer, who was a great preacher of all these doctrines. That is how Latimer dealt with this particular matter.

Now let me quote from John Bradford, a contemporary of Latimer and a fellow-martyr for this great faith and the Protestant confession. He was burnt at Smithfield. This is how he writes, 'If ye feel not faith then know that predestination is too high a matter for you to be disputers of until you have been better scholars in the school-house of repentance and justification, which is the grammar-school wherein we must be conversant and learned before we go to the university of God's most holy predestination and providence.'

Never allow an unbeliever therefore to argue with you about election. Tell him that that is not his business. He will be glad to use it so that he can hide behind it, and evade his real problem. Tell him that this does not belong to him. He has first of all to be born and to become an infant; next he has to grow. Then, and not until then, he may be in a fit condition to apply his mind to such great and wonderful truths.

This great doctrine is meant only for the children of God and for their comfort; it is precious truth for them, but it is not for others. I have sometimes been almost tempted to say that the Bible itself is a Book for the children of God and for the Church only. The unbeliever as such does not understand it, and he cannot understand it unless and until he is born again. We need to remember our Lord's phrase in the Sermon on the Mount about 'casting pearls before swine'. Ignorant people often rend these great doctrines to their own destruction, and are guilty of blasphemy. They do it in ignorance, and so, thank God, they can be forgiven. But let us remind ourselves that this is a precious truth for the children of God, something that should be spoken of only in the family circle.

At the same time we must not come to what we are told here in a spirit of militant partisanship, taking up the cudgels on one side against someone on the other, saying 'I am a great Calvinist' or 'I am a great Arminian'. You should come to this doctrine with a sense of unutterable amazement at what we are told here. You should be filled with a sense of wonder. Then you will be humbled and will say, 'How amazing it is that I should be given a glimpse into this truth!' Such is the man who is likely to understand the Apostle's message. He does indeed take off his shoes. He says, 'It is almost incredible that I should have a part in God's great purpose, that all this is applicable to me.' He is truly astonished, and filled with a sense of wonder. He is utterly humbled by it all, and his heart is filled with praise. Not with the excitement of intellectual argumentation; he is filled with praise to God for His wonderful grace to the children of men.

Ultimately, the proof of a right approach to these doctrines is that you find in them the greatest urge to holiness and sanctification. If your belief of these doctrines has not driven you to holiness you are in a dangerous condition, and they have probably driven you to Antinomianism. You are misusing them to say, 'Well, all is right with me, it matters not therefore what I do. I am saved, and the final perseverance of the saints is assured.'

No one can truly see these doctrines without being humbled, and made to say 'Who is sufficient for these things?' He says with John, 'He that hath this hope in him, purifieth himself even as he is pure' (1 John 3: 3). The more certain I am that I am going to heaven and to glory where I shall see Christ, the more concerned I am about preparing myself for that experience. If the effect of these doctrines upon you is to make you sit back in self-satisfaction, you have never truly known them nor received them aright.

The man whose interest is purely philosophical and whose life is not turned towards godliness, is a believer in philosophic determinism, not in the truth of God. That is counterfeit, and entirely spurious. If you are filled with a spirit of militant partisanship, again you are probably arguing philosophically. This, being the truth of God, always humbles; indeed, because it is the highest, it is the most humbling of all the truths. The higher the truth the more it should humble us; the more glorious the truth, the more ought we to be amazed and astonished at it. What is your reaction to this doctrine? In what manner do you speak of it? Is it a slogan that you wave on a banner? Is it a sort of battle-cry in an intellectual skirmish? Or is it something which is so wonderful to you that at times you almost feel that you cannot speak about it at all, because it is so precious and so glorious?

Are we tarrying too long over this point? Are you waiting patiently for a discussion of election and predestination? If so, beware! We are at the foot of a very holy mountain, and if you imagine that you can run up this mountain you are deceiving yourself. The children of Israel were told to wash themselves before the great revelation was given on Sinai, and I have been urging you to do the same. We have to be clean before we come to this doctrine – clean in mind, and yet more clean in spirit and heart. Then, having cleansed ourselves, the first rule, I would say, is that we must always take these doctrines – this great central theme which, like light passing through a prism, can be broken up into many shades of colour – in their setting and in their context. We must never isolate them, as is done so frequently when they are discussed. Their setting is pastoral; it is comfort for the children of God, for believers faced with trials and tribulations, who do not know what to pray for as they ought.

As long as we discuss them in their setting we shall not go astray.

In the same way it must always be taken as a whole. The particular terms must never be taken in isolation. As you take the whole doctrine in its setting, take every particular statement in its complete setting also. Do not pick out certain terms and argue about them separately or try to understand them separately. They are but individual links in a chain, and they can only be understood in their relationship to other links and to the whole chain. Note the Apostle's words – 'the called according to his purpose. For whom he did foreknow, he also did predestinate to be conformed to the image of his Son, that he might be the first-born among many brethren. Moreover whom he did predestinate, them he also called: and whom he called, them he also justified: and whom he justified, them he also glorified.' The statements are all links in a chain. The whole secret of understanding them is to look at each one in the light of the whole. It is a chain and you cannot divide it; every link is necessary. The Apostle works it out at length in all its glory.

Finally, it is essential for us to examine Paul's statement, and every particular part of it, in the light of all other Scriptures, that is, in the light of the teaching of the Bible as a whole. That is true, of course, not only of this statement but of any other statement in the Scripture. But it is particularly true here because of the elevated character of the teaching. Never was it more essential that we should 'compare Scripture with Scripture', and have a view of the whole, in order that we may be safeguarded from putting too much emphasis on one particular statement.

What is the key to the understanding of this truth? The way to approach it is to ask the question, Why did Paul add verses 29 and 30 after saying, 'We know that all things work together for good to them that love God, to them who are the called according to his purpose'? That is a complete statement in and of itself; why did he add this exposition, this explanation which we have in verses 29 and 30? I have already supplied the answer. Verse 28 is not merely meant to give us comfort in trouble, but to give us the ultimate comfort of knowing that our final salvation is sure, and that everything that happens to us is but a part of that salvation. As each step of our salvation is 'predetermined' and already sure – that is what Paul is saying – we can be sure that God is overruling everything for our good.

In other words it comes to this; if we are in God's plan and purpose, then nothing can be against us. The Apostle tells us so in verse 31 when he writes, 'What shall we then say to these things? If God be for us, who can be against us?' That is the conclusion. It is important to realize it at the beginning. He need not have added verses 29 and 30; there would have been glorious comfort in verse 28 alone; but he explains it, he elaborates it, he works it out, and shows us the various links in the chain. He says in effect: Now this is God's purpose for you, and it will lead to your glorification. Cannot you see that because it is God's purpose He will certainly bring you there? and so everything that happens to you is subservient to, and must be regarded in the light of that purpose.

This, I suggest, is the key to the understanding of this extraordinary and amazing summary of Christian doctrine. The Apostle wants us to see that what matters ultimately is the 'purpose' of God. If we know the purpose of God, and that we are *in* the purpose of God, then there is only one conclusion to come to, that 'all things' must be made 'to work together' for our good; otherwise the purpose of God would never be carried out; God would fail and the devil would be triumphant. Hence the 'purpose' of God must be the starting point. Before predestination and election, before knowledge, before calling, before everything, comes the purpose of God. If this is clear to us, we shall have no difficulty about the glorious promise that 'all things work together for good to them that love God'.

Seventeen

*

And we know that all things work together for good to them that love God, to them who are the called according to his purpose.

For whom he did foreknow, he also did predestinate to be conformed to the image of his Son, that he might be the firstborn among many brethren.

Moreover whom he did predestinate, them he also called: and whom he called, them he also justified: and whom he justified, them he also glorified.   Romans 8: 28–30

We now come to consider this statement or argument more in detail. As we do so we remind ourselves that the vital statement is the phrase at the end of verse 28 about the purpose of God, for it is the key to the understanding of all the other terms – foreknowledge, predestination, calling, justification, glorification. And as we have already seen, the business of verses 29 and 30 is to expound the Apostle's phrase – 'according to his purpose'.

This phrase, first and foremost, is a declaration that God has a definite plan and purpose with respect to salvation. The expression 'according to' means 'in accordance with', or it can be translated 'because of'. The great comforting promise is that God will overrule all things for the good of those who love Him, those who are 'the called'. And they are 'called' and love God 'because of His purpose'. That is the ultimate explanation of the foreknowledge, predestination, calling, justification, and glorification. The phrase means that God has decided and decreed and planned a way of salvation. We sometimes use this term about ourselves, and in the Scriptures it is said about various people that they 'purpose' to do something. It means they intend to, they decide to, they plan to, they make arrangements to do this or that. But here we are told what God has decided and decreed and planned to do.

This is indeed the great theme of the whole of the Bible. The Bible is a collection of books, but it has only one great theme; and this theme concerning God's purpose runs through it from beginning to end. The Bible declares that purpose and shows its unfolding in history. I make bold to assert that a person cannot really understand the Bible and its teaching unless he understands something about this teaching concerning God's purpose. It is implicit in the whole teaching of the Bible and if we fail to see this unifying principle in it – in the plain teaching, in the history, in everything – then we have a wrong or a very inadequate view of the teaching of the Bible. So here we are dealing with something that is basic, not only to the understanding of salvation, but even to an understanding of the Bible itself as the Word of God.

Now while the purpose of God is implicit everywhere in the teaching of the Bible, here we have it stated in an explicit manner. That is an important distinction. The Bible employs both methods of conveying truth. Sometimes it suggests the truth; it is there but you have to find it and extract it. But at other times it states truth plainly and makes an explicit declaration of it. And that is what we have in this particular phrase.

The great truth we are now to examine is not confined to this passage. We shall find the same teaching in chapter 9, verse 11: 'For the children being not yet born, neither having done any good or evil, that the purpose of God according to election might stand, not of works, but of him that calleth.' A particularly clear statement of it is found in the first chapter of the Epistle to the Ephesians, verse 5, where we read: 'Having predestinated us unto the adoption of children by Jesus Christ to himself, according to the good pleasure of his will.' His will and His purpose are, of course, one. What God purposes God wills. It is 'according to the good pleasure of his will', and in verse 9, we read: 'Having made known unto us the mystery of his will, according to his good pleasure which he hath purposed in himself.' God has purposed in Himself the salvation of His people. It is 'according to the good pleasure of his will'. God's own purpose, arising in His own mind, is expressed in His will and in His action. And again in verse 11 of that same chapter: 'In whom also we have obtained an inheritance, being predestinated according to the purpose of him who worketh all things after the counsel of his own will.' Paul is explaining that the Jews had obtained an inheritance in this great salvation because they had been predestinated, and they were predestinated 'because of', 'according to', 'in accordance with the purpose of him who worketh all things after the counsel of his own will'.

Another statement of this great truth is found in the Second Epistle to Timothy, chapter 1, verse 9: 'Who hath saved us, and called us with an holy calling, not according to our works, but according to his own purpose and grace, which was given us in Christ Jesus before the world began.' These explicit statements tell us that God has decided upon a certain course of action. He has taken a decision, He has planned a course of action, and He is putting that plan into operation.

The second point – and one which is evident in some of these quotations – relates to the question as to when salvation was planned and purposed. The answer is that it is 'before the foundation of the world'. This again is emphasized in many places in the Scripture, as, for instance in Genesis 3: 15, where God announces that the punishment of Adam and Eve because of their rebellion would include enmity between the seed of the serpent and the seed of the woman. But He also makes a promise – 'The seed of the woman shall bruise the serpent's head'. In giving that promise God was also indicating His purpose. It was not a sudden decision by God; for it had been determined before that, but God gave expression to it at that time. All the prophecies concerning the coming of the Son of God implicitly indicate the grand and glorious purpose of God in salvation.

A good example of an explicit statement is to be found in 1 Corinthians 2: 6 and 7: 'Howbeit we speak wisdom among them that are perfect; yet not the wisdom of this world, nor of the princes of this world, that come to nought: but we speak the wisdom of God in a mystery, even the hidden wisdom, which God ordained before the world unto our glory.' Nothing could be plainer. God 'ordained' it; that is another way of saying that He 'purposed' our salvation. Before the world was even created God had purposed this and had ordained it. And notice that it is to 'our glory', exactly the same idea as we find in Romans 8: 18. And again, the same truth is found in the Epistle to the Ephesians, chapter 1, verse 3: 'Blessed be the God and Father of our Lord Jesus Christ, who hath blessed us with all spiritual blessings in heavenly places in Christ, according as he hath chosen us in him before the foundation of the world', a statement which corresponds to that which we have already noticed in 2 Timothy 1: 9.

The same emphasis is found in a statement about our Lord Himself in the First Epistle of Peter, chapter 1, verse 20: 'Who verily was foreordained before the foundation of the world, but was manifest in these last times for you.' So all that has happened in Christ, and through Him, was foreordained before the world was made. Then there is that well-known statement in the Book of Revelation about our 'names written in the book of life of the Lamb slain before the foundation of the world'. It is a debatable point as to whether 'the foundation of the world' here refers to the fact that our names are written in the book, or to the Lamb slain before the foundation of the world. It is surely clear that both are true, because both are stated quite explicitly elsewhere in the Scriptures.

It is important that we emphasize that the plan of salvation did not come into the mind of God after the fall of man. It was in His mind even before the creation of the world. The plan of salvation was not conceived after the Fall. There have been no re-adjustments in God's plan. Some have taught and still teach, a notion of a series of re-adjustments in God's plan. They teach that God dealt with the children of Israel in an experimental or empirical manner, trying this and that, and when He found that one plan did not work He tried another. For instance, they say that God gave the Law to the children of Israel as a possible way of salvation; then, when it did not work, He began to give promises through the prophets that He would send a Deliverer. In this way they deny Scripture's emphatic teaching concerning the purpose of God, and give an utter denial to those passages which teach plainly that all was planned 'before the foundation of the world'.

This erroneous teaching is carried even further in the notes of a certain well-known edition of the Bible, which do not hesitate to say that even when eventually God sent His Son into the world the plan had to be changed. They assert that the Son came and preached the Kingdom of God, and offered an entry into the Kingdom of God to the Jews simply on the terms that they should believe on Him and His teaching. Had they done so the Kingdom of God would have been established there and then.

[209]

But unfortunately the Jews rejected the offer, and on that account God had to introduce another way through the death of His Son. And so the Church came into being. The Church had never been thought of before; it came in as an after-thought, as a temporary expedient, because the Jews had rejected the teaching of the Kingdom and the offer of entry into the Kingdom. The Church and salvation through the death of Christ are a kind of improvisation. The death of Christ need not have taken place if the Jews had believed the message of the Kingdom. God's plan had to be interrupted. The 'prophetic clock' was stopped for the time being, and after this 'church age', which is a digression, God's plan and purpose will be continued again.

Such notions are a complete denial of the biblical teaching concerning the 'purpose of God' conceived in eternity before the foundation of the world and the creation of man. They represent the teaching which is known as 'dispensationalism'. We must be clear about these things. God's purpose came into being before the foundation of the world. There is nothing contingent, nothing temporary or expedient about it. It does not come into being because of something unforeseen.

The next matter calling for attention is the agent by whom this purpose is carried out. Quite clearly the answer is that ultimately it is God Himself. Five times in Paul's statement in Romans we are told that it is God who acts – 'We know that all things work together for good to them that love God, to them who are the called according to his purpose. For whom he did *foreknow* he also did *predestinate* to be conformed to the image of his Son, that he [the Son] might be the firstborn among many brethren. Moreover whom he did predestinate, them he also *called*, and whom he called, them he also *justified*, whom he justified, them he also *glorified*.' God Himself not only planned the purpose, and thought of it, and initiated it; it is God ultimately who is carrying out and putting it into operation. Many good Christian people start and end with the Lord Jesus Christ. Let there be no misunderstanding about this; great glory must be given to our Lord, but you must not give all the glory to the Son. The glory is to be given to the three blessed Persons in the Holy Trinity. It is God (the Father) who so loved the world, that He gave His only begotten Son. Those who only and always talk about the Lord Jesus Christ, and pray to Him, and to whom the

Father and the Holy Spirit might very well be non-existent, are not only guilty of great error but are utterly unscriptural.

So far we have noted that believers are the called according to the eternal purpose of God the Father. It is emphatically His purpose. Take the statement made by the Apostle Paul concerning the first Advent. He does not say 'When the fulness of the time was come, the Lord Jesus Christ came to earth from heaven', but 'God sent forth his Son, made of a woman, made under the law, to redeem them that were under the law' (Galatians 4: 4). It is the Father who sent Him. Still less must we, as many have done, represent the Son as having to persuade the Father to forgive us. They concentrate upon the Son to the extent that they even regard the Father as being so much against us that the Son has to plead with Him on our behalf. Such is their false way of interpreting the intercession of the Son, as we shall see later in verse 34. It is the Father who sent Him to do all that He did and still does. 'He spared not his own Son', says verse 32, 'but delivered him up for us all.' From the Scriptures we know something of what this cost the Son – the agony and the shame, the spitting, the crown of thorns, and all else. But we cannot imagine what it meant to the Father. 'He that spared not his own Son, but delivered him up for us all, how shall he not also with him freely give us all things?' So I emphasize that ultimately it is all the work of the Father Himself. It is He, likewise, who sends the Spirit, again through the Son. The Father gives the Spirit to the Son, who sends the Spirit on the day of Pentecost.

The realization of these truths opens up the glorious vista of biblical truth. The Old Testament is but the outworking of this purpose of God as He prepares for the coming of His Son. That coming is the crucial event, but He has to prepare for it, and in the Old Testament we read of the preparation. Ideas are suggested, previews are given, adumbrations are provided. Then in the New Testament we are told of how the Son came, and how He did that essential work which He alone could do, the taking to Himself of human nature, the identifying of Himself with us, the giving of perfect obedience to the Law, the bearing of the punishment of our sins, the conquering of death and the grave, His being raised from the dead to justify us, His ascension to Heaven, and His heavenly session. All this is the special work of the Son. Then the Holy Spirit is sent – that climactic event on the day of Pentecost when the Holy Spirit was shed forth so abundantly. And His work continues. It is the Holy Spirit who convinces and convicts of sin. It is He who brings us into the Church, it is through Him the call comes and we are added to the Church. The purpose of God is carried on and fulfilled through the work of the Spirit, who applies the finished work of the Lord Jesus Christ to us. The final consummation of the purpose will be achieved when the Son comes back again, and all that which we considered when we dealt with verses 17–23 comes to pass, and 'the manifestation of the sons of God' takes place. First it will be the manifestation of the Son Himself, followed by our being transformed into His glory, even our very bodies. But all this is the Father's purpose; it is the Father who began it, it is the Father who is controlling it all, and who guarantees that the grand purpose will be brought to completion.

I must emphasize the absolute certainty of the carrying out of the purpose because it is basic and fundamental. Paul gives us comfort in this way. His argument is that if you are in the purpose of God all is well with you, everything must work together for good for you. There is no meaning in this statement if that end is not absolutely sure and certain to the last iota, with nothing whatsoever missing. The word 'glorified' at the end of verse 30 is enough, in and of itself, to establish this point. I emphasize again the use of the aorists, indicating something already completed once and for ever. 'Whom he did predestinate, them he also called: and whom he called, them he also justified: and whom he justified, them he also glorified.' This has already happened. There are foolish people who say you can be justified and then lose that status. But that is impossible; these are links in an unbreakable chain. If you have been justified you have been glorified – your final glorification has already happened in the purpose of God. These are all past tenses to give us absolute proof of the certainty. In certain ways the most daring statement in the whole of Scripture is this statement that we are already glorified. We are as glorified as we are justified. That is the Apostle's argument; because it is the purpose of God it must be carried out. Verse 31 puts that in the form of a challenge, 'What shall we say to these things?' And the answer is, 'If God be for us, who can be against us?' – that is, 'No one!'

Chapters 9–11 are an elaboration of this theme. Their purpose is similar to that of chapters 6 and 7. They were written to deal with objections. The statement of the doctrine is made here, and chapters 9–11 are not primarily meant to state the doctrine; they supply proofs of it, and answer queries and questions concerning it.

This absolute certainty of the carrying out of God's purpose is proved and demonstrated in many ways in the Scripture. It is proved in all the history of the Old Testament. Look at the story of the children of Israel; at the obstacles and difficulties that confronted them; at the people themselves! God had made a promise that certain things were to happen to them and through them. But as you read the story you feel at times as if they cannot possibly happen; everything seems to be going against them. Nevertheless what God promised comes to pass. That is the message of the Old Testament; what God said He would do, He has done; what God promised, He has fulfilled. That is the real value of the history of the Old Testament. Foolish people say, 'I am not interested in the Assyrians and the Chaldeans and so on'. But we should be interested. These people rose up and tried to frustrate God's purpose; but they failed completely and are brushed aside. God allows much to happen to His people and we are tempted to say, 'Ah, God's purpose is defeated'. Read the history, and you will find that His purpose is not defeated. In spite of all obstacles it goes on. It is the great object, as I say, of chapters 9, 10, and 11, to show that no circumstances whatsoever will be allowed to prevent the carrying out of this great purpose. In strange and unexpected ways God brings it to pass. 'God moves in a mysterious way his wonders to perform.' That is a summary of the teaching of the whole of the Old Testament.

This teaching is seen particularly clearly in the prophetic books of the Old Testament. Were God's purpose not secure and certain there would never have been such a phenomenon as prophecy. The prophets prophesied some eight centuries concerning our Lord's coming before the event happened, often foretelling details that, 'when the fulness of the time was come', came to pass. The only explanation is that prophecy is a part of God's purpose. As the Apostle Peter reminds us in his First Epistle, chapter 1, verses 10, 11, and 12: 'Of which salvation the prophets have inquired and searched diligently, who prophesied of the grace that should come unto you: searching what, or what manner of time the Spirit of Christ, which was in them did signify, when it testified beforehand the sufferings of Christ, and the glory that should follow. Unto whom it was revealed, that not unto themselves, but unto us they did minister the things, which are now reported unto you by them that have preached the gospel unto you with the Holy Ghost sent down from heaven; which things the angels desire to look into.' But this could never have happened if the purpose of God was not absolutely certain and sure. The prophets foretold that our Lord was to be born in Bethlehem; and thus it happened. The exact time is foretold in a mysterious manner in the 9th chapter of the book of Daniel. That is why Paul uses the expression, 'when the fulness of the time was come'. It was all planned to the last detail. Even the fact that the Roman Empire should have conquered other dynasties by then is foretold. We are entitled to speculate that this had to happen in order that the Romans might have made their great highways along which the gospel might spread everywhere throughout the then civilized world. It was all in the purpose of God before the foundation of the world.

The time element is particularly instructive in this connection. Paul in Ephesians 1, verses 9 and 10, sums it up in this manner: 'Having made known unto us the mystery of his will, according to his good pleasure which he hath purposed in himself: that in the dispensation of the fulness of times' – what a phrase! it indicates God's ultimate goal – 'he might gather together in one all things in Christ, both which are in heaven, and which are on earth; even in him'. God, says the Old Testament, sees the end from the beginning; and he has seen 'the dispensation of the fulness of times'. He does not act in a tentative manner, trying, failing, modifying. The whole plan, the whole purpose is certain and secure from the very beginning to the very end.

Nothing has failed, nothing ever will fail, nothing ever can fail for the reason that the character of God demands this. Approach these terms, 'predestination', 'calling', and so on in this way. Start with the character of God. Note how, in the first chapter of Ephesians, the Apostle keeps on repeating the phrase, 'To the praise of the glory of his grace, wherein he hath made us accepted in the beloved' (verse 6). Then again in verse

12: 'That we should be to the praise of his glory, who first trusted in Christ.' Verse 14: 'Which is the earnest of our inheritance until the redemption of the purchased possession, unto the praise of his glory.' The meaning is that all ultimately is designed to manifest the glory of God. The 2nd chapter of the Epistle to the Ephesians brings this out with particular clarity. Paul has been explaining that 'when we were dead in sins, he [God] quickened us together with Christ', that we are 'saved by grace', that 'we have been raised up together with Christ and made to sit together in heavenly places in Christ Jesus'. Why has this happened to us? 'That [in order that] in the ages to come he might show the exceeding riches of his grace in his kindness towards us through Christ Jesus' (verse 7). God's grace and kindness are involved. If anything were to go wrong at this point, it would be a reflection upon the grace and kindness of God. But that cannot happen, and 'the ages to come' are promised a glimpse into the grace and kindness of God. Another statement of the matter is found in Ephesians 3: 10: 'To make all men see what is the fellowship of the mystery, which from the beginning of the world hath been hid in God, who created all things by Jesus Christ: to the intent' – this is the object! – 'that now unto the principalities and powers in heavenly places might be known by (or through) the church the manifold wisdom of God'. God, through the church, through this process of salvation, is showing, and will in the future show to these principalities and powers in the heavenly places his 'manifold wisdom'. What would happen to the 'manifold wisdom' of God if the plan broke down and failed, or if man could frustrate it by saying, 'I will not believe it'? The character of God is involved in this purpose. The grand objective is stated in 1 Corinthians 15: 28: 'And when all things shall be subdued unto him [the Son], then shall the Son also himself be subject unto him that put all things under him, that God may be all in all.'

The certainty of the final consummation is emphasized by the expression 'according to', 'because of', 'in accordance with'. It is God's purpose, God's plan, God's resolve, God's will; and when God decides to do anything God performs it. God is not like us men. You and I propose and start schemes, but we give up, or we can be stopped by another person. But God is God, and when God wills anything it is already virtually done.

These things are identical in God, because God is God. God is 'the Father of lights, with whom is no variableness neither shadow of turning'. In chapter 11 of the Epistle to the Romans, verse 29, the Apostle tells us that 'the gifts and calling of God are without repentance'. God never goes back on his word. This must be so, otherwise God is not God. If anything could prevent or frustrate God's purpose it would mean that this something that is able to frustrate Him is stronger than God, which is inconceivable. Any failure in the carrying out of this purpose would mean the failure and the defeat of God Himself. God's purpose and plan must succeed in order that God may defeat His every enemy, the devil included. Salvation is not ultimately for our sakes; but for the glory of God. God in salvation is vindicating Himself, and manifesting Himself to the whole universe. He is displaying His everlasting and eternal glory. Hence His purpose cannot and will not fail. So we join Augustus Toplady in saying

> *Things future, nor things that are now,*
> *Not all things below nor above,*
> *Can make Him His purpose forego,*
> *Or sever my soul from His love.*

We shall later consider those to whom this purpose applies, and then consider how it is being carried out in detail. But we must never forget or cease to thank God for the fact that our salvation is a part of God's purpose, and the whole character of God is involved in the completion of this purpose. He is vindicating Himself, He is manifesting His manifold wisdom to the 'principalities and powers in the heavenly places'. The ages to come will have to bow before Him in acknowledgment of the fact that He is God, that He is 'all in all', and that beside Him there is none other. We are 'the called according to his purpose'.

Eighteen

*

And we know that all things work together for good to them that love God, to them who are the called according to his purpose.

For whom he did foreknow, he also did predestinate to be conformed to the image of his Son, that he might be the firstborn among many brethren.

Moreover whom he did predestinate, them he also called: and whom he called, them he also justified: and whom he justified, them he also glorified.   Romans 8: 28–30

We come now to consider the people to whom God's purpose applies. The text tells us that it applies to 'the called' – 'the called according to his purpose'. The same people are also described in the terms 'foreknown', 'predestinated', 'justified', and 'glorified'. The principle is that the purpose of God in salvation applies only to these people, not to any others. In other words, to put it negatively, there is nothing in Scripture anywhere to suggest what is called 'universalism', the teaching, very popular today, that at the final consummation every human being who has ever lived anywhere will be saved. Some carry it even further and teach that even the fallen angels and the devil himself will be saved. Such teaching is not based on Scripture, but entirely on philosophy. The philosopher believes that he can work out everything in his own mind; he has a pathetic faith in his own reasoning. He starts by asserting, 'Now you cannot think of God, and the love of God, failing'. He argues that the very notion of the love of God demands that there will be no one outside God's love. People who accept this notion maintain that one cannot imagine a God of love consigning anyone to everlasting perdition and destruction. And because they cannot fit this into their philosophic notion of love they reject it, and proceed to say that, in some marvellous manner, at the end everyone will be saved. They suggest various ways in which this will happen, all of which involve in some shape or form a kind of 'second chance' after death, in which people will see their previous error and will believe and accept salvation. And so, at the end, all will be saved; and even the devil, the first to fall from God, and all the angels who followed him and fell with him, will also be saved. Some go so far as to say that the sole purpose of preaching is to tell people that God loves them whether they believe in Him or not.

The simple reply to such error is that it is a denial of the plain teaching of Scripture; yet it is a most popular teaching at the present time. Many are resting upon it because, they say, it is very comforting and consoling. It more or less allows you to live as you please, and do what you like, for all will be saved in the end. Such people are not interested in other doctrines, in fact they dislike them. This 'love of God', this philosophic notion of that love, covers everything, and all is well. What makes it still more serious is that one of the best-known theologians in the world at the present time (1961), a man described by the late Pope as the 'greatest theologian since Thomas Aquinas' (I refer to Dr Karl Barth) teaches this 'Universalism'. This is not surprising because, in spite of his supposed biblicism, he is in reality philosopher rather than theologian. This is the inevitable result when men substitute their own thoughts, and their own understanding of the love of God, for the plain teaching of the Scripture.

I substantiate my contention by pointing out that everywhere in the Bible the whole of the human race is divided into those who are the people of God, and those who are not. There is a division always between the 'saved' and the 'lost'. Even John 3: 16, the great text on love so frequently quoted – 'God so loved the world, that he gave his only begotten Son, that whosoever believeth in him should not perish, but have everlasting life' – refers by implication to those who do not believe. What becomes of them? It is surely obvious in the remainder of that same chapter. The next verse (17) says that 'God sent not his Son into the world to condemn the world; but that the world through him might be saved'. The world was already condemned: God sends His Son in order that He might save. 'He that believeth on him is not condemned: but he that believeth not is condemned already, because he hath not believed in the name of the only begotten Son of God.' The last verse (36) in that same chapter of John's Gospel clinches the matter: 'He that believeth on the Son hath everlasting life: and he that believeth not the Son shall not see life; but the wrath of God abideth on him.' If we had nothing further to quote, that is more than sufficient in and of itself. In the 10th chapter of John's Gospel this division is emphasized. 'My sheep', says our Lord, 'know my voice'; the others do not. '*My* sheep' – these special people! 'Other sheep I have which are not of this fold' and so on. Christ has been given a definite body of people, and they are contrasted with the others. It is still clearer, perhaps, in the great high priestly prayer in the 17th chapter of John's Gospel. 'I pray not for the world', says our Lord, 'but for them which thou hast given me.' All that He has been doing, He says, He has been doing for the sake of these people whom God has 'given him'. Notice how He expresses it: 'As thou hast given him power over all flesh, that he should give eternal life to as many as thou hast given him' (John 17: 3). It is almost incredible that anyone should assert this doctrine of Universalism in the light of such teaching; and, as I say, there is only one explanation of it, namely, that such teachers brush aside the biblical revelation and substitute for it their own ideas concerning the love of God.

What makes this error yet more serious is that it has influenced certain evangelical people who claim to believe the Bible as the authoritative Word of God. Because they cannot understand the ways of God, they are ready to listen to this doctrine which teaches that, because of the love of God, everyone, everything will be restored in the end. But in the Bible, and especially in its closing book, the Book of Revelation, you find the exact opposite taught; the devil and the beast, and all who follow and belong to them, are finally cast into the lake of fire. It is quite false, therefore, to say that particular redemption is only found in Paul's teaching. It is the teaching found everywhere in the Bible.

But, turning to the Apostle's own teaching, we shall find in chapter 11 of this Epistle that he teaches that, not only is this purpose confined to this particular people 'the called', but that the 'called' constitute a very definite number. We do not know the number, but it is known to God. Paul teaches that there is a 'fulness of the Gentiles' (v. 25) to come in. The number is known exactly. The number of Gentiles who will enter into this final salvation has been known 'before the foundation of the world'. Then 'All Israel shall be saved' (v. 26). That cannot mean every individual Jew, because there are many who are already condemned, and more who will yet be condemned because of their unbelief. 'All Israel' means either the total number of Jews who are to come in; or it has a still more inclusive meaning, and refers to all the redeemed, all the family of God. But whichever it is, it shows that it is a very definite number, and that this is limited. The Apostle says again in 2 Timothy chapter 2, verse 19: 'The Lord knoweth them that are his.' People are falling away, says Paul, nevertheless 'the foundation of God standeth sure'. God knows His people, He has always known them – the exact number is known. Those who were falling away were never among them, they appeared to be, but they were not in reality.

The Apostle John in his First Epistle says of certain people, 'They went out from us'. Why? 'because they were not of us' (1 John 2: 19). They appeared to be, but they were not. 'If they had been of us, they would no doubt have continued with us; but they went out, that they might be made manifest that they were not all of us.' You can make a profession of Christianity, you can be in the visible Church, but that does not mean that you are of necessity among God's own people. The people of God consist only of those who are 'the called according to his purpose'. Their names are written in the Lamb's book of life, and they were written there 'before the foundation of the world'. We read at the end of the 20th chapter of the Book of Revelation that certain books will be opened at the final Assize, and only those whose names are written in the book of life are to be glorified. Further, 'And whosoever was not found written in the book of life was cast into the lake of fire' (v. 15).

All this surely proves beyond any doubt that the universalism which teaches that in the end all are going to be saved, irrespective of what they have done in this life, is a plain contradiction of some of the most explicit statements which are to be found in Scripture. It is not for us to understand these things; we either submit to the biblical teaching or else we do not. If you believe in the Lord Jesus Christ you will not perish. If you do not believe in Him, you are already condemned, and, continuing so, you will perish. So the purpose of God in salvation does not pertain to the entire human race; it only pertains to the people who correspond to the description given of them in the terms we are examining.

What, then, is God's purpose for these people? It is that we might 'be conformed to the image of his Son, that he might be the firstborn among many brethren'. This comes first, and we have to consider it before we come to the terms 'foreknowledge' and 'predestination'. The terms tell us of the mechanism by which the purpose is carried out, but the purpose must first be considered. The Apostle starts by defining 'the purpose', and then proceeds to the means by which that purpose will be achieved. To exalt the means above the purpose is to be unscriptural. We must always follow the Scripture and be led by its logic, and not rush ahead of it.

The Apostle, I believe, defines the purpose in order to show and to guarantee its absolute certainty. It is as if he were saying, When you know what God's purpose is with respect to you, then you will see that He must carry it out. The very nature of the end means that it must certainly and surely and inevitably be brought to completion. What is this purpose? It is not forgiveness only. Forgiveness is but the first step. Thank God for forgiveness, but thank God also that salvation is much more than forgiveness. Many seem to take salvation to mean that your sins are forgiven and that there is no more to be said. Forgiveness is but the initial step in the outworking of this grand purpose that originated in the mind and will of God. Salvation does not even stop at justification. Justification is more than forgiveness as we have seen in the early chapters. Justification is a declaration that we are righteous in the sight of God, that He regards us as such, that He declares us to be such through the righteousness of Christ. But salvation does not stop even at that; it guarantees that something further is going to be done to us. It is not only that the righteousness of Christ is imputed to us, but there is something beyond even that! And it is this something further which gives us our fundamental and final assurance with regard to the certainty of all salvation's blessings. The final blessing for every one of us who is a Christian is that we are to be 'conformed to the image of his [God's] Son, that he might be the firstborn among many brethren'. What a noble, what an exalted statement! Note that there are two elements in it, for the purpose of God is a double purpose. There is the main purpose but also a subsidiary one.

The ultimate purpose is the glory of the Son – 'that he might be the firstborn among many brethren'. The pre-eminence of Christ! The glory of the Son of God! That is the ultimate end and object of salvation. But thank God, in order to establish that end the other purpose comes in, and that applies to us. In carrying out His fundamental purpose of showing His own glory and of glorifying His Son, God gives this wonderful promise to us, that we shall be conformed to the image of His Son.

Let us look first at the purpose of God with respect to us, and then proceed through and from that to the ultimate object of the glorifying of His Son. We are to be conformed to the image of His Son. This is the acme of all teaching concerning salvation, and we must grasp it. The ultimate object of salvation is to bring us to this height. I am not depreciating forgiveness or guidance or comfort and all the other blessings of the Christian life. We need them all more and more in these dark and difficult days. But if you really desire and long to feel 'more than conqueror', and to be able to say with great assurance with the Apostle that you know that 'the sufferings of this present time are not worthy to be compared with the glory which shall be revealed in us', then you must lay hold of this truth.

The trouble is that we all tend to be so subjective. We start and end with ourselves and the particular problems that trouble us – help to overcome some particular sin, or the need of physical healing. We so concentrate on all such blessings that we tend to lose sight of the glory of this ultimate goal – to be 'conformed to the image of his Son'.

It may help us if we look at another statement of this truth which is found in 2 Corinthians 3: 18: 'We all, with open face beholding as in a glass the glory of the Lord, are changed into the same image from glory to glory, even as by the Spirit of the Lord.' Let us examine the terms, the first of which is the term 'image' – 'the image of his Son'. This same word is used with respect to the Lord Jesus Christ Himself. Paul says in 2 Corinthians 4: 4 that 'the god of this world hath blinded the minds of them which believe not, lest the light of the glorious gospel of Christ, who is the image of God, should shine unto them'. Our Lord is 'the image of God'. Colossians 1: 15 says the same thing in reference to our Lord. We there read that Christ 'is the image of the invisible God, the firstborn of every creature'. 'Image' means more than a 'likeness'; it is a very special type of likeness. It is not an accidental likeness, but a 'derived likeness', a likeness that comes to us directly from the object which we resemble. Certain obvious illustrations will help here. Take the head of a monarch on a coin. That is a derived likeness. The head of the monarch on the coin does not vaguely resemble the monarch; it has been derived from the very likeness of the monarch himself. The same applies to the head of a monarch on a stamp; it is derived from the original. We sometimes say of a child, 'He is the exact image of his father'. If that is so, it is because he has derived the likeness from the father. Someone else may be remarkably like this same man, but that is not a 'derived' image. It is the child alone that derives it from the father. It is not an accidental likeness. You may have two objects that look very much alike, two flowers, two stones, two eggs, two apples, for example; but that is not a derived likeness, it is purely accidental. One of them is like the other, not because it has derived its likeness from the other, it just happens that it looks like it, and therefore there is a similarity. The word 'image' is much stronger and indicates something that is always derived directly from another. So when we are told that we are to be 'conformed to the image of his (God's) Son', it means that we are to be like the Son of God in this sense.

The word 'conform' likewise is an interesting word. In the original it means 'to bring to the same form with'. 'Con' means 'together with'; 'form' is the appearance which something or someone has. In other words it means 'to render like', to be like someone else in form, to bring into the same form as someone else. This term, in other words, carries the same fundamental notion as the word 'image'. It does not mean a mere superficial likeness or conformity to the form. It means an inward likeness and conformity. It is not something on the surface, it is down in the depths. That is to say, it is a likeness of essence, and not a mere similarity. Someone has said that this conformity means 'an outward expression of an inward essence or nature'. In other words, what we are told, therefore, is that we are to be 'made conformable to', to be 'like unto' the Son of God in our inward essence. We are to bear His stamp upon us, His likeness in our very nature and, indeed, in the whole of our personality.

The other terms used are really just supporting terms to bring out this whole idea. That is true of the word 'brethren'. He is to be 'the firstborn among many *brethren*', which means a number of brothers. This again adds to the whole notion of the identity of 'essence', and it is a term which is used very frequently in Scripture. We have already met it in chapter 5, verses 12 to 21. We were once 'in Adam', we were children of Adam, we all are by nature brothers as children of Adam. The same general idea applies whichever of the two terms you use. But now we are 'in Christ', a new relationship. We were of the same type as Adam in his fallen condition. In that sense we are all the brethren of Adam as well as being his lineage and posterity. The same applies to our relationship to the Lord Jesus Christ. One of the best statements of this is found in the second chapter of the Epistle to the Hebrews, verse 10; 'For it became him, for whom are all things, and by whom are all things, in bringing many sons unto glory, to make the Captain of their salvation perfect through suffering. For both he that sanctifieth and they who are sanctified are all of one' – one nature, one essence – 'for which cause he is not ashamed to call them brethren'. Then the writer proceeds to quote the words, 'I will declare thy name unto my brethren; in the midst of the church will I sing praise unto thee. And again, I will put my trust in him. And again, Behold I and the children which God hath given me.' This is the very teaching which we have here in our text. So the term 'brethren' – being a more familiar term – helps us to understand the terms 'image' and 'conformity' to the image. Because they have a unity of essence brethren have a certain likeness. It is this community of essence that makes them brethren; and correspondingly there are certain things which characterize them.

The other term which helps us to understand the Apostle's statement is found at the end of verse 30 – 'glorified'. To say that I am to be 'conformed to the image of the Son', to say that I am to become a kind of 'brother' of the Son, is another way of saying that I am to be 'glorified'. This truth is also stated in Hebrews 2: 10: 'It became him, for whom are all things, and by whom are all things, in bringing many sons unto glory, to make the Captain of their salvation perfect through sufferings.' We have already found a reference to glory in chapter 5, verse 2: 'We rejoice in hope of the glory of God', and again in this 8th chapter in verses 18–23: 'Not only they, but ourselves also, which have the firstfruits of the Spirit, even we ourselves groan within ourselves, waiting for the adoption, to wit, the redemption of our body.' The reference is to our ultimate glorification when even the very body itself shall have been delivered.

A similar statement to these is found in Philippians 3: 21 where we are told that, 'He shall change this, the body of our humiliation, that it may be fashioned like unto the body of his glorification, according to that mighty power whereby he is able to subdue all things unto himself.' Glorification! To be glorified means that we shall be like Him; like Him in spirit, like Him even in body. He is already glorified as Hebrews 2: 9 tells us: 'We see not yet all things put under him. But we see Jesus, who was made a little lower than the angels for the suffering of death, crowned with glory and honour.' And we are to be like Him, 'conformed to his image'; not only in spirit, but our glorified bodies will also be like His glorified body.

All this is really contained in the terms 'sons' and 'children' which we have already studied in verses 14–17. 'As many as are led by the Spirit of God, they are the sons of God.' Then, 'The Spirit itself beareth witness with our spirit, that we are the children of God: and if children, then heirs; heirs of God, and joint-heirs with Christ.' Verses 28 to 30 provide a further explanation of those verses. It is as we are glorified, and made conformable to His image, that all this will become true of us in its final fulness.

Now that we have looked at the terms separately, what exactly is the teaching? We have to be careful here, and for this reason, that our Lord is unique as 'the only begotten Son of God'. There is no other such Son of God, and there never will be. As the 'only begotten' Son of God He is co-equal and co-eternal with the Father. He is God the Son, the second Person in the blessed Holy Trinity. Hebrews 1: 3 tells us that He is 'the brightness of his (God's) glory, and the express image of his person' (Authorized Version). A better translation is, 'The radiance of his glory, and the character (or representative) of his reality', which is another way of saying, 'In the beginning was the Word, and the Word was with God, and the Word was God' (John 1: 1).

We must never lose sight of this, and we must never regard Romans 8: 28–30 in such a manner as in any way to detract from it. It is true only of the eternal Son of God, and will never be true of anyone else. So when we are told here that we shall be conformed to the image of his Son, it does not mean that we are to become gods, it does not mean that we are to become sons in the sense that the only begotten One is the eternal Son of God. As we have already seen, our sonship and our relationship to God in this way, is by adoption; and therefore it is different. It is for this reason that our Lord Himself used phrases such as, 'My Father' and 'Your Father'. He never says 'Our Father'. He never puts Himself into the same category as ourselves. He taught us to pray 'Our Father' but He does not include Himself in the expression. He draws a distinction – '*My* Father', and '*Your* Father', '*My* God', and '*Your* God'.

The meaning of the statement that we 'shall be made conformable' to the image of the Lord Jesus Christ, the eternal Son of God, refers to Him as He became the 'second Adam' for our salvation. That is explained clearly in the second chapter of Hebrews, verse 14, where we are told, 'Forasmuch then as the children are partakers of flesh and blood' – as the people whom God is going to bring to ultimate glory are partakers of flesh and blood – 'he also himself likewise took part of the same; that through death he might destroy him that had the power of death, that is, the devil' (verse 14). And further in verse 16: 'For verily he took not on him the nature of angels' – He did not stretch out a helping hand to angels. Well then, to whom? – 'but he took on him the seed of Abraham'. Human beings! The meaning is given us in verse 17: 'Wherefore in all things it behoved him to be made like unto his brethren.' Here we have an exposition of the doctrine of the Incarnation. The eternal Son of God, who was 'in the form of God' and one with the Father, added unto Himself, took unto Himself, human nature. That is what happened in that mystery in the womb of the Virgin; He was born as 'Jesus' – truly man as well as truly God!

But who is this Child, who is this Jesus? Paul gives an exposition of the matter in 1 Corinthians 15, verse 45, where he says, 'So it is written, The first Adam was made a living soul; the last Adam was made a quickening spirit'. He also refers to Him as the 'second Man'. 'The first man is of the earth, earthy; the second man is the Lord from heaven' (v. 47). Originally we all derived our being and our nature from the first Adam, who was the first man. What happens to us in salvation is that we derive a new nature from this 'second Man', this 'last Adam'. There will

never be another. He is the second Adam, and the last Adam.
He is the second Man, but He is the last Adam. That means that
He came into the world in order to start and to found a new
humanity. He is the 'firstborn among many brethren', the
beginner of a new race. A race started in Adam; another race
started in Christ. And the image to which you and I are to be
made conformable is the image of the 'last Adam', that is to say,
this perfect full humanity of the Lord Jesus Christ which is
joined to His eternal Sonship and Godhead. But it is to this that
you and I are to be made conformable. We are to receive, and
we do receive in the new birth, the seed of this new nature; we
receive a part of this new humanity from Him. We are born of
Him, He is the Head, we are the members. The Spirit brings this
to pass. We are 'partakers of the divine nature' in that sense,
and in that sense alone.

We are told that you and I are to be made conformable, in
spirit and in body, to this image of the eternal Son of God, who
has become the God-Man. He is the Son of God; but He is the
Son of Man also; He is the God-Man. In Him there are two
natures in one Person; and as the Son of Man He is the beginner
of this new race. It is to that, that you and I are to be conformed.
He has taken this glorified humanity with Him back to heaven;
it is indissolubly linked to Him; and 'we are members of his
body, of his flesh, and of his bones' (Ephesians 5 : 30). When
God's work is complete, we shall be conformed perfectly to that
very image.

It is as the result of this work that we are 'sons of God',
'children of God', that we know God as Father, that we enjoy
the privilege of this relationship of Father and children and can
address Him as 'Our Father'. But above and beyond that, this
is what we look forward to, because this is God's purpose.
Eventually you and I shall be perfectly conformed in essence to
that perfect glorified humanity that is there at this moment in
the Son of God. Such is the meaning of Hebrews 2, verse 5 to
the end of verse 9. 'What is man, that thou art mindful of him?'
'We do not see everything yet put under him.' 'But we see Jesus',
and because He is there, we shall arrive there. And when we are
there we shall be 'lords of creation', we shall reign with Him,
we shall be seated on His throne, and we shall be sharing this
state of glory with Him for ever and for ever. Now we are being

prepared for that. That is accomplished through the Church, preaching, the reading and exposition of Scripture, prayer, and much else. 'We all, with open face, beholding as in a glass the glory of the Lord, are changed (are being changed) into the same image from glory to glory, even as by the Spirit of the Lord' (2 Corinthians 3 : 18).

Such is the purpose of God with respect to us. Let us hold this in our minds at all times. Meditate along these lines. As John Calvin tells us, 'The Son of God became the Son of man that the sinful sons of men might become the sons of God'. He came down so low and was born as a helpless babe, in order that you and I might ultimately be entirely glorified, might be conformed to His image in spirit and in body, might be like unto the Son of God Himself! The second, the last Adam, came to the conflict and the fight in order to deliver us and to make us ultimately like Himself. Keep this in the forefront of your mind. There is a day coming when you will see Him. 'Beloved, now are we the sons of God, and it doth not yet appear what we shall be: but we know that, when he shall appear, we shall be like him; for we shall see him as he is' (1 John 3 : 2). 'Conformed to the image of his Son'!

Nineteen

*

And we know that all things work together for good to them that love God, to them who are the called according to his purpose.

For whom he did foreknow, he also did predestinate to be conformed to the image of his Son, that he might be the firstborn among many brethren.

Moreover whom he did predestinate, them he also called: and whom he called, them he also justified: and whom he justified, them he also glorified.   Romans 8: 28–30

We now move on to the second aspect of this great purpose of God, namely, that which has reference to the Son Himself – 'That he might be the firstborn among many brethren'. The term 'firstborn' provides at once the key to what the Apostle is saying. The 'firstborn' is always in a position of pre-eminence. That was a great characteristic of family life in Israel as seen in the Old Testament. The firstborn was always in a very special position of privilege, and unusual respect had to be paid to him. So the Apostle says that the glory of the Son is shown in the fact that He is 'the firstborn among many brethren'.

It is most important that we should look at our salvation from this standpoint. We must not only think of it in terms of ourselves, but we must realize that God's ultimate object in ever planning and introducing the scheme of salvation is to glorify His Son. We have already had occasion to emphasize this aspect of the matter in previous expositions, but we are compelled to do so again. We must realize – and there is nothing so comforting as this, nothing so assuring – that the very honour and glory of the blessed Holy Trinity is involved in our ultimate complete salvation. As the chief purpose of salvation is to glorify the Son of God, and as He is the 'firstborn among many brethren', the resulting position if He had no 'brethren' at all, and none to follow

Him, is quite clear. He left the courts of heaven, He came to earth, He gave His teaching, He died on the Cross, He was buried, He rose again, and yet there is no visible result! What would happen to the glory of the Son? There would be no glory; it would be failure. The Apostle wants us to understand this. As God's purpose is to show forth the pre-eminence of His Son, and to glorify the Son – as our Lord Himself emphasized, as we have seen, in His high-priestly prayer – the Apostle emphasizes that truth here.

This is the ultimate and supreme guarantee of our final salvation. The glory of the Son is involved in this; and He will be finally glorified when He and all His brethren are, as it were, 'on view' to the whole cosmos. It is a theme we find repeatedly in the New Testament epistles. We have already quoted the statement in Ephesians 1, verse 10, which tells us that the whole object of salvation is, 'that in the dispensation of the fulness of times he (God) might gather together in one all things in Christ, both which are in heaven, and which are on earth; even in him'. The whole cosmos is to be 'headed up again' in one, in utter absolute perfection, and it is in the Lord Jesus Christ. And in the same manner, at the end of that chapter, Paul says that God, having raised His Son from the dead, 'set him at his own right hand in the heavenly places, far above all principality, and power, and might, and dominion, and every name that is named, not only in this world, but also in that which is to come'. He is supreme above all as the result of the work He has done.

But perhaps the most explicit statement of this matter is found in the Epistle to the Philippians, chapter 2, where we find the famous passage about our Lord's humiliation, beginning at verse 5: 'Let this mind be in you, which was also in Christ Jesus: who being in the form of God, thought it not robbery to be equal with God: but made himself of no reputation, and took upon him the form of a servant, and was made in the likeness of men: and being found in fashion as a man, he humbled himself, and became obedient unto death, even the death of the cross. Wherefore God also hath highly exalted him, and given him a name which is above every name: that at the name of Jesus every knee should bow, of things in heaven, and things in earth, and things under the earth; and that every tongue should confess that Jesus Christ is Lord, to the glory of God the Father.' The word I emphasize is 'Wherefore'. It is as the result of what He has done that He is thus exalted. In other words, the ultimate object of salvation is that the Son might be set in the position in which at His Name 'every knee should bow, of things in heaven, and things in earth, and things under the earth: and every tongue should confess that Jesus Christ is Lord'. He is high and over all.

The Apostle states it again in Colossians, chapter 1, verse 18. Writing about our Lord he says, 'And he is the head of the body, the church: who is the beginning, the firstborn from the dead; that in all things he might have the pre-eminence'. The pre-eminence of the Son of God! 'The firstborn from among the dead'! 'The firstborn among many brethren'! The ultimate end and object of salvation is the glorification of the Son.

The argument, therefore, is that because that is the ultimate object of salvation it is certain and safe and sure; it cannot fail; it cannot go wrong. Everything God has purposed in and through His Son must be fully successful, ultimately triumphant. So if you and I are in this purpose, that is the guarantee of our ultimate glorification. We are to be glorified with the Son, and to be made 'like Him'. And thus all that He does to us and in us and for our salvation will redound to His honour and glory.

Having stated the grand purpose of God in that way, the Apostle, in order to establish the grounds of our assurance yet more firmly, goes on to show in detail how God has put this purpose into operation. He reminds us of what God has done, and is doing, and is yet going to do in order to carry out this great purpose of His. Because He is God, God's purpose is perfect in every respect – perfect as a thought, as a concept, perfect in its inception, and equally perfect in its execution at every stage. 'When the fulness of the time was come, God sent forth his Son, made of a woman . . .' The time was known, known only to God. At the exact moment the Son of God came. That is why exact prophecy was possible in the Old Testament. Everything that had been prophesied was fulfilled to the smallest detail. The Son himself was born perfect, and He never sinned: all He did was perfect. The carrying out of the 'purpose' is perfect in every respect. Everything that had been predicted and prophesied concerning the Messiah was carried out in every single detail.

But this is equally true of the application of what He worked out and achieved to those to whom it applies. It is the theme the Apostle takes up in verse 29. Note that he introduces it with the word 'For'. This word, as we have seen repeatedly, is always important; but it is of crucial importance here: 'For whom he did foreknow, he also did predestinate.' 'For' is here designed to emphasize that every step, every part of this great purpose of God, has been worked out in detail. There is nothing contingent about what God does. He saw it all, He planned it all at the beginning; and there is a sense in which He did it all 'before the foundation of the world'. There is no uncertainty whatsoever with respect to it. Every single step is planned and ordained and will be accomplished. 'For whom he did foreknow [with respect to this purpose] he also did predestinate', and so on.

The carrying out in detail – and every detail in perfection – of this glorious, eternal purpose of God consists of five steps – foreknowledge, predestination, calling, justification, glorification, each one being absolutely vital. Notice the order in which Paul puts them. The five steps can be conveniently arranged as follows. One, the calling, is at the centre, and there are two on each side. On the one side of the 'calling' we find the 'foreknowledge' and the 'predestination'; on the other side we find the 'justification' and the 'glorification'. The Apostle undoubtedly put them in that order deliberately. He did not simply state them as they occurred to him. The order given is that which is in the mind of God. It is the way in which God proceeded to put what He purposed and planned into operation; and it is a very definite, logical order.

The first pair – the foreknowledge and the predestination – have reference to what God has determined and decided with respect to us. The second pair – the 'justification' and the 'glorification' – have a more practical and immediate reference to what is done to us. The calling is a kind of connecting link between the two pairs. An illustration may help at this point. There is a type of machinery known as a 'grab', often seen at docks or in connection with building operations. These great 'grabs' are manipulated electrically and you suddenly see one of them coming down and taking hold of a great crate or mass of earth and lifting it up. That, as it were, represents the 'calling'. The 'grab' represents the plan and the purpose of God, which when set in operation takes hold of us in what Scripture terms our 'calling'. Paul says in Philippians 3 : 12 that he was 'apprehended', he was 'laid hold of', we might even say 'grabbed'! What follows as the result of that grabbing is 'justification' and 'glorification'. The 'calling' is the point at which God's purpose is actually applied to us.

As we study these great terms in detail let us remind ourselves of the importance of guarding our spirits and our hearts. Nothing is more tragic in the history of the Church than the way in which a passage such as this has been abused, and has often become the source of heated, bad-tempered, foolish controversy. Let us remember that we are dealing with the mind and the purpose of God. Let us with humility approach what the Apostle lays before us.

The first term is 'foreknow' – 'For whom he did foreknow'. This is the most important term of the five! Obviously so! The first move in our direction in the application of God's plan and purpose of redemption is determined and controlled by God's 'foreknowledge'. It is interesting to observe that most people do not seem to realize this. They believe that the great term is 'predestination'; but that is the second, not the first. Foreknowledge comes first, as it must do. The actual meaning of the word is 'To know beforehand'. '*Fore*knowledge.' We must be most careful, however, in our interpretation of the term. There are those who say that it simply means that God is omniscient, and knows everything; that there is nothing which God does not know. And because God is omniscient, of necessity He has prescience. If He knows everything; if there is no 'time' where God is, no past, present, or future; and if God knows all and everything at the same time; then from our angle it obviously follows that God knows everything before it happens. Such people argue therefore that all that is meant here is that God, because He is God, knows beforehand what will happen. Then they go further and say that God knows beforehand that certain people will believe the gospel, and therefore He 'predestinated' them to be conformed to the image of His Son. They maintain that this is all that 'did foreknow' means, simply that God knew beforehand who these people were who would in course of time believe.

It is not difficult, however, to show the utter inadequacy of such an explanation of this term. In the first place, the passage does not say that God knew beforehand what certain of his creatures would do. It speaks entirely of God and what He does. There is no reference here to what you or I or anyone else may or may not do. All the statements concern what God alone does – 'Whom *he* did foreknow, *he* did predestinate. Moreover whom *he* did predestinate, them *he* also called: and whom *he* called, them *he* also justified: and whom *he* justified, them *he* also glorified.' It is all the action of God, and to introduce anything that you or I may or may not do is purely gratuitous.

The right way to approach this word 'Foreknow' is to observe the way in which it is used seven times in the New Testament. Twice it is used of the foreknowledge of man, and on the five other occasions, including its use in our text, it is used with respect to God Himself. The first example is found in the Acts of the Apostles, chapter 2, verse 23. Peter is preaching on the Day of Pentecost to the Jews in Jerusalem, and telling them about the Lord Jesus Christ. 'Ye men of Israel, hear these words: Jesus of Nazareth, a man approved of God among you by miracles and wonders and signs, which God did by him in the midst of you, as ye yourselves also know: him, being delivered by the determinate counsel and *foreknowledge* of God . . .' Note that the word is coupled with 'determinate counsel', which carries the same meaning as 'predestination' in our text. The meaning of 'foreknowledge' in Acts 2: 23 is clear. Is Peter simply telling his hearers that God knew from eternity that the Lord Jesus Christ would be crucified? What would be the point of saying that? None whatsoever! The Apostle is saying that Christ died on the Cross because God had sent Him to that death. It was what God had planned. 'You have actually done it', he says in effect, 'and you employed wicked men to do it.' But it was the 'determinate counsel' and 'foreknowledge' of God that caused the crucifixion to take place.

The same statement is repeated in the 4th chapter of Acts. The actual word 'foreknowledge' is not used there, but the same idea is present. 'For of a truth against thy holy child Jesus, whom thou hast anointed, both Herod, and Pontius Pilate, with the Gentiles, and the people of Israel, were gathered together, for to do whatsoever thy hand and thy counsel determined before to be done' (vv. 27, 28). These men were simply carrying out, ultimately, the decision and determination of God. They were doing 'whatsoever thy hand and thy counsel determined before to be done'. In other words, the plain teaching is that the death of the Lord Jesus Christ was planned by God before the foundation of the world. His death was not an accident, a tragedy; He came into the world in order to die. He came 'to taste death for every man'. He came to be 'the Lamb of God'. And this is how the Bible states the matter – all happened according to 'the determinate counsel and foreknowledge of God'.

So 'foreknowledge' means 'foreordination'! The two terms go together. It is interesting to observe the different translations of Acts 2: 23. The New English Bible puts it thus, 'He had been given up to you by the deliberate will and plan of God'. Another translation runs: 'Delivered by the predestined course of God's deliberate purpose.' Never forget in reading the verse that the word 'determinate' governs the 'counsel and foreknowledge'. It was 'determinate counsel', it was 'determinate foreknowledge'. The statement therefore means, not merely that God had knowledge that, when He sent His Son into the world, men would kill Him; but it means infinitely more, thank God! It means that He sent Him in order that that might happen to Him; for if that did not happen to Him there would be no salvation for sinful men. God's way of making salvation possible is to lay our sins upon His Son, and to punish them in Him. He becomes 'the Lamb of God, slain from the foundation of the world'.

The second occurrence of the term is found here in Romans 8: 29, and the third is also in the Epistle to the Romans, chapter 11, verse 2. In chapter 11 Paul is dealing with the case of the Jews. 'I say then, Hath God cast away his people? God forbid. For I also am an Israelite, of the seed of Abraham, of the tribe of Benjamin. God hath not cast away his people whom he *foreknew*.' There surely is only one possible meaning of this statement. Can it possibly mean that God foreknew that they were going to fall away? That would not help the Apostle's argument in any way. He is saying rather, God has not cast away His people whom He has chosen, whom He has foreordained. This is the argument of the entire chapter. It is not merely that God knew certain things about them, and about certain things that they would do. Paul's argument is that it is inconceivable that God, having chosen people, should then cast them away. It just cannot happen. That is the argument, and it is the same word as we find in Romans 8: 29, and exactly the same argument.

The fourth occurrence of the word is in the First Epistle of Peter, chapter 1, verse 2, where in writing to the strangers scattered abroad the Apostle says, 'Elect according to the *foreknowledge* of God the Father, through sanctification of the Spirit, unto obedience and sprinkling of the blood of Jesus Christ: Grace unto you, and peace, be multiplied'. He tells these 'strangers' that because they are Christians certain things are inevitably true of them. They have been 'elected'. How? 'According to the foreknowledge of God.' The translation in the New English Bible rightly has, 'Chosen of old in the purpose of God the Father'. The foreknowledge is implicit in the purpose, for He purposed to save certain particular people whom He subsequently 'called'. The Revised Standard Version uses the word 'destined' instead of 'foreknowledge'.

The final occurrence of the word is found in 1 Peter 1:20. The Apostle is dealing with the way in which we have been saved, so he says in verse 19 that we have been saved 'with the precious blood of Christ, as of a lamb without blemish and without spot: who verily was *foreordained* before the foundation of the world, but was manifest in these last times for you, who by him do believe in God'. I quote from the Authorized Version. The translators of the Authorized Version are at times inconsistent with themselves. In this statement in 1 Peter 1, they very rightly translate it as 'foreordained', and they should have done the same everywhere else. They so translated it there because it is obvious that it could not possibly mean anything else. Peter is writing about Christ as of 'a lamb without blemish and without spot: who verily was foreordained [as the Lamb of God] before the foundation of the world'. It cannot possibly be said that God, because He knows everything, knew before the foundation of the world that His Son would become the Lamb of God. The fact is that it was God who made Him 'the Lamb of God'. It is God who 'foreordained' Him to that! He 'knew' Him in the sense that He specially set Him apart for that work.

In other words there is only one sense and one meaning to 'foreknowledge', and that is 'foreordination'. It is interesting to find, on consulting the various translations, that however much translators may disagree with respect to the other four instances of the use of this word, they are all unanimous in respect of this final usage. For instance, the New English Bible has, 'He was predestined before the foundation of the world'. 'Predestined before the foundation of the world, he was made manifest in this last period of time.' That He should be 'the Lamb of God' was settled and decided upon before the foundation of the world, but it has only been made manifest in historic times. That is the contrast. In the Revised Standard Version translation we read: 'He was destined before the foundation of the world.' Weymouth has, 'He was predestined'. They are all agreed about the matter, because it is so plain and obvious that the word could not possibly mean anything else.

But we can go yet further. This word 'to know', as used in the Bible with respect to God's relationship to human beings, always has a very special meaning. It cannot mean only the knowledge which is inevitably a part of omniscience, because, if so, we would have to say that God knows all people, that there is no individual whom God does not know, and that, from the foundation of the world, and in every respect. So here, in the context of Romans 8: 29, it cannot mean simply that God knows beforehand what these believing people will one day do, because He knows that about everyone. But here the Apostle is writing only of certain special people, people who love God, and are 'the called according to his purpose'. There is obviously something special about them. When we read in the Scripture that God 'knows' someone, or certain people, it means that He has a special interest in them, that He has set His love upon them, that He is planning and has purposed certain things with respect to them.

The classic statement with respect to this is found in the Book of the Prophet Amos, chapter 3, verse 2. God says to the children of Israel, 'You only have I *known* of all the families of the earth: therefore I will punish you for all your iniquities.' Obviously God knows, as a matter of pure knowledge, every family in the earth. But He says that it is because He has known them only, that He is going to punish them for their iniquities. It clearly does not just mean that He knows about them, and knows what they will do, or will not do. It means 'To you only have I given special attention', 'you only have I selected as my own people', 'you are the only ones on whom I have set my heart, and to whom I have given special treatment'. 'You alone – therefore I am going to punish you in an exceptional manner.'

[237]

A parallel on the negative side is found in Matthew 7, verse 23, at the end of the Sermon on the Mount. Our Lord says, 'Many will say to me in that day, Lord, Lord, have we not prophesied in thy name? and in thy name have cast out devils? and in thy name done many wonderful works? And then will I profess unto them I never *knew* you: depart from me, ye that work iniquity.' If that 'knew' is just a question of knowledge in the sense of omniscience and prescience there is no sense or meaning in the statement. But when He says 'I never knew you', He means, 'You have never belonged to me', 'you have never been my people', 'you have never been in this peculiar relationship to me', 'I have never had a special interest in you'. It is the only conceivable meaning there; and it is the common meaning attached to this term 'knowledge' as used in the Bible.

A translation which puts this matter clearly in respect to Romans 8: 29 is that of an American, Charles Williams, who renders it, 'For those on whom he set his heart beforehand he also did predestinate to be conformed to the image of his Son'. The translator points out in a footnote, what is apparently the simple truth from a purely academic point of view, that his rendering carries the meaning which is always attached in the Septuagint to this word translated 'foreknowledge'. 'Invariably', he says, 'in the Septuagint the shade of meaning which is given to the word is – those on whom God has set his heart beforehand.'

To my great interest I find that even Dr James Moffatt, who rejects the doctrine, and also Dr C. H. Dodd, who likewise rejects the doctrine, both have to translate it in this way: 'He decreed of old that those whom he predestined should share the likeness of his Son.' And they carry that translation through quite consistently in chapter 11, verse 2, and in 1 Peter 1: 2 and 1 Peter 1: 20. I conclude that the meaning of 'foreknowledge' corresponds to what we find God saying to the children of Israel in Deuteronomy 7: 7: 'The Lord did not set his love upon you, nor choose you, because ye were more in number than any other people; for ye were the fewest of all people: but because the Lord loved you.' The same idea is expressed in Jeremiah 31: 3: 'Yea, I have loved thee with an everlasting love: therefore with lovingkindness have I drawn thee.' He drew them because He loved them with an 'everlasting love'. It was nothing in them that caused the 'drawing'; His everlasting love is the only explanation.

Here, then, is the consistent teaching of the Bible both in the Old Testament and in the New Testament. 'Foreknowledge' carries the meaning of God setting His love upon, and ordaining and determining certain things for His people. Indeed there is very little difference between foreknowledge and predestination. Hence we almost invariably find the two words being used together, as we have seen in Acts 2: 23; and here and in other places the shade of difference in the meaning is that God first of all sets His heart on these people, and then immediately, because He is God, He determines to do certain things to them and for them. This leads us to the meaning of the term 'predestination'. But 'foreknow' is the first crucial, all-important word. 'For whom he did foreknow [in his purpose], he also did predestinate to be conformed to the image of his Son.' God give us grace to meditate seriously and solemnly and lovingly upon this great word! What it tells us is, that if you and I are lovers of God, if we are 'the called according to his purpose' it is because He 'knew' us 'before the foundation of the world'. Not only before we were born, but 'before the foundation of the world', He 'knew' us and decided and determined these things concerning us. Can you conceive of any greater ground of assurance? But that knowledge does not encourage slackness, or lead to Antinomianism, for what it tells us is that God 'knew' us in this way and determined in eternity that you and I were going to be 'made conformable to the image of His Son', freed from sin completely, and finally glorified.

Twenty

*

And we know that all things work together for good to them that love God, to them who are the called according to his purpose.

For whom he did foreknow, he also did predestinate to be conformed to the image of his Son, that he might be the firstborn among many brethren.

Moreover whom he did predestinate, them he also called: and whom he called, them he also justified: and whom he justified, them he also glorified. Romans 8: 28–30

As we continue our study of these great terms let us remind ourselves that we are not teaching that our understanding of them is essential to salvation. You can be a saved Christian without such understanding. There is a difference between salvation and the assurance of salvation with which at this point the Epistle is particularly concerned. To lack assurance means that you are a defective Christian, that your understanding is not clear. But one thing only is essential to salvation, namely, that we trust utterly and entirely to the Lord Jesus Christ and His perfect work on our behalf. 'Believe on the Lord Jesus Christ and thou shalt be saved.' What the Apostle is here explaining is how you ever come to believe in Him – which is a different matter! For the moment we are simply considering the terms. We shall deal later with some of the difficulties that arise from the teaching. It often happens that a true understanding of the meaning of the terms answers the questions and solves the problems.

There are, of course, real difficulties and problems here, and probably most of them arise from our prejudices and preconceived ideas. So we must try to keep our minds open and to understand what the Apostle actually says and teaches, even if, at the end, you say that you do not agree with him. Our primary business is to expound the Scriptures and to preach the gospel, and to make the truth as plain and as clear as we can. To that end we must approach the truth prayerfully and with humility, and above all avoid a sinful spirit of contention. Our one consuming desire always should be to know God better, to love Him more truly, and to enter as fully as we can into the truth that He has been pleased to reveal to us. As long as we remain in that mood and state of spirit nothing can result but blessing. I refuse to deal with these matters in a controversial manner, for they are inscrutable. Who can understand them in an ultimate sense? I do not claim that I fully understand them, but I believe them, and my task is to expound them.

The next term for us to examine is the word 'predestinate'. There is little difficulty about this word because it follows directly from the first – 'whom he did *foreknow* he also did predestinate'. God, having set His mind and heart upon them, and having selected them, now 'predestinates' them. The word means simply to 'designate before', but as it is a very interesting word let us explore it a little. The Greek word actually used by the Apostle is a compound word. The 'pro' means 'beforehand'. The rest of the word – 'horizo' – is precisely the word from which our word 'horizon' comes. The horizon is that which marks off and separates what we can see from what we cannot see. We can see things that are within the horizon. You look round (for instance, on a boat in mid-Atlantic) and the limit of what you see is always the 'horizon'. The business of the horizon, as it were, is to set a limit. Everything within the limit is in one category, everything beyond that limit is in another category. The word used here, and translated 'predestined' means just that! Now God, having foreknown these people, puts them within a certain horizon, or circle, or limit. Or, to look at it the other way round, it means that He has not only marked them out for something, but He has marked out something for them. God has predestinated them, and has marked them out for this particular purpose and end and object. Or, in other words, He has mapped out a particular destiny for them.

There is a good exposition of this matter in the First Epistle of Peter chapter 2, verse 9. In reminding us of what we are now as Christians the Apostle says, 'Ye are a chosen generation, a royal priesthood' (or 'a kingdom of priests'). Next, Peter describes believers as 'an holy nation'. Israel in the Old Testament was 'an holy nation'. Although she was one of the nations, she was a separate nation, a special nation, an holy nation. Next comes the term 'a peculiar people', that is to say, a people for a 'peculiar possession' of God. God owns the universe and everything in it; but these people are His peculiar possession. In other words, He puts a ring round them, as it were, and He has mapped out a certain special destiny for them.

There are many analogies that suggest themselves here. Think of a shepherd or the owner of sheep. He has a great flock of sheep, perhaps thousands. A time arrives when he decides to sell some of these sheep and to keep others. So he goes out with his dogs and he selects and separates those he intends to sell from those he intends to keep for breeding and other purposes; and having thus taken them out of the great flock, he puts them into a separate pen or fold on their own. That is an illustration of 'predestination'. All we are told by this term is that these people whom God has foreknown He has also set apart for the ultimate destiny He has in His mind for them. He has put a ring round them, and at the same time He has put a ring round what is going to happen to them. That destiny we have already considered. It is, 'To be conformed to the image of his Son, that he might be the firstborn among many brethren'. He has selected them, and has decided that they are ultimately to be brought to that goal, to that final position. All that this term tells us is the goal which God has marked out for us; He has mapped it out, has circumscribed it, has put an 'horizon' around it. It is only these particular people who are ever found in that circle. The really difficult word is not 'predestinate' but 'foreknow'. Predestination is simply a description of the destiny that God has determined and decided upon for the people whom He has foreknown.

So we move on to the third term, 'called'. 'For whom he did foreknow, he also did predestinate to be conformed to the image of his Son, that he might be the firstborn among many brethren. Moreover whom he did predestinate' – note the links in the chain – 'them he also called'. Here is another most important and crucial word. We have already seen the place which it occupies in the list of five terms, and we have already met it in particular in verse 28, where we saw that the second description of a Christian is that he is one who is 'called' – effectually called – 'according to the purpose of God'. So what we are told in verse 30 is that God, because He has foreknown these people and predestinated them for that ultimate destiny, then proceeds to 'call' them in this effectual manner. It is at this point that the great purpose of God becomes actually linked to us, and becomes effectual in our particular case.

But why does the 'call' come as the middle link in the chain? Also, why does it come before justification? The answer is that though all these things, as we have been emphasizing, have been in the mind of God, and have happened in the mind of God before the foundation of the world, yet justification only becomes operative and actual in time. Before time the foreordination and the predestination were in the mind of God with respect to us, and likewise after time began, but they do not affect us until the call comes; then the blessings are applied to us, and they begin with justification. In Scripture 'justification' is always connected with faith, with belief. 'Justification by faith'! We are never declared to be just, or justified, without belief.

We have already seen this truth many times in this Epistle. For instance, in the first chapter, in verse 17: 'Therein', says Paul referring to the gospel, 'is the righteousness of God revealed from faith to faith: as it is written, The just shall live by *faith*'. That is the peculiar message of the gospel. It is different from the Law, which had come to mean to most people 'justification by works'. Again in chapter 3, in verses 21 and 22, 'But now the righteousness of God without the law is manifested, being witnessed by the law and the prophets; even the righteousness of God which is by faith of Jesus Christ unto all and upon all them that *believe*: for there is no difference.' Then in verse 26: 'To declare, I say, at this time his righteousness: that he might be just, and the justifier of him which *believeth* in Jesus.' Justification is always connected with faith. Again in verse 28, 'Therefore we conclude that a man is justified by *faith* without the deeds of the law.'

This explains why the Apostle introduces the 'calling' at this point. It has to come in before the term 'justification' is used. So, clearly, before the Apostle says that God in the working out of His great purpose has 'justified' us, he has to introduce the factor that brings us to faith and belief; and so he introduces this great term, 'calling'. So the meaning can be stated in this way, 'Whom he predestinated, them he also called to believe'; or 'Those whom he predestinated, them he also called to the exercise of faith', or 'called to faith'.

Note once more that the emphasis is upon God. It is God who calls. 'Whom he predestinated, them he also called.' It is not our faith that justifies us. We are not saved *because* we believe, otherwise it would be our action. Faith is but the instrument that God uses in pronouncing our justification, but it is something that He Himself brings into being. He justifies those who have faith, those who believe. But the crucial question is, What brings them to that belief? It follows, of course, by a logical necessity from the statement about foreknowledge. The Apostle expresses the matter very clearly in Ephesians 2, verse 8: 'For by grace are ye saved through faith; and that not of yourselves: it is the gift of God', and he adds, 'not of works, lest any man should boast'.

This is obviously a vital and essential part of the argument the Apostle is using here. He wants us to see that our ultimate and final salvation is absolutely guaranteed; and it is guaranteed because it is the purpose of God with respect to us. Moreover God has ordained every single step in this process that is going to bring us to that ultimate glorification. And one of the steps is this 'calling'. It means that God causes the word of the gospel, which is preached to all creatures, to come to these people whom He has foreknown, with power, the power of the Holy Ghost. We have a statement to this effect in 1 Corinthians, chapter 2, verses 4 and 5, where the Apostle writes: 'My speech and my preaching was not with enticing words of man's wisdom, but in demonstration of the Spirit and of power: that your faith should not stand in the wisdom of men, but in the power of God.' Throughout that chapter he emphasizes that no human reason can ever receive or understand this message; it is the Spirit alone who reveals it or can do so. 'God hath revealed them unto us by his Spirit' (especially verses 8–16). The word comes to these people in the power of the Spirit. We find the same truth in 1 Thessalonians 1:5. 'For our gospel came not unto you in word only' – it did come in word, but not in word only – 'but also in power, and in the Holy Ghost, and in much assurance.' The word came to everyone, to those who did not believe as well as to those who did believe. It comes as a word universally spoken. But it had come 'in power, and in the Holy Ghost, and in much assurance' only to those who had become members of the church at Thessalonica. Paul is not writing to all the citizens of Thessalonica, but only to the members of the church.

The word comes with such power, through the Holy Ghost, that it quickens us, and brings us to life. If it did not do so no one would ever believe it. Were it not for this power that comes in the 'call', the power that comes with the Holy Spirit, no one would ever believe the gospel at all. I base that statement on what we have already seen in the 7th verse of the 8th chapter of the Epistle to the Romans, where we read that 'the carnal mind is enmity against God'. Not merely does it not believe – it is at enmity against God. 'It is not subject to the law of God, neither indeed can be.' That is a description of the natural man or the carnal mind.

But this is not confined to the teaching of the Apostle Paul. Take the statement in John 3: 19: 'This is the condemnation, that light is come [or, has come] into the world, and men loved darkness rather than light, because their deeds were evil.' The light has come in Jesus Christ, in His life and death and resurrection, in His teaching, in all that He is and has done. The only explanation of the fact that the world is in darkness is that men 'love darkness'. It is not merely that they do not believe, they 'love darkness rather than light, because their deeds are evil'. There are two reasons for saying that if this gospel did not come in the power of the Holy Ghost none would believe it. The first is that by nature we are all born in this 'carnal' state; we are all by nature 'enemies' of God. And the second is that we have all by nature 'come short of the glory of God'. 'The whole world lieth guilty before God.' 'There is none righteous, no, not one.' All this has been explained in chapter 3.

Our Lord states the matter in another way in Matthew 18: 3: 'Verily, verily I say unto you, Except ye be converted and become as little children, ye shall in no wise enter into the kingdom of heaven.' There has to be a radical change, otherwise we cannot enter. He says it again to Nicodemus: 'Verily, verily, I say unto thee, Except a man be born again, he cannot see the kingdom of God' (John 3: 3). A rebirth is essential – a new beginning. We have to be 'born of the Spirit', 'born from above', otherwise there is no hope. This is repeated twice in the statement to Nicodemus. We find the same truth in 1 Corinthians 2: 14: 'The natural man receiveth not the things of the Spirit of God: for they are foolishness unto him: neither can he know them, because they are spiritually discerned.' That is a categorical statement.

The man has to become 'spiritual' before he can receive the 'things of the Spirit of God'.

Another explicit statement is found in 2 Corinthians 4, verses 3 and 4, where the Apostle writes: 'If our gospel be hid, it is hid to them that are lost: in whom the god of this world hath blinded the minds of them which believe not, lest the light of the glorious gospel of Christ, who is the image of God, should shine unto them.' They are blinded by the devil who is more powerful than any man. The devil does not allow them to believe; and a power that is great enough to undo the blinding action of the devil is needed before any man can believe. Still more conclusive is the statement in Ephesians 2, verses 1-3: 'And you hath he quickened, who were dead in trespasses and sins; wherein in time past ye walked according to the course of this world, according to the prince of the power of the air, the spirit that now worketh in the children of disobedience: among whom we all had our conversation in times past in the lusts of our flesh, fulfilling the desires of the flesh and of the mind; and were by nature the children of wrath, even as others.' These words describe the condition of all men by nature. Why were not the members of the church at Ephesus still in that condition? The answer is 'You hath he quickened'. Without the quickening they would have remained in their natural condition. Similarly, in that same Epistle to the Ephesians, chapter 5, verse 14, where Paul is contrasting those who have become Christians with those who are still in the darkness and bondage of paganism, he writes, 'Wherefore he saith, Awake thou that sleepest, and arise from the dead, and Christ shall give thee light'. This call that comes to the dead puts life into them; it is the 'quickening' which enables them to believe the gospel.

These are some of the biblical statements which justify my contention that if this call were not effectual no one would believe the gospel. The startling fact is that there is a single Christian in the whole world. The amazing thing is not that most people do not believe; what is astounding is that anyone believes. For we are all born 'natural' men at 'enmity against God', regarding all concerning Him as foolishness – 'dead in trespasses and sins'. What God has predestined for these people whom He has foreknown would never come to pass in a single instance were it not that God in His infinite love and mercy quickened us and awakened us by His Spirit through His effectual calling. The Holy Spirit operates upon our souls, and puts in a new principle of life, a new disposition. He changes us from being 'natural' to being 'spiritual'. And as the result of this we begin to see the truth; more than that, we desire the truth, and that which we formerly regarded as foolishness we now regard as most precious, that which we regarded as offensive nonsense we now glory in, and delight in, and we wish to understand it more and more.

That is how the Spirit acts, and that is the meaning of the effectual call. 'But does not this mean that a man's will is forced?' asks someone. The will is never forced. What happens is that the Holy Spirit, by putting this new disposition within us, this new ability, enables us to appreciate the truth. What used to be 'foolishness' suddenly becomes meaningful to us, becomes wonderful; and because we now see what it is, we desire it. The important factor is not the will itself, but that which governs and controls the will. The will is merely a kind of executive faculty; it is always determined by something else. Formerly it was determined by the devil; but now the Holy Spirit reveals these things to us and we desire them. No man is ever saved against his will, or browbeaten into salvation. You are given such a view of it that you want it with the whole of your being. You who formerly rejected it, and regarded it as folly, now see its glory and embrace it with all the energy of your will.

That is how the call becomes effectual. It is not a forcing or a coercing of the will; it makes one will and desire that which one formerly hated and rejected. What the Apostle is emphasizing here in Romans 8: 29 is that it is God who brings this to pass. If we were left to ourselves we would none of us desire it. We would all reject it, we would all say that it is foolishness, and we would remain in that carnal state in which we hate God. Unless the call is made effectual not a single human being would ever have believed this gospel. God has to make it effectual, otherwise His own purpose would never really come into operation, and would be a gigantic failure. But God, having purposed it, guarantees that it does become effective and efficacious. 'Whom he did foreknow, he also did predestinate: and whom he did predestinate, them he also called' – in an effectual and certain manner.

Let me now adduce some supporting statements in the Scriptures

[247]

to show how this is taught everywhere. In addition to what I have already quoted in John's Gospel, take chapter 6, verse 44: 'No man can come to me, except the Father which hath sent me draw him: and I will raise him up at the last day.' Our Lord was arguing with the unbelieving Pharisees and in effect He says to them: 'You are where and what you are because you have not been drawn to me. No man can come to me, except the Father which hath sent me draw him.' And then He adds immediately, 'And if a man is drawn unto me by the Father, I will raise him up at the last day'. Another interesting statement is found in Acts 13: 48 concerning Paul's preaching at Antioch of Pisidia. He preached the same gospel to everyone, and some believed it; but others did not, and rejected it, and persecuted the Apostle. The comment that is added is, 'And as many as were ordained to eternal life believed'. No others believed. The only people who believed were the people who had been 'ordained' to eternal life.

The word translated as 'ordained' in Acts 13: 48 is most interesting. It is not the same word precisely as we have in our text, but it has the same meaning. The New English Bible translates it: 'Those who were marked out for eternal life became believers.' 'Marked out for . . .' If they had not been 'marked out' for eternal life they would never have believed at all. In other words they were effectually called. Another instance is found in Acts 16: 14 where the first real preaching of the gospel in Europe by Paul at Philippi in the women's prayer-meeting outside the city wall by the river on a Sabbath afternoon is described. He sat down among them and began to speak to them. This is what we are told: 'A certain woman named Lydia, a seller of purple, of the city of Thyatira, which worshipped God, heard us; whose heart the Lord opened, that she attended unto the things which were spoken of Paul.' Notice the order. The Lord opened her heart, so that she attended to the things that were spoken by Paul. If the Lord had not opened her heart she would not have attended.

In Acts, chapter 11, verse 15, we find Peter in trouble because he had baptized certain Gentiles. The Jews said that he should not have done this, because these people were uncircumcised. They questioned his right to bring Gentiles into the Christian Church and to give them Christian baptism. Peter gave this explanation: 'The Holy Ghost came on them as on us at the beginning, so what was I, that I could withstand God?' If God had marked them out by giving them the gift of the Spirit, it was enough, says Peter, it was a proof that they were Christians. And after he had spoken, we read: 'When they heard these things, they held their peace' – that is, these Jews who, before, could not understand what Peter had done – 'and glorified God, saying, Then hath God also to the Gentiles granted repentance unto life'. What an interesting statement! Many say, 'I thought that repentance was entirely the action of man'. But those early Christians 'glorified God, saying, Then hath God also to the Gentiles granted [or given] repentance unto life'. It is God who grants repentance. Even repentance is a gift. No man would ever repent were it not for the 'effectual call' of God.

My last quotation is found in the Second Epistle to Timothy, chapter 1, verse 9: '[God] who hath saved us, and called us with an holy calling, not according to our works, but according to his own purpose and grace, which was given us in Christ Jesus before the world began.' It is an 'effectual calling', it is an 'holy calling'. It is not the result of our actions; it is entirely of the grace of God. If God did not make this call effectual for the people whom He has marked out they would not believe. This is the way in which God guarantees their full salvation and glorification. He calls them in such an effectual manner by the Spirit that this is what they now desire above everything else.

All this is seen clearly as in a picture in the conversion of Saul of Tarsus who became the Apostle Paul. First we see him going down from Jerusalem to Damascus, 'breathing out threatenings and slaughter', regarding Christ as a blasphemer, hating Christians, rejecting with contumely and scorn the Christian message. Never did a man regard the gospel as such unutterable foolishness, indeed as blasphemy, as Saul of Tarsus. How did he ever become the Apostle Paul? Did he 'decide' to believe in Christ? Did he decide to accept the message? We know what happened. The Lord of glory appeared to him. He saw Him in His glorified state! And immediately he believed, immediately his will desired Him. 'What wilt thou have me to do, Lord?' A perfect picture of the effectual call! The Apostle did not decide to believe, his conversion was not the result of his own activity. But when he saw Him who is the Truth there was the inevitable response.

The Holy Spirit does the same work in us in a spiritual manner; He manifests Christ to us. And nothing short of that can make anyone believe. The change that takes place in all who become Christians is the change from Saul to Paul – not as regards office, of course, but as regards nature. It happens to every one of us who is a Christian, but it would never happen to anyone were it not that the Spirit reveals these things unto us. 'Eye hath not, seen, nor ear heard, neither have entered into the heart of man the things which God hath prepared for them that love him. But God hath revealed them unto us' – not to everyone, but 'unto us' – 'by his Spirit: for the Spirit searcheth all things, yea, the deep things of God.' 'We have received, not the spirit of the world, but the Spirit that is of God; that [in order that] we might know the things that are freely given to us of God' (1 Corinthians 2: 9–12). This is just another way of saying, 'Whom he did predestinate, them he also called' – by the Spirit, in the effectual manner that leads them to faith and to belief.

Twenty-one

*

And we know that all things work together for good to them that love God, to them who are the called according to his purpose.

For whom he did foreknow, he also did predestinate to be conformed to the image of his Son, that he might be the firstborn among many brethren.

Moreover whom he did predestinate, them he also called: and whom he called, them he also justified: and whom he justified, them he also glorified.   Romans 8: 28–30

We have seen that God makes the call effectual through the Spirit. Enlightenment comes, the understanding is opened, a new desire is created within, a new principle of life is put within us, and we see everything differently. The result is that we are made willing and anxious to believe the truth concerning ourselves. There is nothing the natural man hates more than to be told that he is a sinner, and that his nature is twisted and perverted. He believes in himself, and that he is a good fellow; all the teaching of psychology encourages him to believe in himself. He hates a doctrine which tells him that he is a sinner, and a vile one at that, and that he is so bad that nothing will remedy matters but to be born again and to be given a new nature. But once the Spirit operates effectually we not only do not hate such teaching, we agree with it entirely. We see that it is true, and that nothing but the Christian salvation can deal with our plight. We become aware that all our righteousness is but as 'filthy rags'. We agree with teaching which formerly we hated, teaching which tells us that, in our natural state, we are hopeless and helpless, under condemnation, and deserving it richly; and that we can contribute nothing to our own salvation. Thus we become more than ready to believe the gospel concerning the Lord Jesus Christ, the Son of God. We believe the truth concerning His person and as to what He has done; we see the meaning of His atoning death, and learn the power of His resurrection. The truth of God concerning our salvation, and our relationship to Him, becomes plain to us, and, voluntarily and willingly, we desire it and we believe it and begin to rejoice in it.

It is in this way that what God has purposed and planned for His people in eternity becomes operative in them in time. The relationship between the 'foreknowledge' and the 'predestination' on the one hand, and the 'calling' on the other, is illustrated by what the Apostle says about himself in writing to the Galatians. In showing them his credentials as an apostle he writes: 'When it pleased God, who separated me from my mother's womb, and called me by his grace, to reveal his Son in me, that I might preach him among the heathen; immediately I conferred not with flesh and blood' (Galatians 1: 15 and 16). He says that he was 'separated from his mother's womb'; but we know that for years he was a proud, self-righteous pharisee, Saul of Tarsus. Nevertheless, he had been separated from his mother's womb, and he was 'called' at a particular moment in history on the road to Damascus.

The next term for our consideration is 'justified'. This, as we have seen, is always associated with belief and faith. The term has become familiar – 'Justification by faith only'. That they are in a state of justification, or justified, is true of all who believe, who exercise faith. Christian people are often troubled and confused about 'foreknowledge' and about the 'calling', but no Christian should ever be in trouble concerning 'justification', for it is the foundation of our whole position and standing with God. The first four chapters of this Epistle to the Romans are devoted to this subject of 'justification by faith only'. The Apostle introduced it in the 17th verse of the 1st chapter; but because of the failure of the Jews to see it, and a corresponding failure on the part of the Gentiles, he had to argue it out in detail and demonstrate it with a multiplicity of proofs in those four chapters.

Justification in its essence is a legal or forensic term, a term that belongs to the realm of the Law Court. It means 'to declare just', and 'to declare righteous'. It is the opposite of condemnation. The Christian has moved from a state of 'condemnation' to one of 'justification'. For this reason the Apostle starts this 8th chapter by saying, 'There is therefore now no condemnation to them that are in Christ Jesus'. He is taking up again the argument he had left off at the end of chapter 5, where he had been working out some of the consequences of justification. His constant emphasis concerning this is that it is something which is done by God. 'Moreover whom he did predestinate, them he also called: and whom He called, them he also justified.' In other words we do not justify ourselves before God. God justifies us, and He does it – and this is the argument of the first four chapters – entirely apart from us and our works. It is not the result of any merit that is in us. One verse that states this clearly and beyond any doubt is the 5th verse in the 4th chapter: 'But to him that worketh not, but believeth on him that justifieth the ungodly, his faith is counted for righteousness.' God justifies the 'ungodly'; not the 'righteous', but the 'ungodly'. He argues the same point in chapter 5, verses 6–8: 'When we were without strength, in due time Christ died for the ungodly. For scarcely for a righteous man will one die: yet peradventure for a good man some would even dare to die. But God commendeth his love toward us, in that while we were yet sinners, Christ died for us.' It is the action of God, and exclusively the action of God. This is the central argument of this Epistle. It is the declaration made by God concerning those who believe in Christ. We are justified in Christ, but through faith and belief. The belief is the instrument.

Let us emphasize again certain other aspects of this doctrine. Justification does not merely mean forgiveness. It includes forgiveness, but it is much bigger than forgiveness. It means in addition that God declares us to be entirely guiltless; He regards us as if we had never sinned at all. He pronounces us to be just and to be righteous. In doing so He is answering any declaration that the Law may make with respect to us. It is the judge upon the bench not merely saying that the prisoner at the Bar is forgiven, but that he pronounces him to be a just and righteous person. In justifying us God tells us that He has taken our sins and their guilt, and has 'imputed' them to, 'put them to the account of', the Lord Jesus Christ and punished them in Him. He announces also that, having done that, He now puts to our account, or 'imputes' to us, the perfect righteousness of His own dear Son. The Lord Jesus Christ obeyed the Law perfectly; He never broke it in any respect. He gave a full and a perfect satisfaction to all its demands. That full obedience constitutes His righteousness. What God does is to put to our account, to put upon us, the righteousness of Jesus Christ. In declaring us to be justified, God proclaims that He now looks on us, not as we are, but as clothed with the righteousness of the Lord Jesus Christ. A hymn by the Moravian Count Zinzendorf, and translated by John Wesley, expresses it thus:

> *Jesus, Thy robe of righteousness*
> *My beauty is, my glorious dress;*
> *'Midst flaming worlds, in this arrayed,*
> *With joy shall I lift up my head.*

The Count proceeds in the hymn to defy anyone and anything to bring a charge against us, because we are clothed and robed with this 'righteousness' of the Lord Jesus Christ. Such, then, is the meaning of justification, and it is entirely the action of God. It is, I repeat, the forensic, legal declaration of God that we are not only forgiven but guiltless, and that as we are clothed with the righteousness of Christ we shall continue in that condition. In other words, we are given a new standing and a new status in the presence of God.

I emphasize all this because it is a vital and essential part of the Apostle's argument in the verses we are examining. If the truth concerning us were simply that we have been forgiven, we would still be left exactly where we were without any real change in our relationship to God. I may sin at any moment, and thus become guilty once more, and fall out of and break the relationship with God, and all my misery and unhappiness would come back upon me again. And I would have to go through the whole process once more. My entire life would be one of repeatedly falling out of relationship with God, and then returning to it temporarily, and back and fore and in and out. But the Apostle's whole object here is to impress upon us the staggering truth that justification puts us into an entirely new relationship with God, changes our status and standing before Him, and even though we may sin, it cannot affect that standing because our justification is based upon the declaration of God. I am clothed with the righteousness of Christ; and His robe of righteousness covers all my sins – future sins as well as past sins.

It is the essence or kernel or nerve of the argument in these verses, that God's act of justification is once and for all. It is not something that can be annulled and re-established, and annulled and re-established. That would be chaos. It is God's act, and it is 'once and for all'; the Apostle has already worked it out in chapter 5, where he lays the foundation for the argument he develops here; hence our prolonged and detailed study of that chapter. As we suggested there, it is the key to the whole Epistle. It begins by telling us, 'Therefore being justified by faith we have peace with God through our Lord Jesus Christ'. But the Apostle continues, 'by whom also we have access by faith into this grace wherein we stand' – that brings out the status, the standing, the position – 'and rejoice in hope of the glory of God'. The Apostle has really said it all there in chapter 5; here, he repeats it, puts it in a slightly different manner, and works it out for us.

Actually in chapter 5, verses 12 to 21, he emphasized that, because we are justified, we are 'in Christ', and shows what that implies. We were in Adam, we are now in Christ. The moment you are justified you are 'in Christ'. This is an indissoluble relationship. We are involved in the 'reign of grace' with the consequence expressed in the 21st verse: 'That as sin hath reigned unto death, even so might grace reign through righteousness unto eternal life by Jesus Christ our Lord.' Nothing so robs us of the joy of salvation and assurance, as the failure to realize the full content of 'justification'. Justification is not only forgiveness; that is preliminary. If you are justified, you are 'in Christ', incorporated into Him, a part of Him. And that, as Paul points out, implies and involves our 'adoption' as children of God, sons of God, and all that follows from that, as we have already seen.

These things must be differentiated and distinguished in thought, but they must never be separated as facts. Of course in order to get a clear conception in our minds we have to differentiate between the terms, but it is being impressed upon us that the action, as far as God is concerned, is one – 'whom he did foreknow, he also did predestinate: whom he did predestinate, them he also called: whom he called, them he also justified; and whom he justified, them he also glorified'. We cannot rise to such heights; as creatures of time we are slow, and we have to take truth in separate portions. But while it is right to draw these distinctions intellectually, it is fatal to separate these things as facts concerning what God does to us. Above all, the Apostle wants us to realize that all these blessings are not dependent upon us and upon what we may do. God does all, and His act does not vary with what we do. We are fallible, we fall into sin and are liable to error, we misunderstand circumstances and are ready to grumble and to complain in our tribulations. That does not change the end, says Paul; in spite of you, God is bringing His great purpose to pass. You cannot see it now, but you will see it ultimately.

Have you not often looked back in your life and said, 'I did not understand that event then, but I see it now, and I thank God for it'? You say with the Psalmist, 'It is good for me that I have been afflicted, because before I was afflicted I went astray'. You did not see at the time what God was doing; afterwards you came to understand it. It is the central glory of this salvation, that though we do not understand it, it is still a fact, and it continues. If this were not so, not a single soul would be saved. Thank God, we are not saved by our understanding. If we were, we would soon be lost again. We are saved in spite of our failure to understand; and that is why I said earlier that an understanding of this doctrine is not essential to salvation. It is God who does all from beginning to end. Nothing, perhaps, proves this doctrine of 'foreknowledge' and 'election' more clearly than the case of Christian people who do not believe these doctrines. In spite of all their muddle-headedness they have been saved by the grace of God, and one day they will come to see the truth. They are the greatest proofs of the doctrine they deny.

But we move on to consider the last step – 'and whom he justified, them he also *glorified*'. We have dealt with this term previously, and more than once. We dealt with it in verses 16 and 17, and particularly also from verse 18 to verse 23. It is inevitable, as a part of God's purpose, that we should be 'conformed to the image of his Son'; that implies glorification. And glorification means that we shall be like the Lord Jesus Christ. Let us not forget that it includes the body, as verse 23 reminds us: 'And not only they, but ourselves also, which have the firstfruits of the Spirit, even we ourselves groan within ourselves, waiting for the adoption, to wit, the redemption of our body.' It means, in other words, that we shall be delivered finally and completely from every conceivable effect and result of sin and evil. We are not glorified in this life. The body will not be glorified until the resurrection morning, as we have already seen more than once in this Epistle; for instance in verses 10 and 11 of this 8th chapter: 'If Christ be in you, the body is dead because of sin; but the Spirit is life because of righteousness. But if the Spirit of him that raised up Jesus from the dead dwell in you, he that raised up Christ from the dead shall also quicken your mortal bodies by his Spirit that dwelleth in you.' The quickening has not happened yet; but it will happen. Before man is completely redeemed and glorified every part of him has to be, and must be, delivered. We are delivered already in the realm of the spirit and soul; but the body still needs to be redeemed; and it shall be! That is the ultimate glorification. We shall be entirely delivered, body, soul, and spirit.

We must emphasize the way in which the Apostle states the truth. Those justified, he says, 'he [God] also glorified'. 'You have been saying', says someone, 'that we are not yet glorified, but Paul says "he also glorified". He has done so already.' This is a most important point. We have already drawn attention to the fact that in each of these statements the Apostle used the past tense. 'Whom he did foreknow', not 'whom he does foreknow'. It happened before the foundation of the world. 'He also did predestinate.' It has happened. 'Whom he did predestinate, them he also called: whom he called, them he also justified and whom he justified, them he also glorified.' It has all happened in the past; each time Paul uses the aorist tense. This is true of all the terms; the reference is to a series of completed acts of God, but it is particularly striking and interesting with respect to glorification. We know that as Christians we have already been called; we know that we have already been justified. We know that we would not be interested in these things and believe the gospel if we had not been called. But we know that we are not glorified; and yet the Apostle says that God has glorified us, that it has happened in the past.

How is this to be explained? There is only one explanation. The Apostle deliberately uses this aorist tense in order to give us this final unshakeable assurance. In the mind of God it has already been done; it is as certain as our justification. There was a time when you and I were unbelievers, but even then we had been called in God's purpose. It actually happened to us in time – 'separated from my mother's womb', but 'called' on the road to Damascus. The Apostle's argument is that as we know most certainly that we have been called and justified, we can be equally certain of our glorification. Nothing can prevent it because it is a part of God's purpose for us.

Let me substantiate what I have said by quoting certain authorities, several of whom do not actually believe this doctrine. Take Dr James Denney, for instance. 'The tense', he says, 'in the last word' (that is, glorification) 'is amazing. It is the most daring anticipation of faith that even the New Testament contains.' That is an excellent comment; but in a sense there is nothing at all daring about it. The Apostle had been given a revelation concerning this, so no daring was involved. But looking at it from the human standpoint, it is indeed a most daring asseveration and affirmation; nothing goes beyond it in the whole range and realm of Scripture. Dr Denney continues, 'The life is not to be taken out of it by the philosophical consideration that with God there is neither before nor after'. The philosopher who does not believe in revelation and who dislikes this doctrine says, 'There is no difficulty here, as regards God, because God is outside time in eternity, and everything is the same to God. With Him there is no past, present or future.' But Denney says, and very rightly, that the life must not be taken out of this aorist by the philosophical consideration that with God there is neither before nor after. You do not get rid of it in that way; the statement goes beyond that. In other words the Apostle's statement is that the glorification is already consummated, though still in the future in the fullest sense and as regards our experience. But in God's mind and purpose it is as complete as every other part of His action.

Sanday and Headlam in their well-known commentary say, 'The step implied is both complete and certain in the Divine counsels'. Yet they do not go on and see the inevitable implication. There is no contradiction in all they have to say on the word; but on sheer grounds of grammar they have to say that the step implied is both 'complete' and 'certain' in the divine counsels. Henry Alford, a great commentator of the last century says: 'He did not merely, in his premundane decree, acquit them of sin, but also *clothed them with glory*: the past tense being used, as the other past tenses, to imply the completion in the divine counsel of all these – which are to us, in the state of time, so many successive steps – simultaneously and irrevocably.'

The conclusion we must draw, therefore, is that the act of

glorification is irrevocable, it is absolutely certain. Nothing can cause it to fail, for it is the action of God. God has glorified us, and if God has glorified us, how can we ever fall from grace and salvation? How can anything ever change our position? In other words, because we are in the purpose of God our eternal future is certain and sure. This is the Apostle's way of giving us complete certainty and assurance. He says that if we are certain of our calling, we can be certain of our ultimate glorification. If God has called us it means that He has justified us, and if He has justified us, it means that He has glorified us; because if we are in any one of these positions we are in them all. They are joined together indissolubly, irrevocably, as links in a chain forged by God Himself.

The one thing that matters, therefore, from our experimental standpoint is to be sure that we are in the purpose of God. Do we know that we have been called? We have already suggested some nine tests by which that can be determined. Let me name one of the most important of them. Do you accept God's verdict on yourself that you are a sinner, vile, unworthy and deserving of nothing but hell? Do you see that, if you lived to be a million years old, and strove with all your might as a monk or a hermit to live a godly life, you would be as lost at the end as you are now, and that you have no hope whatsoever but that the Son of God has died for you and your sins, and that God clothes you with His righteousness and gives you new life? If you do so believe, you are 'called'. Only the 'called' accept God's verdict. The natural man hates it and abominates it; he resents it and regards it as insulting, and pours his vituperation upon it. If you believe and accept what the Bible tells you about yourself, and about the only way to be reconciled to God and to come to a knowledge of God, I assure you that you are 'called'. And if you are called, you are justified, and if you are justified, you are glorified. Your glorification is as certain as the fact that you are now a Christian. No matter what may happen to you, or what the world, the flesh, the devil and all hell may do to you, nothing can ever make any difference to your position. As Toplady expresses it:

> *The terrors of law and of God*
> *With me can have nothing to do;*
> *My Saviour's obedience and blood*
> *Hide all my transgressions from view.*

The Perseverance of the Saints

Things future, nor things that are now,
Not all things below nor above,
Can make Him His purpose forego,
Or sever my soul from His love.

At this point let me call your attention to a most interesting and significant fact, namely, the omission from verse 30 of the term 'sanctification'. 'Moreover whom he did predestinate, them he also called: and whom he called, them he also justified: and whom he justified, them he also glorified.' But not a word about sanctification! Does not that surprise you, and especially so when you contrast it with what we find at the end of the first chapter of the First Epistle to the Corinthians, in verse 30: 'But of him are ye in Christ Jesus, who of God is made unto us wisdom, and righteousness [justification] and sanctification and redemption.' There 'sanctification' comes between 'righteousness' and 'redemption' (which stands for 'glorification'). Why then does the Apostle omit sanctification here? Surely there is some significance in this. The explanation is that sanctification is not a vital step in the argument the Apostle has in mind at this point. And that is so because sanctification makes no vital difference to our status and standing, as justification does. We were originally under the wrath of God, but the moment we are declared to be just our whole position is changed. Sanctification does not affect that position. It is not an essential step in the argument pertaining to assurance and final perseverance. Indeed I make bold to say that sanctification is not a step at all, it is a process. If it were a step it would be included here.

But secondly, the Apostle has no need to mention sanctification here for the reason that it is inevitable because of justification. The moment a man is justified the process of sanctification begins. Chapter 6, verses 1 and 2, have already dealt with the matter. 'What shall we say then? Shall we continue in sin, that grace may abound? God forbid. How shall we that are dead (that died) to sin, live any longer therein?' And the rest of that chapter answers the Apostle's question. The moment you are justified, sanctification has already started – it is implicit in justification. So there is no need to mention it as a separate step. Indeed, as Paul points out, the very facts that we have the new nature and the new outlook, that we are dead to sin and risen with Christ, that we are 'in Christ' and 'alive unto righteousness' – all this guarantees sanctification.

But not only so, sanctification is inevitable from the standpoint of glorification also. What is sanctification but the preparation for our glorification? So it is implicit everywhere. As the Apostle John says: 'He that hath this hope in him, purifieth himself, even as he is pure' (1 John 3 : 3). The man who believes in the ultimate glorification is of necessity concerned about sanctification. He strives to become sanctified; he 'cleanses himself from all impurity of the flesh and of the mind', he 'mortifies the members of his body'. Any man who believes in glorification must have this great impetus to sanctification; the one is implicit in the other. You cannot separate the two.

Therefore I suggest in the fourth place, that to make sanctification a distinct and a separate step is clearly quite wrong and unscriptural. Hence there should never be a separate movement for sanctification or holiness, for it shows that you are looking at sanctification from too subjective a standpoint. The way to preach holiness is not to preach about 'me' and 'my feelings' and to propound various theories as to how I can be delivered; it is, rather, to preach justification and glorification. By so doing you will include sanctification. Such is the Apostle's method – 'whom he justified, them he also glorified'. It is because certain people do not know the truth about justification and glorification as they ought that they are defective in their teaching about sanctification. A man who has his eye on his future state of glorification will spend his time in preparing himself for it. How often are sermons on glorification heard in holiness meetings or in conferences in connection with sanctification? It is surely most significant that the Apostle does not mention sanctification here. It is implicit in justification; justification leads to it, and it prepares for glorification. Both of them include it between them; therefore there is no mention of it in our text.

Lastly, to say, as a popular teaching has done so often, that you can be justified without being sanctified, and then proceed to appeal to people and say, 'Now as you took your justification by faith, so take your sanctification by faith' – this is entirely without foundation in the teaching of the Scripture. There is nothing else to be said about it. As we have seen earlier, we are nowhere exhorted to 'receive' our sanctification by faith.

Nothing condemns that wrong teaching more strongly than the fact that sanctification is not even mentioned here. It cannot and must not be isolated in that way; it is implicit in justification, and involved of necessity in glorification. Let us be Scriptural and never divide, isolate, or separate things which are never separated in the Scripture. You cannot just take justification alone from Christ. If you are 'in Christ', you are in Him, and Christ is in you, and He cannot be only partly in you. You cannot divide Christ, and you cannot separate and isolate sanctification from justification and glorification. We should be governed and controlled in all our thinking and activity by the thought of glorification. Then the words of John will follow inevitably: 'Whosoever hath this hope in him, purifieth himself, even as he is pure.'

Twenty-two

*

And we know that all things work together for good to them that love God, to them who are the called according to his purpose.

For whom he did foreknow, he also did predestinate to be conformed to the image of his Son, that he might be the firstborn among many brethren.

Moreover whom he did predestinate, them he also called: and whom he called, them he also justified: and whom he justified, them he also glorified. Romans 8: 28–30

Though we have spent some time in considering the exact meaning of the particular terms which the Apostle uses, it is important for us to remember that these three verses are essentially one great statement with a number of subsidiary clauses. The statement, which is a reasoned argument, is that we can be certain, we can 'know', that 'all things work together for good' for us because we are 'the called according to his purpose'. The Apostle wrote these words in order to comfort these Roman Christians and the background is the problem of suffering in the Christian life.

The fundamental truth is the purpose of God which He conceived for us in eternity, and all the steps of which were planned in eternity before the foundation of the world. God planned for His people this ultimate salvation, this final glorification. He did not merely plan the first steps, and then wait to see what would happen; He planned it right through to the end. The daring statement, 'them he also glorified', reminds us of this. In other words we are considering here what is called the doctrine of the final perseverance of the saints. Their arrival in the glory everlasting is guaranteed by this one great fact that it is God's purpose with respect to them.

Let us now attempt to deal with some of the difficulties certain people seem to have with regard to this doctrine. I must confess that I am not doing so of choice. I have always admired the type of preacher and Bible teacher who simply says what he believes and never deals with any difficulties; but, for myself, I feel compelled to deal with them. The business of a pastor and teacher is not to enjoy himself or to do what he likes, it is to help people. In so doing he has to take risks, and especially the risk of being misunderstood. If he really desires to build up his hearers, and have them 'grounded' and 'established' in the truth, it is essential that he should help them to face the difficulties and the problems.

I do this therefore, not merely for the sake of argument, or that we may indulge together in some kind of intellectual gymnastics and fencing. The truth should never be dealt with in that way; though doubtless many of us have done so frequently, and have argued about these things, and enjoyed the argument *qua* argument. But these things are too precious to be dealt with in that spirit; they are not merely matter for clever intellectual disputation. But we must consider the difficulties were it merely that we should always be concerned to be accurate in our exposition; we should have an inward desire to arrive at the exact meaning of any statement. That compels us to consider various points of view.

Another reason for our doing so is that so much depends upon this doctrine. We shall be in endless difficulties if this doctrine is not true. We shall be confronted by apparent contradictions in the Scripture, and any interpretation which makes you feel that Scripture is contradicting itself is inevitably wrong. Scripture does not contradict itself.

My chief reason, however, and one that I have been emphasizing repeatedly is that there is no more glorious truth than this. No higher form of assurance is possible to anyone in this world than that which is given here. It is very sad that there should be anyone who does not enjoy the assurance which is given by this sublime doctrine. I am concerned only with those people who are genuinely perplexed and who really desire to be taught. I am not interested in those who are merely concerned to defend a position, or to enjoy an argument and to prove that they are right. Not a few are utterly impatient with this doctrine; they resent it, and speak with bitterness about it. Indeed I have heard people speaking of it in a blasphemous manner. The moment the doctrine of 'final perseverance' is mentioned they begin to scowl and become furious. They pronounce it 'terrible', and with scorn they reject it. I have nothing to say to such except very seriously to warn them to be careful. I would repeat the warning given to such people by Charles Simeon of Cambridge. Simeon was a mild man, and sometimes he adopts positions which are not clear; that is why I deliberately quote him at this point. This is what he says: 'The subject of predestination is confessedly very deep and mysterious, nor should it be entered upon without extreme caution, both as to the mode of stating it and to the persons before whom it is stated.' We have already emphasized that very point. 'It is much to be lamented', he continues, 'that there exists in the minds of many a strong prejudice against it, insomuch that the very mention of it is deemed by them little short of heresy, I had almost said blasphemy. But this, surely, is not a way in which any part of God's revealed will is to be treated.' To harbour a violent prejudice against anything taught in Scripture is obviously wrong. There should never be a violent approach to any aspect of truth. That is always wrong. To become heated and excited, and to display bitterness is always wrong in this realm. Simeon continues, 'That the inspired writers do speak of it is undeniable, and that our own church' – he was an Anglican – 'also has made it an article of faith which all her ministers and members are to receive, is also certain. On these counts we must not discard the doctrine through fear of offending any who may be hostile to it; though on the other hand we ought not so frequently or so strongly to insist upon it as unnecessarily to wound and grieve them. The true medium which a minister should aim at is to give to this doctrine, as well as to every other, as precisely as possible that measure of prominence and importance which it bears in the sacred writings.' That is precisely my own attitude. It is essential to avoid both foolish extremes. A prejudiced person never really listens, is not prepared to listen. His mind is shut, a mental shutter comes down. He does not want to be enlightened, and never will be enlightened, of course, as long as he remains in that condition. God have mercy upon all such.

The second kind of person to whom I have nothing to say is he who rejects this teaching, this doctrine, because of his philosophy, and because he cannot reconcile it with his philosophical view of God. There are many such persons at the present time and their views are found in most modern commentaries. They do not really believe in the unique inspiration of the Bible, though some claim to do so. They come to the Bible with their intellect and their knowledge and philosophy; if anything in the Bible agrees with what they think they accept it, if it disagrees they reject it. With regard to a particular teaching they may say, 'I cannot reconcile that with my idea of a God of love. Therefore this teaching is wrong and I reject it.' Their fundamental trouble is not really with the doctrine of perseverance at all; it is their wrong view of the Bible. And until they are clear on that you cannot expect them to believe this or many another doctrine. If we do not start on the common basis that the Bible is the divinely inspired, inerrant Word of God, there is no basis for a discussion. These teachers grant that the Apostle Paul clearly teaches the doctrine we are examining, but they think that he was mistaken. They explain his 'false' teaching in terms of his being a Jew, still under the influence of rabbinical teaching, who brought much of his old legalistic notions with him into Christianity. Such teaching is found, for instance, in the popular commentaries of Dr C. H. Dodd or Prof. William Barclay. The point at issue here, as I say, is not this particular doctrine, but their view of revelation and inspiration, their whole view of the authority of the Scriptures.

Similarly there is but little to say to those who reject this doctrine because they are universalists, a view that is becoming increasingly popular. These people believe that everyone is going to be saved at the end, that no one will be finally lost. They believe in a universal salvation, even including the devil himself. Obviously it is a waste of time to argue with such people concerning this particular subject of the final perseverance of the saints, because, according to their view, everyone finally enters the Kingdom of God; so ultimately there is no problem. We have already dealt with the problem of universalism in chapter 5, verses 12-21, when dealing with the phrase 'all men' which Paul keeps on repeating in that section; also in more recent chapters.

Turning to those who have a genuine difficulty, let us try to be patient with one another. One difficulty that perplexes many is expressed in these terms: 'Does not your teaching of necessity imply that God has also predestined some people to damnation?' There is but one answer to that as far as I am concerned; the teaching does not involve that conclusion. I do not believe in 'double predestination'. There is but one statement in the whole of Scripture, that I am aware of, that lends any countenance to the teaching that some are predestined to damnation. It is in the First Epistle of Peter, chapter 2, verse 8. Verses 7 and 8 in that chapter read: 'Unto you therefore which believe he is precious: but unto them which be disobedient, the stone which the builders disallowed, the same is made the head of the corner, and a stone of stumbling, and a rock of offence, even to them which stumble at the word, being disobedient: whereunto also they were appointed'; but even that is not strong enough to make me believe it. All I know is that God has foreknown the people who are to be finally glorified. What of the others? Surely they are left where they were. They are already damned because of the sin of Adam, and because of their own personal sin, and because they do not desire salvation and are not interested in it. There is no need to 'determine' their damnation, they are already damned. What we have here in Romans 8: 28–30 is a statement concerning those who are saved, those who 'love God', those who are 'the called according to his purpose'. And it does not follow that to accept this statement means of necessity that you have to believe in predestination to damnation.

A second difficulty which troubles Christian people who believe the Bible to be the Word of God, and who are ready to submit to its teaching, is how to reconcile this doctrine with the love of God. They cannot understand, they say, how God can set His affection on some people and not on others. My answer to such people again is quite simple – I also cannot understand it! But I am not called upon to understand. This is something in the mind and the heart of the eternal God. He is infinite, He is absolute, and I am not. And not only am I finite, I am also sinful – and so are all of us. We should not be surprised that we do not understand the ultimate mind and heart of God; we are not in a position to do so. The moment we try to resolve such difficulties, we are entering into the realm of pure speculation where one man's opinion is as good as another's. The fact is that none of us know, and we must realize that we are not meant to know, all things. God has been pleased to reveal certain things to us, and we are to know them. But we are not meant to know the things which He has not revealed. Deuteronomy 29: 29 expresses the final truth concerning this matter: 'The secret things belong unto the Lord our God: but those things which are revealed belong unto us and to our children for ever.' We must keep ourselves to that! I have sometimes thought that the best definition of faith is, that faith means that a man is prepared and content to be ignorant where the Bible does not provide him with revelation. The man who lacks faith says, 'I want to know; I will not believe until I understand'. That attitude is the opposite of faith. Faith is to 'become like a little child' and to say, 'These matters are high and infinite and absolute and eternal; and I am finite and small and sinful. All I know is what I am told in the Word of God, and I believe that because it is the Word of God. I do not understand many things and I am content not to understand.'

The ultimate sin is intellectual pride, and for that reason the Apostle Paul says in the 1st chapter of the First Epistle to the Corinthians, verse 26, 'You see your calling, brethren, how that not many wise men after the flesh, not many mighty, not many noble, are called'. Not the wise, because they insist upon understanding; because they are philosophers! The moment you say, 'I cannot believe that because I do not see or understand' you become a 'wise' man, a philosopher. You are pitting your pygmy mind and understanding against the mind of God, and you are saying to God, 'I am not going to believe until I fully understand what you are saying and what you are doing'. That is the antithesis of faith; so let us be careful. There is no point in saying that you accept the Bible as the Word of God if you are determined to reject statements which you cannot understand. We must submit ourselves to the teaching, and be content not to understand.

I repeat that I do not claim for a moment to understand this doctrine. I believe that in the glory we shall have a perfect understanding and a perfect explanation, but not until then. All I can say in the meantime is that not a single human being deserves salvation, for 'There is none righteous, no, not one'. If God had consigned the entire human race to hell and eternal perdition no one would have a right to complain. If God sent all to perdition He would be exercising perfect justice. We have all sinned against Him, none of us have glorified Him as we should have done – none of us! There is a natural hatred against God in every person born into this world; and that is more than enough to damn us all to all eternity. No one deserves to be saved. The fact that a single soul is saved is an absolute proof of the love and the grace and the mercy of God. There is no obligation on God's part to save anyone, not a single person! That is enough for me! What amazes me is not that certain people are not saved! what astounds me is that anyone is saved, and particularly myself.

Others who are in trouble about this say: 'Surely if you teach that doctrine you are inciting people to sin and encouraging what is called Antinomianism and carelessness. If you tell people that their ultimate glorification is guaranteed, that all things work together for good to them that love God, are you not inciting them to say, "Well, it does not matter what I do, I can go out and sin as much as I like; all is well, even sin is going to turn to my good"? Surely that is the high road to Antinomianism!?' There was a great argument in the 18th century concerning these matters, the great argument between John Wesley and John Fletcher of Madeley on the one hand, and Augustus Toplady and others on the other hand. The titles of their tracts and books and sermons bear eloquent testimony to this. The very crux of that argument – and it is still heard frequently – was that if you teach this absolute certainty, people will be careless.

Our reply to that is to start by admitting freely that that can happen, and that it has often happened. There are some people who have espoused this great truth only in their minds, and who have been interested in it solely in an intellectual sense, paying no attention to applying it to their lives. The result has been that this doctrine has done them great harm. But that does not mean that there is anything wrong with the doctrine; the trouble is entirely in the people who abuse it. Food is good for us, and essential to life, but you can abuse food, and greatly harm yourself by gluttony. But you do not blame the food as the cause of the harm; you blame the man who eats too much. Every single doctrine in the Bible can be abused, and is frequently abused. The fact that certain people become 'heady and high-minded' and get so drunk on their own knowledge of doctrine that they become guilty of Antinomianism and carelessness, tells us nothing about the doctrines.

Furthermore, there are people in the Church who not only do not believe this doctrine of final perseverance, but who almost hate it, who are equally guilty of the same Antinomianism. I am referring to the people who are guilty of what is known as 'easy believism'. They teach 'All you have to do is to say "I believe on the Lord Jesus Christ" and you are saved. You may not feel anything; you just have to speak these few words.' Having thus 'taken their decision' or 'taken Christ' they are perfectly happy, and are never troubled. Should they happen to hear a convicting sermon they dislike it because it makes them feel uncomfortable, and they doubt 'whether the gospel was being preached'. Such people are Antinomians. They do not believe this doctrine of the final perseverance of the saints, but they are guilty of the same carelessness, because they are abusing the doctrine of 'justification by faith only' in exactly the same way as they charge those who believe this particular doctrine.

Finally, under this heading, I would say, after pastoral experience of some thirty-five years (1962), without any hesitation at all, that the people who are most concerned about the state of their souls and their lives are the people who believe this doctrine. The more you believe in the 'effectual call' the deeper will be your concern about your soul. The people who are most careless about their souls and their lives are those who have been most ignorant of doctrine and who are not aware of these profundities. They rarely think or meditate, they read little and assume that all is well. They have 'taken a decision', and rest upon that decision. Not on the purpose of God, but upon their decision, or upon some experience they once had! Past history, and present pastoral experience, bear testimony to the fact that Arminianism can be as productive of Antinomianism as Calvinism. May God preserve us from labels!

As we turn to some particular difficulties we are confronted by the fact that there are statements in the Scriptures which on the surface seem to contradict this doctrine. Here we have a Scriptural difficulty, not some general philosophical difficulty. Quite recently I read a book published in America called '*Life in the Son*' by a man named Shanks. It is a book of some 380 pages, and on the dust cover it was recommended by someone who thought this might perhaps be considered eventually the greatest book ever written! I was the more interested in reading it when I found that the claim made was that this book 'could disprove the doctrine of the final perseverance of the saints'. The author lists some 85 passages in the New Testament which he claims disprove this teaching. I read the book carefully but time prohibits us to consider the 85 passages. Nevertheless we should address ourselves very carefully to these difficult passages. If you believe this doctrine of the final perseverance of the saints you must not brush aside passages of Scripture which appear to disagree; you must produce a careful exegesis of them, and have an explanation of them.

I have sub-divided the important passages into three groups. The first group contains passages that seem to teach the possibility of 'falling away' from grace. The first is the Parable of the Sower, where we are told that some seed fell on to thorny ground and sprang up but was eventually choked. The parable is found in three of the four Gospels in the New Testament. Another is our Lord's parable of an 'unclean spirit' being driven out of a man, and the house swept and garnished, but because no one came to occupy it, the spirit came back and brought seven other spirits with him worse than himself, so that the last state of that man was worse than the first. This parable is found in Luke's Gospel, chapter 11, verses 24–26. Another is found in Matthew 18, verses 21–35: the case of the servant who was in debt to his master. The master was taking hold of the servant's throat and was about to punish him when he pleaded for mercy, and the master forgave him. But then another servant serving under the first servant owed him just a little sum, nothing like what the first had owed his master. But the wicked servant took hold of this other man's throat and insisted he must pay him every farthing, though he himself had received grace. Our Lord's comment upon that is that we shall all be rejected unless we also forgive others their trespasses, even as ours have been forgiven by God.

Another favourite quotation is Matthew 25: 1 to 13: the Parable of the Ten Virgins telling us how the five foolish virgins who had been invited to the wedding feast and had accepted the invitation were finally shut out from the feast. Another is John 6: 66. Our Lord's teaching became very deep on one occasion and at that point some of the people said, 'This is a hard saying; who can hear it?' We read that 'From that time many of his disciples went back, and walked no more with him'. Then there is John 15: 1–6, beginning with 'I am the vine, ye are the branches', and going on to say that the unfruitful branches will be torn off and burned in the fire. We have already met another in the 8th chapter of Romans, verse 13, 'If ye live after the flesh, ye shall die; but if ye through the Spirit do mortify the deeds of the body, ye shall live'. In Romans 14: 15 we read: 'But if thy brother be grieved with thy meat, now walkest thou not charitably. Destroy not him with thy meat, for whom Christ died.' The implication on the surface is that it is possible for a man for whom Christ has died to be destroyed by us and our false teaching. It has its parallel in 1 Corinthians 8: 11.

Then in 1 Corinthians 10: 1–14 the Apostle reminds the Corinthian Christians that many of the children of Israel who were travelling from Egypt to Canaan perished in the wilderness, and never got to the land of Canaan, and he warns them against a like fate. In 1 Timothy 1: 19 the Apostle writes of certain people who have made 'shipwreck of the faith' – 'Holding faith and a good conscience; which some having put away concerning faith have made shipwreck: Of whom is Hymenæus and Alexander; whom I have delivered unto Satan that they may learn not to blaspheme.' 1 Timothy 4: 1 and 2 reads: 'Now the Spirit speaketh expressly, that in the latter times some shall depart from the faith, giving heed to seducing spirits and doctrines of devils; speaking lies in hypocrisy; having their conscience seared with a hot iron.' In 1 Timothy 5: 11, 12 we have, 'But the younger widows refuse: for when they have begun to wax wanton against Christ, they will marry; having damnation, because they have cast off their first faith'. 2 Timothy 2: 11–13 is considered to be most important: 'It is a faithful saying: For if we be dead with him, we shall also live with him: If we suffer, we shall also reign with him: if we deny him, he also will deny us. If we believe not, yet he abideth faithful: he cannot deny himself.' Then the Apostle proceeds to say: 'But shun profane and vain babblings: for they will increase unto more ungodliness. And their word will eat as doth a canker: of whom is Hymenæus and Philetus; who concerning the truth have erred, saying that the resurrection is past already; and overthrow the faith of some. Nevertheless the foundation of God standeth sure' (vv. 16–19).

Turning to the general epistles we find similar examples in 2 Peter 2: 1–22, and especially verse 1: 'But there were false prophets also among the people, even as there shall be false teachers among you, who privily shall bring in damnable heresies, even denying the Lord that bought them, and bring upon themselves swift destruction.' And in the last verse of that chapter, 'But it is happened unto them according to the true proverb, The dog is turned to his own vomit again; and the sow that was washed to her wallowing in the mire.' Something similar is found in 2 Peter 3: 16, 17, where Peter, referring to Paul's epistles concerning these matters, says '. . . in which are some things hard to be understood, which they that are unlearned and unstable wrest, as they do also the other scriptures, unto their own destruction'.

In 1 John 5: 16 we read: 'If any man see his brother sin a sin which is not unto death, he shall ask, and he shall give him life for them that sin not unto death. There is a sin unto death: I do not say that he shall pray for it.' Read also the Epistle of Jude from verse 3 to verse 19 In the Book of Revelation in chapter 3, verse 5 we read: 'He that overcometh shall be clothed in white raiment; and I will not blot his name out of the book of life' – implying that there are some who are to be blotted out – 'but I will confess his name before my Father, and before his angels'. Revelation 3: 15 says, 'I know thy works, that thou art neither cold nor hot: I would that thou wert cold or hot. So then because thou art lukewarm, and neither cold nor hot, I will spue thee out of my mouth.' These are some of the passages which seem to teach quite specifically the possibility of 'falling away from grace', or falling away from your final glorification.

Next I quote some passages which belong to the next group, passages which seem to teach that our salvation is uncertain and that it depends upon us. There are not so many in this group. I have selected the following: Matthew 24: 13 says, 'He that shall endure unto the end, the same shall be saved'. In Philippians 2: 12 we find, 'Work out your own salvation with fear and trembling', and in Philippians 3, verses 12–14 the following: 'Not as though I had already attained . . . but I press toward the mark.' Again, Colossians 1: 20–23: 'And, having made peace through the blood of his cross, by him to reconcile all things unto himself; by him, I say, whether they be things in earth or things in heaven. And you, that were sometime alienated and enemies in your mind by wicked works, yet now hath he reconciled in the body of his flesh through death, to present you holy and unblameable and unreproveable in his sight: if ye continue in the faith grounded and settled.' '*If* ye continue in the faith grounded and settled.'

Then in the Epistle to the Hebrews, chapter 5, verses 8, 9 we read: 'Though he were a Son, yet learned he obedience by the things which he suffered; and being made perfect, he became the author of eternal salvation unto all them that obey him.' Great emphasis is put upon this. Again, James 1: 12: 'Blessed is the man that endureth temptation', – and emphasis is placed on the 'enduring'. In James 2: 20 we read, '. . . faith without works is dead' and in James 4: 4–10 we find the same kind of teaching. Similarly in 2 Peter 1: 10 we read: 'Wherefore the rather, brethren, give diligence to make your calling and election sure: for if ye do these things, ye shall never fall.'

In the third, and last, group we have what are commonly referred to as the warning passages. There is one in Romans 11: 21 where the Apostle warns the Gentiles that, if God spared not the natural branches, which were cut off through unbelief, then they must not presume, the suggestion being that the same thing could happen to them. Perhaps the most famous of these statements is 1 Corinthians 9: 27, where Paul says, 'I keep under my body, lest having preached to others, I myself should be a castaway'. And again in 1 Corinthians 11: 29–32, in the passage about the Communion Service, there is the same suggestion. In 1 Corinthians 15: 1 and 2 we find: 'Moreover, brethren, I declare unto you the gospel which I preached unto you, which also ye received, and wherein ye stand; by which also ye are saved, if ye keep in memory what I preached unto you, unless ye have believed in vain.' In Galatians 5: 4, in the Authorized Version, the phrase 'fallen from grace' is used. Galatians 6: 7–9 is also quoted in this connection. Then, of course, the Epistle to the Hebrews, chapter 2: 1–3 with the question in verse 3, 'How shall we escape, if we neglect so great salvation?' is frequently adduced. Other passages in Hebrews are 3: 17–19 and 4: 1–16. But in many ways the words most frequently quoted and relied upon are the classic passages in Hebrews 6: 1–9 and 10: 26–31.

These, then, are some of the passages in the Scripture itself which most frequently bring people into difficulties. The argument is, 'Do not these passages seem to be a contradiction of the teaching concerning the final perseverance of the saints, which you say means that, because we are in God's purpose, our ultimate salvation is absolutely guaranteed and cannot possibly fail?' In humility of spirit, and with a desire above everything else really to understand the teaching of God's Word, and not merely to prove that we are right and others mistaken, and with a desire to know the truth which makes us free, let us meditate upon and ponder these statements of God's most holy Word.

Twenty-three

*

> *And we know that all things work together for good to them that love God, to them who are the called according to his purpose.*
>
> *For whom he did foreknow, he also did predestinate to be conformed to the image of his Son, that he might be the firstborn among many brethren.*
>
> *Moreover whom he did predestinate, them he also called: and whom he called, them he also justified: and whom he justified, them he also glorified.*　　　　　　　　　　　　Romans 8: 28–30

It is clear that we cannot possibly deal with each one of the Scripture passages quoted at the end of the previous chapter which on the surface seem to contradict the doctrine of the final perseverance of the saints. But we can lay down certain canons or principles of interpretation which will help us not only to interpret these particular scriptures but any other scripture which is difficult and perplexing in this respect. In so doing we shall incidentally not only be dealing with the particular scriptures I have mentioned but also providing a method whereby any problem which causes perplexity in biblical study can be dealt with.

Incidentally a book which is of great help when one is studying these particular passages is a book entitled *The Cause of God and Truth.* It was written about two hundred years ago by Dr John Gill, preacher and theologian, who was one of Charles Haddon Spurgeon's predecessors at the New Park Street Baptist Church in South London.

As we come to these 'principles of exposition' let me make it clear that while I say that these verses can be dealt with and expounded I am not for a moment suggesting that there are no difficulties in doing so. Any man who claims that he can understand every word in the Bible is hardly worthy of our consideration. All honest expositors admit that there are residual problems in interpretation with respect to certain aspects of the teaching of the Bible. Divine truth is so great that no one man, nor indeed all of us together, can finally compass it. Having done our best there will still remain certain questions and queries in people's minds. I am not claiming for a moment that I can explain everything. The more I study the Bible the more I discover what Thomas Carlyle called 'infinities and immensities'. But I thank God that we understand what we do understand, and that includes all that is necessary to our salvation, and much more. There are certain final ultimate matters which, while not essential to salvation, are of very great importance in the matter of assurance, confidence and certainty, and, therefore, in the enjoyment of the Christian life while we are passing through this world of time.

Our first principle of interpretation is that we must deal with Scripture alone. I mean that when you are dealing with a difficult passage of Scripture you must keep to the Scripture and not allow philosophy to intrude itself. A failure to do so leads to most of the sterile argumentation. For instance, those who believe in what is called 'Conditional immortality' constantly act in this way. In their books and conversation they start by saying that they base their position on the Scripture, but when you show them that, quite plainly, the terms 'eternal' and 'everlasting' are used in precisely the same way as related to 'life' and 'destruction', they fall back upon a philosophical argument and say that they cannot imagine a God of love ever consigning anyone to endless destruction. But at that point they have ceased to argue from the Scripture only; they have sought refuge in philosophy. In expounding Scripture we must keep to the Scripture and not go outside it and begin to reason in terms of our failure to understand. For the moment you begin to import anything from the realm of philosophy, you are not only of necessity confusing the issue, but also in a sense denying the sufficiency of revelation. You are invoking something beyond it.

A second principle is that we must compare Scripture with Scripture. There are not, and cannot be, any contradictions in Scripture. It is God-breathed, it is God-inspired, it is God's Word, it is infallible. Scripture does not contradict Scripture, therefore we must always be careful to compare Scripture with Scripture in any interpretation, and make certain that any conclusion at which we arrive does not contradict what is clearly taught elsewhere.

A third principle is that we should start with the great positive statements of the Scripture. The Protestant Fathers of the 16th century, the Puritans of the 17th century, and the Evangelical Fathers of the 18th century, used to refer to what they called 'proof texts'. I am well aware of the fact that the whole notion of proof texts is ridiculed today. It is anathema to those described as 'liberals' and 'modernists'. They pour scorn upon the various Confessions of Faith of former centuries, and especially upon the footnotes containing the 'proof texts'. They regard that kind of procedure as an abuse of the Bible, which they constantly assert is not a 'collection of proof texts'. In one sense I agree; nevertheless I assert, and assert very strongly, that there are proof texts in the Scriptures. I mean that there are certain statements in Scripture which are plain and explicit and quite unambiguous; and it is a wise rule of interpretation to start always with such certainties. It is indeed a good rule not only in interpreting Scripture, but in any kind of investigation, and particularly in the realm of science. In science a cardinal rule is to proceed from the known to the unknown. You start with the known and advance from it, and build upon it as you approach the unknown possibilities.

Let me illustrate what I mean by these great positive statements, these unambiguous proof texts, particularly as related to the doctrine of the final perseverance of the saints. Take, for instance, what we find in John 10: 27-29: 'My sheep hear my voice, and I know them, and they follow me: and I give unto them eternal life; and they shall never perish, neither shall any man pluck them out of my hand. My Father, which gave them me, is greater than all; and no man is able to pluck them out of my Father's hand.' I call that a 'proof text' because it is explicit and unambiguous. Our Lord there gives a guarantee that His flock, His people, His sheep, shall never perish, that no man shall ever pluck them out of His hand. Another example is found in John 17: 11, 12, in our Lord's high-priestly prayer: 'And now I am no more in the world, but these are in the world, and I come to thee. Holy Father, keep through thine own name those whom thou hast given me, that they may be one, as we are. While I was with them in the world, I kept them in thy name; those that thou gavest me I have kept, and none of them is lost, but the son of perdition; that the Scripture might be fulfilled.' That, again, I would call a 'proof text'. The falling away of 'the son of perdition' as prophesied is a proof that 'His own' will not and cannot fall.

Another example is found in this 8th chapter of Romans, in verse 7, where the Apostle says: 'The carnal mind is enmity against God: for it is not subject to the law of God, neither indeed can be.' That again is an explicit and clear statement with regard to the 'carnal mind'. Then later we shall come to the famous argument in chapter 9, leading up to the Apostle's question to a man who objects: 'Nay but, O man, who art thou that repliest against God? Shall the thing formed say to him that formed it, Why hast thou made me thus?' The statement is clear and plain and explicit. Then there is the familiar statement, already quoted, in 1 Corinthians 2: 14, which is crucial in this matter: 'The natural man receiveth not the things of the Spirit of God: for they are foolishness unto him: neither can he know them, because they are spiritually discerned.' Nothing could be clearer and more explicit. We are all either carnal, natural men, or else we are spiritual. The natural man cannot believe; it is impossible. Therefore if you are a believer you must be spiritual. You cannot believe until you become spiritual; therefore if you believe, it is a proof that you have become spiritual already. The realization of this has often been used, I have found in experience, to bring people who had been living in uncertainty and unhappiness about their whole position to great assurance and joy in the Lord, and as a direct consequence it has prompted their growth in grace and in holiness.

A parallel statement in Ephesians 2: 1–3 says much the same thing. 'You hath he quickened, who were dead in trespasses and sins' – and much more follows. Again, consider the First Epistle of Peter, chapter 1, verses 3–5. Having said that Christians are 'elect according to the foreknowledge of God the Father, through sanctification of the Spirit' – that is to say, having been set apart by the Spirit because God had chosen them – 'unto obedience [the Spirit separates them unto obedience] and sprinkling of the blood of Jesus Christ', Peter goes on to say, 'Blessed be the God and Father of our Lord Jesus Christ, which according to his abundant mercy hath begotten us again unto a lively hope by the resurrection of Jesus Christ from the dead, to an inheritance . . .' Note that we are begotten to the inheritance, predestinated to this conformity to the image of God's Son. The inheritance, he maintains, is 'incorruptible, and undefiled, and that fadeth not away, reserved in heaven for you'. For whom? For those 'who are kept by the power of God'. It is the power of God that keeps us; it is an explicit statement – 'through faith'. That is the instrument, as we have seen, which is always used by God. But it is God who keeps us through the faith which He gives us; and we are kept 'unto salvation ready to be revealed in the last time'. Here we have a clear and explicit statement.

Notice also the words found in the First Epistle of John, chapter 5, verses 18, 19: 'We know that whosoever is born of God sinneth not' – that is to say, he does not go on sinning, he does not habitually sin, he does not dwell in sin, he does not lie in sin – 'but he that is begotten of God keepeth himself, and that wicked one toucheth him not.' Many authorities say that a better translation at this point is, 'he that is begotten of God keepeth him'; in other words it is a reference to the Son of God keeping us. But whichever it is, it comes to the same thing – 'that wicked one toucheth him not'. The devil cannot regain control over the Christian. 'We know that we are of God, and the whole world lieth in wickedness.' The world is lying in the arms, in the embrace of the wicked one; but we are not, because we are 'of God', and the devil cannot touch us. Such is the teaching of that First Epistle of John summarized at its end in this striking manner.

Here then are a number of great positive statements which can have only one possible meaning. These are what I call, therefore, 'proof texts'; and we must start with them.

My fourth principle of interpretation is as follows: Deal with the difficult statements, or the doubtful statements which do not seem to be quite clear to you, in the light of such great statements as I have quoted. Our principles follow one another in a logical sequence. You start with Scripture only, you exclude your philosophy or anything else; you compare Scripture with Scripture; and then start with these fundamental statements. Then you take the perplexing statements and consider them in the light of these fundamental postulates that are stated in such an unambiguous and clear manner. In so doing try to find an explanation or an exposition of your difficult passage that is consistent with these foundational principles of the Bible. Obviously this is essential, because Scripture does not contradict itself. Whatever interpretations we arrive at we must be able to demonstrate that they are consistent with these great foundational statements. If they disagree with them, your interpretation is wrong, because you are making Scripture contradict Scripture.

To put this in a different form, there is nothing that is so dangerous, and as a consequence there has been nothing in the long history of the Church that has been so prolific in the production of heresies and error, as the founding of a doctrine or a body of truth on an isolated text. That could be illustrated from Church history with great ease. Men have taken one text of Scripture, have prized it right out of its context, and have established their whole doctrine on it without any concern about reconciling it with other doctrines. This is always the high road to heresy. We must never try to establish a doctrine or a position upon an isolated text; still less upon an ambiguous text, or a difficult text, a text which does not seem to be clear on the surface.

We now move on to a fifth principle which is a more practical one. Be careful, when you are dealing with a particular verse or paragraph, always to pay great attention to details. Be careful to observe exactly what is being said, and to consider the context. This sound quite elementary, of course, but far too often, difficulties have arisen because people refuse to do just that. They do not pay sufficient attention to what is actually before them, or to the context of the verse or verses they are investigating.

As an illustration of this weakness take the case of the Parable of the Sower which I formerly quoted. Some people say that this parable teaches the possibility of falling away, and they quote our Lord's words: 'Hear ye therefore the parable of the sower. When anyone heareth the word of the kingdom, and understandeth it not, then cometh the wicked one, and catcheth away that which was sown in his heart. This is he which received seed by the wayside. But he that received the seed into stony places, the same is he that heareth the word, and anon with joy receiveth it; yet hath he not root in himself, but dureth for a while: for when tribulation or persecution ariseth because of the word, by and by he is offended. He also that received seed among the thorns is he that heareth the word; and the care of this world, and the deceitfulness of riches, choke the word, and he becometh

unfruitful. But he that received seed into the good ground is he
that heareth the word, and understandeth it; which also beareth
fruit, and bringeth forth, some an hundredfold, some sixty, some
thirty' (Matthew 13: 18–23). But if we observe carefully what our
Lord is saying here, it will solve the problem. Take the phrase
which He uses in verse 21. He is talking about those who received
the seed into stony places, and of them he says: 'Yet hath he not
root in himself.' The root is absent; there is no true life in the
man. There is an appearance, but no real life. Remember that in
this parable our Lord was illustrating one matter in particular,
namely, that not all that 'appears' to be Christian is Christian.
Certain people appeared to be Christians but He says that they
never had any root in themselves. Then in speaking of the last
group He says, 'He that received seed into the good ground is
he that heareth the word, and understandeth it'. This is the only
group that does understand it; and therefore it is the only one
that really represents the Christian. The danger is to think of the
Parable of the Sower in an abstract manner, and to say that it
indicates clearly that there are certain types which produce a
genuine result but in the end come to nothing, and then to add,
'Is not that a clear picture of a man who has become a Christian
and then falls away and ceases to be a Christian?' I am arguing
that if you read the words carefully, and pay attention to what
is being said, you will see that our Lord Himself makes it perfectly
clear that only the last group is really Christian. You find an
'appearance' in the others; but there is no real root, there is no
real life in them.

Let me give some further illustrations of this most important
point. Take what we have at the end of the 2nd chapter of John's
Gospel, verses 23 to 25: 'Now when he was in Jerusalem at the
passover, in the feast day, many believed in his name, when they
saw the miracles which he did. But Jesus did not commit himself
unto them, because he knew all men, and needed not that any
should testify of man: for he knew what was in man.' Surely
that explains itself, if you allow it to do so. The people described
did not truly believe in Him. They give a kind of intellectual
assent, they seemed to believe in Him; but He knew that they
had not believed in Him in reality, and that is why He did not
commit Himself to them. Note that the Evangelist uses the
expression that they 'believed' in him. A similar example is

found at the end of the 6th chapter of John's Gospel, verses 60–66: 'Many therefore of his disciples, when they heard this, said, This is an hard saying; who can hear it? When Jesus knew in himself that his disciples murmured at it, he said unto them, Doth this offend you? What and if ye shall see the Son of man ascend up where he was before? It is the Spirit that quickeneth; the flesh profiteth nothing: the words that I speak unto you, they are spirit and they are life. But there are some of you that believe not' – and yet they have been called disciples! It simply means that they had been following Him; they were interested, intrigued, attracted, and thought that they believed what He said – 'There are some of you that believe not, for Jesus knew from the beginning who they were that believed not, and who should betray him. And he said, Therefore said I unto you, that no man can come unto me, except it were given unto him of my Father' – that is, coming to Him as true believers. You can be a follower, interested and taking notes of sermons and addresses, as it were, and apparently believing it all; but He says that no man can really come unto Him except it is 'given unto him of my Father'. 'From that time many of his disciples' – disciples! – 'went back, and walked no more with him.' What so many do is to pick out verse 66 only and say, 'Now there you are! Isn't it perfectly clear, "From that time many of his disciples went back, and walked no more with him"'! They had been Christians but they ceased to be Christians.' But in the context it is made quite clear that they had never been Christians at all. They were followers but not true believers, and resemble the people at the end of chapter 2. We must not fasten on certain words out of context, but allow the context and what the writer himself says to make the actual meaning clear to us.

For a further illustration of this type let us turn to 1 Timothy 1: 19, 20, which is often quoted in this connection: 'Holding faith', says the Apostle, 'and a good conscience; which some having put away concerning faith have made shipwreck: of whom is Hymenaeus and Alexander; whom I have delivered unto Satan, that they may learn not to blaspheme.' The opponent of perseverance emphasizes that these men, disciples, believers, had made shipwreck of their faith, which means they had fallen away and ceased to be Christians. The answer is that all the Apostle is actually telling us is that their faith at this point was in a state of shipwreck. In other words, with respect to their belief, and their statements of their belief, they were in a state of chaos, 'shipwreck', utter muddle. The Apostle does not say that they were reprobate; all he says is that they have got into this indescribable muddle, a shipwreck, a shambles, call it what you will. He is using a figurative term. And the Apostle tells us that he has handed them over to Satan, a statement which, when compared with the parallel passage in 1 Corinthians 5, shows that he means 'for their correction', thereby suggesting that they were not apostates. He is handing them over that they may learn a lesson. They are going to suffer at the hands of Satan, and that will bring them to their senses, and cause them to see the importance of 'holding faith with a good conscience'.

Take a similar example in 1 Timothy 4: 1 and 2: 'Now the Spirit speaketh expressly, that in the latter times some shall depart from the faith, giving heed to seducing spirits, and doctrines of devils; speaking lies in hypocrisy; having their conscience seared with a hot iron; forbidding to marry, and to abstain from meats, which God hath created . . .' These words have a close parallel in 2 Timothy 2, verses 15 to 18: 'Study to show thyself approved unto God, a workman that needeth not to be ashamed, rightly dividing the word of truth. But shun profane and vain babblings, for they will increase unto more ungodliness. And their word will eat as doth a canker (a cancer) of whom is Hymenaeus and Philetus; who concerning the truth have erred, saying that the resurrection is past already; and overthrow the faith of some.' All that is really being said is that there were certain people in the church who were being regarded as Christians and good church members, yet who had gone astray in their doctrine, and as a result others had been shaken and their faith had been upset. We have no means of proving that these people – Hymenæus and Philetus and others – had ever been true believers at all. All we do know is that they had been church members and that now they were teaching false doctrine. They were in the same position as the people described in the 1st Epistle of John, chapter 2, verse 18, 19: 'Little children, it is the last time: and as ye have heard that antichrist shall come, even now there are many antichrists; whereby we know that it is the last time. They went out from us, but they were not of us; for if they had been of us, they would no doubt have continued with us: but they went out, that they might be made manifest that they were not all of us.' Here again were people who had been members of the church. They had been 'of us', they seemed to be perfectly good Christians, they had been subscribing to the faith. They would never have been received into the early church if they had not claimed to believe. The early Church was very careful about these matters, people had to become catechumens, and were tested before they were received. These people had been in the church, but they had been teaching false doctrine and they had left the church. The Apostle John says that although they 'were among us; they were never of us'. 'For', he says, 'if they had really been of us, they would no doubt have continued with us.' The fact that they had gone out proves that they had never really belonged; they were merely within the realm of the Church, and appeared to be Christian.

Now these people – Hymenæus and Philetus, and the others to whom the Apostle is referring in 2 Timothy 2 – belong to the same category. All the Apostle states is that these people who were in the Church were now teaching false doctrine and thereby were upsetting the faith of others. That does not mean that these others had 'fallen from grace'; they are simply in a muddle for the time being, and they can be put right. As for the others, they had never been right at all; if they had been right they would have continued so. The fact that they have gone out is proof positive in itself that they had never truly belonged at all.

For our next example I turn to the famous passage in Hebrews 6 and the parallel passage in Hebrews 10. Here again the answer is that we are not told that the people described were regenerate. There is no statement to the effect that they had been born again, though they had had wonderful experiences. The history of the Church helps us to understand these two passages. History shows that in times of great revival, when the Holy Spirit is poured out, in addition to the people who were truly converted and born again, there have been a number of others who are, as it were, 'carried in by the tide'. They appear for a while to be true Christians but they do not continue in the faith. When the tide of revival recedes these people fall away. During the revival you cannot determine their true state; they seem to be having great experiences, and are moved in the meetings and enjoy them. But that in and of itself does not prove that they are truly regenerate.

It is what happens subsequently that reveals their true state and condition. As we read in Hebrews 6, verse 7, the test is as follows: 'For the earth which drinketh in the rain that cometh oft upon it, and bringeth forth herbs meet for them by whom it is dressed, receiveth blessing from God.' At a time of revival you cannot tell who is saved and who is not; the fruit alone will reveal the fact of the matter. As our Lord says, 'By their fruits ye shall know them.' And as Hebrews 6; 8 says conversely: 'That which beareth thorns and briars is rejected, and is nigh unto cursing; whose end is to be burned.' The same rain falls upon both types, and they have the same experiences apparently. The Holy Spirit can give general experiences to people which are quite genuine, but they fall short of rebirth, regeneration, or a true reception of the principle of life.

One other matter in connection with Hebrews 10 often causes confusion. It is assumed that, when the author writes about sin and falling away, he is referring to some failure in practice and in daily living. But that is not the case. The whole of the Epistle to the Hebrews is concerned about belief. The problem of those Hebrew Christians was not so much failure in practice and in life, as the tendency to go back to Judaism, the tendency to go back to the temple and the burnt offerings and the sacrifices, and to deny the pre-eminence of Christ and justification by faith only. That is the one great theme of the Epistle to the Hebrews. The realization of it solves many problems. The people referred to in chapters 6 and 10 appear to believe in the same way as those in 1 John 2: 19. But it is clear that they have never been truly Christian. These are illustrations of the principle that if we read carefully, and consider the context, we shall be led to the true exposition.

That brings us to the last example under this heading. It is in many respects the most difficult of all. It is in 2 Peter 2: 1: 'But there were false prophets also among the people, even as there shall be false teachers among you, who privily shall bring in damnable heresies, even denying the Lord that bought them, and bring upon themselves swift destruction.' Similarly, at the end of the same chapter in verses 20-22: 'For if after they have escaped the pollutions of the world through the knowledge of the Lord and Saviour Jesus Christ, they are again entangled therein, and overcome, the latter end is worse with them than the beginning.

For it had been better for them not to have known the way of
righteousness, than, after they have known it, to turn from the
holy commandment delivered unto them. But it has happened
unto them according to the true proverb, The dog is turned to
his own vomit again; and the sow that was washed to her wallowing in the mire.' Let us take them in the reverse order, starting
at the end and going back to the beginning. With regard to
verses 20–22, I argue that if you read them carefully the problem
will be solved. Take the word 'pollutions' which is used in
verse 20. Compare it with what we read in 2 Peter 1: 4: 'Whereby
are given unto us exceeding great and precious promises: that
by these ye might be partakers of the divine nature, having
escaped the corruption that is in the world through lust.' Peter
is there writing to believers, those who are 'partakers of the divine
nature', and he says of them that they have escaped the 'corruption'
that is in the world. But in writing about the other people at
the end of chapter 2, he does not use the word translated 'corruption' but the word translated 'pollutions'. Obviously that is done
quite deliberately. The people in chapter 2 had never been delivered
from the 'corruption' but they had been delivered temporarily
from the 'pollution'. The Apostle himself uses two different
words, and 'corruption' is a much stronger word than 'pollution'.
Pollution affects the surface, as when a man who happens to
fall into a bog or into mud is covered with mud and dirt.
Corruption is something deep within, down in the very depths of
the nature. So the Apostle, in writing of the people who seem
to be falling away as Christians, uses the word 'pollution' instead
of 'corruption'. But not only so, in verse 22 he says, 'But it has
happened unto them according to the true proverb, The dog is
turned to his own vomit again; and the sow that was washed to
her wallowing in the mire'.

The truth about those people was that they had been washed
on the surface. They had got rid of the pollution – the sow had
been washed and is no longer covered with mud. But she is still
a sow; a clean sow is still a sow and has not changed her nature.
All the Apostle is saying is that these people for the time being
had got rid of the pollution. This is something one has seen
many times in the Christian Church. I have known it in the case
of drunkards and other types of obvious sinners. Poor fellows,
they have been in trouble, perhaps proceeded against in a court

or sent to gaol, and as a result they say, 'I am going to live a better life'. We tell them that that is not enough, and that they must believe the gospel. Then they say that they do believe the gospel; and for weeks and months they do not drink, or gamble or whatever it is that troubles them. But, alas, far too often, unfortunately, people who have to work with such poor creatures find that it is but a case of 'the sow being washed' temporarily; they have got rid of the pollution for the time being. There is no real change of nature. Thank God, there are the many cases where there is a true deliverance from the corruption; but there are many cases in which it is merely a washing away of the pollution and there has never been any real change. The dog goes back to his vomit because he has never ceased to be a dog. So there is no teaching concerning 'falling away from grace' in these passages.

Turning now to the first verse in that same 2nd chapter of the Second Epistle of Peter, let me show how John Gill deals with it in a most illuminating and interesting manner. He writes: 'This passage of Scripture is often produced as a proof both of the saints' final and total apostasy and of universal redemption; or that, besides those that are saved, Christ died also for them that perish.' The words 'even denying the Lord that bought them' appear to say that; and this is how John Gill deals with the problem: 'Christ is not here at all spoken of, nor is there one syllable of his dying for any persons, in any sense whatsoever.' What enables him to say that? This is his answer: 'The word "despotes", translated Lord ("denying the Lord that bought them"), does not designate Christ but God, the Father of Christ. The only places besides this where this word is used, when applied to a divine person, are Luke 2: 29, Acts 4: 24, 2 Timothy 2: 21, Jude verse 4, Revelation 6: 10, in all which places God the Father is plainly intended, and in most of them manifestly distinguished from Christ. Nor is there anything in this text or context which obliges us to understand it of the Son of God, nor should this be thought any diminution of the glory of Christ, since the word "despotes" is properly expressive only of that power which masters have over their servants, whereas the word "kurios", which is used whenever Christ is called Lord, signifies that dominion and authority which princes have over their subjects.' I have checked John Gill on this and find that he is strictly

accurate. The only case which is in any way doubtful is Jude 4,
which reads, 'There are certain men crept in unawares, who were
before of old ordained to this condemnation, ungodly men,
turning the grace of our God into lasciviousness, and denying
the only Lord God, and our Lord Jesus Christ.' I quote the
Authorized Version translation, and there it seems quite clear,
as John Gill says; but the authorities are not all agreed about this.
Some of them say that it should read thus: 'turning the grace
of God into lasciviousness, and denying the only Lord and God
our Saviour Jesus Christ'. It seems to me, having again looked
at the evidence, that a dogmatic pronouncement cannot be made
as to which of the two readings is correct. Incidentally it makes
no difference to John Gill's argument. I am calling attention to
this to show that in all the other instances the position is clear,
that the reference is to 'God the Father'. So I am prepared to
stand with the Authorized Version translators who undoubtedly
translated it in this manner – 'denying the only Lord God' –
because 'the Lord God' is 'despotes theon', and then add 'and
our Lord Jesus Christ'.

Gill next proceeds to say: 'When these persons are said to be
bought' – 'denying the Lord God that *bought* them' – 'the meaning
is not that they were redeemed by the blood of Christ, for, as
before observed, Christ is not intended. Besides, whenever
redemption by Christ is spoken of, the price is usually mentioned,
or some circumstances or another which fully determines the
sense of it.' For instance, Acts 20: 28, where we have the expression 'purchased to himself by his blood'; again, 1 Corinthians
6: 20, 'Ye are not your own, ye are bought with a price'; and
again, Ephesians 1: 7, 'In whom we have redemption through
his blood, the forgiveness of sins, according to the riches of his
grace'; and yet again, 1 Peter 1: 18, 19, 'Ye have been redeemed
from your vain conversation, inherited by tradition from your
fathers, not with silver or gold, but with the precious blood of
Christ'. John Gill's argument is, that when there is a reference
to being 'bought' by Christ Jesus, there is always some reference
to the 'precious blood' or to the price paid. Revelation 5: 9 and
Revelation 14: 3, 4 further illustrate this point. John Gill goes
on, 'Whereas, here, is not the least hint of anything of this kind.
Add to this that such who are redeemed by Christ are never left
to deny him, so as to perish eternally, for could such be lost, or

bring on themselves swift destruction, Christ's purchase would be in vain and the ransom price be paid for nought.' 'But' – and this is to me the most interesting part of his answer – 'the word "buying" regards temporal deliverance, and particularly the redemption of the people of Israel out of Egypt, who are therefore called the people the Lord had purchased.' He continues, 'The phrase is borrowed from Deuteronomy 32: 6, "Do ye thus requite the Lord, O foolish people and unwise? Is not he thy Father that hath bought thee?" ' The reference is to God as related to the Children of Israel, 'Is not he thy Father who hath bought thee? hath he not made thee?' God has 'bought' them; their deliverance out of the capitivity of Egypt is described in this pictorial manner. John Gill proceeds, 'Nor is this the only place the Apostle Peter refers to in this chapter; see verses 12 and 13 and compare them with Deuteronomy 32: 5'. This last-mentioned verse reads thus: 'They have corrupted themselves, their spot is not the spot of his children; they are a perverse and crooked generation.' In 2 Peter, chapter 2, verses 12 and 13, we read: 'But these, as natural brute beasts, made to be taken and destroyed, speak evil of the things that they understand not; and shall utterly perish in their own corruption; and shall receive the reward of unrighteousness, as they that count it pleasure to riot in the day time. Spots are they' – 'spots,' a word derived from the 32nd chapter of Deuteronomy – 'and blemishes, sporting themselves with their own deceivings while they feast with you.'

In other words, John Gill's argument is that Peter, in warning these early believers, is taking and applying what he found in Deuteronomy 32. His second chapter opens with the words, 'There were false prophets also among the people, even as there shall be false teachers among you' and he then proceeds to describe what was true of the false prophets. Obviously as Peter writes the 2nd chapter of his Epistle, the words of Deuteronomy are in his mind. The term 'denying the Lord that bought them' is an exact quotation from Deuteronomy 32, verse 6, where we are told that God had 'bought' the Children of Israel when He brought them out of the captivity of Egypt, and was leading them towards Canaan. But as the Scripture tells us in many different places, all those who came out of Egypt were not truly the children of God. 'They are not all Israel that are of Israel.' They were not all redeemed, but they were all brought out. In that sense they were all 'bought'. But they were not bought in the sense of being redeemed and regenerated and becoming the children of God. This is the explanation of 2 Peter 2: 1. Compare Scripture with Scripture, and when you find the word 'bought', discover its meaning elsewhere in Scripture, and you will find that you have the key to the solution of your problem. It is found in the 32nd chapter of Deuteronomy in this particular instance.

Twenty-four

*

And we know that all things work together for good to them that love God, to them who are the called according to his purpose.

For whom he did foreknow, he also did predestinate to be conformed to the image of his Son, that he might be the firstborn among many brethren.

Moreover whom he did predestinate, them he also called: and whom he called, them he also justified: and whom he justified, them he also glorified. Romans 8: 28–30

As we continue our examination of various passages of Scripture which seem to contradict the doctrine of the final perseverance of the saints we come to another principle which should guide us in our interpretation. You will find, sometimes, that your difficulty is solved if you but realize that the author is referring, not to individuals, but to churches. An illustration of this is found in the Book of Revelation, chapter 2, verse 5. It is in the letter to the church at Ephesus: 'Remember therefore from whence thou art fallen, and repent, and do the first works.' Though fallen she can still repent. The word 'fallen' must be construed in a sense which allows for repentance, it is not a final falling away. The important statement for our purpose, however, is 'or else I will come unto thee quickly, and will remove thy candlestick out of its place, except thou repent'. There lies the stumblingblock, the difficulty for many. 'Here', they say, 'is a clear statement to the effect that the candlestick which has been there in position may be removed.' But there, clearly, we are dealing not with individuals, but with a church, as is proved by Revelation, chapter 1, verse 20: 'The mystery of the seven stars which thou sawest in my right hand, and the seven golden candlesticks. The seven stars are the angels of the seven churches: and the seven candlesticks which thou sawest are the seven churches.'

So a 'candlestick' stands for a church as a whole, not individuals in the church, the church at Ephesus in this particular case. Another example of the same thing is found in Revelation, chapter 3, verse 16, in the letter to the church of the Laodiceans, where we read: 'So then because thou art lukewarm, and neither cold nor hot, I will spue thee out of my mouth.' That statement has worried, upset and stumbled many people – the possibility of being spued out of His mouth. But, once more, it is addressed to a church, and not to individuals who are members of the church. It is a generic expression with regard to what may be done to a particular church. This is helpful, not only in the context of what we are actually considering at the moment; it is an important principle to lay hold of in the understanding of the history of the Church throughout the centuries. Indeed it helps us to understand the situation of the Christian Church at the present time. The threatenings addressed to the seven churches of Asia have been carried out in the case of many churches, as history reveals. The very churches to which the letters were originally addressed are churches that have ceased to exist. In addition there is the classic example of the great Christian Church that flourished at one time in North Africa, including those under the care of the great Saint Augustine – Augustine of Hippo. He exercised his ministry in the great and prominent churches of North Africa for 40 years; but they have vanished altogether; their candlesticks have been removed, for they had become guilty of the very things against which Christians and Christian Churches are warned in the letters to the seven churches.

So we find that actually, in history, what had been threatened has literally taken place; churches as churches have simply gone out of existence altogether. More recent history provides examples of the same thing. I was privileged to spend a part of my youth in the village where the great Daniel Rowland – one of the leaders of the Methodist awakening in Wales, two hundred years ago, and the greatest preacher of them all – preached for over fifty years. The church was renowned throughout Wales, and to some extent in England, at that time, and for some time afterwards. But by the time I came to live there, it was, of all churches that I have known, the most lifeless. The same holds true of Trevecca, the district where Howel Harris lived. There are many illustrations of this phenomenon. You can visit districts where remarkable outstanding men of God once lived and ministered; you go there full of enthusiasm and keenness, expecting to find something remarkable, but you often find nothing but utter barrenness. The candlestick may be removed because of what has become true in the life of the church.

May not this be the explanation of the condition, for instance, of the Roman Catholic church at the present time? A church can continue to exist as an organization; but it does not mean that the candlestick has not been removed. This is a most disturbing thought. You cannot guarantee the continuity of any church, or even of any group of churches; history shows us the exact opposite. Though they may have been greatly blessed at one time, if they fail to observe the conditions set by the Lord they cease to be, the candlestick is removed, they are spued out of His mouth. So when we come across certain passages in Scripture let us be quite sure whether they have reference to churches or to individuals. We have no right to apply teaching meant for churches to our own individual case or to the case of any other individual.

We now come to a group of passages which refer to office and function rather than to personal salvation. There are many such passages. Under this heading the most notable example is the familiar statement in 1 Corinthians 9: 27, where the Apostle Paul says, 'But I keep under my body, and bring it into subjection: lest by any means, when I have preached to others, I myself should be a castaway.' Faced by such a text many say, 'The matter is as plain and as explicit as you could ever desire. The Apostle Paul does not hesitate to say that he has this fear, this horror, lest he who had preached so much to other people should find himself ultimately unsaved, lost, cast out of God's kingdom, and suffering everlasting punishment and torment.' They say, 'He is so afraid of such a calamity that he is prepared, as it were, to mutilate his body, to hit it until it is black and blue'. (Such is the meaning of the phrase which he uses – 'keep under my body'. He beats it; the analogy is that of a boxer hitting and bruising.)

I have already hinted at the answer to this particular problem in the general principle I have laid down. The whole of the 9th chapter of First Corinthians is concerned with 'office'. It starts with the words, 'Am I not an apostle? am I not free? have I not seen Jesus Christ our Lord? If I be not an apostle unto others, yet doubtless I am to you.' Such is the theme and Paul continues with it. I am picking out verses at random. Verse 14: 'Even so hath the Lord ordained that they which preach the gospel should live by the gospel.' This refers to the office of preachers. Verse 16: 'Though I preach the gospel, I have nothing to glory of: for necessity is laid upon me; yea, woe is unto me, if I preach not the gospel.' Verse 18: 'What is my reward then?' Verse 19: 'For though I be free from all men, yet have I made myself servant unto all, that I might gain the more.' Verse 20: 'Unto the Jews I became as a Jew.' All along he is referring to his work as a preacher and as an apostle, as a propagator of the gospel message and as a man who establishes churches and teaches them. The whole chapter, right on to its end, deals with his office, his position as a preacher, teacher and apostle. Surely we must take all this into consideration, and not suddenly isolate the last verse? It is there he brings his entire case and argument to a climax. That is the first point.

A second is that we must exercise great care with the word 'castaway' which is the translation in the Authorized Version. The word actually means 'disapproved'. The Apostle uses the illustration of people running in a race: 'Know ye not that they which run in a race run all, but one receiveth the prize?' So he says that, as a preacher, he is determined to succeed, to win. He is greatly concerned about it. So the statement means that he is anxious that he should not find that all his labour and work as a minister and preacher and apostle would ultimately turn out to be useless; in other words, lest he should prove a complete failure and not receive any prize whatsoever.

He has already said very much the same thing earlier in his Epistle in chapter 3 beginning at verse 9: 'For we are labourers together with God: you are God's husbandry, you are God's building. According to the grace of God which is given unto me, as a wise masterbuilder, I have laid the foundation, and another buildeth thereon. But let every man take heed how he buildeth thereupon.' Here again he is concerned about ministry, about building, about Apollos and himself as preachers. 'For other foundation can no man lay than that is laid, which is Jesus Christ. Now if any man build upon this foundation gold, silver, precious stones, wood, hay, stubble; every man's work shall be made manifest' – note it is his 'work' that is going to be made manifest – 'for the day shall declare it, because it shall be revealed by fire; and the fire shall try every man's work of what sort it is. If any man's work abide which he hath built thereupon, he shall receive a reward. If any man's work shall be burned, he shall suffer loss:' – that is, as regards his work – 'but he himself shall be saved; yet so as by fire'. A man may be a complete failure as regards his work, and obtain no reward at all. He may 'suffer loss' and receive no prize as a preacher. As a man who has been building upon the only foundation he is a complete failure, he is utterly disapproved. This is precisely what the Apostle says in 1 Corinthians 9: 27; in both cases he is dealing with the work of God's servants. In 1 Corinthians 3 he himself draws the vital distinction between a man being disapproved utterly in respect of his work, even while he himself remains a saved man. How important it is that we should pay very careful attention always to the context, and make quite sure whether the Apostles or others are dealing with our personal salvation or with what happens to our work and ministry. Let every preacher pay careful attention to this. It is possible to spend a lifetime in the Christian ministry, and at the end to be disapproved as ministers and have nothing to show for all our labour. But thank God we may still be 'saved' ourselves, even though it be as 'by fire'.

To complete this particular argument I assert that this must of necessity be the case. I do not start with this assertion; I finish with it. We must deal with these problems in the first instance in terms of the actual text and context. That must be worked out, and any other passage that throws light on it or is parallel to it, must be considered also. It must all be done in a thoroughly expository manner. By then you should have arrived at a conclusion which agrees with the great foundational passages, the unambiguous passages, from which the whole discussion has started. What we have just been saying illustrates this perfectly. You cannot find any parallel to this statement in 1 Corinthians 9: 27 in all the writings of the great Apostle if it refers to his personal salvation. What we find in the writings of the Apostle Paul everywhere is a strong note of certainty and assurance both in regard to his present salvation and his ultimate destiny. Take, for instance, the closing words of this 8th chapter of the Epistle to the Romans: 'I am persuaded, that neither death, nor life, nor angels, nor principalities, nor powers, nor things present, nor things to come, nor height, nor depth, nor any other creature, shall be able to separate us from the love of God, which is in Christ Jesus our Lord.' Or take what he says at the end of his life, in what is generally agreed to be his last Epistle – the Second Epistle to Timothy, chapter 4, verses 7 and 8: 'I have fought a good fight, I have finished my course, I have kept the faith: henceforth there is laid up for me a crown of righteousness, which the Lord, the righteous judge, shall give me at that day: and not to me only, but unto all them also that love his appearing.' There is no doubt whatsoever in these words! The Apostle Paul had an absolute assurance of his relationship to God, who had separated him even from his mother's womb, and to the Son of God who had loved him and given Himself for him, the Christ of whom he could say, 'To me to live is Christ, and to die is gain'. 'I know whom I have believed and am persuaded that he is able to keep that which I have committed unto him against that day' (2 Timothy 1: 12). Our exposition of 1 Corinthians 9: 27 puts it into line with the teaching of the Apostle concerning his personal salvation everywhere in all his writings.

For another example we turn to the 15th chapter of the Gospel according to St John, verses 1–11, where we have another passage which refers to office or function in the Church rather than to personal salvation. There is, however, disagreement as to whether this should be included under this heading. Some agree that it should be included, others take it as referring to personal salvation. We must therefore look at it from both standpoints. The two verses on which attention is concentrated are the second and the sixth. Verse 2: 'Every branch in me that beareth not fruit he taketh away: and every branch that beareth fruit, he purgeth it, that it may bring forth more fruit.' Verse 6: 'If a man abide not in me, he is cast forth as a branch, and is withered; and men gather them and cast them into the fire, and they are burned.' I suggest that here again we are dealing with 'office', 'function', 'work' rather than with personal salvation, for, in my view, chapters 14, 15, and 16, in John's Gospel deal with that aspect.

In these chapters our Lord is speaking in particular to his own disciples who had been troubled when He told them that He was about to leave them. In chapter 14 He says, 'Let not your heart be troubled, ye believe in God, believe also in me.' He goes on to tell them, 'Greater works than these shall ye do; because I go unto my Father'; and He explains that He is about to give them 'another Comforter', who will help them and aid them. In the 15th chapter He tells them in verses 18 and 19: 'If the world hate you, ye know that it hated me before it hated you. If ye were of the world, the world would love his own: but because ye are not of the world, but I have chosen you out of the world, therefore the world hateth you.' Then in verse 20: 'Remember the word that I said unto you, The servant is not greater than his Lord. If they have persecuted me, they will also persecute you; if they have kept my saying, they will keep yours also.' All this is said in the context of the work they were about to do. He had been doing the work; now they will have to continue with it. He is warning them of what is going to happen, and giving them the comfort and the consolation which will enable them to continue. In the 16th chapter He says in verses 1 and 2: 'These things have I spoken unto you, that ye should not be offended. They shall put you out of the synagogues; yea, the time cometh, that whosoever killeth you will think that he doeth God service.' Verse 4: 'But these things have I told you, that when the time shall come, ye may remember that I told you of them.' Verse 12: 'I have yet many things to say unto you, but ye cannot bear them now. Howbeit when he, the Spirit of truth is come, he will guide you into all truth: for he shall not speak of himself; but whatsoever he shall hear, that shall he speak: and he will show you things to come. He shall glorify me: for he shall receive of mine, and shall show it unto you. All things that the Father hath are mine; therefore said I, that he shall take of mine, and shall show it unto you.'

I suggest that here our Lord was addressing His disciples as the future teachers and preachers and establishers of churches. I admit that I cannot prove this; but it seems clear to me that that is the context in the light of which every particular statement must be interpreted. If that be the case, then the statements in chapter 15 about the branches being taken out of the tree and burned and destroyed must be interpreted in exactly the same way as the statement in 1 Corinthians 9: 27 and the parallel in 1 Corinthians 3. The statements refer to 'office' and to 'function'. Indeed there is a word in verse 6 of chapter 15 which seems to justify this interpretation to the hilt. 'If a man abide not in me, he is cast forth as a branch.' He does not say simply that he is 'cast forth', but he is cast forth 'as a branch', as a branch that is meant to bring forth fruit. He tells them that apart from Him they can do nothing; and this is surely a reference to ministry. The whole picture is that of branches as parts of a tree upon which they depend for everything, and which are to bear fruit. Therefore if they do not function as branches and bear fruit they are useless, and are cast away and burned in the fire. The Lord argues out the full imagery in detail, but it is the principle that here concerns us. I argue therefore that He is referring here to Christians who are engaged in ministry and service. The words apply primarily to the apostles, but can be applied also to all who are now engaged in a similar manner. Looking thus at the statements we arrive at precisely the same interpretation as in the case of the passages already explained.

But let us now assume that these statements refer to the matter of our personal salvation. Do they suggest the possibility of 'falling away from grace'? and do they teach that you can be saved and born again at one time, but yet end in hell and in perdition, having lost the eternal life you once had? Let us consider the position that results if we regard them in that way and not in terms of service. The first conclusion to which we must come is that there are two classes of persons dealt with here, and that they are contrasted with each other. They all *seem* to be in the same position, but they are essentially different. A superficial glance at them suggests that they are identical, but the whole point of the picture is to show that they are not identical but that they differ essentially in their nature, and for this reason they will differ in their ultimate fate. In other words, on that second interpretation chapter 15 is addressed to the visible Church and is a test of profession. In the visible Church you have two kinds of people. Looked at superficially they all appear to be identical; nevertheless they consist of two types of people, though their names are on the same church roll. On this interpretation therefore our Lord is simply saying that in the Church there are those who are truly Christian and those who only appear to be Christian, and that what shows the difference is this matter of fruit-bearing. There are those who bear fruit, and there are those who do not bear fruit.

Let me show how this exposition cannot be justified. Take, for instance, what our Lord says in the third verse of this 15th chapter of John. 'Now ye are clean through the word which I have spoken unto you.' He had already said something similar in the 13th chapter in verse 10. Our Lord was washing the disciples' feet and Peter, in trouble, says to Him, 'Thou shalt never wash my feet'. 'Jesus answered him, If I wash thee not, thou hast no part with me. Simon Peter saith unto him, Lord, not my feet only, but also my hands and my head. Jesus saith to him' – here is the important point! – 'He that is washed needeth not save to wash his feet, but is clean every whit: and ye are clean, but not all.' There we have the general statement and then the qualification – 'ye are clean, but not all; for he knew who should betray him; therefore said he, Ye are not all clean.' It is clear that He had in mind the case of Judas; and that is vital in this exposition.

Anyone taking a general glance at the twelve apostles would have said that there were no differences among them, but that all were followers of the same Master. He speaks of them as His disciples, and He has sent them out with the same commission. Judas, remember, was included in the commission. He went out, as the others did, to preach and to cast out devils, yet our Lord says, 'but not all'. He knew from the beginning about Judas. At the end of chapter 6 we read: 'Jesus answered them, Have not I chosen you twelve, and one of you is a devil? He spake of Judas Iscariot the son of Simon: for he it was that should betray him, being one of the twelve.' So in chapter 13 the Lord expresses Himself quite explicitly over this question of washing the feet. Surely we have an exact parallel to that in the phrase in chapter 15, verse 3: 'Now ye are clean through the word which I have spoken unto you.' In chapter 15 our Lord is speaking of those who are already cleansed and washed and saved. He is not concerned about testing profession of faith and of Christianity but about functioning and ministering.

At the same time these statements, and the whole picture in John chapter 15, does teach by implication that our profession of Christianity as members of the Church has to be tested. The mere fact that we appear to be in the Vine does not prove that we are in the Vine. Our Lord is using a picture, a very dramatic picture; but we must remember always that it is a picture. He says that the test of whether we are true members of Christ is that we bear fruit. He makes it quite plain that the branches that are torn off, and burned, have never borne any fruit at all; 'I am the true vine, and my Father is the husbandman. Every branch in me that beareth not fruit' – it has never borne any fruit at all – 'he taketh away.' It appeared to be a true branch; but it proves that it is not, because if it were it would bear fruit. It is only the branches that do not bear fruit that are thrown away. 'If a man abide not in me, he is cast forth as a branch, and is withered.' It is all a question of fruit bearing; 'I am the vine, ye are the branches: He that abideth in me, and I in him, the same bringeth forth much fruit.' In other words it comes to this, that if you are born of God, born of the Spirit, if you are 'in Christ', you will bear fruit; but if you are merely a church member who has never been born again, you will never bear fruit, and your end is destruction. There is no question of a true believer falling away.

There are certain parallel statements which establish my point. Take what our Lord says in the Sermon on the Mount, Matthew's Gospel, chapter 7 beginning at verse 15 : 'Beware of false prophets, which come to you in sheep's clothing.' There are two types of prophets, true prophets and false prophets. When you first look at them you conclude that there is but one kind of prophet, for to outward view they all appear to be sheep wearing 'sheep's clothing'. But what matters is that, inwardly, some of them are 'ravening wolves'. It is the inward nature that matters, not the outward appearance only; and the nature always expresses itself. Our Lord says in Matthew 7 : 16, 'You shall know them by their fruits', exactly as in John 15. He continues: 'Do men gather grapes of thorns, or figs of thistles?' That is impossible. Whatever the appearance may be, it is the nature that tells. You will never find grapes on thorns, you will never find figs on thistles. 'Even so', He says, 'every good tree bringeth forth good fruit' – that is a categorical statement – 'but a corrupt tree bringeth forth evil fruit.' Our Lord is speaking about the appearance of the false prophet; his argument is that it is the nature that matters, and that the nature shows itself in the fruit. 'A good tree cannot bring forth evil fruit, neither can a corrupt tree' – however good it may look – 'bring forth good fruit.' In other words a man who is only a Christian in appearance never brings forth good fruit. It is impossible for him to do so. If you are not 'in Christ' you cannot ever bear spiritual fruit. 'Every tree that bringeth not forth good fruit is hewn down, and cast into the fire.' 'Wherefore by their fruits ye shall know them.' Then still more explicitly in verses 21–23: 'Not every one that saith unto me, Lord, Lord, shall enter into the kingdom of heaven but he that doeth the will of my Father which is in heaven. Many will say unto me in that day, Lord, Lord, have we not prophesied in thy name? and in thy name have cast out devils? and in thy name done many wonderful works? And then I will profess unto them, I never knew you: depart from me, ye that work iniquity.' They appeared to be Christians but they had no life, and so they will have to depart from Him because they are 'workers of iniquity'.

Lastly, I suggest that we have an exact parallel to John 15, verses 1–11, in this very Epistle to the Romans, in chapter 11 beginning at verse 13: 'For I speak to you Gentiles, inasmuch as I am the apostle of the Gentiles, I magnify mine office: If by any means I may provoke to emulation them which are my flesh, and might save some of them.' Then, 'For if the casting away of them be the reconciling of the world, what shall the receiving of them be, but life from the dead.' At the moment I am not interested in these words from the standpoint of prophecy, but simply as an illustration of our present point. The Apostle continues, 'For if the firstfruit be holy, the lump is also holy, and if the root be holy, so are the branches.' The same principle holds good everywhere! 'And if some of the branches be broken off, and thou, being a wild olive tree, were grafted in among them, and with them partakest of the root and fatness of the olive tree; boast not thyself against the branches. But if thou boast, thou bearest not the root, but the root thee. Thou wilt say then, The branches were broken off, that I might be grafted in. Well; because of unbelief they were broken off, and thou standest by faith. Be not high-minded, but fear: For if God spared not the natural branches, take heed lest he also spare not thee. Behold therefore the goodness and severity of God: on them which fell, severity; but toward thee, goodness, if thou continue in his goodness: otherwise thou also shalt be cut off. And they also, if they abide not still in unbelief, shall be grafted in: for God is able to graft them in again. For if thou wert cut out of the olive tree which is wild by nature, and were grafted contrary to nature into a good olive tree: how much more shall these, which be the natural branches, be grafted into their own olive tree?'

The people of God are this 'olive tree'. At one time the whole nation of Israel was represented by this good olive tree, and the other nations were 'wild' olive trees. Israel was the tree that God had planted. But the Apostle teaches quite plainly that some branches of the tree had been torn off. Many at this point say, 'Does not that mean that people who were once saved can be finally, lost?' No! The Apostle is really teaching the exact opposite! His argument can be stated thus: The nation of Israel is God's olive tree. But 'They are not all Israel which are of Israel' (9: 6). Not all the children of Israel were true children of God. They were regarded as such as a whole; they were the 'good olive tree'. But many did not really belong to it, and these are the people who are torn off and burned. So, in effect, Paul says to the Gentile members of the church: 'You Gentiles have been admitted now into the Christian Church; but do not assume that because you have become members of the Christian Church you are therefore of necessity Christians. If God casts out even the children of Israel, who were actually physical descendants of Abraham, He may certainly do the same with you.' In other words, the members of the nation of Israel who were cast out had never been true children of God at all. They belonged to Israel, but they were not truly Israel; 'they are not all Israel' who belong to it in an external manner. So the Apostle's argument can be stated thus: 'If God deals in that way even with those who were the "natural" branches, much more will He do so with you who have simply been grafted in to this parent trunk.' What matters is the trunk and the relationship to the trunk. That is the picture, and if we remember that it is a picture, the meaning becomes plain.

Once more I quote 1 John 2: 19: 'They went out from us, but they were not of us.' They had been in the Church as members, but John says, 'If they had been truly of us, they would no doubt have continued with us: but they have gone out, in order that it might be made manifest that they were not all of us'. So, to return to John 15, verses 2 and 6, the branches that are thrown out and burned in the fire have never borne any fruit at all; because they have never been regenerate they could not bear fruit. They are like those Israelites who were not truly of Israel; they are like the false prophets described at the end of the Sermon on the Mount. So, even if we were to grant that John chapter 15 not only deals with function and ministry but with profession of faith also, it still does not teach the possibility of 'falling from grace' or deny the final perseverance of the saints.

Twenty-five

*

And we know that all things work together for good to them that love God, to them who are the called according to his purpose.

For whom he did foreknow, he also did predestinate to be conformed to the image of his Son, that he might be the firstborn among many brethren.

Moreover whom he did predestinate, them he also called: and whom he called, them he also justified: and whom he justified, them he also glorified.   Romans 8: 28–30

In our consideration of the objections to the doctrine of the final perseverance of the saints we come now to the famous 'warning passages' which, perhaps, above all others, cause people to stumble. I have noticed that those who write books against this doctrine always fall back upon these warning passages. This is very true of the book by Shanks to which I have referred, published in the U.S.A. In other words, I suggest that there is little that can be said against the doctrine of the final perseverance of the saints, apart from the warning passages. They constitute the main difficulty in the exposition and elucidation of this great doctrine. The best known examples of these warning passages are the three parables found in chapter 25 of the Gospel according to Matthew – that of the ten virgins, the talents and the final judgment of the nations. These three parables as I hope to show really teach the same truth.

As we come to examine these warning passages I can but suggest lines of interpretation. The first principle, and it is absolutely essential, is that we bear in mind the state and condition of the visible Church. For some curious reason little is heard these days about the visible Church and the invisible Church. But it is a vital distinction much emphasized by the Protestant Reformers and their followers. For our immediate purpose we must realize the truth concerning the state of the visible Church. I have already touched on this in dealing with the statements in John 15, verses 1-11, because it helped us at that point. We return to it because I am more and more convinced that the difficulty people feel with respect to the doctrine of perseverance is due to the fact that they have not grasped this point about the state and the condition of the visible Church. I refer not only to the visible Church today, but still more to the visible Church in New Testament times. As we read the New Testament, and especially the epistles written to churches, we have to remember that they were written, not to the invisible, but to the visible Church – 'the church which is at Corinth', 'the church at Ephesus' and so on. This is of vital importance because it reminds us that we must not assume that every individual who belongs to a church is of necessity a Christian. There is such a thing as what the Puritans used to call 'a temporary faith'. It might equally well be described as 'a false profession'. The Puritans wrote much about the false professor, and differentiated between the false professor and the true professor of the Christian faith. I would add that you can also have a false or a spurious experience. All religious experiences are not of necessity produced by the Holy Ghost. The Bible itself is full of warnings with regard to this matter; yet many are prone to think that any experience produced in a church building must be a true experience. But that is a real fallacy. We have our Lord's authority for saying that, when the 'seed' is being sown, the devil is always present and watching and ready to do his nefarious work. So we must always hold in our minds this broad principle that the 'warning passages' deal with the 'visible' Church, and that the visible Church, like the children of Israel journeying from Egypt to Canaan, is a 'mixed multitude'. If we assume that all church members are Christian we have no hope of understanding these passages.

This principle is taught in many places in Scripture. Let us start with what is stated in this Epistle to the Romans, chapter 2, verses 28 and 29. The Apostle has been arguing about the relationship of the Jews to the Law. The mistake the Jews made was to think that, because the Law had been given to them, somehow or other it meant that they had satisfied the Law. This was their foolish mistake. So the Apostle says in verse 17, 'Behold, thou art called a Jew, and restest in the law, and makest thy boast of God, and knowest his will, and knowest the things that are more excellent, being instructed out of the law; and art confident that thou thyself art a guide of the blind, a light of them which are in darkness, an instructor of the foolish'. But then comes the question, 'Thou therefore which teachest another, teachest thou not thyself? thou that preachest that a man ought not to steal, dost thou steal?' In other words a mere knowledge of the Law is nothing in and of itself; the question is, What is a man's relationship to it in terms of obedience? It is precisely the same, says the Apostle, with circumcision: 'Circumcision verily profiteth, if thou keep the law; but if thou be a breaker of the law, thy circumcision is made uncircumcision.' And then he sums up the argument in verses 28 and 29, by saying, 'For he is not a Jew that is one outwardly'. The fact that a man had been circumcised when he was an infant does not mean that he is of necessity a Jew. 'He is not a Jew which is one outwardly, neither is that circumcision which is outward in the flesh: but he is a Jew, which is one inwardly; and circumcision is that of the heart, in the spirit, and not in the letter; whose praise is not of men, but of God.' Essentially the error of the Jews was that they assumed that they were in a true relationship to God because they had been born 'of the seed of Abraham', because they had been circumcised, because they were people to whom the Law of God had been given. The Apostle's argument is that all this may be true of a man, but it does not constitute him a Jew. That which makes a man a Jew is not something outward, but inward. It is not in the flesh, but in the spirit.

This same principle is equally applicable in the Church. Nothing is so fatal as the notion that because we were born of Christian parents, and were christened when we were infants, and have been brought up in the Church and 'received into membership', therefore we are Christians. Nothing has done so much harm to true Christianity as just that teaching, and everything that encourages such an error. Another illustration of this truth is found in the 9th chapter of this Epistle in verse 6: 'For they are not all Israel, which are of Israel.' All the Jews were 'of Israel'. They were not Gentiles, they belonged to Israel, they were in the company of Israel; yet 'they are not all Israel, which are of Israel'.

Indeed Paul proceeds to say in chapter 11 that at that time the true Israel was but a very small remnant, 'a remnant according to the election of grace'.

All this is equally true of the Christian Church; it is a principle which is absolutely essential to our understanding of these particular warning passages. It is because of this truth that we have so many exhortations in the Scriptures to 'examine ourselves'. Take, for instance, 2 Corinthians 13: 5: 'Examine yourselves, whether ye be in the faith; prove your own selves. Know ye not your own selves, how that Jesus Christ is in you, except ye be reprobates?' Remember that the Apostle was writing, not to the world, but to church members, to professors of the Christian faith. The Corinthians are exhorted on these lines because of the possibility of their having a temporary faith or a false profession. The same is found in essence in 1 John 4: 1: 'Beloved, believe not every spirit, but try the spirits whether they are of God.' This pertains more in the realm of experience, but it is the same principle; we must not assume that because we have had certain experiences in the realm of the Church that they are of necessity produced by the Spirit of God. We have to 'prove' these spirits. There is a 'spirit of antichrist', a false spirit, that can simulate the Christian experience and thus mislead us. Such exhortations become necessary because of the state and condition of the visible Church. It always has been, and always will be a 'mixed multitude' until the Church is finally purified and glorified. So keep that in mind as you examine these difficult passages.

We move on from that to the second principle which is closely akin to the first. The primary purpose of the warning passages is to test our profession of faith in order that we may know whether it is true or spurious. They are given to us to warn us against the terrible danger of having a false profession. The ultimate test is as to what kind of fruit our profession produces. It is not difficult to make a profession of faith, but the question is, Is it real? So the test, ultimately, is the test of continuance, the test of conduct and behaviour, the test of 'fruit'. We do not make ourselves Christians, we do not become Christians by anything that we do. It is not even our belief that makes us Christians, still less our good works. It is the action of the Spirit of God in us that makes us Christians. No man can make himself a Christian whatever he may do. But while we emphasize all this, we have nevertheless to emphasize the other side also. We must test our belief, our profession, by the various tests which can prove its genuineness, namely, continuance, endurance, and certain fruits and results which necessarily accompany it. In a word, the controlling test at this point is the famous statement in the Epistle of James, 'Faith without works is dead' (James 2: 26).

Faith and works must always go together. 'We are justified by faith only'; 'faith without works is dead'. The business of the 'warning passages' is to help us to discover whether we have this living faith, and not merely a dead faith, a temporary faith, or a false profession. James, far from contradicting Paul, is saying the same thing in a different way; he is supplementing Paul. The danger facing the man who sees the faith principle is to say, 'As long as I confess that I believe, nothing else counts and everything is right with me.' Such a man needs to be warned against a faith unaccompanied by works. The Scripture always maintains a perfect balance; it warns us against the two false extremes at one and the same time.

The principle works in this way. Take, for instance, the statement we have been examining in 1 Corinthians 9: 27. If you did not accept the exposition I then suggested, you are driven to this, that the Apostle teaches that what really saves him, and keeps him, is his own action in 'keeping under' his body. But if you say that, you are back to 'justification by works', which is the exact opposite of what the Apostle teaches in all his writings. It has to be one thing or the other. If we are responsible at any point for our salvation, then the credit must be given to us. But that is not the Apostle's teaching. He uses the expression in 1 Corinthians, as we have seen, in order to show how he did his work efficiently and effectively, and in order to shew that his faith was genuine.

In the light of this let us now examine the parables in Matthew, chapter 25, starting with the 'Parable of the Ten Virgins'. Many who read that parable say, 'Here we have a picture of ten virgins, all professed members of the Christian Church; and yet we are told that at the end five were outside and not admitted to the feast. In other words, it is clearly possible to be a Christian and yet at the end to be outside, to be lost. The parable is commonly interpreted in this way. But let us now examine it in the light of the principle I have been laying down. The wrong interpretation arises because people are ensnared by the fact that up to a certain point these two types of virgins are apparently identical. At first one cannot see any difference between them. We are told, incidentally, that five of them were wise, and five were foolish, but by just looking at them you could not tell that that was so. What you see is a group of ten girls, and each one has a lamp. Not only so, they were all awaiting entrance to a wedding feast. They were all waiting for the same bridegroom to arrive. Furthermore, they all slumbered and slept. All these things were true of every single virgin; and for that reason many assume that we are looking at an account of ten people who are true Christians. But alas, we find at the end that five of them are refused admission to the feast, and the conclusion is drawn that you can be in a state of grace, and yet, by falling out of grace, you can be everlastingly lost. But such an interpretation at once presents us with a complete contradiction of the plain teaching of Scripture elsewhere.

The difference between the two groups is that the five wise virgins took oil with them, and the others did not. What does that mean? In the usual interpretation you are driven to say that it means 'justification by works'; because these five virgins were wise enough to take sufficient oil with them they were saved. The others failed to do so, and therefore they were lost. So the five wise virgins saved themselves by their action in taking the oil! That is unadulterated teaching of 'justification by works'; that you become a Christian because of the good life you are living, because of your good works. The Apostle wrote the Epistle to the Romans in order to give the lie to such teaching. The whole object of the Epistle is to show that that is the ultimate error. Nothing that a man can do can justify him in the sight of God. The Apostle 'concludes' at the end of chapter 3 'that a man is justified by faith', and by faith alone. So to accept this interpretation of the parable of the ten virgins makes Scripture contradict Scripture.

What then is the point of the parable? Using the key of the truth concerning the visible Church, you find ten people in the visible Church. They appear to be identical; they are members of the same church, and they go to the same meetings, they seem to do everything in exactly the same way. Nevertheless there is an essential difference between them. It is that the profession made by the foolish virgins is entirely selfish and self-centred.

They desire the privileges, they want the pleasures, they want to be present at the feast, they want to welcome the bridegroom and to enjoy the banquet and all that is involved in it. But, obviously, they are not interested in anything else. They have their eye only on the benefits. This attitude is always the chief characteristic of the 'false professor'. There are people who do not want to go to hell, they desire to be blessed by God, and they want to enjoy the blessings that God offers His people. They covet all the blessings of Christianity, but they do not want anything else. They do not want any responsibilities; they are not truly interested in the faith, they do not think it out. That was why five of these virgins were 'foolish'. They pick up their lamps and rush off, but then they feel tired and fall asleep; and so, when the bridegroom comes and the call is given, they suddenly find they have no oil. They have never troubled about that! They were 'foolish', thoughtless!

Many such people are found in the Christian Church. They do not like searching sermons. They say that they make them feel uncomfortable, and doubt whether any one should preach in that way. They claim to be Christians, they assume that they are Christians. That was precisely the trouble with the foolish virgins – assuming, taking things for granted! Not making sure, not examining, not 'proving their own selves', not 'examining their own selves' as the Scriptures tell us to do! Their attitude is, 'I am a Christian, I have always been a Christian, I have never done anybody a wrong.' Such people always resent anything that searches and examines them; they merely want to enjoy the benefits as did the foolish virgins. The parable of the ten virgins is nothing but a test of profession. People may be banded together in the visible Christian Church, and yet there may be this vital difference between them, the difference between wisdom and folly, or a living and a dead faith. The true Christian is always concerned and careful; he examines himself, and wants to make sure of his position; the other does not. He is in the realm of the Church, but is quite careless, and not really interested in truth.

Such, it seems to me, is the only adequate interpretation of this matter of the oil. It must not be interpreted as 'works', but it can and must be interpreted as a concern about the things in which you are involved and the benefits you are enjoying. This is a useful test, and a very comforting test. If you are concerned and worried and troubled about your salvation, I would say to you in the name of God, and on the basis of this parable, that you have very good presumptive evidence that you are a 'wise virgin'. But if you are heedless and thoughtless, and never examine yourself at all, and resent any call to self-examination, then I suggest very seriously that you had better examine the very foundation as to whether you are a Christian at all. 'Foolish' virgins never like such advice, they simply desire ease and benefits. This is confirmed by what our Lord says at the end of the parable: 'Afterward came also the other virgins (the foolish), saying, Lord, Lord, open to us. But he answered and said, Verily I say unto you, I know you not.' It does not mean that He did not know 'about' them, He knows all; it means that He has never known them in the sense that this word always has in Scripture – 'I have never known you, I have never been interested in you; you have never really belonged to me.' He never says that to anyone whom He has ever known. Never! That is quite impossible. But He has never known these foolish virgins, and for this reason we are exhorted at the end of the parable, 'Watch therefore!' In other words, 'Examine yourselves'.

Similar teaching is found in the second parable. Look particularly at the man who had been given the one talent. At first he appears to be like the others. He comes forward and receives the talent as they had done. There is no significance in the numbers five, two, and one. The fact is that this man received a talent in exactly the same way as the others. Hence it is very difficult to differentiate in the visible Church between true Christians and those who are merely temporary believers or false professors. But a very valuable test is suggested here. Note the attitude of this man with the one talent. His whole attitude is revealed to be entirely different from that of the others. The first two, given their talents, desire to do something for the benefit of their master. Not so the last man: 'He that received one talent went and digged in the earth, and hid his lord's money.' And later he gives the reasons for his conduct and displays that his entire attitude has been wrong. We read: 'Then he which had received the one talent came and said, Lord, I knew thee that thou art an hard man' – such is his attitude! – 'reaping where thou hast not sown, and gathering where thou hast not strawed: and I was afraid, and went and hid thy talent.' His whole attitude is one of antagonism and of fear. There is no love, no desire to please his lord. The man betrays himself; though he appears on the surface to be like the others he shows in his spirit, in his heart, in his whole attitude that he is different.

Alas, there are people in the Christian Church who call themselves Christians but who really hate God. They talk about the true Christian life being 'narrow', and when they are exhorted to holiness and sanctification they dislike it. They desire all the benefits that Christianity can give, but they feel that it is a hard life, a narrow life; it is 'against the grain'. They rebel against it, though they are church members. It is only to such people that these words are addressed, 'Thou wicked and slothful servant, thou knewest that I reap where I sowed not, and gather where I have not strawed: thou oughtest therefore to have put my money to the exchangers, and then at my coming I should have received mine own with usury. Take therefore the talent from him, and give it unto him which hath ten talents. For unto every one that hath shall be given, and he shall have abundance: but from him that hath not shall be taken away even that which he hath.' This is paradox; but the meaning is perfectly plain. This man has never really had life, he appeared to have it but what he appears to have is taken from him, and he has really nothing at all. 'And cast ye the unprofitable servant into outer darkness: there shall be weeping and gnashing of teeth.'

The third and last parable in the chapter teaches precisely the same thing. It is a picture of the great last judgment and of the two groups, the sheep and the goats. This is how the final verdict is recorded: 'Then shall the King say unto them on his right hand, Come, ye blessed of my Father, inherit the kingdom prepared for you from the foundation of the world: for I was an hungred, and ye gave me meat: I was thirsty, and ye gave me drink.' 'Then shall the righteous answer him, saying, Lord, when saw we thee an hungred, and fed thee? or thirsty, and gave thee drink? When saw we thee a stranger, and took thee in? or naked, and clothed thee? Or when saw we thee sick or in prison, and came unto thee? And the King shall answer and say unto them, Verily I say unto you, Inasmuch as ye have done it unto one of the least of these my brethren, ye have done it unto me. Then shall he say also unto them on the left hand, Depart from me, ye cursed, into everlasting fire, prepared for the devil and his angels. For I was an hungred, and ye gave me no meat, I was thirsty . . . Then shall they also answer him, saying, Lord, when saw we thee an hungred, or athirst, or a stranger, or naked, or sick, or in prison, and did not minister unto thee? Then shall he answer them, saying, Verily I say unto you, Inasmuch as ye did it not unto one of the least of these, ye did it not to me. And these shall go away into everlasting punishment: but the righteous into life eternal.'

This parable is the most frequently misunderstood, perhaps, of all the parables. The opponents of final perseverance say, 'It teaches quite plainly that what saved the first group was that they had done these good deeds unto our Lord's brethren. Because of that they are saved and are praised.' But it cannot be so, for such an interpretation takes us back to 'justification by works' again. The Son of God need never have come into the world, need never have died on the Cross on Calvary's hill, if that is true. The interpretation cannot be that we save ourselves by doing good. Scripture becomes nonsense if that is true. What then is the meaning? We already have the key to the parable. The interesting thing to note about the people who are praised is that they had done all this good without knowing it, without realizing it. They ask 'When did we do this?' That is the great characteristic of the true Christian. The man who is not a Christian, the false professor, always boasts of his works. The 'goats' say in effect, Had we but known, we would have done this, and thereby we would have put ourselves right.

The true Christian never speaks in this way. He is never aware of what he does. He thinks nothing of what he does, he feels he is an 'unprofitable servant'. The chief characteristic of the action of the Christian is that it is unselfconscious. The Christian produces 'fruit', and is not aware of doing so. The attitude of the Christian to himself is, How little I am doing! how little do I love the Lord! He is aware of his deficiencies and defects, and he is amazed when the Lord praises him or chooses to smile upon him, and to embrace him. But the false professors demand it as a right, and are always ready to defend and to justify themselves. The way to tell the difference is to test the spirit. 'Justification by works' must not be introduced at any point. The three parables in Matthew 25 are meant to test the professors in the Christian Church. At the outset the people in each parable all appear to be identical, but on careful examination we find a very real difference. 'Examine yourselves,' says the Apostle, 'prove your own selves', make sure that you belong to the right group.

A second and notable illustration of this is found in the Book of Revelation, chapter 3; verse 5, in the letter of the Lord to the church at Sardis: 'He that overcometh, the same shall be clothed in white raiment' – then the statement, 'and I will not blot out his name out of the book of life, but I will confess his name before my Father, and before his angels.' The opponents of the doctrine of perseverance emphasize the negative statement, 'I will not blot out his name out of the book of life.' That implies, they argue, that there are others whose names will be blotted out of the book of life. Also, 'I will confess his name before my Father, and before his angels' implies that there are others in whose case He will not do so.

Let me show that this is a false and totally unjustifiable interpretation. We start by asking whether there are any other references to this 'book of life', and to names in the book of life, in this same Book of Revelation? We find in the 13th chapter, verse 8: 'And all that dwell upon the earth shall worship him' – that is, one of the beasts – 'whose names are not written in the book of life of the Lamb slain from the foundation of the world.' There are some authorities who say that the verse should be read thus: 'All they that dwell upon the earth shall worship him, whose names are not written from the foundation of the world in the book of life of the Lamb slain.' In other words, they argue – and there is a great deal to be said for it, although in my opinion it cannot be proved one way or the other – that it does not mean that the Lamb was slain from the foundation of the world, but that the names are written in the book of life from the foundation of the world. If I had to choose one or the other, my choice would be the second.

Again, in chapter 17, verse 8, we read: 'The beast that thou sawest was, and is not; and shall ascend out of the bottomless pit, and go into perdition: and they that dwell on the earth shall wonder, whose names were not written in the book of life from the foundation of the world.' There is nothing here about the Lamb slain. It is an unambiguous and clear statement to the effect that the names were written in the book of life from the foundation of the world.

The last reference is in chapter 21, verse 27: 'And there shall in no wise enter into it anything that defileth, neither whatsoever worketh abomination, or maketh a lie: but they which are written in the Lamb's book of life.' Only those whose names are written in the Lamb's book of life will be admitted into the heavenly Jerusalem.

There is but one deduction to draw from the verses I have quoted and it is that the names are written in the Lamb's book of life before the foundation of the world, a truth that is exactly parallel with the statement made in Ephesians 1: 4: 'Blessed be the God and Father of our Lord Jesus Christ who hath blessed us with all spiritual blessings in heavenly places in Christ; according as he hath chosen us in him before the foundation of the world.' The Lord's people were chosen before the foundation of the world, and their names were then written in the Lamb's book of life. The only names put into the book are the names of those who were chosen, and both acts were performed before the foundation of the world. Obviously this is an action taken on the basis of God's 'foreknowledge'.

The conclusion we must draw is that, if it is possible for anyone's name to be blotted out of the book of life, God must have been mistaken when He wrote it there. If you interpret 'foreknowledge' as meaning only that God knows everything that is to happen beforehand, then if He has put anyone's name in the book of life and later has to blot it out, it means that He could not have known that they were going to fall. In both cases the position becomes ridiculous and impossible.

But notice, further, that the statement is a negative one, not a positive one. There is no statement in the Scripture anywhere that anyone's name will be blotted out of the book of life. All we are told here is this: 'He that overcometh, the same shall be clothed in white raiment; and I will not blot his name out of the book of life.' In other words what we have here is the figure of speech known as 'litotes', which means that a statement is made negatively in order to give emphasis to it. A perfect example of this is found in Romans 1: 16: 'I am not ashamed of the gospel of Christ', says the Apostle. Actually he means that he is very proud of it. He has just been saying, 'I am a debtor both to the Greeks, and to the Barbarians; both to the wise and to the unwise. So, as much as in me is, I am ready to preach the gospel to you that are at Rome also. For I am not ashamed of the gospel of Christ.' He is not apologizing for the gospel but rejoicing in it. It is a negative used to supply a positive emphasis.

This manner of speaking is said to be the great characteristic of the Englishman, who delights in understatement. It is not confined to the English. It is a characteristic also – I think members of the medical profession would agree with me in saying – of most patients. When the doctor asks the patient whom he has been treating, 'How are you?' the patient is very fond of saying, 'I am no worse, thank you'. That is litotes, and that is what we have in Revelation 3: 5: 'I will not blot his name out' – Of course I will not! The Lord is praising the kind of person in view, but He puts it in that dramatic manner in order to give it additional emphasis.

I add that as an extra argument to show how unthinkable the other explanation is. The ultimate argument is the one I have already given, namely, that, on any showing, if God has put a name into the book of life before the foundation of the world and later has to erase it, He has no foreknowledge in any sense; for He would never have put it there if He had known what was later to happen.

I say once more, as I have said several times in dealing with this matter, that we must take time with the Scriptures and not jump to conclusions. Then, remember the central fundamental doctrines. Never arrive at an interpretation that queries 'justification by faith only', because if you do so, you are already wrong. Then come back and take another look at the statement; also, take Scripture with Scripture and you will find that Scripture will lead you.

There are yet other passages for us to examine before we round off this argument concerning the glorious doctrine of the final perseverance of the saints. The 'warning passages' are really for our comfort and consolation when properly understood. Those who misinterpret them are generally those who are troubled and unhappy. They are designed by God to keep us from straying, and to ensure that His purpose to make us conformable to the image of His Son shall be perfectly carried out.

Twenty-six

*

And we know that all things work together for good to them that love God, to them who are the called according to his purpose.

For whom he did foreknow, he also did predestinate to be conformed to the image of his Son, that he might be the firstborn among many brethren.

Moreover whom he did predestinate, them he also called; and whom he called, them he also justified: and whom he justified, them he also glorified. Romans 8: 28–30

There are two main reasons why I am dealing with the doctrine of the final perseverance of the saints in such a detailed manner. The first is that we may all enjoy the positive value of this doctrine. That is certainly my main interest in it; and I am sure that it was the Apostle's main interest. In other words I am moved by a pastoral interest; not a mere intellectual interest. Primarily this is a pastoral matter; for it emphasizes the importance of having an assurance of salvation and of knowing that a believer's salvation cannot suddenly be lost at any moment. It is implicit and inherent in the whole notion of assurance that it should continue. You cannot be 'assured' of something which may be lost at any moment. It is therefore vital to a true enjoyment of the Christian salvation that we should be clear about this great doctrine. I am not concerned primarily to defend it; I am interested in it because of what it does for us. God has revealed it to us in order that, as His children, we may enjoy the fruits of His grace, and of His dealings with us through our blessed Lord and Saviour.

My second and subsidiary pastoral reason for handling it in such detail is that the passages which we are considering, and which seem to militate against this doctrine, are of all passages in the Scripture those that most frequently cause distress and trouble to God's people. In other words, I have a positive reason and a negative one; the positive being that there is no more glorious doctrine than this; and the negative, that the devil attacks us strongly at this point because of its great importance. He holds many of God's children in a state of captivity because of their failure to understand the meaning of some of these passages.

With regard to the 'warning passages' I have been asked why I did not refer to the statement found at the very end of the Book of Revelation, chapter 22, verse 19, where we read: 'And if any man shall take away from the words of the book of this prophecy, God shall take away his part out of the book of life, and out of the holy city, and from the things which are written in this book.' My answer is that it is generally agreed that the translation found in the Authorized Version is not correct at this point. It should not read 'the book of life', but the 'tree of life'. I was concerned to deal only with passages that referred to the 'book of life'. But quite apart from that, what was said with regard to the other passages is as applicable here as it was there.

We must also glance at our Lord's words to the seventy disciples when He sent them out to preach and to cast out devils. We are told in Luke 10: 17–20 that when the disciples came back they were elated and full of boasting, saying 'even the devils are made subject unto us'. And our Lord said to them, 'In this rejoice not that the devils are subject unto you, but rather rejoice because your names are written in heaven'. There, instead of saying that our names are in the book of life He says that our 'names are written in heaven'. And as we have seen, if your name is once written there it is permanent, otherwise God's omniscience and foreknowledge are meaningless.

We must now look at two other passages to which I have already referred. I can say definitely after some 35 years of pastoral experience that there are no passages in the whole of Scripture which have more frequently troubled people and caused them soul agony than the passage in Hebrews 6: 4–8, and the corresponding passage in Hebrews 10: 26–29. Large numbers of Christian people are held in bondage by Satan owing to a misunderstanding of these particular statements. I do not say that these are the two most difficult passages in the Bible – I do not regard them as such – but I do assert that they are the passages the devil seems to use most frequently in order to distress and to trouble God's children.

In Hebrews 6: 4–8, we read, 'It is impossible for those who were once enlightened, and have tasted of the heavenly gift, and were made partakers of the Holy Ghost, and have tasted the good word of God, and the powers of the world to come, if they shall fall away, to renew them again unto repentance; seeing they crucify to themselves the Son of God afresh, and put him to an open shame.' And in Hebrews 10: 26–29: 'For if we sin wilfully after that we have received the knowledge of the truth, there remaineth no more sacrifice for sins, but a certain fearful looking for of judgment and fiery indignation, which shall devour the adversaries. He that despised Moses' law died without mercy under two or three witnesses: Of how much sorer punishment, suppose ye, shall he be thought worthy, who hath trodden under foot the Son of God, and hath counted the blood of the covenant, wherewith he was sanctified, an unholy thing, and hath done despite unto the Spirit of grace?'

First, let us consider the wrong explanation and exposition of those two portions of Scripture. It is the view which says, 'Here we have plain, clear, explicit teaching that it is possible for someone who has been truly Christian to fall away altogether and to be finally reprobate'. I came across another false explanation quite recently in a certain journal. A writer dealing with this passage contended that it could be explained quite simply as follows: that the author of the Epistle to the Hebrews was not dealing here with Christians at all in any sense, but was dealing simply with the unbelieving Jews to whom the gospel had been preached, but who would have nothing to do with it. He felt that he was thereby safeguarding this doctrine of the final perseverance of the saints by saying that Hebrews 6 has nothing whatsoever to do with Christians. But I regard this also as a false exposition. I cannot possibly accept it for the reason that the letter is addressed to members of churches. The whole assumption of the entire Epistle is that it is written to those who belonged to Christian churches.

Furthermore, the terms which are used in describing these people will not admit of such an explanation. I cannot believe that the people described here in these terms are people who have never had anything to do with the faith and with the gospel, and have rejected it from the beginning, and have remained entirely unaffected by the gospel as unbelieving Jews. We are told certain things told about them here which make that view quite impossible. As I am going to show, they are not Christians; but they are certainly not unbelieving Jews who have never had anything to do with the gospel. Verse 9 of itself is sufficient to prove that we are certainly in the realm of the Church here for it runs, 'But beloved, we are persuaded better things of you, and things that accompany salvation, though we thus speak'. The entire matter is dealt with in terms of the profession of the Christian faith.

An interpretation that has been put forward frequently by writers and preachers in the Christian Church is the argument that depends entirely upon the word 'If' at the beginning of verse 6: 'It is impossible for those who were once enlightened, . . . *if* they shall fall away, to renew them again unto repentance.' According to this exposition the little word *if* solves the problem. The argument runs thus: The Epistle is not saying that anyone ever does, or has done, or ever will do this. All the author is saying is purely suppositional, and it is, of course, impossible. But if anyone really did act in this way, then he would become 'reprobate'. The supposition is merely for the sake of argument, the thing itself is quite impossible and cannot happen. Thus they feel that the solution to the problem is found in the word *if*.

But that explanation must be rejected for the reason that there is no 'if' in the original. It is, once more, a matter of translation. I believe that the translators of the Authorized Version introduced the 'if' for a very good reason. They were men who believed in the infallibility of the Scripture, and its unique inspiration; they were fine evangelical men and also theologians who believed in the doctrine of the final perseverance of the saints. And at this point their theology obviously governed their translation. The particular theological views of the translator or translators always tend to govern the translation. That is abundantly clear in the multiplicity of modern translations. There is no such thing as 'pure' scholarship. The translators of the Authorized Version believed in the final perseverance of the saints, so, in order to safeguard the doctrine, they inserted the little word 'if'. But it should be 'And'. 'It is impossible for those who were once enlightened, and have tasted of the heavenly gift, and were made partakers of the Holy Ghost . . . *And* falling away . . .' Not 'If they fall away', but, '*And* falling away'. So we must reject this second explanation also. I confess that at one time I myself used it but it is quite inadmissible. You do not get over the difficulty by saying that the statement is purely hypothetical, a supposed impossible case introduced in order to bring out the truth. The 'if' is an importation in the interest of the doctrine; and must be rejected because it involves arguing in a circle. An argument should be linear not circular; otherwise you can prove anything, and you rely upon what you are trying to prove in order to prove it.

What then is the correct exposition of this passage? As we have seen with respect to other statements the way to approach it is to look at it fairly and examine the terms, and avoid jumping to conclusions. 'It is impossible for those who were once enlightened.' 'Enlightened' is taken to mean that they were fully regenerate. But it does not say so. All the term says is that at one time they had received the light of the gospel, and in using the word 'received' I mean that they had heard it and had said that they believed it. Here again some people say that there is another simple explanation, namely, that in New Testament times the word 'enlightened' was used concerning all those who were baptized. So 'enlightened' just means, 'It is impossible for those who were once *baptized*'. While there may be something to be said for that view, we need not accept it. It cannot be proved one way or the other. It is a fact, quite definitely, that the baptized were referred to as the 'enlightened'; the two terms were used synonymously and interchangeably. But it seems to me to be quite unnecessary to fall back on that explanation. It is helpful, of course, because all must agree that baptism does not guarantee that a man is truly Christian. The fact that a man has been baptized as an infant does not prove him to be a Christian; and the fact that a man has been baptized by immersion as an adult does not prove that he is a Christian. The baptized may be Christians, or they may not be Christians. However, I hold the view that it is much more likely that the author is referring here to people who say that they believe the teaching of the gospel. 'Once enlightened.'

The second term is 'tasted of the heavenly gift'. Here again we have an interesting but difficult expression. Some of the authorities, and among them even the great Dr John Owen, the Puritan, seem to me to attempt to get out of the difficulty by a way that is not legitimate. Dr Owen suggests that the trouble with these people was that the truth only went into their mouths. They never swallowed it, they only 'tasted' it. They 'flavoured' it and 'savoured' it, but it never went further than the mouth. If they had thoroughly masticated it and swallowed it, all would have been well. I cannot accept that suggestion, because it puts me into difficulty immediately with the statement of the same author in chapter 2, verse 9: 'But we see Jesus, who was made a little lower than the angels for the suffering of death, crowned with glory and honour; that he by the grace of God should *taste* death for every man.' It is the same word exactly as in this passage in the 6th chapter; and I cannot accept an explanation that detracts from the value of 'tasting death for every man'. Our Lord did not merely taste death in His mouth, He experienced death in a manner that none other will ever be called upon to know. He knew it in all its fulness, in all its bitterness, in all its terrible character. We must not reduce the value of this word. A further reason for rejecting Owen's view is the use of the word in 1 Peter 2: 2 and 3: 'As newborn babes, desire the sincere milk of the word, that ye may grow thereby: if so be ye have *tasted* that the Lord is gracious.' We must give this word its full value. We cannot therefore solve our problem in that way.

The word translated 'tasted' stands for 'being acquainted with', and even 'experiencing'; and we must give it that value here. These people have experienced something of the 'heavenly gift'. We must not be too dogmatic about the meaning of the expression 'heavenly gift'; there are many possible explanations. But it seems to represent all that is offered and given us by the gospel. These people had experienced something of that.

The next phrase, the most difficult of all, is, 'and were made partakers of the Holy Ghost'. This, to all who object to the doctrine of final perseverance, is quite conclusive, and can have but one meaning, namely, that these people were regenerated by the Holy Ghost. But we must examine the meaning of 'partaker'. The Scofield Bible has a very good note at this point. It very rightly points out that 'partaker' means 'going along with', and such is its meaning here. It means 'participant' or 'sharer'. It is sometimes used for an 'associate', a 'partner'. A partner is a man who goes along with another man in a business or whatever it may chance to be. So here it means that they had been 'going along' with the Holy Ghost in certain respects.

Let me illustrate what that means. Think of Saul, the first King of Israel. You remember that he received a gift which enabled him to prophesy. The saying was 'Is Saul also among the prophets?' That gift was given to him by the Holy Spirit, and we can say therefore of Saul that he was a 'partaker of the Holy Ghost'. The same is true of a man like Balaam, a hireling and a false prophet; but he by the Holy Ghost was given a certain ability. In other words the Holy Ghost for a given purpose, 'took him into partnership'. Then, coming to the New Testament, we have similar illustrations and examples. Judas, though he was 'the son of perdition', was nevertheless a 'partaker of the Holy Ghost'. Our Lord sent out certain men, Judas among them, and gave them power to preach and to cast out devils, as we have seen already in Luke chapter 10. Judas was among them, and it is clear that he had the same power as the others to cast out devils. There seemed to be no difference between him and the others. When at the Last Supper with His disciples our Lord said, 'One of you shall betray me', we are told that each one was in trouble, and each one asked 'Is it I?' Everything the others had done Judas had done, they all seemed to be identical. There is no doubt but that Judas was a true 'partaker of the Holy Ghost' in that sense. The Holy Ghost used him. He was in this kind of 'partnership', he 'went along with' the Holy Ghost for a particular function and purpose.

Another statement by our Lord Himself settles the matter finally. I have already quoted it from the Sermon on the Mount as recorded in Matthew 7: 21 and 22: 'Not every one that saith unto me, Lord, Lord, shall enter into the kingdom of heaven; but he that doeth the will of my Father which is in heaven. Many will say to me in that day, Lord, Lord, have we not prophesied in thy name? and in thy name have cast out devils? and in thy name done many wonderful works?' He does not say to them that they had not done those wonderful works; what He says is, 'Then will I profess unto them, I never knew you: depart from me, ye that work iniquity.' They were 'partakers of the Holy Ghost', but they did not belong to Him, and He had never 'known' them.

The phrase means that power had been given to them. Some say that it is a reference primarily to miraculous gifts. That is possible; but we do not of necessity have to say that. The Holy Ghost has many gifts to give us; He can 'take us along with him' in many respects. He can do so in understanding, and in feeling, and in gifts of power, and in many other ways; and still we are only 'partakers of the Holy Ghost'.

The next term is, 'tasted of the good word of God'. This seems to be a reference to an ability to follow and to understand the message and the reasoning of the Word of God, the whole content of the Scripture. The people in question had the ability to comprehend and to understand in a measure the message of the Bible. That was true even of the Pharisees. They were not only well versed in the Scriptures, they had an understanding of the Scriptures in many respects, even though, at the same time, they were guilty of a profound misunderstanding. It is possible for us to know the 'letter' of the Scripture, and to go even further. There are people who, on grounds of sheer intelligence and natural ability, having read textbooks on theology can grasp the arguments and statements, and can repeat them. They have a grasp and an understanding of them; they have 'tasted of the good word of God'.

The final phrase is that they had 'tasted the powers of the world to come', that is to say, the powers of the spiritual realm. Some expositors say that the reference is to this present age. There is much to be said for the idea that when the Epistle to the Hebrews refers to 'the age to come' it means 'the age of the gospel'. The Jews spoke about 'the age to come', 'the age of the Messiah'. There are those who argue, therefore, that this refers to the Christian era. While I believe that it includes the Christian era, I hold that it refers also to the age that is yet to come, when the Lord returns and ushers in His everlasting kingdom. Whenever there is an outpouring of the Spirit of God, as in revivals, the Church experiences something of 'the powers of the world to come'. In other words the Holy Spirit is not only 'the seal' but also 'the earnest' of our inheritance. Everything the Spirit gives is a foretaste, a first instalment, an earnest of that world to come, and its powers. These people, therefore, had had some experience of these powers of the world to come.

Let me just glance at one or two of the difficult expressions in chapter 10 before we deal with the subject as a whole. 'If we sin willingly after that we have received the knowledge of the truth . . .' This statement I have already explained; indeed it is a good way of expressing what I have already said concerning the receiving of the knowledge of the truth. It does not say that they had received the truth, but that they had 'received the knowledge of the truth' – a good explanation of the phrase 'once enlightened'. Then in verse 29, 'Of how much sorer punishment, suppose ye, shall he be thought worthy, who hath trodden under foot the Son of God, and hath counted the blood of the covenant, wherewith he was sanctified, an unholy thing, and hath done despite unto the Spirit of grace?' The difficult phrase is, 'who hath counted the blood of the covenant, wherewith he was sanctified, an unholy thing'. The opponents of perseverance give strong emphasis to these words.

There are a number of possible answers to this difficulty, including that at which we looked in connection with 2 Peter 2: 1, where the Apostle, quoting a statement from Deuteronomy 6, says, 'There were false prophets also among the people, even as there shall be false prophets among you, who privily shall bring in damnable heresies, even denying the Lord that bought them.' All it may mean is that they once claimed to believe, they once took up their position with the true believers in the 'mixed multitude' that constitutes the Church. They were among Christian people and said with all other members of the Church that they were 'saved', 'set apart' for God by the blood of Christ. But later they showed clearly that it was never really true of them. This is a sufficient explanation.

But there is another explanation, namely, that the statement should be read thus: 'counted the blood of the covenant, where-with *he* was sanctified.' This interpretation emphasizes that the 'he' does not refer to a man who claims to believe, but to the Lord Jesus Christ Himself. It is He who is 'sanctified by the blood of the covenant'. 'But', says the objector, 'how can the Lord Jesus Christ be sanctified'? Our Lord Himself answers the question in His high-priestly prayer as recorded in John 17: 'For their sakes I sanctify myself' (v. 19). It means that He 'sets Himself apart' for this work that He is going to do as our great High Priest. The High Priest under the old dispensation was sanctified by the blood that was put upon him. So the Lord Jesus Christ was sanctified for His work by the blood that was upon Him, and it was His own blood. Neither of these interpretations can be proved. In terms of language it can be either; but surely if we take the whole tenor of Scriptural teaching we must agree with those who say that the 'He' who was sanctified is none other than the Lord Jesus Christ Himself.

Thus we have looked at the particular terms of these statements in Hebrews, chapters 6 and 10. The important thing to notice is that all these terms taken together have a definite limit to them. Nowhere are we told that these people were 'born again', that they were regenerate; nowhere are we told that they have been justified; nowhere are we told that they have been sanctified; nowhere are we told that they have been sealed by the Spirit; nowhere are we told that they have been adopted into God's family. I emphasize this for the reason that when references are made to true believers it is always the case that the terms 'justified' and 'sanctified' and so on, are used. Take examples to prove the point. In 1 Corinthians, chapter 6 beginning at verse 9, we read: 'Know ye not that the unrighteous shall not inherit the kingdom of God? Be not deceived: neither fornicators, nor idolaters, nor adulterers, nor effeminate, nor abusers of themselves with mankind, nor thieves, nor covetous, nor drunkards, nor revilers, nor extortioners, shall inherit the kingdom of God. And such were some of you.' But you are no longer people who can be thus described, says Paul. Why so? What does he say about them? Does he say 'You were enlightened, you have tasted of the heavenly gift, you have been made partakers of the Holy Ghost, you have tasted the good word of God, and the powers of the world to come'? No! what he says is this: 'But ye are washed, but ye are sanctified, but ye are justified in the name of the Lord Jesus, and by the Spirit of our God.' Or take what Paul says of believers in Ephesians 1:13: 'In whom also, having believed, you were sealed with that Holy Spirit of promise.' The believer is said to be 'justified', to be 'sanctified', to be 'sealed'. 'Of whom are ye in Christ Jesus, who of God is made unto us wisdom, and righteousness, and sanctification, and redemption' (1 Corinthians 1:30). These are the terms used, but not one of them is used in Hebrews 6. What we are told about these people is not that they are regenerate, not that they are justified, not that they are reconciled to God; but that they have had certain experiences which had brought them into the Church and made them think, and made everyone else think, that they were truly Christian. They had claimed to believe the truth; they had had some remarkable experiences in the realm of the Church together with others, some indeed may even have had some of the miraculous gifts. But all that does not necessarily prove that a man is a Christian, that he is regenerate.

This is surely the only adequate explanation of the Hebrews passages, however you may regard the doctrine of the final perseverance of the saints. The people described in them were not unbelieving Jews who had never had anything at all to do with the gospel. They were Jews who had claimed to have seen the truth and to have believed it, and had been accepted into the Church. They are exactly like the people described in John's first Epistle chapter 2, verse 19: 'They went out from us, but they were not of us; for if they had been of us, they would no doubt have continued with us.' But they had been baptized, they had been received into the membership of the Church. They seemed to be truly Christian but they had never been truly Christian. It is possible for the Holy Ghost to influence us to a certain point and still leave us short of regeneration.

The history of revivals throughout the centuries supplies abundant confirmation of this fact. Whenever there is a great outpouring of the Spirit of God there are always a number of people who, as it were, are 'carried in by the tide' and *seem* to be truly Christian for a while. But you discover later that they have never been Christians at all. I have known many such instances, but one in particular comes to my mind. It is the case of a man who was quite young at the time of the Welsh Revival of 1904/5. He was a leader of the Revival in his own district, particularly among the young people. After the Revival he decided to become a minister of the gospel and went to a theological college. Very soon he was denying everything that is essential to the faith, and he is still doing so. But he had had extraordinary experiences during the Revival. The Holy Spirit can do remarkable things, can give the gift of prophecy to Balaam, to Saul king of Israel, and to many a Judas. The Holy Spirit can do many things to us short of regeneration. He can and does produce general as well as saving effects. It is a complete fallacy to imagine that an unbeliever has never been touched by the Spirit at all. These

[327]

more general influences of the Spirit are often seen in evangelistic campaigns. Many think that they have been converted who have never been converted. They find out afterwards that they have never been changed; but they thought so at the time. They claimed to have had marvellous feelings, they seemed to see the truth, everything seemed to be clear; and yet they say afterwards, 'I have nothing at all. What happened to me formerly?' It may have been nothing but a psychological experience; but it may also have been this general work of the Spirit. Whenever He is acting in great power there are always those who, as it were, are carried in, as I put it, by the tide; but they have never been Christians at all, they have never been regenerated.

I would argue that verses 7 and 8 in this 6th chapter of Hebrews really prove the whole point: 'For the earth which drinketh in the rain that cometh oft upon it, and bringeth forth herbs meet for them by whom it is dressed, receiveth blessing from God. But that which beareth thorns and briers is rejected, and is nigh unto cursing; whose end is to be burned.' There are two types of earth; the same rain falls upon both, and they both belong to the same Master. But the results are very different because the earth is very different. Remember that the writer of Hebrews uses the illustration to illustrate what he has just been saying in verses 4–6. In other words he is saying that these people have always remained natural people; they have never been spiritual, they have never been regenerate. They are like this bad type of earth that bears nothing but its own natural product, though for the time being it may appear to be fruitful. They are, in fact, like the people to whom our Lord will say, in spite of all their claims and the fact that they call Him 'Lord, Lord' and have done many things, 'I never knew you'. They have never belonged to Him at all. All these passages confirm one another; they all point the same great lesson.

This then is our conclusion, that these people have never had any vital change, they have never become regenerate, there has never been any divine life within them. They have simply been carried along for a period in this strange kind of 'partnership' with the Holy Ghost. They are like the people depicted by our Lord in the Parable of the Sower. The only ground that is of value is the last type where there is a depth of earth which brings forth fruit. So we come to the same conclusion again: it is the fruit that finally lets us know the condition. Some may think this to be a good argument for not pressing for decisions at the close of a meeting. People are often given the impression that because they 'come forward' in a meeting they are therefore regenerate and are Christians. No one is in a position to say so. To assume this to be the case is to mislead the persons themselves and the Church. Our business is to sow the seed in the power of the Spirit, knowing that it is He alone who can give the increase. When He does so, it always shows itself.

I conclude this exposition by putting the truth in the following way: What does the author of the Epistle to the Hebrews really say about people who fail to persevere? I suggest that his answer proves my contention. When he writes saying '(If) they fall away', or 'falling away', most people seem to assume that it refers to committing sins, and they claim that in chapter 10 it says so explicitly – 'If we sin wilfully after that we have received the knowledge of the truth'. Surely, they argue, such words refer to the committing of certain sins. But neither of these two passages has any reference to the committing of particular sins. The 'falling away' to which the author of the Epistle always refers is a 'falling away' from the truth! That is quite clearly and plainly the theme in chapter 6 and chapter 10. He is not dealing with conduct. He is writing about people who, once having claimed to believe the Christian message, are now denying it. They are denying the Person of the Lord Jesus Christ, they are ridiculing His shed blood on Calvary's Cross as the blood of atonement, they are turning back to the Jewish sacrifices and 'the blood of bulls and of goats and the ashes of an heifer'. This is made quite explicit in the Epistle.

The kind of person depicted is not a Christian who happens to fall into some grievous sin, whatever it may be, even including murder. That is not the theme, for even a murderer can be forgiven by God. These are not people who have committed particular sins; these are people who are denying Christ, trampling Him underfoot, regarding His blood as something cheap and profane. They are denying the essence of the Christian message, and doing so deliberately, and are pleased with themselves for doing so. Such is the theme of the Epistle, and it is the point at issue in chapters 6 and 10. As the writer has already said at the end of chapter 5 and the beginning of chapter 6, 'When for the time ye ought to be teachers, ye have need that one teach you again which be the first principles of the oracles of God . . . Therefore leaving the principles of the doctrine of Christ' – and 'principles' here means elementary principles, the first beginnings of the gospel of Christ – 'let us go on unto perfection; not laying again the foundation of repentance from dead works, and of faith towards God'. The writer is saying that if a man goes back upon, and denies the fundamental principles of the gospel, he has nothing more to say to him. There is nothing to say to such a man except the very thing he has rejected. He has nothing further to say to people who, having claimed to understand the gospel, then go back to Judaism. All he can do is to keep on telling them about the Lord Jesus Christ, about His death upon the Cross, and the atonement. If they do not believe his message, he has no further message to give them. Such is the meaning of this passage.

When the writer of Hebrews says, in chapter 6, that, if they 'fall away', it is 'impossible to renew them again unto repentance' – and that he can do nothing more for them – he is even saying that they can do nothing more for themselves. But he does not say that God the Holy Spirit cannot. There is still that possibility. They cannot do it, he cannot do it, but it does not shut out the other possibility. Let me say this, that if anyone reading these words has ever denied this truth, but now hates himself or herself for having done so, and wants to believe it, I assure you that that is the work of the Holy Spirit within you. If ever a man wants to believe this truth it is always the work of the Holy Spirit; for the natural man never receives it, the carnal mind is 'enmity' against it. Any man who ever desires to receive it, and who is grieved and sore vexed by his unbelief, can be quite sure that the statement in Hebrews chapter 6 has nothing at all to do with him. All the writer is saying is that when people go back on these first principles and do not want to have anything to do with them, but reject them and take pride in doing so, and in treating them with contumely and scorn, then what he says in chapters 6 and 10 is applicable to them. But it is not applicable to those whose greatest desire is to believe and to grow in knowledge, even though they may have fallen into grievous sin. Such *can* renew themselves to repentance.

We are now in a position to state the purpose of these warning passages, and do so in a threefold way. In the first place, this is one of God's ways of keeping us from presumption and Antinomianism. The danger is to regard these doctrines intellectually and to say, 'What I do does not matter'. The answer is 'Faith without works is dead'. These great passages, I repeat, are given to warn us against presumption, mere intellectual belief, and the terrible sin of Antinomianism.

Secondly, this is God's way of ensuring our perseverance. It is by warning us that He keeps us to the narrow way. When the Christian tends to become slack he suddenly reads one of these statements and is terrified. God also accomplishes this through His chastisements – 'Whom the Lord loveth he chasteneth'. God's way of keeping His people is to warn them and to punish them, as the 12th chapter of this Epistle reminds us. The same truth is taught in 1 Corinthians, chapter 11, in connection with the Communion Service. Because of the failure in their lives the Apostle says, 'Some are weak, and some are sickly among you, and some sleep'. He does not say that they are lost; but that because these are the Lord's people He intends to bring them to the final glory. He will do so by terrifying them with these passages, by chastising them, by punishing them, even sending sickness sometimes in order to keep them, and in order to preserve them. It is God's way therefore of ensuring the perseverance of His saints.

God has yet another way, which is mentioned in 1 Corinthians 5 : 4–5 in connection with the man in the Church at Corinth who was guilty of a terrible sin. He is to be treated in the following manner: 'In the name of our Lord Jesus Christ, when ye are gathered together, and my spirit, with the power of our Lord Jesus Christ, (to) deliver such an one unto Satan.' Paul does not mean that he is completely lost and hopeless, and going to hell. No! – 'to deliver such a one unto Satan for the destruction of the flesh, that the spirit may be saved in the day of the Lord Jesus'. They are to 'hand him to Satan', not to destroy him, but to bring him to his senses. When he will not listen to the warnings, when he is headstrong in his Antinomianism, Paul hands him over to Satan. Satan will deal with him, perhaps in or through his body, but he will lead him to suffering in some form. The purpose and object of this is that the man's spirit may be preserved. That is how the final perseverance of the saints is effected. It is a very strange way, but it is one that is clearly taught by the Apostle.

The final proof of the correctness of our interpretation is that the only people who are ever troubled by these two passages in the Epistle to the Hebrews are Christian people, God's saints, and no one else. The false believer is never troubled by them. If he had been troubled, he would not have continued to be a false believer. The real trouble with the false believer is that he always believes that everything is well with him. He claims to have believed God, therefore he does not need to be searched or examined. He never examines himself, and is never worried about his soul. The false believer never doubts whether he is a Christian at all. Whenever anyone tells me that he (or she) is worried about his (or her) soul's salvation, I always say, 'You are a believer, for you would not be worried if you were not'. False believers are never worried. They say, 'Lord, Lord, have we not done this, that, and the other?' They may be very active and busy persons in the church; but they are never worried, never troubled, and they dislike preaching that disturbs and causes them to examine themselves.

The proof of the soundness of our interpretation is, I repeat, that the only people who are troubled by these passages are the saved, the children of God. God uses that very trouble to preserve them. It will drive them nearer to Him, it will help them to hate sin more than ever, it will lead them to pray that they may know the sealing of the Spirit in all His abundance. So if you are worried and troubled by these passages take it as proof of the fact that you are a Christian. God's threatenings found in the Scriptures are always promises to His children.

So we come to the final conclusion, that to be concerned and troubled about the state of our soul when we read passages such as these is in and of itself evidence that we are sensitive to God's Word and to His Spirit, that we have spiritual life in us, and that our chiefest concern is to know that we are children of God. The only people who long to know, and to know for certain, are those who are the children of God. The people who belong to the world never desire this. It is only God's children who really want to know. The little child, after you have had to chastise it, generally pleads saying, 'Tell me that you love me'. The lover always wants to be told that the one he loves also loves him.

Romans 8: 28–30

Tell me Thou art mine, O Saviour,
Grant me an assurance clear

cries William Williams in one of his hymns.

Banish all my dark misgivings

he cries. In the natural realm the child invariably wants assurance and certainty: and it is the same with the spiritual child. So to be worried and troubled by these warning passages, far from proving that you are reprobate, is a proof that you are not reprobate, but rather a child of God, 'the called according to his purpose' and one who is to be 'made conformable to the image of his Son'.

Twenty-seven

*

And we know that all things work together for good to them that love God, to them who are the called according to his purpose.

For whom he did foreknow, he also did predestinate to be conformed to the image of his Son, that he might be the firstborn among many brethren.

Moreover whom he did predestinate, them he also called; and whom he called, them he also justified: and whom he justified, them he also glorified.   Romans 8 : 28–30

Having considered the main difficulties with respect to the 'final perseverance of the saints' we are now in a position to look at this great and most encouraging doctrine once more as a whole, and to adduce certain further arguments which support it. The argument of these verses alone, I suggest, is really quite sufficient in and of itself to establish the doctrine, even if we had no other Scriptures. The fact that this is God's purpose is sufficient – 'We know that all things work together for good to them that love God, to them who are the called according to his purpose'. God will make all things work together for His people's good, He will overrule everything for their good, because He has a specific 'purpose' with respect to them and, of itself, that suffices to guarantee the end. When God purposes anything He always carries it through. That is axiomatic; 'He is the Father of lights with whom is no variableness, neither shadow of turning.' Anything God proposes or purposes will most certainly be carried out. We can certainly say with Toplady,

> *Things future, nor things that are now,*
> *Not all things below nor above,*
> *Can make Him His purpose forego,*
> *Or sever my soul from His love.*

[334]

We have also seen that, whatever view you take of 'foreknowledge', the other terms of Romans 8 : 29–30 make it quite impossible for a child of God finally to be cast away. Take the word 'predestinate'. We are told that God's purpose for His people whom He has foreknown is that He has 'predestinated them to be conformed to the image of his Son'. For the sake of argument only, I maintain that whatever view you may take of 'foreknowledge' – even if you interpret it merely as prescience – you have to realize that all whom God has foreknown in that way He has predestinated to this great purpose and end of being conformed to the image of His Son. In other words God does not merely propose to forgive such people. Many go wrong at that point and think of salvation solely in terms of forgiveness; but all whom God foreknows, He 'predestinates to be conformed to the image of his Son, that he might be the firstborn among many brethren'. If God has 'known' you as one of His people, then He has taken this great decision with respect to you. He has already predestinated you to that ultimate end, to be glorified like His Son. If therefore it is possible for anyone to fall away, it means that God made a mistake when He predestinated such a person to that glory. For the moment I am arguing on the supposition that 'foreknowledge' simply means that God knew that you would decide at a certain point of time to believe in the Lord Jesus Christ. On the basis of that foreknowledge He then predestinated you to this ultimate glory. So if it is still possible for you to fall away and to be lost and reprobate, then what was the point of predestinating you to this ultimate glory? It was a mistake! You cannot reconcile predestination with 'foreknowledge' even on that definition of it. It makes it quite ridiculous.

Then take the term 'called'. Granting once more, for argument's sake, that foreknowledge in this context simply means divine prescience, what we are told is that God 'calls' these people. 'Whom he did predestinate, them he also called.' We have seen that that means an 'effectual call', a call that brings people to belief and makes of them believers in the Lord Jesus Christ. But if you argue that you can depart from Him and end as a reprobate, finally cast out, then you are left once more in the same impossible position. If God knew, as He must know in His prescience, that you are going to end by denying the truth, and becoming reprobate, why did He ever call you? What is the object of giving a temporary effectual call to those who, He knows, are finally going to be reprobate? That leads to sheer confusion, not only intellectual confusion but confusion from every conceivable standpoint. It makes the work of God utterly chaotic. We must always remember that it is God who does each one of these things; so you are left in the position that God had 'called' these people to belief quite pointlessly. It leaves you with a contradiction concerning the mind and purpose of God.

The same argument applies in the case of the term 'justified'. Justification is the act of God. It means that God 'declares' that we are just, and that He regards us as just because He has imputed to us the righteousness of our Lord and Saviour Jesus Christ. There is no suspicion of a suggestion anywhere that is conditional. It is an act, a declaration by God. He justifies 'the ungodly' (Romans 4: 5). He does not justify us because of our state and condition; He does it in spite of that state and condition. But if there is a possibility that a believer may finally fall away, then God has made an error in declaring such a person to be just. Surely, once more, there would be no purpose in the making of such a declaration concerning the righteousness of this person if God knows that subsequently he is going to fall away. It is to introduce an element of confusion and chaos into God's planning and activity which the whole Bible proclaims to be an utter impossibility, and totally inconceivable. God acts always in every realm in a manner which is, above everything, orderly. His ways are always perfect in every respect. The very idea of being 'temporarily justified' is not only foreign to the whole of biblical teaching but also to our understanding of the being and nature of God. God does not go back on His decisions; God does not 'repent' in that sense. When the word 'repent' is used in the Scripture with respect to God, you will always find in such cases that God is using an anthropomorphism; He is speaking as if He were human in order to teach a lesson to the people. God does not change, and cannot change, by His very nature. His purposes therefore are for ever 'sure'.

And finally, even if we were to grant, for the sake of argument, that it was possible for a justified person to fall away – I do not grant it, I cannot grant it, but concede it momentarily as a supposition – the next word clinches the entire argument. '. . . whom he hath justified, them he hath also glorified.' We have seen that the tense used by the Apostle is the aorist tense – it has already happened. If God has foreknown us as people who are going to be Christians, then, according to the Apostle, He has *already* glorified us. Glorification does not belong to this life and this world; it belongs to the next world, to the life that is yet to come. So glorification cannot possibly be a temporary condition. It applies to our mortal bodies; they will be glorified when we are fully conformed to the image of His dear Son. This is beyond time, beyond the grave, beyond anything that we can do in this world; and the argument is that those whom God has foreknown He has already glorified. You cannot reconcile 'falling from grace' with that fact. How is it possible for such a person finally to fall away?

You cannot believe what is taught here about 'foreknowledge', on any explanation of that word, and still say that it is possible for a true believer to fall away. Every single term used makes that completely impossible. In other words this statement constitutes an unbreakable chain, each link of which is unalterably joined to the next and there is no room left for falling away at any point.

But we need not step at this point. There is complete confirmation of all that I have asserted in many other statements that are made concerning believers; not about temporary believers, but about those who truly believe in the Lord Jesus Christ. As we look at these statements we shall see that the cardinal error into which many tend to fall is to think of ourselves as Christians in terms of our believing and our 'holding on', instead of looking at ourselves in the way in which Scripture always presents the position to us. This is the ultimate cause of most of our troubles. There has been so much emphasis upon 'decision', 'receiving', 'yielding', 'being willing', and 'giving ourselves' that salvation is regarded almost exclusively in terms of our activity. Whereas as we see in these three verses – without going any further – the emphasis in Scripture is always on the other side, the God-ward side, and that we are saved ultimately in the life of the Lord Jesus Christ. That, as we have seen, is the great emphasis in the 5th chapter of this Epistle. Anyone who has grasped the teaching of that crucial chapter should find no difficulty here. The statements in chapter 8, verses 28–30, are an inevitable consequence of the teaching of that chapter. There the Apostle was laying the foundation, and here we have a kind of coping-stone. In chapter 5, verses 9 and 10, he says, 'Much more then, being now justified by his blood' – that is to say, by the blood of the Lord Jesus Christ – 'we shall be saved from wrath through him'. Having started the chapter with the words, 'therefore being justified by faith, we have peace with God', he emphasizes in verse 9 that that has been accomplished for us by the death of Christ, 'by the blood of Christ'. The argument then is that if we are now 'justified by his blood', how much more shall we be brought completely to that final glory destined for us. Paul states the certainty in terms of our being saved 'from wrath', which means from the final judgment. We have nothing to fear, we are saved 'from wrath'. And it is 'through him'. Justified by His blood, and ultimately saved through Him.

Verse 10 in chapter 5 expounds the matter in greater detail. 'For if, while we were enemies, we were reconciled to God by the death of his Son, much more, being reconciled, we shall be saved by his life.' We suggested that a better translation is 'in his life'. His death upon the Cross for us, even while we were enemies, has reconciled us to God. Then it follows of necessity, and by a logical inevitability, that if He has reconciled us to Himself by the death of His Son, He will save us completely 'in' the life of that Son. But what I would emphasize chiefly is that it is 'in' the life of Christ that this is going to happen to us. It is not in the realm of 'my faith', 'my holding on' – I am in an entirely new realm, that of God's activity.

From that certain other things also follow inevitably. The Christian is already 'dead to sin'. That is the argument of chapter 6. The Apostle starts by asking, 'What shall we say then? Shall we continue in sin, that grace may abound?' He answers 'God forbid. How shall we that are dead to sin, live any longer therein?' I quote the Authorized Version, but the true translation is, 'God forbid. How shall we, that died to sin, live any longer therein?' As Christian people we have 'died' to sin. The aorist tense is used; it is something that has happened once and for ever in the past. When Christ died on the Cross, we died with Him. That is the argument from verse 2 to verse 6 in the sixth chapter. 'Know ye not that so many of us as were baptized into Jesus Christ were baptized into his death? Therefore we are buried with him by baptism into death: that like as Christ was raised up from the dead by the glory of the Father, even so we also should walk in newness of life. For if we have been planted together in the likeness of his death, we shall be also in the likeness of his resurrection: knowing this, that our old man was crucified with him.' That is the best translation – 'our old man was crucified with him'. It has happened. The idea that the Christian is an 'old man' who is holding on by faith is an utter denial of the Scripture. That old man has gone, he is 'dead', finished with, buried with Christ; he is no longer in existence.

The argument continues from verse 8 onwards. 'Now if we be dead with Christ, we believe that we shall also live with him: knowing that Christ being raised from the dead dieth no more; death hath no more dominion over him' – and not over us, therefore, because of this relationship. 'For in that he died, he died unto sin once: but in that he liveth, he liveth unto God. Likewise reckon ye also yourselves to be dead indeed unto sin, but alive unto God through Jesus Christ our Lord.' In verse 18 the Apostle repeats it all again, 'Being then made free from sin, ye became the servants of righteousness'. There is only one conceivable explanation of all this; it means that we are dead to the 'realm' and the 'dominion' of sin. It does not mean that we are sinless, it does not mean that we cannot fall into sin; but it does mean that whereas, until our conversion, we were under the dominion of sin and Satan, we are no longer in that condition. It is because many do not realize this that they talk about the possibility of 'falling away'. They will persist in thinking of 'my decision', 'my believing', 'my abiding'. But we must not think of these things in that way; it is but childish thinking. The truth is that we have 'died unto sin', we have finished with it, we no longer belong to that realm.

But in the third place, Paul proceeds to say that we are also 'dead to the law'. He says in verse 14, 'For sin shall not have dominion over you, for ye are not under the law, but under grace'. This vital change has taken place in the Christian. All who are not Christians are 'under the law'; but the Christian has finished with it, he is dead to the law, and is now 'under grace'. The early verses of chapter 7 are given exclusively to a further exposition of that statement. 'Know ye not, brethren, (for I speak to them that know the law,) how that the law hath dominion over a man as long as he liveth?' An illustration follows: 'For the woman which hath an husband is bound by the law to her husband as long as he liveth; but if the husband be dead, she is loosed from the law of her husband. So then if, while her husband liveth, she is married to another man, she shall be called an adulteress: but if her husband be dead, she is free from that law; so that she is no adulteress though she be married to another man.' Next comes the application: 'Wherefore, my brethren, ye also are become dead to the law by the body of Christ.' The death of Christ has separated us from our union with the Law. We are dead to the law by the death of Christ, 'that we should be married to another, even to him who is raised from the dead, that we should bring forth fruit unto God'. The result of this is next stated: 'For when we were in the flesh, the motions of sins, which were by the law, did work in our members to bring forth fruit unto death. But now we are delivered from the law, that being dead wherein we were held; that we should serve in newness of spirit, and not in the oldness of the letter.' Nothing could be more explicit or clearer than that! We have been entirely delivered from the Law; and therefore there is nothing left that can condemn us. As an inevitable consequence it is impossible that we should become reprobate. So Paul says in the 1st verse of chapter 8, 'There is therefore now no condemnation to them which are in Christ Jesus'. We are in the realm of grace, this entirely new relationship. The 'old man' has gone once and for ever; he died with Christ; 'our old man is crucified with Christ' (Romans 6: 6). What a vital statement that is! He cannot come back because he has died and been buried with Christ. We can never die again because we are in Christ. I am no longer an 'old man' but a 'new man', and as a 'new man' I can never be reprobate, it is a sheer impossibility.

Is it not extraordinary that we fail to grasp these great terms and realize their meaning and significance! It is because we are so anxious about 'our part' that we get into this state of intellectual confusion. The old man has gone; and has gone for ever. We have finished with the Law, we have finished with every form of condemnation. And to make it doubly certain, it has happened to us as the result of God's action. It is God who has crucified us with Christ. 'I am crucified with Christ' says Paul to the Galatians (chap. 2: 20). We did not perform the action, it was the Father who did it. 'God hath made him to be sin for us, who knew no

sin; that we might be made the righteousness of God in him'
(2 Corinthians 5 : 21). We are in this entirely new realm, and it is
impossible for us to return to the old realm, for we are where
we are as the result of the action of God.

But there is yet more to be considered. We turn our attention
to the new birth, which is suggested in Romans 8: 2: 'For the
law of the Spirit of life in Christ Jesus hath made me free from
the law of sin and death.' Many are in trouble simply because
they do not realize the truth concerning the new birth and
regeneration. Of course, if you ask them as from a catechism,
'Do you believe in the new birth?' they would say, 'Yes, certainly!'
But somehow or other, though they believe it intellectually, they
seem to forget all about regeneration and rebirth when the devil
attacks them. The danger is to think of salvation as if it were
only a matter of forgiveness, and of our deciding for Christ,
and taking up the Christian life. We must learn to think of it in
an entirely different manner as the action of God. Nothing is more
glorious than the doctrine of the rebirth; and this is obviously
the work of God in us through the Spirit. We do not give birth
to ourselves, we are not reborn because we believe. We believe
because we are reborn; and rebirth means that God puts a new
principle of life into us. 'You hath he quickened', says the Apostle
in Ephesians 2: 1, 'who were dead in trespasses and sins.' God
'quickens' us, puts new life into us, puts this new principle into
us. Or, to take another term, the Christian is a 'new creation'.
The God who created man at the beginning creates us who are
Christians, anew. 'If any man be in Christ, he is a new creature
(a new creation): old things are passed away; behold, all things are
become new'. God brings to birth a new being, a new creature.
Is that but temporary? If it were to be only temporary, then I
ask with reverence, why does God ever do it at all? If God knows
that I am going to be finally reprobate why does He bring me to a
birth at all? It means, again, either that God has made a mistake
concerning me in giving me this new life and this new birth,
or He lacks the power to keep me and to help me. Thus you
are driven to conclusions which are monstrously impossible.

Again, in this 8th chapter of Romans, consider verses 5–10:
'For they that are after the flesh do mind the things of the flesh;
but they that are after the Spirit the things of the Spirit' (the
Christian is no longer 'after the flesh', he is 'after the Spirit').

'To be carnally minded is death; but to be spiritually minded' (as is the Christian) 'is life and peace. Because the carnal mind is enmity against God: for it is not subject to the law of God, neither indeed can be. So then they that are in the flesh cannot please God. But you are not in the flesh, but in the Spirit' – this great change has taken place; the Christian is an entirely new being, no longer in 'the flesh', but 'in the Spirit' – 'if so be that the Spirit of God dwell in you. Now if any man have not the Spirit of Christ, he is none of his.' (The man who does not have 'the Spirit of Christ' may well be a temporary believer, he may give the impression that he is a Christian; but he has never been such. The man who has the Spirit of God and of Christ in him is the Christian.) 'And if Christ be in you, the body is dead because of sin; but the Spirit is life because of righteousness.' And then the argument follows: 'If the Spirit of him that raised up Jesus from the dead dwell in you, he that raised up Christ from the dead shall also quicken your mortal bodies' (verse 11). Because the Spirit is in you the redemption of your body is inherently guaranteed.

The doctrine of the rebirth in and of itself, it seems to me, should be sufficient to settle this matter of final perseverance once and for ever. If to be a Christian only means that for the time being you believe in Christ, and therefore you are forgiven, but that your final deliverance is contingent upon your holding on, then there would be a possibility of a 'fall from grace'. But that is not the position. A man who is a Christian has already been 'born again'. He is no longer 'in the flesh', he is 'in the Spirit'. He has finished with the Law, he is dead to the whole realm and dominion of sin and Satan, he is in this entirely new position. God has given him this new gift of life; and to believe that such a man can finally fall away is to believe that all that God has done can suddenly be undone, that God's own creative act can be undone. It is a terrible and monstrous suggestion!

We must cease to put our emphasis upon what we do. What we do follows what God has done. 'We are his workmanship, created [anew] in Christ Jesus unto good works, which God hath before ordained that we should walk in them' (Ephesians 2: 10). God's Word gives us the right order. We do not maintain our position by our good works at any point. He has made us, we are His workmanship, and He has created us anew in Christ Jesus in order that [with the object and intention that] we should do these good works, and always, of course, 'to the praise of the glory of his grace'. If it is possible for such people to fall away, then God's work has failed, God's workmanship is imperfect. Such a suggestion is impossible!

I am stating these arguments in an ascending scale; and the last great argument is what we are told about ourselves in terms of our union with Christ. It has already been introduced in the Epistle in chapter 5, verses 9 and 10. 'Much more then, being now justified by his blood, we shall be saved from wrath through him. For if, when we were enemies, we were reconciled to God by the death of his Son, much more, being reconciled, we shall be saved in his life.' This goes even beyond the new birth and regeneration. It is what the Apostle works out in detail in his 5th chapter from verse 12 to verse 21. That is basic, and, as I have said, chapter 8 is nothing but an extension of that. There we find the key to it all. We can summarize the argument thus: we were all by nature 'in Adam', united to him, and what Adam did applied to all of us. Verse 12: 'Wherefore, as by one man sin entered into the world, and death by sin; and so death passed upon all men, for that all have sinned.' Adam was our representative, and when he sinned we all sinned with him, and became involved in the consequences of his action. But the amazing and glorious truth, says Paul, is that if you are a Christian you are no longer 'in Adam', you are now 'in Christ', this 'new man' who is the beginning of a new humanity. We are dead to Adam. The 'old man' means the man that was in Adam. The man I was in Adam is dead, I am a new man, and my new man is the man that is 'in Christ'. We are united to Him, we are in Him, in His life; what we are told about Him becomes true of us. Such is the argument worked out, as we have just seen, in chapter 6. We are involved in His death, we are involved in His resurrection. We are 'planted' with Him, united to Him, and all that has happened to Him has happened to us. That is how my old man died, that is how I am risen, and so on. As a Christian I am not merely forgiven, I am 'in Christ', I am a part of Christ, I am united to Him. This same Apostle puts it in this way in the 1st Epistle to the Corinthians, chapter 6, verse 17, 'He that is joined to the Lord is one spirit'. He is 'one spirit' with the Lord.

To see it stated in a similar irrefutable manner look at the statement in Ephesians 2 : 6. Paul has been reminding the Ephesians of what has happened to them. While they were 'dead in trespasses and sins, God quickened them together with Christ'. And then the Apostle proceeds to make this amazing statement: 'And hath raised us up together, and made us sit together in heavenly places in Christ Jesus.' He is not saying that this is to happen to us in the future, he is asserting that it has happened to us already. As certainly as they had been 'quickened' they are now 'seated in the heavenly places in Christ Jesus'. God has done all this. Because we are 'in Christ', at this very moment we are not only sitting in our homes or in a church building, we are seated in the heavenly places in Christ Jesus. So if you reject the doctrine of the 'final perseverance of the saints' you must believe that it is possible for a man to be seated in the heavenly places in Christ Jesus at one stage in life and yet to fall from that position and to be cast into hell! God does not work in that manner! God does not make mistakes! I may appoint a man to a post and discover afterwards that I have made a mistake, and I may have to dismiss him. But God is not man. To believe that one of God's children can finally fall away is to believe that it is possible and conceivable that God should actually raise a man to the heavenly places in Christ and yet for that man finally to be lost. To believe that that can happen is proof that we have no conception of what 'the heavenly places' represents, and of what is meant by being 'in Christ', to be joined to Him indissolubly, to become a part of Him. The Church is 'the body of Christ', and we are all 'members in particular'. This is an absolute, indissoluble unity. We are not only forgiven, we are not merely believers; God has done these things to us. He has not only given us new life, He has 'united' us to Christ; we are bound to Him by bonds that are indissoluble. Everything we are told about the true Christian makes it impossible for him ever to fall away. The only people who can fall away from the Church are those who are temporary believers, false professors, people with just an intellectual, temporary faith. But the man who is given new life, who is a 'partaker of the divine nature' and who is 'in Christ', by definition of terms cannot fall away. Other arguments remain which substantiate this yet further.

Twenty-eight

*

And we know that all things work together for good to them that love God, to them who are the called according to his purpose.

For whom he did foreknow, he also did predestinate to be conformed to the image of his Son, that he might be the firstborn among many brethren.

Moreover whom he did predestinate, them he also called: and whom he called, them he also justified: and whom he justified, them he also glorified.   Romans 8: 28–30

We can sum up what we have found so far by saying that everything we are told about the Christian, about the believer, carries with it this inevitable implication of 'the final perseverance of the saints'. This same truth has been stated clearly by our Lord Himself in the statement in John chapter 5, verse 24, 'Verily, verily, I say unto you' – that formula always indicates a grave statement and can be translated as 'Amen, Amen' – 'he that heareth my word, and believeth on him that sent me, hath' – not 'he shall have' – 'hath everlasting life, and shall not come into condemnation; but is passed from death unto life'. That one statement should really be sufficient in and of itself to prove final perseverance. It gives two clear assertions – the believer *has* everlasting life; the believer will not be condemned. But to make the truth yet more sure, the Lord gives us the additional statement, 'he is passed from death unto life'. The New English Bible translation is almost amusing in this instance. It starts by saying, 'Anyone who gives heed to what I say and puts his trust in him who sent me, has hold of eternal life'. They do not seem to be very sure at that point. They do not say that he has it, which is what the original says; they say he 'has hold' of it. That might give the impression, of course, that he may lose his hold of it. But then they proceed to translate '[he] does not come up for judgment', and they end with a statement that is even stronger than the Authorized Version translation – '(he) has already passed from death to life'. They introduce the word 'already' which is not in the original, making the statement even stronger. But it comes to the same thing. The statement is unequivocal and can only carry one meaning.

Our Lord's words should be enough, but knowing the difficulty some people find in accepting this doctrine and indeed their opposition to it, I must produce some further arguments. My next argument is based upon the nature of the Christian Church. A chief cause of trouble is to think of salvation too much and too exclusively in individual terms. The whole emphasis today is upon the individual aspect. That is right up to a point; we should all enjoy assurance of personal salvation; but to regard the whole of salvation in exclusively personal terms, and in terms of the benefits we desire to enjoy, is not Scriptural. Individually as Christians we are parts of a greater whole. The Apostle Paul says in 1 Corinthians 12: 27: 'Ye are the body of Christ, and members in particular.' We are individual, particular, members, but not in isolation. The New Testament places great emphasis on the doctrine of the Church as 'the body of Christ'. As members of the Church we are not a loose collection of odd individuals bearing some relationship to the Lord. That is quite a wrong conception. We must think of ourselves as being 'members in particular' of a body which is one complete whole.

The analogy of the body brings out the truth very clearly. A finger has no meaning in and of itself; it is a part of a whole. It is a part of a hand, and a hand is not something in itself; it is joined to a forearm and to an arm and so to the whole body. This is something which we are prone to forget. The exclusively personal, individual, emphasis can be most misleading and damaging in experience. Believing that they can come in an individual manner to Christ certain people believe also that they can fall out of that individual relationship to Christ. And this is largely because they fail to understand and to remember the New Testament emphasis upon the Church as a 'body', and that the individual aspect is only an aspect of the whole, not something complete in and of itself. The Apostle emphasizes it repeatedly in the 12th chapter of the First Epistle to the Corinthians, as, for instance in the 13th verse, in which we are told that we are baptized 'by' the one Spirit 'into' this one body of Christ. A similar statement is found in Ephesians 4: 4 where we read: 'There is one body, and one Spirit, even as ye are called in one hope of your calling.' Earlier in that Epistle Paul says: 'And [God] hath put all things under his feet' – the feet of the Lord Jesus Christ – 'and gave him to be the head over all things to the church, which is his body, the fulness of him that filleth all in all' (1: 22–23). Again in Ephesians 4: 15–16 we find a very clear statement: 'Grow up into him in all things, which is the head, even Christ, from whom the whole body fitly joined together and compacted by that which every joint supplieth, according to the effectual working in the measure of every part, maketh increase of the body unto the edifying of itself in love.' So that as you think of yourself as an individual Christian you must be careful to remember always that you are not in isolation. We are all a part of this body of Christ, the church. The whole is more than a mere summation of the parts, and we are parts of the whole.

The importance of this is seen when we realize that the Lord Jesus Christ did not die primarily for us as individuals, He died for His people. Of course it is true that He has died for you as an individual – thank God for that – but He died for you as an individual because you belong to the people for whom He has died as a body. Let me substantiate this contention. In the 17th chapter of John's Gospel it is taught in almost every verse. Here are some of the crucial statements. Take the 2nd verse: 'As thou hast given him power over all flesh, that he should give eternal life to as many as thou hast given him.' God has given Him a people and He has come to give eternal life to these same people. Verse 6: 'I have manifested thy name unto the men which thou gavest me out of the world: thine they were, and thou gavest them me: and they have kept thy word.' Again verse 9: 'I pray for them: I pray not for the world, but for them which thou hast given me; for they are thine.' God has given Him a people, and all that He does He does for these people. Once more in verses 10 and 11: 'All mine are thine, and thine are mine; and I am glorified in them. And now I am no more in the world, but these are in the world, and I come to thee. Holy Father, keep through thine own name those whom thou hast given me, that they may be one, as we are.'

The 17th chapter of John has been appropriated by the so-called Ecumenical Movement today as a statement of their position. It is one of the greatest statements of ultimate unity, but not in the sense in which they use it. The unity of which our Lord speaks is not a mere coming together of all who call themselves Christian; it is a unity of the same character as the unity between Father and Son – 'that they may be one, even as we are one'. And it is in that sense that *we* are to be one. Verse 12: 'While I was with them in the world, I kept them in thy name: those that thou gavest me I have kept and none of them is lost, but the son of perdition; that the scripture might be fulfilled.' The end of the 'son of perdition' was prophesied and known. Judas Iscariot was never truly one of them. But the Lord continues his prayer: 'And for their sakes I sanctify myself, that they also might be sanctified through the truth. Neither pray I for these alone' (vv. 19–20). He adds these words lest anyone might think that He was speaking these things of the apostles alone. He was speaking of them primarily, but He says that his prayer not only relates to them, but to 'them also which shall believe on me through their word' – and that comes right down to us today – 'that they all may be one; as thou, Father, art in me, and I in thee, that they also may be one in us' (v. 21). That is union; it is the union of believers, their union with Christ, and His union with the Father. It is not a mere union of organizations or of denominations; it is essentially an organic, spiritual union. Verse 22: 'And the glory which thou gavest me I have given them; that they may be one, even as we are one.' There is nothing higher than that! The unity between the Father and the Son is akin to the unity that exists between those who are members of His body and who are all joined to Him, the living Head. Our Lord continues: 'I in them, and thou in me, that they may be made perfect in one; and that the world may know that thou hast sent me, and hast loved them, as thou hast loved me' (v. 23). God's love to us as Christians is the same as His love to His own Son. If His love to us can somehow be frustrated, then His love to the Son can be frustrated in the same way. The very idea is impossible! These are His own words in verse 24: 'Father, I will that they also, whom thou hast given me, be with me where I am; that they may behold my glory, which thou hast given me: for thou lovedst me before the foundation of the world.' The whole of that chapter is in reality an exposition of this doctrine of the final perseverance of the saints. Our individual perseverance is guaranteed by the fact that we are parts of that body of people for whom our Lord came into the world that He might save them. We are among those whom God had given to Him.

The Apostle Paul repeats this teaching in Ephesians 5 from verse 25: 'Husbands, love your wives, even as Christ also loved the church, and gave himself for it.' A similar statement was made by the Apostle in his farewell address to the elders of the church at Ephesus as recorded in Acts 20, verse 28, where, referring to the Church, he says, 'which he hath purchased with his own blood'. Christ died for the Church, and He died for us individually as we are parts of the Church. The Apostle, in the same 5th of Ephesians, proceeds to say: 'He gave himself for it; that he might sanctify and cleanse it with the washing of water by the word, that he might present it to himself a glorious church, not having spot, or wrinkle, or any such thing; but that it should be holy and without blemish.' He is referring to the Church throughout; not to a collection of individuals, but to the Church as the bride, His own bride whom He is preparing for Himself. Then comes the extraordinary statement, 'He that loveth his wife loveth himself'. How can that be? How is it true to say that a man who loves his wife is thereby 'loving himself'? The Apostle answers, 'No man ever yet hated his own flesh'. A man's wife is 'his own flesh'. So 'he nourisheth and cherisheth it, even as the Lord the church: for we are members of his body, of his flesh, and of his bones'. Here we see the relationship. We are not 'holding on to' Christ, or merely loosely attached; we are a part of Him, of His body. It is a difficult argument; 'this is a great mystery' as the Apostle himself says. Then returning to the state of matrimony he says: 'For this cause shall a man leave his father and mother, and shall be joined unto his wife, and they two shall be one flesh.' That is a sublime statement concerning marriage. But the Apostle adds: 'I speak concerning Christ and the church.' Such is the relationship between Christ and the Church: 'one flesh'; 'members of his body, of his flesh, and of his bones'. Christ died for the people given to Him, that is to say, for the Church; and nothing that belongs to the Church can therefore be lost. The intimate relationship is such that separation or falling away is quite impossible.

If we grasp this teaching, and cease to think of our salvation in an atomistic manner, it will not only help us to understand this doctrine, it will also save us from much trouble in a variety of ways. Let us ever remember that Christ died for the Church, the full, the complete Church, to redeem it and to perfect it, and finally to present it to Himself. Ultimately it will be absolutely perfect; no part will be missing; it will not be minus a finger or minus a foot. It will be 'perfect and entire', a complete whole, 'without spot, or wrinkle, or any such thing'. Such is the argument. It gives immense support to the doctrine of the final perseverance of the saints. If any of us could 'fall away' the Church would no longer be perfect; it would be a mutilated, truncated Church minus various parts and portions. The idea is quite inconceivable; and especially in the light of this great doctrine of the Church.

My next argument is that the doctrine of the final perseverance of the saints is entirely confirmed by the teaching of the Scriptures concerning chastisement. This is stated with particular clarity at certain points. For instance in I Corinthians, chapter 11, where we find teaching concerning the Lord's Table, and how to partake of the Lord's Supper: 'Wherefore whosoever shall eat this bread, and drink this cup of the Lord unworthily, shall be guilty of the body and blood of the Lord. But let a man examine himself, and so let him eat of that bread, and drink of that cup. For he that eateth and drinketh unworthily, eateth and drinketh damnation to himself . . .' (the Authorized Version reads 'damnation' but it should read 'judgment'). 'For this cause' – here we have the element of chastisement – 'many are weak and sickly among you, and many sleep.' Because they had not examined themselves and prepared themselves, he says that 'many are weak', physically weak, many are ill – 'sickly among you', and some have even died – 'many sleep. For if we would judge ourselves we should not be judged.' 'But when we are judged' (in this way, by the Lord afflicting us with weakness or sickness or even death) 'we are chastened of the Lord, that we should not be condemned with the world.' In other words, the Lord does this to His own people because they belong to Him, and He will not permit them to become involved in the condemnation of the world.

Again, in the Epistle to the Hebrews, chapter 12, verses 5 to 11, there is a notable passage about chastisement. The author writes, 'Ye have forgotten the exhortation which speaketh unto you as unto children, My son' (note the emphasis!) 'despise not thou the chastening of the Lord, nor faint when thou art rebuked of him: for whom the Lord loveth he chasteneth, and scourgeth every son whom he receiveth. If ye endure chastening God dealeth with you as with sons; for what son is he whom the father chasteneth not? But if ye be without chastisement, whereof all [sons] are partakers, then are ye bastards, and not sons.' In other words, if you are not receiving chastisement you are not a child of God at all, you are a 'bastard'. You may think that you are a child of God, but you are not, and never have been such; you are a 'bastard' and not really a 'son'. 'Furthermore we have had fathers of our flesh which corrected us, and we gave them reverence: shall we not much rather be in subjection unto the Father of spirits, and live? For they verily for a few days chastened us after their own pleasure, but he for our profit, that [in order that] we might be partakers of his holiness.' This explains why God chastises us. It is a part of His process of preparing His children for the glory He has prepared for them.

In other words, the argument from chastisement is that if we are chastised it is proof positive that we are children, because if we were not children we would not be chastised. And God chastises His children because He is preparing them to share in the glory of His Son when He appears. We therefore argue that the very employment of chastisement is a proof of the final perseverance of the saints because it is the way in which God enables them to persevere, or, to use a stronger term, 'compels' them to persevere. Because we are His children He does not leave us alone. Because we are His children He intends to bring us by various means and methods to that place which He has originally designed for us, 'conformity to the image of His Son'.

By way of illustration, take the reference to Judas as 'the son of perdition' in the 17th chapter of John's Gospel, and contrast our Lord's dealing with Judas with His dealing with Peter. The Apostle Peter denied His Lord three times, even with oaths and curses. There is nothing to be said in defence of Peter; his action was cowardly, dastardly, and inexcusable. He deliberately denied his Lord in order to save his own life. But notice the extraordinary difference in the treatment of Peter and Judas. Our Lord prepared Peter beforehand as we are told in the Gospel according to Luke chapter 22, verses 31 to 34. Our Lord tells Peter that He knows exactly what he is about to do, how he will deny Him, and so on, but He gives him this great assurance, 'I have prayed for thee, that thy faith fail not'. Our Lord is taking care of Peter. He knows Peter's weakness, He knows what is about to happen to him, He knows that he will deny Him; He says, 'Simon, Simon, behold, Satan hath desired to have you, that he may sift you as wheat'. But He assures him, 'I have prayed for thee, that thy faith fail not: and when thou art converted, strengthen thy brethren.' Peter then foolishly says, 'Lord, I am ready to go with thee, both into prison and into death', but our Lord replies, 'I tell thee, Peter, the cock shall not crow this day, before thou shalt thrice deny that thou knowest me'.

Our Lord knows what both Judas and Peter are about to do, but He does not handle Judas in the same way. Judas is allowed to go his own way. He is 'the son of perdition', he has never really belonged. But Peter does belong, and therefore our Lord prays for him. He is caring for him, and He assures him even before his fall that he will be restored, and tells him to strengthen his brethren after he has been restored. Peter did not understand it; but, thank God, our ultimate salvation does not depend upon our understanding. It depends upon the fact that He holds on to us and will never let us go. We are held by Him, and not by what we do; otherwise, beyond any question we should all be ultimately lost.

A very good statement concerning the chastisement of God's children is found in Psalm 89, verses 31–34: 'If they break my statutes, and keep not my commandments, then will I visit their transgression with the rod, and their iniquity with stripes. Nevertheless my loving-kindness will I not utterly take from him, nor suffer my faithfulness to fail. My covenant will I not break, nor alter the thing that is gone out of my lips. Once have I sworn by my holiness that I will not lie unto David. His seed shall endure for ever, and his throne as the sun before me. It shall be established for ever as the moon, and as a faithful witness in heaven.' Here is mention of chastisement, and it can be very severe. The teaching in 1 Corinthians 11 is clearly that some Christian people had died because of their lack of self-examination and self-discipline. But though they are dead, they are not lost. Note the distinction. Even their death, in a sense, is a part of the chastisement that ultimately saves the soul. In the same way, in this psalm we are told, 'Nevertheless my loving-kindness will I not take from him, nor suffer my faithfulness to fail. My covenant will I not break, nor alter the thing that is gone out of my lips.' And, as we saw earlier, the teaching concerning 'handing over to Satan' in 1 Corinthians, chapter 5, is a proof of the same thing. The Christian is 'handed over to Satan' that the 'flesh' might be dealt with and corrected, and the soul saved. Chastisement is clearly one of the ways by which God preserves His people, and perfects them, and prepares them for the final glory which He has predestined for them in the Lord Jesus Christ.

Another argument to prove the same doctrine is the teaching concerning the remnant found in the Scriptures; for example, in this very Epistle to the Romans, in chapter 9, verse 29, which is a quotation from Isaiah 1, verse 9: 'And as Esaias said before, Except the Lord of Sabbaoth had left us a seed, we had been as Sodoma, and been made like unto Gomorrha.' In other words, if the Lord of hosts Himself had not left us a seed all of us would have perished. The first chapter of Isaiah is a description of the fall and failure and sin of the nation of Israel. They are left, we are told, like a tent in a garden of cucumbers; everything else has gone. And here it is quite plainly stated by the prophet, and the Apostle quotes it, 'If the Lord of hosts had not left [preserved] us a seed, we had been as Sodoma, and been made like unto Gomorrha'. It is the Lord of hosts who preserves the remnant. The remnant does not preserve itself.

In chapter 11 of the Epistle to the Romans Paul deals with the same matter in the first six verses, 'I say then, Hath God cast away his people? God forbid.' The problem is that the vast majority of the Jewish nation had rejected Christ, had crucified their own Messiah. So the question arises, 'Hath God cast away his people?' Away with the thought, says the Apostle, 'For I also am an Israelite, of the seed of Abraham, of the tribe of Benjamin. God hath not cast away his people whom he foreknew. Wot ye not what the Scripture saith of Elias? how he maketh intercession to God against Israel, saying, Lord, they have killed thy prophets, and digged down thine altars; and I am left alone, and they seek my life. But what saith the answer of God unto him? I have reserved to myself seven thousand men, who have not bowed the knee to the image of Baal. Even so then at this present time also there is a remnant according to the election of grace. And if by

[353]

grace, then is it no more of works: otherwise grace is no more grace. But if it be of works, then is it no more grace: otherwise work is no more work.' The Apostle explains how Elijah had thought in his day that he was the only true believer left, and God had told him that he was not alone, not the only one left who was faithful to God, 'I have reserved to myself seven thousand men, who have not bowed the knee to the image of Baal.' God did not say to Elijah that there were another seven thousand who were 'holding on' and who had not fallen away with the others. Not at all! 'I have reserved to myself . . .' And then, to put it still more plainly, the Apostle adds, 'Even so then at this present time also there is a remnant'. What accounts for this remnant who believed? It is 'a remnant according to the election [the choice] of grace'. As God had reserved seven thousand in addition to Elijah, He was reserving to Himself even now (in Paul's time) 'a remnant according to the election of grace'. Then, in order to make quite sure that we should be clear about the matter, and that we should not give the glory to the Jews who had 'taken a decision' to believe, Paul says, 'If it is of grace, then it is no more of works'. It is not the works of the Jews, it is not even the fact that they believe. It is of grace. 'If it is of grace, then is it no more of works: otherwise grace is no more grace. But if it be of works, then it is no more grace.' It has to be the one thing or the other. The belief of the remnant of the Jews implies no merit in them. It is all of grace, it is all according to God's election; God reserves unto Himself this remnant in Israel.

Take with that what the Apostle has said in Romans 9, verses 6 and 7, where we find another way of teaching the truth concerning the remnant: 'Not as though the word of God hath taken none effect.' Do not say that, because the whole of the nation of Israel seems to be in unbelief, all that God did in the Old Testament has been a waste of time, a frustrated effort that has come to nothing. No! 'Not as though the word of God hath taken none effect. For [because] they are not all Israel, which are of Israel: neither, because they are the seed of Abraham, are they all children: but, In Isaac shall thy seed be called.' We must not run away with the notion that all who belong to the nation of Israel are children of God. There is a true Israel within the larger visible Israel, 'They are not all Israel, which are of Israel'.

Applied to our situation today, this means that not all who

say they are Christians are of necessity Christians; they are not all Christians who are members of the visible Christian Church. God knows who are His people; and it is this 'true' Israel that constitutes the 'remnant according to the election of grace'. The teaching, then, quite clearly is that there would be no remnant at all were it not that God kept it. If God did not 'preserve' a remnant all would be 'like Sodoma and Gomorrha'. The teaching concerning the remnant always is that it is a remnant that God Himself reserves and preserves; it is 'a remnant according to the election of grace'.

How do we react to such teaching? My own reaction is, 'Thank God that it is so'. If I thought that my eternal future depended upon myself and my faithfulness, I would be of all men most miserable. God calls, God keeps, God preserves; and God will never leave us nor forsake us.

> *I grasp Thy strength, make it mine own,*
> *My heart with peace is blest;*
> *I lose my hold, and then comes down*
> *Darkness, and cold unrest.*
> *Let me no more my comfort draw*
> *From my frail hold of Thee;*
> *In this alone rejoice with awe –*
> *Thy mighty grasp of me.*

Twenty-nine

*

We know that all things work together for good to them that love God, to them who are the called according to his purpose.

For whom he did foreknow, he also did predestinate to be conformed to the image of his Son, that he might be the firstborn among many brethren.

Moreover whom he did predestinate, them he also called: and whom he called, them he also justified: and whom he justified, them he also glorified.   Romans 8: 28–30

A further general argument in confirmation of the doctrine of the final perseverance of the saints is the consideration of the position by which we are confronted if this doctrine is not true. That is always a good way of approaching any difficulty that may arise with respect to any doctrine. It is not an argument with which to start, but it is a useful confirmatory argument. The ultimate question that faces us is, What is it that keeps any Christian from falling away? If it is not what we are told here, namely, that we are 'the called according to his purpose', and that because it is His purpose He Himself keeps us from falling, well then, what is it that keeps us from falling? Consider the position of those who believe that it is possible for a regenerated, born-again Christian finally to go to perdition, to fall away from this position of being 'in Christ'. What they believe is that you have two types of Christians. One type of Christian will hold on to the truth and to the faith and will finally arrive in the glory; the second loses his hold for some reason or another, falls away, and goes to perdition. They account for the difference between these two Christians by asserting that it was the will and the desire of the one Christian to hold on, and that it was not the will and the desire of the second. The difference is entirely determined by the will and the desire and the determination of the particular Christian.

[356]

This is the only conclusion to which you can come on that supposition.

But if that were true then it would follow that such a person is stronger than Adam was. Adam was perfect and was sinless. He had complete free will, yet he chose deliberately to listen to the devil and thereby fell and produced those consequences, with which we are familiar, in himself and in all his progeny. So it follows that the type of Christian who holds on has a stronger will and determination than Adam had. But the reply may be made, 'The Christian is in a better position than Adam; he has received divine life from Christ and therefore has something beyond what Adam had. He has received new life from God in his soul, and it is this that enables him to stand in a way that Adam was incapable of.' But that argument does not help us at all, for all Christians, by definition, have received that selfsame new life. So that does not account for the difference. It cannot be the divine life that has been received because both parties possess it. We are driven to the inevitable conclusion that what keeps one Christian faithful to the Lord in the last analysis is nothing but the man's own will-power and determination. It is a natural quality, and therefore your ultimate conclusion is that what determines a man's final salvation is not regeneration at all, it is a natural strength of will and of understanding, a man's inherent power. In other words, you are driven to a conclusion which is a complete contradiction of the doctrine of grace. A man is not saved finally because of God's action in giving him new life and regenerating him. The determining factor is man's own power to hold on; some have it, and others have not. It is a natural quality, and so it is a final contradiction of the whole biblical teaching concerning salvation, and especially regeneration. That is the conclusion to which you are driven inevitably if you reject this doctrine of the final perseverance of the saints based on the purpose of God.

In other words, we arrive at the conclusion that it is the failure of the opponents of the doctrine to realize the ultimate purpose of God's plan of salvation that brings them into conflict with the doctrine. We can state it in the following way: What is the ultimate purpose of the great and glorious plan of salvation? The opposers of the doctrine will probably say: 'Oh, it is that I may be saved, that I may be forgiven and go to heaven.' But that is not a correct answer; it is not the main purpose, it is a subsidiary purpose. The ultimate object and purpose of the plan of salvation is the glory of God, the vindication of the glory and the sovereignty and the character of God. If that is not clear to us then it is not surprising if we go astray at many points. That the chief object of salvation is to vindicate the glory and the character of God is the central theme of the Bible. And because that is so, it cannot and will not fail; otherwise the devil will have defeated God.

The way therefore to look at this great matter is to face the question as to why there has ever been a plan of salvation at all. There is only one answer, it is to vindicate the character of God, the God who is the Creator of all things in heaven and earth, the God who made everything perfect, and saw that everything was 'good' and was well pleased with it. But, as we know, a fall took place among some of the highest angelic beings, the devil, Satan, and his followers. Then followed the temptation by Satan of the man whom God had made in His 'own image and likeness', which led to the Fall of man and all its disastrous consequences. But God had already planned and now He introduced the way of salvation in order that everything should be restored to its original condition. Such is the meaning of the statement we have quoted repeatedly from Ephesians 1: 9 and 10: 'Having made known unto us the mystery of his will, according to his good pleasure which he hath purposed in himself; that in the dispensation of the fulness of times he might gather together in one all things in Christ, both which are in heaven, and which are on earth; even in him.' In other words, the glory of God demands that this whole universe, the entire cosmos, cannot be left in its present fallen, evil, sinful condition; that would not be consistent with the glory of God. As to why God ever permitted evil to enter in, we do not know, we are not told, and we cannot go beyond what has been revealed. But in His own inscrutable wisdom God gave freedom of choice to the perfect creatures He had created, and that contained within it the possibility of a wrong choice. The argument then is this, that the glory of God demands and insists that that condition should not be allowed to remain. We may say with reverence that God, because He is God, must restore all He has made to its original perfection. According to Ephesians, chapter 1, verse 10, He has purposed to head up again all things in Christ, and to restore them to their original perfection and glory. It is purposed 'according to his own good pleasure', 'according to the glory of his grace'. These are the great terms the Apostle always uses when he introduces this theme. It is all being done in order to establish the character and the glory and the sovereignty of God who made all and who owns all and who is ruler over all.

It follows, therefore, that if this is the ultimate object and purpose of salvation, it is inconceivable for a moment that the result should be dependent upon our power to hold on and to persevere. To believe that is to believe that ultimately the glory of God is in our hands, and that it is our power and capacity to hold on, and to continue and to persevere, that maintains, and will finally establish, the glory of God. Regarded in that way the very idea is obviously ridiculous. We know ourselves, our frailty and our proneness to sin; we are aware of our ignorance, our smallness; we know something of the power of the devil, and all the forces set against us; and yet we are asked to believe that the ultimate glory of God rests upon some natural ability that resides in us to hold on by our own will-power. Such a supposition is not only ridiculous and laughable, it is contrary to the entire teaching of Scripture itself.

The Apostle has already stated this very clearly in the 4th chapter of this Epistle to the Romans, in the 16th verse; 'Therefore it is of faith, that it might be by grace; to the end the promise might be sure to all the seed.' It is not of works or of anything that depends upon man. It is 'of faith' in order that it might be 'by grace', the ultimate object being, that 'the promise might be sure to all the seed'. In other words, it has been so arranged that it could not be a matter of works, it could not be dependent upon man's works or man's decision or anything else of man, because then it would not be 'sure' to anyone. But it has to be 'sure', says the Apostle, and the only way to make it sure is that it should be 'by grace through faith'. This verse supplies one of the answers to those who are troubled by the doctrine of the final perseverance of the saints. Salvation has to be guaranteed, it has to be 'made sure to all the seed', whether they are Jews or Gentiles. 'Not to that only which is of the law, but to that also which is of the faith of Abraham; who is the father of us all.'

Let us work this out a little further, for I know of nothing more comforting and consoling. The plan of salvation not only cannot fail, it will not fail because the glory of God is involved in it. It must succeed. The proof of this is that the whole of salvation depends upon the Lord Jesus Christ Himself, the Son of God. The significance of that fact can be seen in the following way. Man is fallen; he has become the slave of sin. The highest pinnacle of God's creation, the 'lord of creation', he fell and everything fell with him; the ground was cursed and chaos entered. How can God restore this fallen universe? In answer, I begin by quoting what the Apostle says in chapter 6, verse 19, of this Epistle to the Romans: 'I speak after the manner of men because of the infirmity of your flesh.' The infirmity of their flesh led him to use an illustration, and I shall use an illustration for the same reason.

Think of the fallen universe; God's glory demands that this be rectified. How can He do so? Let us assume that the first possibility that occurred to the mind of God was to create another man. But that proposition would have to be rejected for this reason, that if God had made another man He could not have made a better man than Adam. Adam was perfect, sinless, completely innocent. Even God could not make a more perfect man than Adam, for Adam was made 'in the image of God'. So when God purposed and planned a way of salvation He did not create another perfect man like Adam, for that would have led to the same result, and His glory would not have been vindicated. God has to introduce a plan of salvation that cannot fail; and what He has done is the amazing thing which is at the very heart of the Christian gospel. He does send a 'second man', a 'last Adam', but this time He is not only a man, He is God's own Son. The 'Lord from heaven' becomes the 'second man', the 'last Adam'. Here is the key to the understanding of the gospel. God has acted in this way in His Son because the plan must succeed and failure must be impossible. A 'man' is not sufficient; it needs a God-man. It has to be done in human nature, but human nature alone is not enough. The human nature must be joined to the divine nature; thus we have the miracle and marvel of the incarnation, and two natures in the one Person.

This is the sole explanation of why the Son of God ever came into this world. God has acted in this way because no mere man could have taken upon himself the guilt of those who had sinned against God in Adam; it needed a God-man to do that. But the gospel does not stop at this point. It takes a God-man also to defeat the devil, and to conquer death and the grave; and beyond that, to continue to act as our high priest and intercessor and advocate in the presence of God. The Lord Jesus Christ's work for our salvation did not end upon the Cross, the application of that work is still continuing. As the Epistle to the Hebrews chapter 7 states it, 'He ever liveth to make intercession for us' and so saves us 'to the uttermost'. This means that He does not merely start the process of salvation, He continues it, and He will continue it until 'the uttermost', in other words, until we are completely glorified. Because He is alive, He is still carrying on the work of our salvation. He did not die for us and then leave us; He maintains us and sustains us. He is working in us still, and He will go on doing so through the Holy Spirit until the work terminates in our final glorification.

We must understand and realize that God's whole purpose in sending His only begotten Son into this world was to ensure that His plan of salvation could not fail. It cannot go wrong or fall short in any respect. God has chosen the people whom He has given to His Son; and the Son has said that He came into the world to do this work for them at the behest of His Father. It cannot fail; otherwise the glory of God would not be vindicated, and the devil would still be triumphant. Christ is 'the firstborn among many brethren', and, as we have seen, we are saved not only because He died for us, but because we are united to Him. We are 'in Him' and He is 'in us'. 'As thou, Father, art in me' so are we in Him and He is in us. This is the relationship that subsists between us. We are bound to Him by this indissoluble bond. God saves us in this particular way in order to make certain that His purpose could never fail, and that 'the promise' shall indeed 'be sure to all the seed'. Man could never accomplish such a work, but the God-man has come and the result is secured. It cannot possibly fail; the Lord Jesus Christ is the guarantee of its success. What matters is not our frail grasp of Him, but His almighty grasp of us!

Our Lord Himself has taught this in very plain and explicit terms in the 6th chapter of John's Gospel. I emphasize this because of the ridiculous teaching which says that this doctrine is confined to the teaching of the Apostle Paul and that it is not found in the Gospels. There are no contradictions in the

Scripture. In the Gospel of John, often described as the Gospel of love, we read in chapter 6, verse 37: 'All that the Father giveth me shall come to me; and him that cometh to me I will in no wise cast out. For I came down from heaven, not to do mine own will, but the will of him that sent me. And this is the Father's will which hath sent me, that of all which He hath given me I should lose nothing, but should raise it up again at the last day. And this is the will of him that sent me, that every one which seeth the Son, and believeth on him, may have everlasting life: and I will raise him up at the last day.' If that does not satisfy, what can do so? These are the words of the Son of God Himself. But again in the same chapter at verse 46 we read: 'Not that any man hath seen the Father, save he which is of God, he hath seen the Father. Verily, verily, I say unto you, he that believeth on me hath everlasting life' – and everlasting means everlasting. It refers not only to a quality of life, but there is the time element in addition. It means that it will last for ever. Then: 'I am that bread of life. Your fathers did eat manna in the wilderness, and are dead.' The Jews were interested in the manna that Moses had given to their forefathers; and argued that our Lord was not as great as Moses. They said, 'Moses gave us manna, what are you giving?' He replies that the bread He was offering was altogether different from the manna. 'Your fathers did eat manna in the wilderness, and they are dead. This is the bread which cometh down from heaven, that a man may eat thereof, and not die.' The argument is clear. Earthly manna could not keep them alive; but if they ate the bread that He gave, it would keep them alive, and they would never die. Note the difference between the two breads. Yet we are asked to believe that people who have received this 'heavenly manna', this 'bread from heaven', even the Lord Jesus Christ, can yet die. He says, 'This is the bread which cometh down from heaven, that a man may eat thereof, and not die. I am the living bread which came down from heaven: if any man eat of this bread, he shall live for ever: and the bread that I will give is my flesh, which I will give for the life of the world. If any man eat of this bread he shall live for ever.'

In reality there is nothing to be said in favour of any objections to this doctrine of the final perseverance of the saints. They are based on a complete misunderstanding of, or a failure to understand the glory and the greatness of the plan which God has carried out in and through His only begotten beloved Son. The Son, after He had risen from the dead, said to His disciples, 'All power is given unto me in heaven and earth'. Failure on His part is an impossibility. God's own Son is the guarantee of success. He has conquered all our enemies; and we are joined to Him. He is a 'King'; He came to establish a Kingdom; and the success of His Kingdom, thank God, does not depend upon us, it depends upon Him alone. It is the King who determines the character of the Kingdom. Charles Wesley, better in his hymns than in his polemical statements, has expressed it well in the lines:

> *His Kingdom cannot fail;*
> *He rules o'er earth and heaven;*
> *The keys of death and hell*
> *Are to our Jesus given.*
> *Lift up your heart, lift up your voice:*
> *Rejoice, again I say, Rejoice!*

'His Kingdom cannot fail.' Of course it cannot! And yet we are asked to believe that salvation depends upon us and our capacity to hold on, and that if a sufficient number of us do not hold on His Kingdom will fail. His Kingdom cannot fail because He is who He is, the Lord from heaven. What is important is the contrast between the first Adam and this last Adam, the first man and the second Man. The first Adam was 'of the earth, earthy'. The second Adam is 'a quickening Spirit'. The first Adam could give us physical being, but here is One who gives us spiritual being, who renews us spiritually and gives us eternal life. The contrast is absolute. The first Adam could not give me the spiritual life that guarantees my persistence. The 'Lord from heaven' can, and does. Hence the magnificent note of glory and of triumph in 1 Corinthians chapter 15 and especially in the closing verses: 'But thanks be unto God which giveth us the victory through our Lord Jesus Christ. Therefore, my beloved brethren, be ye steadfast, unmoveable, always abounding in the work of the Lord, forasmuch as ye know that your labour is not in vain in the Lord.'

It is thus alone that the glory of God is not only vindicated but also manifested. If this doctrine of final perseverance is not true, then, if you ever find yourself in glory, the glory will have to go to you for holding on. You, like many other people, have been given the same gift of salvation and eternal life; they foolishly did not hold on to it, but you are doing so: therefore the glory goes to you for holding on. But that is a complete contradiction of the teaching of the Scripture from first to last. No man can boast with regard to this matter. 'He that glorieth, let him glory in the Lord.' Man has nothing whatsoever to boast of. And when you and I arrive in heaven we shall realize fully that we are there, not because we held on when others gave up, but because He held on to us, and because we are in the purpose of God, and that He kept us in spite of ourselves and our weakness and waywardness. And we shall give Him all the praise and the honour and the glory. We shall see that it is His glorious plan from beginning to end, and we shall worship the Lamb, the Son of God who has done it all. He must have all the glory. Salvation is entirely His doing, and the praise and the glory must be to Him, and to Him alone.

To all this I would add a little footnote. The history of this doctrine is most interesting. You will never find an unbeliever who accepts the doctrine of the final perseverance of the saints. Unbelievers not only do not believe it, they ridicule it and pour scorn upon it. 'You are making man an automaton', they say. It is always good to believe something that the unbeliever rejects with scorn!

The same applies to those who are known as higher critics, or liberals in their theology; none of them believes in the doctrine of the final perseverance of the saints. None of those who say 'I accept this in Scripture, but I do not accept that' believes in the doctrine of the final perseverance of the saints. This is not surprising, for they only believe what they think they can understand and what tallies with their philosophy and preconceived ideas. They do not accept the revelation of the Scripture.

But the doctrine of final perseverance is not only taught plainly, as I have demonstrated, in the Scripture, it has been the sheet anchor of the noblest and greatest souls the Church has ever known. St Augustine believed this doctrine and that explains why his teaching was the one light that illuminated the darkness of so much of the dark Middle Ages. It was also the doctrine of the Protestant Reformers. Martin Luther believed it with all his soul, as also did John Calvin. The men who founded Protestantism in this country believed this doctrine, and saw its vital importance. They did not rest any longer upon the Church of Rome and her priesthood, but upon the glorious doctrine of God's sure purpose. John Knox, I need scarcely say, also believed it and taught it. It is in the formularies of the various churches—the Church of England's Thirty-nine Articles and the Westminster Confession of Faith. The great Puritan preachers of the 17th century taught it. There was but one exception among them – John Goodwin. All the others believed it, preached it and taught it. Those profound expositors of the Scriptures exulted in it and were sustained by it. Isaac Watts and Philip Doddridge, the great hymn-writers, also believed it. George Whitefield, the greatest evangelist and preacher that England has ever produced, believed it, preached it and rested upon it. All the great Methodist Fathers in Wales in that same 18th century were unanimous in maintaining it. Charles Haddon Spurgeon preached it, as all volumes of his sermons testify. He went as far as to say that he really doubted whether a man who did not believe the doctrine was a Christian at all! I would hesitate to say that, because I believe that there are some Christians who are so muddle-headed and so badly instructed that they do not think clearly. Many, I believe, like Charles Wesley, know it in experience, but when they try to think it through they become muddled and introduce their own philosophical ideas.

The fact is that throughout the centuries, with the exception of Roman Catholics, and Protestants such as Arminius and the Wesley brothers – John in particular – and their followers, there has been this great unanimity. Surely that should carry some weight with us. Many today, ignorant of the history of the Church and the history of doctrine, are not aware of the fact that until about 1860, apart from the Methodists, this doctrine was believed universally among the foremost Free Church Christian bodies in this country and by most of the evangelicals in the Church of England. I have already quoted Charles Simeon of Cambridge on this very doctrine. It is tragic therefore that during this present century, and especially at the present time among evangelical people, this is regarded as some 'strange new doctrine'. It has been the doctrine in which those who have understood the way of salvation have gloried throughout the centuries, a doctrine which they have often prized above all others. Be careful therefore, lest you classify yourself with the unbelievers who do not believe the Bible to be the Word of God, inerrant and inspired. Be careful lest you begin to insinuate your philosophy into these matters, and to pit your own little puny mind against this glorious revelation from God. Go back to the chapters from which I have quoted in John's Gospel, and remember that our Lord said that the Father had sent Him on a mission and that of all those who had been given to Him none was to be lost, and how He said with thankfulness in His high-priestly prayer that none was lost! He rejoiced that all who had been given to Him should have eternal life and that He would raise every one of them up at the last day. 'In Christ' we have already passed through judgment into life. 'There is therefore now no condemnation to them that are in Christ Jesus.'

> *Rejoice, the Lord is King;*
> *Your Lord and King adore;*
> *Mortals, give thanks and sing,*
> *And triumph evermore.*
> *Lift up your heart, lift up your voice:*
> *Rejoice, again I say, Rejoice.*

Rejoice in Him, and give Him who deserves it all the glory for your salvation from the very beginning to the very end. We have nothing in which to glory. It all belongs to Him, and to Him alone in whom the glory and the character of God are for ever vindicated, and in whose glory we shall rejoice in eternity.

Thirty

*

What shall we then say to these things? If God be for us, who can be against us?
                                                              Romans 8:31

In this verse we come to a new sub-section in the 8th chapter of this Epistle to the Romans. I use the term sub-section deliberately because, as we have seen repeatedly from the very beginning of the chapter, it really has but one great message. The Apostle states this message in a number of sub-sections all of which are linked together.

He starts this new sub-section by putting this question, 'What shall we then say to these things?' Then he proceeds to answer the question in the remainder of the sub-section, which goes on to the end of the chapter. In doing so he also winds up and puts in a different form the argument contained in the next assertion of verses 28, 29, and 30. He states it now in a negative way in order to enforce it and to make it doubly sure. At the same time he brings to a grand climax the massive doctrinal portion of this Epistle, that which began in the first chapter in verse 16. Prior to that he had been giving his customary preliminary salutations, but in verse 16 he introduces his great theme, 'I am not ashamed of the gospel of Christ: for it is the power of God unto salvation to every one that believeth; to the Jew first, and also to the Greek'. Then in verse 17 he introduces the doctrine of justification by faith only. From there on until the end of this 8th chapter he works that out in various ways, as we have seen. My contention is that at the end of chapter 8 he really completes what he principally set out to do, namely, to state fully the great doctrine of salvation. But some may say, What of the remainder of the Epistle? My reply is that chapters 9 to 11 are a kind of postscript dealing with one specific question, namely, the problem of the position of the Jews as a nation in the light of the doctrine the Apostle has been teaching. That is not a part of the doctrine of salvation as such. It is an explanation of how the particular case of the Jews fits into this great purpose, this great scheme of salvation. Chapters 12 to 16 are obviously but the practical application of the doctrine to daily life. That again is not doctrine as such, but the application of it, showing how it should be worked out in our ordinary daily life.

This closing sub-section, however, here in chapter 8 is a very important part of the Apostle's exposition of the way of salvation. Once more we observe that he handles his theme in a manner which is very typical of himself. Every man has his particular style, and in the case of the Apostle Paul it is especially obvious. One can almost anticipate what he intends to do. Here, as always, he first makes his positive statement of doctrine, putting it before us in a number of grand assertions. But he never stops at positive assertions, he always goes on to prove what he has said, and to convince the people to whom he is writing. Remember that the Apostle's primary object was always a pastoral one. We must not think of him as an academic theologian. He was an evangelist and teacher, but his chief characteristic is his pastoral interest. He was not interested in doctrine in an abstract manner; He was no mere intellectual or doctrinaire theologian, but always takes trouble to make his meaning plain and clear to all his readers. He does not content himself with a positive assertion of his principles. He states them, and then he puts them in another way in order to establish them, and to prove them. He deals with difficulties and objections; he supposes them, and then takes them up and answers them. His design always is to prove matters so abundantly to the people to whom he is writing that they will never be in trouble concerning them any more, but will rejoice in their great salvation and be ready for whatever may chance to meet them.

This is exactly what he does at this point. Having stated the proposition positively in verses 28–30 – 'We know that all things work together for good to them that love God, to them who are the called according to his purpose' – he proceeds to speak of foreknowledge, predestination, calling, justification and glorification. And next he states the proposition negatively by anticipating certain objections and difficulties that arise in people's minds with regard to these doctrines, meeting them beforehand. That is, of course, an excellent way of presenting and teaching truth. It is not popular today. The great slogan today, and especially in evangelical circles, is 'Always be positive, never be negative'. That is utterly unscriptural; it is the exact opposite of the Apostle Paul's method. If you desire people to know the truth, and to be able to withstand all the heresies and the cults that surround us at the present time, then, if you are a teacher worthy of the name, you will mention these negatives and deal with them. In doing so you will probably be charged with not having a nice Christian spirit, and with being negative. But my observation over the years is that it is the people who have not been taught the truth negatively as well as positively who always get carried away by the heresies and the cults, because they have not been fore-warned and forearmed against them.

Do not be misled by this spurious notion of 'love'. We must not only assert the truth; we must attack the evil and the false; we must 'prove' our truth and demonstrate it; and that can only be done by means of a negative. State the truth, consider the objections, answer them, and so you establish the truth yet more firmly. This is the method of the Apostle himself.

We have seen an example of this earlier in chapter 4. In the first three chapters Paul laid down positively the doctrine of justification by faith only. Then in chapter 4 he raises a problem, 'What shall we say then that Abraham our father, as pertaining to the flesh, hath found?' He devotes the whole of chapter 4 to that challenge to what he has been saying. He answers it and then proceeds further. In chapter 5 he lays down another great doctrine, and having done so he again raises objections and difficulties in chapters 6 and 7. In chapter 6: 1 we read: 'What shall we say then?' This was his customary formula, following on an assertion, meaning, What is true in the light of this? Then at the beginning of chapter 8 he starts a series of positive assertions, beginning with the resounding statement, 'There is therefore now no condemnation to them which are in Christ Jesus'.

Such is the Apostle's method and he uses it both with respect to the grand, massive sweeps of doctrine and also the more detailed aspects. All preachers and ministers should try to emulate this magisterial example. This is the way to convey the truth of God, and to bring it home to the minds and the hearts of men and women. A particularly good way of doing so is to put up a series of questions, and then deal with them one by one. The Apostle does it in striking fashion.

In this particular instance we find that he raises five or even six questions or queries concerning what he has been saying. They are presented in the Authorized Version with question marks. The first is, 'What shall we then say to these things?' The second: 'If God be for us, who can be against us?' The third: 'He that spared not his own Son, but delivered him up for us all, how shall he not with him also freely give us all things?' The fourth: 'Who shall lay anything to the charge of God's elect?' The fifth: 'Who is he that condemneth?' I propose to regard the last two as one. Then comes the sixth and final question: 'Who shall separate us from the love of Christ?' Some maintain that there is yet one more, namely, 'Shall tribulation, or distress, or persecution, or famine, or nakedness, or peril, or sword?' That, to me, is but an elaboration of the main question which is asked in 'Who [or, What] shall separate us, from the love of Christ?' Having presented the questions, the Apostle in the grand climax of verses 38 and 39 makes his ultimate assertion and asseveration of the glorious truth of the absolute security of, and the final perseverance of all believers. All objections having been answered and demolished he says, 'I am persuaded that neither death, nor life, nor angels, nor principalities, nor powers, nor things present, nor things to come, nor height, nor depth, nor any other creature, shall be able to separate us' – we who are 'the called' and so on – 'from the love of God, which is in Christ Jesus our Lord'.

For the sake of clarity of understanding it may help if we state the five questions in the form of four problems or challenges to the doctrine the Apostle has been enunciating. The first is found in verse 31 which asks, Is there any conceivable power that can prevent our arriving at that ultimate glorification? The second question asks whether there is any danger that God's love to us may undergo a change or be diminished? (verse 32). The third question, asked in verses 33 and 34, is whether someone or something may not finally convict us of sin and bring us to final condemnation? In other words, I regard as one the two questions, 'Who shall lay anything to the charge of God's elect?' and 'Who is he that condemneth?' The Apostle deals with the matter and answers it in the same two verses 33 and 34. The fourth and last challenge is, May we not fail or falter, owing to our weakness, as we face the trials and the tribulations of life? What if we should fail? This challenge Paul states and refutes in verses 35-37. Then follows the final glorious asseveration that there is nothing in any direction or from any quarter that can possibly separate us from the love of God, which is in Christ Jesus our Lord.

Let us now examine the first challenge of verse 31, 'What shall we then say to these things? If God be for us, who can be against us?' This translation, which is that of the Authorized Version, adds certain words which are not found in the original, and rightly so. The translators did so in order to clarify the meaning. The words 'be' and 'can be' are added for the sake of interpretation. They are printed in italics in order that we may know that they have been added by the translators. Such is the method of the Authorized Version translators in contradistinction to that of most modern translators. This first question arises from a challenge to the power of God. The Apostle's assertion has been that God has done everything in connection with salvation. It is God who 'foreknew' us, and therefore 'predestinated' us, and therefore 'called' us, and therefore 'justified' us, and therefore 'glorified' us. And the argument is that, because God has done so, salvation is certain. But the challenge asks whether it is not possible that some power may arise and rob us of the ultimate goal? The Apostle states that challenge in the words, 'If God be for us, who can be against us?'

But that challenge is introduced by the more general question, 'What shall we therefore say to these things?' To what does the expression, 'these things', refer? That it refers to the immediately preceding argument is beyond question; but it does not stop at that. It also refers to everything that the Apostle has been saying in this chapter. But again it does not stop at that; it also includes everything that has been said from chapter 1, verse 16. 'These things' includes Paul's entire exposition of the way of salvation. Of course he divides it into sub-sections, and we have to do so, but that is done simply for the convenience of our minds. It is ultimately one big statement, and it is vital for us to see the matter in that light. In this sub-section the Apostle is summing up God's great plan and purpose of salvation which he first announced in the 17th verse of the 1st chapter in the words, 'For therein is the righteousness of God revealed from faith to faith: as it is written, The just shall live by faith'. This is the gospel, the gospel of which he is not ashamed; this righteousness from God which is by faith; justification not by works, not by Law, but by faith in the Lord Jesus Christ only and in His perfect work on our behalf. This is argued out in the first three chapters.

The next great theme is that of our union with Christ, stated in chapter 5 and especially in verses 12–21. Paul works out the implications of this union and answers objections in chapters 6 and 7. Then in chapter 8 he shows how this is actually worked out in our experiences by the work of the Holy Spirit in us. All this, he says, is in preparation for our complete redemption, including even our bodies. Sanctification, he says, is not an end in itself; its ultimate object is not only to give us personal victory over particular sins, it is to prepare us for the glory which is coming. To Paul sanctification is an essential preliminary to, and preparation for, the final glory of believers as sons of God.

The Holy Spirit in us is also a guarantee of our sonship, and of our adoption into God's family and because of these twin blessings our ultimate salvation is certain. This is so because our sonship means that we are also 'heirs, heirs of God and joint-heirs with Christ'. Christ is already glorified; and we shall be glorified also. 'If we suffer with him that we may be also glorified together.' Even the sufferings can be used as an argument to prove that all this glory that awaits us is certain and sure. Suffering is a part of our preparation quite as much as our sanctification.

The Apostle then proceeds to tell us how the Spirit also helps our infirmities, in the matter of prayer in particular. This again is a proof of the absolute certainty of our ultimate glorification. Then we come to the great assertion beginning at verse 28 with the words 'We know'. The highest proof of our final glorification is the fact that it is God's purpose, and that it is God who has worked out this purpose in its every part, and above all in the sending of His only begotten Son into this world to live and die and rise again.

Now the Apostle pauses, as it were, and says, 'What shall we then say to these things?' At what conclusion do we arrive in the light of all this? For himself, he says, there is only one conclusion, 'If God be for us, who can be against us?' Let us follow him in his argument. 'If God be for us . . .' This 'if', of course, is not an 'if' of doubt; indeed, it is an 'if' of certainty, meaning 'since'. 'Since God is for us'; 'In view of the fact that God is for us'. 'Since God is for us, who can be against us?' Paul means, Who can be against us in the sense that they can ever rob us of our glorification, or thwart the purpose of God, or 'make him his purpose forego', or 'sever our souls from his love'? In asking 'Who can be against us?' the Apostle is not, as is the fashion of the modern cults, saying in a glib and superficial way that all is well. His is not a shallow, easy optimism; it is indeed the exact opposite. The Apostle reminds us repeatedly that there are terrible forces against us, and their might and malignity is almost indescribable. But taking them as they are, and at their worst, he asks, 'What are the forces against us if the power of this God is for us?'

The New Testament never claims that the Christian life is an easy life; and a teaching that maintains that the Christian can never be in a position in which he has no struggle, no fight, no difficulty at all, and that all he has to do is to sit back passively, is sheer heresy. There are terrible forces against us – the world, the flesh, and the devil. As Paul says in Ephesians 6: 12, 'We wrestle not against flesh and blood, but against principalities, against powers, against the rulers of the darkness of this world, against spiritual wickedness in high places.' We are faced with the devil in all his power and malignity. We must not underestimate the power of the enemy; to do so is no part of New Testament teaching. Scripture constantly urges us to face our problems in a realistic manner; it indicates no short cuts to final victory. We are faced by a powerful and subtle enemy, whom we are required to 'withstand', and there is but one way of doing so, namely, to realize that, though he is so powerful, he is as nothing face to face with the One who is on our side and who is working on our behalf. 'If God be for us' he challenges. God is the almighty God, God is the omnipotent One, God is the creator and maker and sustainer and controller of all things. He is 'Lord of all', He is from eternity to eternity, and He reigns. 'If God be for us . . . .'

This, then is something of the content the Apostle puts into his question. The comfort of the message is that this God *is* for us. We would not know Him at all if He was not 'for us'. It is He who has 'called' us and done everything for us. We would be still 'dead in trespasses and sins' were it not that He has 'quickened' us. He is interested in us, He is concerned about us in a very special way. In 'us' remember; not in everyone; only in those who are 'in Christ Jesus', those who 'love God', those who are 'the called according to his purpose'. In spite of all that is against us, God is on our side, working on our behalf. We are fighting on His side against our terrible foes.

This is the comfort that is given to us so abundantly in the Scriptures. Consider the case of Abraham, especially after he had fought the mighty enemies of his people, and of Lot in particular. After the great effort of the battle a kind of reaction set in and Abraham was afraid, but we read in Genesis 15:1: 'After these things the word of the Lord came unto Abram in a vision, saying, Fear not, Abram: I am thy shield, and thy exceeding great reward.' Do not be afraid of your enemies, says God, 'I am thy shield', standing between you and them. God 'for us'.

The same comforting truth is found in the 23rd Psalm, verse 4: 'Yea, though I walk through the valley of the shadow of death, I will fear no evil: for thou art with me; thy rod and thy staff they comfort me.' God is for us; and the mere sight of His rod and His staff is enough. Take also the 27th Psalm: 'The Lord is my light and my salvation; whom shall I fear? the Lord is the strength of my life; of whom shall I be afraid?' (v. 1). Once we realize who the Lord is, there is no-one to fear. So the psalmist continues: 'When the wicked, even mine enemies and my foes, came upon me to eat up my flesh they stumbled and fell.' The psalmist did not stumble or fall but the enemy did. 'Though an host should encamp against me, my heart shall not fear: though war should rise against me, in this will I be confident.' The source of comfort and consolation is always the same. 'For in the time of trouble he shall hide me in his pavilion.' What a place of safety! God as a fortress! No atomic bombs can in any way affect such a refuge. 'In the secret of his tabernacle shall he hide me; he shall set me up upon a rock.' No enemy can ever reach you there. The psalmist ends by saying in the last two verses (13 and 14): 'I had fainted unless I had believed to see the goodness of the Lord in the land of the living. Wait on the Lord: be of good courage, and he shall strengthen thine heart: wait, I say, on the Lord.'

For the same reason the 46th Psalm has often proved to be a bulwark for God's persecuted and afflicted saints. 'God is our refuge and strength, a very present help in trouble. Therefore will not we fear, though the earth be removed, and though the mountains be carried into the midst of the sea; though the waters thereof roar and be troubled, though the mountains shake with the swelling thereof. There is a river, the streams whereof shall make glad the city of God, the holy place of the tabernacles of the Most High. God is in the midst of her; she shall not be moved; God shall help her, and that right early. The heathen raged, the kingdoms were moved: he uttered his voice; the earth melted.' What had been so great before, melts like a morning mist the moment God utters His voice. 'The Lord of hosts is with us; the God of Jacob is our refuge.' 'Come', says the psalmist, 'look at the works of the Lord, what desolations he hath made in the earth. He maketh wars to cease unto the end of the earth; he breaketh the spear in sunder; he burneth the chariot in the fire. Be still' – stop talking, give in – 'and know that I am God: I will be exalted among the heathen, I will be exalted in the earth.' The One who commands all the hosts of heaven is with us, 'The God of Jacob is our refuge'. Then think of that phrase in Psalm 84, verse 11: 'The Lord God is a sun and shield.' What more can be desired?

Then turn to the 40th chapter of the Book of the prophet Isaiah. You who are trembling and afraid, or who feel that some power may arise and take you out of the hands of God, and cast you into final perdition, listen to verse 10 in that chapter: 'Behold, the Lord God will come with strong hand, and his arm shall rule for him: behold, his reward is with him, and his work before him.' Then verses 12–14: 'Who hath measured the waters in the hollow of his hand, and meted out heaven with the span, and comprehended the dust of the earth in a measure, and weighed the mountains in scales, and the hills in a balance? Who hath directed the Spirit of the Lord, or being his counsellor hath taught him? With whom took he counsel, or who instructed him, and taught him in the path of judgment, and taught him knowledge, and showed to him the way of understanding? Behold, the nations are but as a drop of a bucket, and are counted as the small dust of the balance.' That is the measure of all the potentates and powers – communism, humanism, materialism, and everything that you can think of, that are set against you – 'a drop of a bucket, small dust of the balance'. 'Behold, he taketh up the isles as a very little thing. And Lebanon is not sufficient to burn. All nations before him are as nothing; they are counted to him less than nothing, and vanity.' Such is the truth concerning them in God's sight. Again, verse 22: 'It is he that sitteth upon the circle of the earth, and the inhabitants thereof are as grass-hoppers;' – the great men who strut about as if they were some kind of colossus – 'that stretcheth out the heavens as a curtain, and spreadeth them out as a tent to dwell in: that bringeth the princes to nothing' – emperors, kings, princes, dictators – 'He maketh the judges of the earth as vanity. Yea, they shall not be planted; yea, they shall not be sown; yea, their stock shall not take root in the earth; and he shall also blow upon them, and they shall wither, and the whirlwind shall take them away as stubble.'

Then comes the final challenge: 'To whom then will ye liken me, or shall I be equal? saith the Holy One. Lift up your eyes on high, and behold who hath created these things, that bringeth out their host by number: he calleth them all by names by the greatness of his might, for that he is strong in power; not one faileth. Why sayest thou, O Jacob, and speakest, O Israel, My way is hid from the Lord, and my judgment is passed over from my God? Hast thou not known? hast thou not heard, that the everlasting God, the Lord, the Creator of the ends of the earth, fainteth not, neither is weary? There is no searching of his understanding. He giveth power to the faint; and to them that have no might he increaseth strength. Even the youths shall faint and be weary, and the young men shall utterly fall: but they that wait upon the Lord shall renew their strength; they shall mount up with wings as eagles; they shall run, and not be weary; and they shall walk, and not faint.' God is for us, and His Son tells us, 'All power is given unto me in heaven and in earth'. 'All power!' So if God be for us, who can be against us?

What do you say to these things? I have put the case before you in the words of the Apostle Paul and in other words from Scripture. Do you still say that it is possible for you to lose your salvation? Do you still dispute the doctrine of the final persever-ance of the saints? This is not a theoretical matter. The Apostle calls for a verdict from us. I am not interested in theoretical truth. I ask the simple question, What do you say to these things? Are you clear about the truth? Are you certain of your salvation? Do you know that nothing can ever rob you of it?

There is no real enjoyment of these great statements if you do not come to that conclusion. Do you realize that the one thing that matters is that you should know that you are in this great purpose of God? That is what matters ultimately; not the world, the flesh, the devil, nor your own weakness. Nothing matters but to know that you are in His 'purpose', that you are one of 'the called according to his purpose'. Can you say 'My God'? Can you say, 'God is for me. I know He is for me, because I would not believe in Him at all if He were not for me. I am His child because He is for me. And if God be for me, no one and nothing can be against me in the sense of ever separating me from Him'? What do you say to these things? Can you shout exultantly with the Apostle Paul and the saints of the centuries, 'If God be for us, who can be against us?'

Thirty-one

*

> *He that spared not his own Son, but delivered him up for us all, how shall he not with him also freely give us all things?*
>
> Romans 8 : 32

In this verse we come to the second challenge to the doctrine of the final perseverance of the saints which the Apostle considers. Is there any danger of God's love to us lessening or waning, or, indeed, ceasing altogether? This is obviously a most important question because our whole position is dependent upon the love of God. If there is any possibility of a change in God's love then we are again in jeopardy and are left in a state of complete uncertainty. Nothing is more important than that we should know, and know beyond any doubt, that it is impossible for the love of God toward us ever to change at all. That is the question with which the Apostle deals here. He never takes anything for granted, he always supplies us with proofs, with demonstrations of his pronouncements. This verse is not only a masterly argument in and of itself, it is at the same time one of the greatest statements of the doctrine of the atonement, and one of the most comforting and re-assuring statements to be found anywhere in Scripture. Sanday and Headlam in their Commentary say, 'A number of emphatic expressions are crowded together in this sentence'. We can go still further. A number of the most wonderful and crucial Christian doctrines are crowded together in the space and confine of this one verse: 'He that spared not his own Son, but delivered him up for us all, how shall he not with him also freely give us all things?'

Let us for a moment look at the argument in general. Its very mechanics are full of interest, while its object is to prove and to demonstrate that God's love to us can never possibly fail or grow less. The method Paul employs is often found in his writings;

he argues from a greater to a lesser proposition. He has done so, for example, in chapter 5, verses 8, 9 and 10: 'But God commendeth his love toward us, in that, while we were yet sinners, Christ died for us. Much more then, being now justified by his blood, we shall be saved from wrath through him. For if, when we were enemies, we were reconciled to God by the death of his Son, much more, being reconciled, we shall be saved by [in] his life.' Here the Apostle starts with the greater and from that he then deduces the lesser. In other words, he is saying that if God has already done for us the greatest thing that even He Himself could possibly do, how can He conceivably fail or refuse to do for us anything less than that! That is the argument: If God has already done the greatest thing of all for our salvation then it is quite unthinkable that He should fail to continue His work in us until He has brought us to the final goal of ultimate perfection and glorification. Such is the character, the nature, of the argument.

This shows itself in a very striking way in the actual words the Apostle uses. It is interesting to observe that the Authorized Version, the Revised Version, the Revised Standard Version and the New English Bible all fail to pay any attention to a word the Apostle actually used, a little but important word found in the original at the beginning of the verse. It is an intensive particle which the Apostle used in order to magnify what God has done. So a word should be added to the translation, and it is the word 'Surely'. 'Surely, he that spared not his own Son, but delivered him up for us all, how shall he not with him also freely give us all things?' The word 'Indeed' is also suitable. A famous American grammarian, A. T. Robertson, translates as follows: 'Who as much as this . . .' It is intensive. Dr James Moffatt has 'Surely'. J. N. Darby has also seen the significance of this and uses the word 'Yea' in order to introduce emphasis. 'He who, yea, has not spared his own Son, but delivered him up for us all, how shall he not also with him grant us all things?' The whole object and purpose of this little particle is to intensify. The God who has done that for us, 'Surely . . .' That is the effect of what the Apostle is saying. The translation found in the N.E.B. not only misses that word of emphasis but also misses the argument. The way in which it splits up the statement loses the whole point and intensity of the argument as the Apostle states it. Another way of stating the argument is: The God who has already done that supreme thing for us, surely cannot fail to do anything less than that in order to lead us to the ultimate goal for which He did that greatest thing. Such, then, is the form of the argument.

Next we must pay attention to the way in which the Apostle gives us this assurance. Every believer needs to know for certain that God's love toward us can never vary and can never fail. Notice that the Apostle does not merely say, 'You need not worry about that matter, because God is love'. People speak in this way today; but that is not how the Apostle states the matter. He does not give us the assurance only on the basis of the fact that God is love. The fact is true; but the Apostle knows us well; he knows that we are liable to doubts and fears, and that the devil is always ready to suggest questions and to insinuate queries when untoward things happen to us, and to make us say, 'Does God love us after all?' If our comfort were left merely as a vague, general statement we would soon lose our assurance. So the Apostle bases our assurance on facts, on certain things which God has already done, and in particular on the fact of the death of the Lord Jesus Christ on the Cross on Calvary's hill. He is never satisfied with mere general statements about the love of God. He always comes down to particulars, to facts. Consider this blessed Person, he says, and remember His death on a Cross! We are to look at an event, at a fact which belongs to the realm of history.

But the Apostle does not stop at a bare recital of the facts, he bases the assurance also on the meaning and the significance of the facts. In other words, he bases his comfort on doctrine, because doctrine, after all, is the explanation of the meaning and the significance of facts and events. To look at a fact, an event, without understanding its meaning and its purpose does not help us. Doctrine is that which explains the object and the meaning and the purpose of the facts. So the Apostle, in addition to giving us the facts, gives us explanations concerning God's plan, the Person of Christ, and the meaning of Christ's death upon the Cross. These explanations constitute the great cardinal, central doctrines of the Christian faith.

This is the biblical method from beginning to end, and I emphasize it in order to show that it is essentially different from what is so popular at the present time. There is a popular teaching on the Continent of Europe today – it is largely followed in the theological colleges of Germany and in most other parts of the Continent – which teaches that facts do not matter at all, and that actually we cannot be sure of most of the purported facts with regard to the Lord Jesus Christ. To Bultmann and his followers the facts do not matter as long as we hold on to certain religious truths. But that is the exact opposite of what the Apostle does here and everywhere. This new teaching says that the facts do not matter, that it makes no difference whether Christ literally rose in the body or not; what matters is His experience of God and the influence He still exerts. Some go so far as to say that all we can be sure of is that the man Jesus died on a Cross – no virgin birth, no miracles, no substitutionary atonement, no physical resurrection. But the Apostle's arguments are always based solidly and entirely upon historical facts.

Another departure from the Pauline and biblical method is even more common in this country than the Bultmann teaching. It announces that doctrine does not matter at all. It is the teaching – far too common in evangelical circles – which says, 'We are not theologians, we are just simple evangelical people; we do not bother about theology. Our fathers wasted much time over theology and divided from one another.' I once heard a well-known evangelical say, 'I am only a simple evangelist; I do not understand doctrine. I just offer Christ to people. I do not understand the doctrine of the atonement, I confine myself to reciting certain verses referring to Christ's death.' But here we find that the comfort and the assurance the Apostle gives us is based directly upon doctrine. If you desire to have real assurance of your salvation, the firmer your grasp upon Christian doctrines the greater your assurance will be. Facts are essential, plus exposition. To leave out either is wrong. We need the facts, and we also need the doctrines that explain the facts. And here in this 32nd verse of Romans, chapter 8, the Apostle provides us with both.

There is nothing more foolish or self-defeating than for a Christian to say that he is not interested in doctrines. Such a man is on the high road to becoming a victim of the latest plausible teaching that offers itself and its spurious blessings. Ignorant and innocent Christians often think that as long as a preacher talks about the Cross all is well; but what matters is not that a preacher talks about the Cross, but what he says about the Cross. There are many who carry crosses on their persons, but the question is, What do they believe about the Cross?, what is their doctrine of the death of Christ? The Apostle's entire argument depends upon the meaning, and upon our understanding, of what was happening when our Lord died upon the Cross. The way to combat doubts, and the way to resist the devil, and to 'rejoice in hope of the glory of God', is to work out the kind of argument the Apostle presents here, an argument based solidly upon events that have taken place in the realm of history and upon an understanding of their meaning. I have thus emphasized the mechanics of the argument because I find constantly that it is the people who do not trouble to do this who are always in difficulties. I refer to people who go to a service, or who go to a minister 'just to get a word of comfort'. If they understood the doctrine they would be able to work out the argument for themselves.

We now come to consider the argument itself. Each of the terms used by the Apostle is full of meaning and significance, and we must therefore take them one by one and give them their full value. The first assertion of the Apostle is that what was happening on the Cross on Calvary's hill was the action of God. 'He that spared not his own Son, but delivered him up for us all.' He – God! The argument is that as God has already given his Son to death for us, He cannot refuse to do for us anything else that is necessary. Most people are clear about the second half, 'How shall he not with him also freely give us all things?' Here it is quite clear that it is God who gives, but it is essential to the Apostle's argument that the first part is also the action of God. Otherwise there is no parallel. His parallel is, the God who has already done this, cannot refuse to do that! It is the same Person who acts in both parts of the statement. This needs to be emphasized in view of the popular teaching with regard to Good Friday. What is taught popularly and commonly about the crucifixion and death of Christ is that it was solely and entirely the action of men. It is regarded as the greatest tragedy. An intelligent man once asked me the question, 'Why do you call it *Good* Friday? I would have thought it was the worst Friday that has ever been – *Bad* Friday!' I said, 'Why do you say that?' He replied, 'Surely there is nothing to be said for it. Look at those cruel men, those ignorant men, those men who did not recognize Him, could not understand Him, and did not see His significance; look at their jealousy and their envy and their malice and their spite.' That is the teaching which tells us all about the characters round the Cross, and which explains the Cross solely and entirely in terms of the action of men. 'Were you there when they crucified my Lord?' says the popular negro-spiritual song, and the answer is that we were. It is we who put the Son of God to death.

There are others who say that it was not so much the action of men as the action of the devil and the 'principalities and powers', the fallen angels and all the powers that are governed and controlled by the devil. They say that the devil used men but the action was ultimately his. He set out at the very beginning to try to destroy the Son of God. He tried through king Herod to kill Him when He was a babe, and he followed Him, he tempted Him, he tried to trap Him; and at long last he manipulated the people in such a way that he encompassed and brought about His death. If you ask them, in the light of such an approach, to explain what happened on the Cross, they say 'Its meaning is that God is there saying to us, indeed to all men, "Though you did that – even that – to my Son, I still forgive you".' This is probably the commonest form of teaching with respect to the meaning of the death of Christ upon the Cross today. I once heard a clever young preacher stating it thus – 'God was not making a way of forgiveness on Calvary: God forgives Calvary'. God in reality was doing nothing on Calvary; He was entirely passive, according to that teaching. Men were acting and God was passively looking on, and saying to us, 'Though you have done even that, I am still ready to forgive you'.

Such teaching, and all the variants of it, is entirely wrong and utterly false. It misses the whole glory of the Cross, and is a complete contradiction of the teaching of Scripture. We cannot afford to be vague and uncertain as to the meaning of the death on the Cross. I have heard evangelical people accepting that false teaching and praising it. I have heard men described and welcomed as evangelical who taught that and no more. But it is not evangelical teaching. It misses the whole glory of the evangelical teaching about the Cross. Evangelical teaching is a proclamation to the effect that it is God who acted on Calvary. *He!* He who acted there is the One who is going to give us all these other things. And I know and am certain of this, because of what He has already done there! God acted through men, through the instrumentality of men, but the action was the action of God!

We must demonstrate this because it is the very nerve of the Apostle's argument. Let us start with the 53rd chapter of Isaiah's prophecy where this is stated several times. There the prophet gives a preview, under the inspiration of the Spirit; he sees it all. Take for instance, verse 4: 'Surely he hath borne our griefs, and carried our sorrows: yet we did esteem him stricken, smitten of God, and afflicted. But he was wounded for our transgressions, he was bruised for our iniquities: the chastisement of our peace was upon him; and with his stripes we are healed.' Then verse 6: 'All we like sheep have gone astray . . . and the Lord hath laid on him the iniquity of us all.' It is God the Lord, the Father, who is acting and putting on Him the iniquity of us all. The prophet continues, 'Yet it pleased the Lord to bruise him; he hath put him to grief', and so on. There we have the prophetic foreview of the great event of the Cross. There is much more to the same effect in the Old Testament, but that is the classic and crucial passage.

In the New Testament we read of our Lord Himself addressing Pontius Pilate, who claimed that our Lord's fate was in his hands entirely. Our Lord turns to him and says, 'Thou couldest have no power at all against me, except it were given thee from above' (John 19: 11). The Apostle Peter expounds the meaning of the Cross in his sermon on the Day of Pentecost, as recorded in the 2nd chapter of Acts, beginning at verse 22: 'Ye men of Israel, hear these words; Jesus of Nazareth, a man approved of God among you by miracles and wonders and signs, which God did by him in the midst of you, as ye yourselves also know; him, being delivered by the determinate counsel and foreknowledge of God, you have taken, and by wicked hands have crucified and slain.' The inspired apostle, filled with the Holy Spirit, explains to the people at Jerusalem that, though it was their hands that had actually done the deed, it was God's purpose that was being carried out – 'the determinate counsel and foreknowledge of God'.

The same truth is found in Acts 4 with its account of the prayer of the persecuted early Church. Peter and John had been threatened by the authorities that if they continued to preach or teach in the name of Jesus they would not only be arrested again, but probably be put to death and the entire Church would be exterminated. So the Church met together and we are told how they prayed:

'The kings of the earth stood up, and the rulers were gathered together against the Lord, and against his Christ. For of a truth against thy holy child Jesus, whom thou hast anointed, both Herod and Pontius Pilate, with the Gentiles, and the people of Israel, were gathered together, for to do whatsoever thy hand and thy counsel determined before to be done' (Acts 4: 26–28). The believers are addressing God, and what they say in this prayer is that Herod and Pontius Pilate, and the Gentiles, and the people, were simply carrying out 'whatsoever God's hand and God's counsel determined to be done'.

Then there is a very explicit statement concerning this matter in 2 Corinthians 5: 21: 'For he [God] hath made him [Christ] to be sin for us, who knew no sin; that we might be made the righteousness of God in him.' This follows Paul's statement that 'God was in Christ, reconciling the world unto himself', and is an exposition of it. The same truth is taught in Colossians, chapter 2, verses 13 to 15: 'And you, being dead in your sins and the uncircumcision of your flesh, hath he quickened together with him, having forgiven you all trespasses; blotting out the handwriting of ordinances that was against us, which was contrary to us, and took it out of the way, nailing it to his cross; and having spoiled principalities and powers, he made a show of them openly, triumphing over them in it.' God was not passive. The death on the Cross was not ultimately the work of the principalities and powers; indeed, it was putting them to an open shame.

The Apostle Peter teaches the same doctrine in his epistles. In his 1st Epistle, chapter 2, verse 6, he quotes from Isaiah 28: 16: 'Wherefore also it is contained in the Scripture, Behold, I lay in Sion a chief corner stone, elect, precious: and he that believeth on him shall not be confounded.' The context speaks of men rejecting Him – 'Disallowed indeed of men, but chosen of God, and precious . . . . the stone which the builders disallowed, the same is made the head of the corner' (vv. 4 and 7). It is all an exposition of the death on the Cross, and the resurrection, and it is clear that it is God Himself who is acting.

So the teaching is that what happened on the Cross was something God had planned and foreordained before the foundation of the world. The Cross is not an accident; it is not only the result of the malice and the jealousy and the envy and the blindness and the folly of men; it was according to the 'determinate counsel and foreknowledge of God'. And so it is stated here in Romans 8: 32, 'He that spared not his own Son, but delivered him up for us all'. That the death on the Cross was God's action is essential to this argument. What God has done is my guarantee of what God will yet do. If it be argued that God was but looking on passively, and saying 'Even though you have done that, still I forgive you' there is no argument here at all, and no assurance for us.

Let us allow Peter to have the final word about this matter. In his First Epistle, the first chapter, verse 18 he says: 'Forasmuch as ye know that ye were not redeemed with corruptible things, as silver and gold, from your vain conversation received by tradition from your fathers; but with the precious blood of Christ, as of a lamb without blemish and without spot: who verily was foreordained before the foundation of the world, but was manifest in these last times for you, who by him do believe in God that raised him up from the dead, and gave him glory; that your faith and hope might be in God.' It is God who smote Him, it is God who raised Him up. 'He that spared not his own Son . . .' Failure to understand this robs us of the glory of the Cross and of our own assurance. Teachers who deny this do so because they do not believe the Scriptures, but substitute for the teaching of the Scriptures their own ideas of God and His love. They do not believe in 'the wrath of God', they do not believe that God punishes sin; indeed they tell us that that is impossible because of the love of God. There is no justice, there is no righteousness in God according to their view, and love and wrath are to them mutually exclusive. So they explain our Lord's death on the Cross in human terms. The simple answer is that what happened at Calvary was the action of the Almighty, God the Father, an action pre-determined before the foundation of the world.

Let us take one further step. 'His own Son!' Who died upon the Cross? This again is vital to the argument. Was He merely a good man? Or just a great religious teacher, someone like Socrates? According to popular teaching 'Jesus was one of the great religious teachers – one of the martyrs',

> *Truth for ever on the scaffold,*
> *Wrong for ever on the throne.*

They put Him into the category of a good man dying for his

principles, a good man 'before his time', whom the ignorant people could not follow and appreciate. But was He only a good man, only a godly man? We have the answer here! Was He the Son of God in some general sense, as we are all sons of God in terms of the universal Fatherhood of God and the universal Brotherhood of man? I was reading recently of someone who had asked one of the sceptical writers who nevertheless pass under the name of Christian, 'Do you or do you not believe in the divinity of Jesus Christ?' The answer was, 'Of course I do; I believe in the divinity of all men'. Is that what the Apostle is asserting here?

Take one further step. Earlier in this chapter the Apostle has been telling us that Christians are the sons of God. 'As many as are led by the Spirit of God, they are the sons of God. For ye have not received the spirit of bondage again to fear; but ye have received the Spirit of adoption, whereby we cry, Abba, Father. The Spirit itself beareth witness with our spirit, that we are the children of God (sons of God).' Is our Lord the Son of God in that sense only? Is He but one who, according to the modern phrase, 'achieved divinity'? Paul answers that He is unique and separate even from those of us who are Christians, who have become the children of God by adoption. He is 'the only begotten of the Father', 'His own Son'. Not created, not adopted into the family of God as we are who are Christian, He was the Son of God from all eternity. He has always been the Son of God. He is the eternal Son of God. He is 'in the bosom of the Father'. 'In the beginning was the Word, and the Word was with God, and the Word was God' (John 1 : 1). He has been God from all eternity. 'This is my Son, the beloved'. God has never said these things about anyone except about this One. Here is the One who is God's 'own Son', He is a partaker of God's own nature, He is 'the brightness of his glory, and the express image of his person' (Hebrews 1 : 3). That is true of no-one except this Person. This is the One who said, 'I and the Father are one'. No-one has ever dared to say that except this Person. He was charged with claiming that God was His own Father. He did so claim, and His claim is true; and it is only true of Him. We are sons of God by adoption; He is Son by eternal generation.

We must pay close attention to every word. 'He that spared not his own Son . . .' It is a vital essential part of the argument.

[387]

It was not a man only that God was not sparing on the Cross; it was not even an adopted son; it was His 'own Son'. The amazing doctrine of the Incarnation is found in those two words *His own* Son. 'When the fulness of the time was come God sent forth his Son, made of a woman, made under the law' (Galatians 4: 4). The Apostle's argument loses its cogency and its power to convince and to comfort us, unless we realize who it was that God did not spare on the Cross. It was none other than His only begotten beloved Son, the One who was one with Him from eternity, sharer of His divine eternal nature with the Holy Ghost, the One whom He loved with all the intensity of the divine nature. That is the One whom the Father did not spare, but rather 'delivered him up' for us all on the Cross on Calvary's hill.

I repeat that every single word in this verse is of inestimable importance, charged with the glorious doctrines of the Christian Faith. Is anything more reprehensible than the way in which men rob this of its glory, evacuate it of its meaning, but still go on using the language. And is anything more sad than that foolish people should say, 'I cannot be bothered about doctrine; all I know is, I have my experience'? Lay hold on every word here; do not yield anything, not a single letter of any word. If you would see something of the glory, if you really want to know something of the love of God, and if you would have an unshakable assurance, hold on to every detail, every word, every letter. Learn to view your salvation in terms of the mind and the eternal purpose of God.

Thirty-two

*

He that spared not his own Son, but delivered him up for us all, how shall he not with him also freely give us all things?

Romans 8 : 32

We have seen how essential it is that we should understand clearly each of the terms used by the Apostle in this most reassuring statement. The first is that it was God who ordained the death on Calvary's hill, and not men. The second is that it was God's eternal Son who died there, and not a human martyr. It was 'His own Son'.

The third term that confronts us is 'spared'. 'He that spared not his own Son.' What was happening at Calvary must be construed in terms of God not 'sparing' His own Son. 'Spared' is an old word which is used in connection with the offering up of Isaac by Abraham in Genesis 22: 16. The Septuagint translators who translated the Old Testament into Greek used this very word in Genesis 22: 16. In the Authorized Version it reads: 'By myself have I sworn, saith the Lord, for because thou hast done this thing, and hast not withheld thy son, thine only son: that in blessing I will bless thee.' The offering of Isaac by Abraham is a type of what God Himself did on Calvary's hill. Abraham was offering his son, his specially beloved son Isaac, his only true son. He was ready to offer him up at the behest and the commandment of God – 'thine only son'. He did not *withhold* him. This is the very word the Apostle uses here, 'He that *spared not*'. He did not hold anything back with respect to Him. The same word is used in Acts 20: 29, where the Apostle prophesies to the elders of the Church at Ephesus that 'grievous wolves shall enter in, not *sparing* the flock'. These rebellious, rapacious people are going to attack them and maul them; nothing will be spared, nothing is going to be held back.

What it means is that God the Father did not spare His Son anything in this world, either in His life or (and more particularly) in His death; He did not hold back from Him anything that was a part of the process by which He could save us. Everything that was essential to our salvation came upon the Son of God. Though He was God's own Son, His dearly beloved Son, He did not spare Him necessary suffering. How different from our customary practice! We spare people whom we like, we keep things back from them. If we can spare them any suffering we are always ready to do so; but what we are told here is that God did not hold anything back from His Son, nothing was kept from Him. He was spared no suffering.

That brings us to the next term. Far from sparing Him, 'He delivered him up'. The Apostle uses a negative first and then the positive and so brings out this strong contrast between them for the sake of emphasis. Far from sparing His own Son anything He delivered Him up. This is a vital part of the Apostle's argument. This is the 'greater' thing which God has done, and from which Paul deduces that, because God has so done, He cannot refuse anything smaller. It is essential therefore that we should understand this greatest of all acts, 'delivered him up for us all'. The Apostle has already introduced this thought to us in the last verse of the 4th chapter where he says, '[Christ] was delivered for our offences, and raised again for our justification'. This is the term, '*delivered* for our offences'. We are face to face here with the great mystery of the atonement, and what happened to our blessed Lord and Saviour in order that you and I might be saved. But it is essential to the Apostle's argument that we should understand something of what was involved; and as there is so much confusion with regard to it, as there is with regard to most matters connected with our salvation, we must handle it with special care. As we have seen in connection with the other terms the whole modern tendency is to evacuate it of its glorious content.

'Delivered him up' – to whom? to what? Turn to the phrase used in Luke 22, verse 53. When the chief priests and others came to arrest our Lord He said to them, 'When I was daily with you in the temple ye stretched forth no hands against me: but this is your hour, and the power of darkness'. It is clear therefore that our Lord was delivered up as it were to 'the power of darkness'. He was telling those cruel men that 'the hour' had come when He would have to suffer at the hands of 'the power of darkness' as a part of our salvation. The Apostle Paul in Colossians 2, verses 14 and 15, refers to the same matter, saying that our Lord 'triumphed over principalities and powers, putting them to an open shame'. But before He triumphed over them He was 'in their power'. He had said to His own followers that 'the prince of this world cometh and hath nothing in me' (John 14: 30). In other words, a part of this 'delivering up' clearly means that He was held for a time in the hands of the powers of darkness.

To obtain a fuller understanding of this we must remind ourselves of what happened to our Lord in the Garden of Gethsemane. The terms used are most important. 'He was withdrawn from them about a stone's cast, and kneeled down, and prayed, saying, Father, if thou be willing, remove this cup from me: nevertheless not my will, but thine be done.' He offered that prayer three times. 'And there appeared an angel unto him from heaven, strengthening him. And being in an agony he prayed more earnestly: and his sweat was as it were great drops of blood falling down to the ground' (Luke 22: 41–46). That throws light on 'delivered him up'. Then we come to the Lord's cry upon the Cross, 'My God, my God, why hast thou forsaken me?' (Matthew 27: 46). This again is essential to a true understanding of what is meant by 'delivered him up for us all'.

Then we have the statement of the Apostle Paul in 2 Corinthians 5: 21: 'He [God] hath made him to be sin for us, who knew no sin; that we might be made the righteousness of God in him.' 'Delivered him up for us all' includes that also. Similarly the statement in Galatians 3: 13 which is most expressive: 'Christ hath redeemed us from the curse of the law, being made a curse for us: for it is written, Cursed is every one that hangeth on a tree.' He was 'made a curse' for us. Then there is the expression in Philippians 2: 8: 'He humbled himself, and became obedient unto death, even the death of the Cross.' Finally, in Hebrews 12: 2 we read that 'He endured the Cross, despising the shame.'

I have quoted these statements in order that we may see something of the content of the expression, 'delivered him up for us all'.

Any view of the Cross which does not include the teaching of these verses is false. They mean nothing less than this, that He was 'delivered up' by God the Father to bear the full wrath of God Himself against sin. He was 'delivered up' to bear the full penalty of God's holy Law pronounced upon sin and transgression. Nothing was withheld. I am amazed that anyone should try to detract from this doctrine. I read recently in a popular morning newspaper what is called 'A one-minute Sermon' by a well-known writer. In dealing with 'My God, my God, why hast thou forsaken me?' he said, 'The cry from the Cross was not in grief or protest; it echoed the Psalmist's prophetic song of thanksgiving, praise and triumph'. That is a typical expression of the modern view. Men seem to have a fear of saying that the cry of our Lord on the Cross was a cry of dereliction. That they regard as impossible; it could not have happened to the Lord Jesus Christ. As the Son of God He knew everything. He knew that He was going to triumph, hence He cannot have meant, 'Hast thou really left me?' So to explain the words they say that He was but quoting the opening words of Psalm 22 which is ultimately a song of triumph. There was no grief there, they say, no agony; the Lord was simply quoting Psalm 22 as if to say to the people, 'All is well, this is happening to me now but I know that it is going to lead to triumph'. He was not in any way giving expression to what He Himself was feeling at the time.

One can well understand the object of such people; but in their anxiety to safeguard our Lord's knowledge they detract from what is perhaps the greatest glory of what happened on the Cross, the very thing the Apostle Paul goes out of his way to emphasize here. Psalm 22 is certainly a wonderful prophetic foretelling of all that our Lord would endure upon the Cross – the thirst, the bodily pain, the consciousness of all the agony in His bones, and so on. It is an amazing description of death by crucifixion. And it ends on a note of triumph, just as our Lord on the Cross was able to say, 'Father, into thy hands I commend my spirit', and 'It is finished'. But the pity is that they are so concerned about the ultimate note of thanksgiving, trust and triumph, that they do not recognize that before our Lord arrived at that point of triumph He had to pass through terrible agony and through an experience in which He felt utterly abandoned and forsaken of His Father. He felt it to the very depths of His being. We must always be true to Scripture.

Let us look again at Isaiah 53, and at some of the terms that are used there in order to refute the suggestion that there was no element of grief in the cry on the Cross. Isaiah, who was given a preview of the Cross, expresses it in terms such as these: 'Surely he hath borne our griefs, and carried our sorrows'; 'the chastisement of our peace was upon him'; 'He was oppressed, and he was afflicted'; 'Yet it pleased the Lord to bruise him; he hath put him to grief'. In view of such expressions, how can it be true that our Lord was not suffering any grief, but was just quoting Psalm 22 and its ultimate triumph. We cannot dismiss Isaiah's terms – 'He hath borne our griefs, and carried our sorrows'; 'He was smitten of God, and afflicted'; 'the travail of his soul'; 'wounded', 'bruised', 'chastisement', 'oppressed'; 'he hath put him to grief'. To take out such terms is to miss the central glory of the Cross. In other words we have to realize that our Lord experienced at Calvary all the torment and the suffering and the agony that results from the punishment of sin.

Let me add further proof. Why was our Lord in an agony of soul in the Garden of Gethsemane? According to the modern idea there was no grief, no agony. He knew, they say, that He was ultimately going to triumph, that He was going to be raised from the dead. He had told the Apostles that He was not only to be slain but that He would rise again on the third day. Certainly He did so, but we cannot by-pass the agony in the Garden of Gethsemane. Why did our Lord, 'being in an agony', sweat great drops as of blood? If there was no grief there is no explanation. And if there was no grief upon the Cross there was obviously none in the Garden, because what happened in the Garden was an anticipation of what He was going to experience on the Cross. However great the agony in the Garden, it was much greater on the Cross, the difference between anticipation and actual experience. The fact is that there was real agony in the Garden and on the Cross.

What is the explanation of the agony? To what is our Lord referring when He prays three times to His Father saying, 'If it be possible, let this cup pass from me'. There is only one adequate answer. It is not that He was afraid of death. To say so is to make Him inferior to the saints, indeed inferior to many a man who is not a Christian at all. There is but one answer. He knew that there was to be a moment when God His Father, having 'made him to be sin', having placed our sins on Him, would smite Him, would strike Him and avert His face from Him. He realized that He who had ever looked into the face of His Father, and loved Him from all eternity, would be separated from His Father, and would experience the agony and the grief and the suffering of any soul under the wrath of God against sin. To suggest that our Lord had no such experience, that He knew no grief, is to take away the central glory of what happened on the Cross. It also vitiates and nullifies the Apostle's argument in our text. The Apostle is asserting that God delivered Him up, and did not spare Him any suffering. When God put our sins upon His own Son He did not withhold any part of the punishment from Him; He poured it all upon Him, everything that it deserved. God kept nothing of it back, and the Son submitted Himself to it willingly. That God 'delivered him up for us all' means that He poured all the vials of His wrath against sin upon Him. He smote Him, He struck Him, He wounded Him, He oppressed Him, He afflicted Him. He 'put him to grief', nothing was withheld.

How important it is that we should take the Scriptures as they are, and not allow our philosophies to control our thinking. Those who are guilty of the latter argue always from the love of God which they think they understand, and they fondly imagine that they magnify the love of God. Actually they are making it very much smaller, and robbing it of its greatest glory. The love of God is so great that He delivered up His Son for us. He put Him to grief, He smote Him, and caused Him to pass through that moment of dereliction in which He cried 'My God, my God, why hast thou forsaken me?' Our Lord was forsaken at that moment. Sin – yours and mine – came between Him and His Father and He felt utterly forsaken, and so He cried out in His agony. What He experienced on the Cross was altogether greater even than what He had experienced in the Garden. He is 'the Lamb of God' being put to death, separated from His Father, experiencing the wrath of God against sin to its very depths.

The next word for us to examine is the word 'for'. 'Delivered him up *for* us all.' It actually means 'on behalf of'. It is not merely that it was done for our benefit. I agree that the actual word used here by the Apostle is not the word he normally uses when he wants to convey this notion of 'on behalf of', but the whole context here makes it perfectly plain that that is its real meaning.

It was 'on our behalf' that He bore our sins in His own body on the tree. God delivered Him up 'instead of ' us. We should be 'delivered up' to the punishment, for we are the sinners; but instead of delivering us up for the punishment, God delivered up His Son in our stead and in our place.

But we move on to the word 'us'. 'He delivered him up for *us.*' We must give the right content of this word again – 'for us'. What is the truth about 'us'? Is it that we are nice, good, godly, religious people? No, it is what we were, by nature, every one of us, 'the children of wrath, even as others'. It is what we are by our natural descent from Adam, and also as the result of our actions, our own unworthy deeds. Paul has already described us in the 5th chapter, verse 6: 'When we were yet without strength, in due time Christ died for the ungodly.' And in verse 8: 'God commendeth his love toward us, in that while we were yet sinners, Christ died for us.' Indeed verse 10 goes further and says we were 'enemies'.

So the Apostle is asserting that God delivered up His own Son, kept nothing back from Him, but allowed all that should have come upon us, guilty, vile rebels, deserving nothing but hell, to fall upon Him. He 'delivered up' His own Son, 'for us', even while we were enemies and haters of God. How important is every single word in this verse! Put the full content into that 'us' here as in chapter 5, verse 10: 'If, while we were enemies, we were reconciled to God by the death of his Son, how much more, being reconciled, shall we be saved in his life!'

The last word is 'all', 'delivered him up for us *all*'. Is the Apostle referring to the whole of mankind? Obviously he is not. The 'us' refers to the people of whom he has been speaking earlier, 'We know that all things work together for good'. To whom? To the whole world? No! 'to them that love God, to them who are the called according to his purpose'. The 'us all' of verse 32 refers to the same 'us' as in the previous verses, and to no one else. Christ was delivered up for us as a whole; but He was also delivered up for every single one of us in particular. I emphasize this because it is where the final perseverance of the saints comes in. If God has delivered up His Son for me in particular, He is not going to abandon me. Every one of 'us' is covered by this action of God which He undertook on the Cross on Calvary's hill.

There is one other word I feel I must include. The commentators do not agree about this, but I feel that there should be no hesitation. 'He that spared not his own Son, but delivered him up for us all, how shall he not with him also freely give us all things?' I believe that the *freely* belongs to the first part of the statement as much as it does to the second. He not only gives us freely the 'all things' we need, he also freely gave up His Son for us all. This is where we really see the love of God; He did it all 'freely'. There was nothing in us to recommend us; God did not do it in response to our cry or to anything in us. We were 'enemies', and 'alienated in our minds by wicked works'; we were 'the children of wrath, even as others'. Why did God do all this for us? He did it 'freely', He did it of His grace. That element is in the very word the Apostle used, translated here 'freely'. It is 'grace'. The freeness of God's grace. Everything is the result of the grace of God. And so He spared not His own Son, but delivered Him up for us all 'freely', moved by nothing but His own eternal and glorious grace.

Such, then, is the measure of God's love, and it is the only adequate measure of a love which is 'beyond measure'. How pathetic and hopeless is the position of people who think that they safeguard the love of God by denying the substitutionary theory of the atonement, who say that our Lord did not cry out in an agony, and who imagine that the measure of the love of God is that God says, 'Though you have killed my only Son, I still love you, and am still ready to forgive you'! They believe that they safeguard and magnify the love of God by denying the truth concerning the wrath of God, and that God must and does punish sin. I trust that I have shown that what they actually do is to detract from the love of God. The love of God is only truly seen when we realize that 'He spared not His own Son', but, the Son having offered Himself as the Lamb of God, having given Himself up that God might lay our sins upon Him and punish them in Him, God meted out the full punishment upon Him, withholding nothing.

This is what magnifies the love of God and makes it appear infinitely greater. It was not that God allowed cruel men to kill His Son; it was God Himself who smote His Son, as Abraham had been prepared to do with Isaac. It was God's action; it was 'the determinate counsel and foreknowledge of God' that brought Christ's death to pass. It was the only way to forgive sin. Sin must be punished, as the entire Bible teaches. God is a God of righteousness and justice and holiness. He cannot wink at sin, He cannot pretend that He has not seen it, He cannot simply say, 'I forgive you because I love you'. The whole character of God demands justice and righteous retribution; and on the Cross that was meted out. So, as the Apostle has already told us in the third chapter of this Epistle in verses 25 and 26, 'Whom God hath set forth to be a propitiation through faith in his blood, to declare his righteousness for the remission of sins that are past, through the forbearance of God; to declare, I say, at this time his righteousness: that he might be just, and the justifier of him that believeth in Jesus'. It is in such an action that you see the love of God. He loved such as we are, and to such an extent, that for us He punished His only Son, did not spare Him anything, 'delivered him up for us all', and poured upon Him the final dregs of His wrath against sin and evil, and the guilt involved in it all.

The rest of the Apostle's argument follows inevitably. If God has already done these things for us, even when we were His 'enemies', His love to us can never fail, and nothing can ever separate us from it. 'But what if I fall into sin?' asks someone. The answer is, that you had fallen into sin much more while you were an enemy and an alien and a rebel, but God sent His Son to die for you even then. Can He possibly reject you now, when you are no longer an enemy but a child? It is quite inconceivable. But it is only inconceivable if you give the full content to 'spared not' and 'delivered up'. If you fail to do so, you have no argument, and you miss the comfort and the consolation of the statement. Follow the argument very closely. I say with reverence that even the almighty and eternal God can never show His love in a greater manner than He did on the Cross on Calvary's hill when He delivered up His own Son for us all and kept nothing back. We can therefore be certain that, in view of what has already been done. He will surely 'with him also freely give us all things'.

What are these *all things*? The same 'all things' as in verse 28! 'We know that all things work together for good to them that love God . . .' The Apostle is proving here what he said before. God will over-rule everything for our benefit. 'All things' are made to work together for good to us who love God in order that we might come to final glorification. Here, the Apostle repeats that 'all things' that are necessary to bring us to an ultimate conformity to the image of God's Son will be done. The God who has 'delivered up his own Son for us' cannot refuse anything less than that. He cannot give us up, cannot lose interest in us, cannot cease to love us whatever we may do or say. His act upon the Cross guarantees it. If He has already 'delivered up' His Son, He will do everything else. 'Surely he will also with him freely give us all things.' All things that are necessary for our perseverance, every grace that we can ever need, we shall have. Whatever my circumstances, wherever I am, whatever the trials, troubles, tribulations, whatever my weakness, frailty, whatever my sin, it makes no difference; He who freely gave up His Son for me, will with Him also freely give me all things.

Thus the Apostle is able to write later to the Philippians and say, 'My God shall supply all your need according to his riches in glory by Christ Jesus' (4: 19) – everything whatsoever! Again in 2 Corinthians 9: 8 he writes: 'God is able to make all grace abound toward you; that you, always having all sufficiency in all things, may abound unto every good work.' John Newton expresses it very well in one of his hymns:

> *His love in time past*
> *Forbids me to think*
> *He'll leave me at last*
> *In trouble to sink:*
> *Each sweet Ebenezer*
> *I have in review,*
> *Confirms His good pleasure*
> *To help me quite through.*

He will help me to the very end, until I am perfect and entire. In the light of this John Newton concludes:

> *Since all that I meet*
> *Shall work for my good,*
> *The bitter is sweet,*
> *The medicine food;*
> *Though painful at present,*
> *'Twill cease before long;*
> *And then, O how pleasant*
> *The conqueror's song!*

There is surely only one thing to say; it can be best expressed in the words of the Apostle: 'Thanks be unto God for his unspeakable gift', His indescribable gift when He gave up His own Son, and 'delivered him up for us all'. But its special glory is that from it I can reason and argue that, with His greatest gift, He will also freely give me everything I shall ever need, in health, in sickness, in pleasure, in pain, in plenty, in penury. Whatever my circumstances may be, He will 'freely' give me all that is necessary to keep me, to hold me, to guide me, to mould me, until at last I shall see Him as He is, and be made like Him, and be with Him in the everlasting glory.

Christian people, work out this argument. Are you assured of your salvation? Are you assured of your final perseverance? That is what the Apostle desired for the Christians in Rome. If you do not have this assurance, if you are not certain of your final perseverance, if you still believe that you can fall away from grace and go to final perdition though you are now a Christian, it simply means that you have never really understood what happened on the Cross on Calvary's hill. That is the real explanation as to why many deny this doctrine of final perseverance. They think they know and understand the love of God; but that is where they are most ignorant. They have never realized the depth of that love, because they do not realize what God did at the Cross. The moment you come to that realization you are driven to the inevitable conclusion that 'He that spared not his own Son, but delivered him up for us all, how shall he not with him also freely give us all things?' It is guaranteed. If He has 'foreknown' you He has 'predestinated' you, and if He has 'predestinated' you He has 'called' you, and 'justified' you: and if He has 'justified' you He has already 'glorified' you. His love sees the end from the beginning, and He has given you an absolute proof of it on the Cross in order that you might enjoy the assurance and the happiness of salvation even while you are in this world of sin and woe and evil and shame. Do you constantly work out this mighty logic?

Thirty-three

*

Who shall lay anything to the charge of God's elect? It is God that justifieth.

Who is he that condemneth? It is Christ that died, yea rather, that is risen again, who is even at the right hand of God, who also maketh intercession for us.   Romans 8: 33, 34

These two verses contain what I have described as the third of the challenges which the Apostle himself puts up to test the doctrine of the final perseverance of the saints which he had enunciated in verses 28, 29, and 30. Though there are two questions here, one in verse 33 and one in verse 34, I put them together and describe them as 'one challenge', because in essence they deal with one big issue, namely, the possibility of our finding ourselves ultimately in a state of condemnation or of rejection by God. Is it really the case that there is no possibility whatsoever of anything ever arising that can again bring us into condemnation, and leave us finally outside the love of God and outside His great salvation? Paul considers that issue in terms of two questions. One is the possibility of anyone bringing a charge against us, and the other, the possibility of someone somehow condemning us or proving that we are in a state of condemnation.

Before we come to details there is one mechanical point with which we have to deal, namely, the relationship of the particular terms the Apostle uses to one another. Many of the commentators take up this point and it merits attention. The main point at issue is the relationship between the end of verse 33 and the beginning of verse 34: 'It is God that justifieth' and 'Who is he that condemneth?' In the Authorized Version – indeed in all the versions where the statement is divided up into verses – the phrase, 'It is God that justifieth', in verse 33 is an answer to the question at the beginning of that verse, 'Who shall lay anything to the charge of God's elect?'; and 'Who is he that condemneth?', at the beginning of verse 34, is put as the question that is followed by the answer, 'It is Christ that died, yea rather, that is risen again, who is even at the right hand of God, who also maketh intercession for us'. Certain commentators, however, disagree with this, and put together the end of verse 33 and the beginning of verse 34. They maintain that 'Who is he that condemneth?' is the answer to the statement, 'It is God that justifieth', and that we should read the two sentences thus: 'It is God that justifieth; who is he that condemneth?' In the light of the fact that it is God that justifies, who is there that can condemn? Otherwise, they say, it would mean that the Lord Jesus Christ is regarded as the one who justifies. So on those grounds they rearrange the statement and say that the statement, 'It is Christ that died, yea rather, that is risen again, who is even at the right hand of God, who also maketh intercession for us' answers by anticipation the question at the beginning of verse 35, 'Who shall separate us from the love of Christ?'

Though it is true that both views ultimately teach the same great truth, the question is worthy of a brief examination. I find myself in entire agreement in this matter with Martin Luther, John Calvin, and the Authorized Version, as against the other view, and for the following reasons. In the first place, what is suggested by those who take the other view, completely upsets the symmetry of the Apostle's statements. Beginning again at verse 31 we have, 'If God be for us, who can be against us?' This is a complete statement in itself. Then comes the second statement in verse 32: 'He that spared not his own Son, but delivered him up for us all, how shall he not with him also freely give us all things?' This also is complete in itself. I argue that the Apostle goes on to do exactly the same thing in verse 33, and therefore agree with those who divided what the Apostle wrote into the verses as we find them. He propounds the question, 'Who shall lay anything to the charge of God's elect?' and answers it by saying, 'It is God that justifieth'. The next question then follows, 'Who is he that condemneth?' and this receives its answer in the same verse, 'It is Christ that died, yea rather, that is risen again, who is even at the right hand of God, who also maketh intercession for us' – another complete statement. Then comes the next question, in verse 35, 'Who shall separate us from the love of Christ? shall

[401]

tribulation, or distress, or persecution, or famine, or nakedness, or peril, or sword?' – and the elaboration in verse 36 – and it receives its answer in verse 37, 'Nay, in all these things we are more than conquerors through him that loved us'. Thus we have a natural sequence of questions and answers. But to connect the end of verse 33 with the beginning of verse 34 entirely upsets the symmetry; it means that you sometimes have an answer before the question.

But what of the argument that the rearrangement is necessary because otherwise the statement makes the Lord Jesus Christ the One who justifies and not God? That does not seem to me to follow. In verse 34 the Apostle is concerned not with justification but with judgment. God the Father is the justifier, and that is always the answer to anyone who brings a charge against us. But when you are thinking in terms of condemnation, although in a sense you are still in the realm of justification, the main idea is that of judgment; and here it is entirely appropriate to speak of the Lord Jesus Christ as the judge.

Here is the evidence I adduce for that statement. Take the teaching of our Lord Himself in John's Gospel chapter 5, verses 26 and 27. 'For as the Father hath life in himself; so hath he given to the Son to have life in himself; and hath given him authority to execute judgment also, because he is the Son of Man.' The Father has handed over the question of judgment to the Son. The Father is ultimately the judge but He has committed the execution of it to the Son.

The Apostle Paul gave similar teaching in his sermon at Athens as recorded in Acts 17, verses 30 and 31: 'The times of this ignorance God winked at; but now commandeth all men everywhere to repent: because he hath appointed a day, in the which he will judge the world in righteousness by that man whom he hath ordained; whereof he hath given assurance unto all men, in that he hath raised him from the dead.' Then there is the statement in 2 Corinthians 5:10 and 11: 'We must all appear before the judgment seat of Christ, that every one may receive the things done in his body, according to that he hath done, whether it be good or bad. Knowing therefore the terror of the Lord [the Lord Jesus Christ], we persuade men . . .' Again, it is taught clearly in the Book of Revelation, chapter 1, verse 7: 'Behold, he cometh with clouds; and every eye shall see him, and they also which pierced him: and all kindreds of the earth shall wail because of him. Even so, Amen.' But still more specifically in the 6th chapter of the Book of Revelation, verses 15–17: 'And the kings of the earth, and the great men, and the rich men, and the chief captains, and the mighty men, and every free man, hid themselves in the dens and in the rocks of the mountains; and said to the mountains and rocks, Fall on us, and hide us from the face of him that sitteth on the throne, and from the wrath of the Lamb: for the great day of his wrath is come; and who shall be able to stand?' The Lord Jesus Christ has had judgment committed to Him; He is to exercise the judgment on behalf of His Father. So it seems to me that the Apostle here raises the question of justification in terms of God the Father, and the possibility of condemnation in terms of God the Son, to whom judgment has been committed.

I would even venture a third argument, namely, that the answer in verse 34 refutes the possible suggestion that the Lord Jesus Christ, as a result of the incarnation, and of His taking on human nature and living a perfect life as a man in the flesh, becomes a source of condemnation to us. People might say that He was truly man, but He never sinned, He obeyed God perfectly, and so He condemns us. The answer is that He has died for us, has risen for our justification, and is interceding for us at the right hand of God.

For these reasons, and there are others, I would defend the verse division we have in our Bibles, and express my entire agreement with the view of Luther and Calvin as against those who suggest the other. As I have said, there is no ultimate difference between the two parties, but it seemed to me to be worthy of just that amount of attention in passing.

Let us now look at the actual statements. We start with verse 33 which, I am arguing, is a complete statement in and of itself, 'Who shall lay anything to the charge of God's elect?' The answer is, 'It is God that justifieth'. Notice, first, the way in which we are described as Christians. We are 'God's elect'. As Christians we should always think of ourselves in this way. The very term is a part of the Apostle's argument; it is a very good summary of all he has said in verses 28, 29, and 30. It is really another way of saying, 'Whom he foreknew' because that means 'Whom he had chosen beforehand'. We have seen that 'foreknow' as used in the Old Testament carries the meaning, not of omniscience, but of 'choice beforehand', the setting of God's affection in particular upon certain people. So Christians are those whom God has chosen beforehand. They are 'God's elect', and the Apostle uses the term as a part of his great argument concerning assurance of salvation and the certainty of the final perseverance of the saints.

I ask a question at this point: Do you habitually think of yourself as one of 'God's elect', one of God's chosen people, or, if you prefer it in the language of the Apostle Peter, one of God's 'peculiar' people, one of those whom God has chosen to be 'a peculiar possession for himself'? Many of our troubles arise from the fact that we do not think of ourselves in this way, and that we think of the Christian as one who has 'decided for Christ'. The emphasis should be the other way round. The Christian is one who has been 'elected', 'chosen of God' and 'precious' for that reason; God's 'peculiar possession', 'His purchased possession', one of the people whom He has set apart for Himself. If we learn to think of ourselves in these terms, with the dignity and everything else that belongs to the position, it will revolutionize our Christian life and all our thinking. What unworthy views we often have of the Christian! – a 'good man', 'one trying to live a good life', 'one who has taken his decision' – all the emphasis is on men! But that is not the Apostle's teaching. A Christian is one of 'God's elect'.

In the light of that the Apostle issues his challenge, 'Who shall lay anything to the charge' of such a person? He presents the challenge in the form of an illustration of a case being tried in a court of law. He says, 'Who shall come forward, or can come forward, as an accuser of God's people?' The court is in session and a challenge is issued: Is there anyone who can come forward and bring a charge that he can substantiate against the people of the Lord? Who can act as accuser of these people? The interesting word the Apostle used is found several times in the New Testament; all other examples being in the Acts of the Apostles. One occurrence is in Acts 19, verse 40. There was an uproar in the assembly at Ephesus as the result of the work of Paul, and the town clerk addressed the people saying, 'We are in danger to be *called in question*' – 'accused' – for this day's uproar, 'there being no cause whereby we may give an account of this concourse'.

Another occurrence of the word is in Acts 23, verse 29, in the letter sent by 'Claudius Lysias unto the most excellent governor Felix'. Writing about Paul he says, 'Whom I perceived to be *accused* of questions of their law'. The term is always used in a legal manner. A further example is in Acts 26: 2, where Paul appearing before Agrippa says, 'I think myself happy, king Agrippa, because I shall answer for myself this day before thee touching all the things whereof I am *accused* of the Jews'. The Jews were bringing their charge against him, and clearly it was a legal charge.

The Apostle's challenge, therefore, 'Who can come forward and accuse any one of these people?' is a legal challenge. The Bible tells us that Satan is the chief accuser, or, in legal terms, the chief prosecutor. He is 'the accuser of the brethren' (Rev. 12: 10). He sets about his work in many different ways. He does so sometimes by playing upon our consciences, at other times he works through other people. They come along and say, 'Do you call yourself a Christian? A fine Christian you are! Look at what you have done, look at what you are!' They are thus acting as junior counsel – 'devils' of the devil, to use a legal term. But the devil is the chief prosecutor, the chief 'accuser of the brethren'.

The challenge being given, what is the answer to it? The Apostle has already given us part of the answer in calling us 'God's elect'. In a sense that is enough in and of itself. If you are one of God's chosen people, then, because God is God, no one can ever rob you of your position. It is for this reason that the Apostle used the term 'God's elect'. He does not say, 'Who shall bring any charge against those who believe in the Lord Jesus Christ'. That is not strong enough; it leaves the position dependent upon my belief. No, 'Who shall bring any charge against *God's elect?*' But the Apostle does not stop at that point. He says in effect that as this is a legal matter it must be dealt with in a legal way. And this he proceeds to do. His method is to ridicule the charge out of court. The Apostle employs this type of argument frequently. Notice it in verse 31, 'If God be for us, who can be against us?' The suggestion is foolish, ridiculous, impossible! Here we have the same thing, 'It is God that justifies'. The actual words used by Paul mean, 'God, the One justifying'. The rest has been added by the translators in order to make it clear to us. The words can be taken in two ways; and again the learned commentators are divided. Some say it is a question 'Who shall lay anything to the charge of God's elect – God, the one justifying?' Impossible! Or it can be taken as a statement as in the Authorized Version – 'Who shall lay anything to the charge of God's elect? God is the one who justifies'. Once more, of course, it comes to exactly the same thing, but I prefer the question form, because it seems to me to be much stronger, and it brings out this element of ridicule. 'Who shall lay anything to the charge of God's elect? what, God the one justifying us?' The ridicule, the hammer stroke, comes out more strongly if you put it in the form of a question rather than in the form of a statement.

The Apostle's argument is compressed into those few words, 'God, the One justifying'; but take note of the content. First, man's relation to God is a legal one. In His dealings with men God has always acted in terms of a covenant; and a covenant is a legal document. Even when He placed man in perfection in the Garden there was a covenant, a Covenant of Works. He must not eat of a particular fruit, and was to behave in a given manner. We must hold firmly to this legal concept, because the Apostle's argument is essentially a legal one. God has chosen to deal with man and to have relationships with man in this particular way.

Secondly, God Himself has made and constructed and fashioned the Law which governs His relationship with man. The Law is not made by man; the Law is made by God. It is He who has thought of it. It is He who has promulgated it. It was He who gave it originally to the first man. It was He who renewed it with Noah. It was He who renewed it with Abraham. It was He who made it still more plain to Moses, and through Moses. It is God's Law, not man's. And God has worked out and determined every single detail of this Law.

The third step is that God not only is the administrator of the Law, God is also the judge. He is described as the Judge everywhere in the Bible. 'Shall not the Judge of the whole earth do right?'(Genesis 18: 25). God is the Judge eternal, He has revealed Himself as such. He is the One who judges man in terms of the Law which He Himself has promulgated. All these principles are implicit in Paul's few words.

The fourth principle is that any charge that can ever be brought against a man must always be in terms of this Law, and nothing else; either that I have broken the Law, or that I have failed to keep the Law. A person who comes along and merely says that he or she does not like me has no standing; the sentiment does not count in man's law. You cannot go to a law-court in England and say, 'I do not like such a person, therefore I ask that that person be punished'. If you do so you will be told, 'Whether you like or dislike Mr So-and-So does not matter here. Can you prove that this person has broken a law or has failed to keep a law?' In a court of law everything has to be done in terms of law and nothing else. Likes and dislikes and motives do not matter, do not count. If anyone is to accuse us before God it has to be always in terms of this Law which God Himself has given to determine the state and condition of man, and His relationship to Him. Any accuser – the devil or anyone else – who is anxious to accuse us has to be able to establish his charge in terms of what the Law says.

This principle always governs procedure in a law court. Sometimes this appears to us to be almost ridiculous. I read of two cases recently that illustrate my point. A man was in court of whom it was said that he was guiltless in that he had done everything he could to avoid knocking down a woman on a Pedestrian Crossing. It was agreed that it was the woman's fault for she had foolishly run across the road; yet the man was punished, because he was guilty of a contravention of the law on one particular point. So that, though it may seem unjust to us, legally speaking the man was in transgression as the law now stands. In other words, what matters is not what you and I think, not what you and I may even regard as right and just; the question is, What does the law say? That is why we have the saying that 'The law is an ass'. It sometimes appears to us to be quite contrary to common sense. But while the law is the law, you have to abide by it, and you will be punished according to it. All this has a bearing upon problems in the realm of things spiritual.

With these thoughts in mind we are now in a position to consider the statement that it is God Himself who justifies us. This is the crux of the matter. The New English Bible translates, 'It is God who pronounces acquittal'. That is certainly true, but the translation does not go far enough. Indeed it leaves out what is the most glorious aspect of justification. It identifies justification with acquittal, with a pronouncement of 'Not guilty'. But we need more than that. Thank God, He does pronounce an acquittal;

otherwise we would all be damned. The first thing we need to know is that we are acquitted. But God goes further than that! To justify means more than to pardon; it means more than to forgive. As we have seen repeatedly in our study of the first four chapters of this Epistle, it means that God makes a declaration, a judicial declaration, to the effect that He has not only forgiven us, but that He now regards us as just and righteous and holy, as if we had never sinned at all. And that is what the Apostle is emphasizing at this point. God justifies in a legal manner; He always acts in terms of Law; He must be just. If God cannot forgive me without abrogating His own justice, then there is no forgiveness. In chapter 3, verses 24 to 26, we read: 'Being justified freely by his grace through the redemption that is in Christ Jesus . . . that he (God) might be just and the justifier of him which believeth in Jesus.' God has justified us in a legal manner, in a just manner. He has taken my sins and put them upon His Son. He said that He would punish sin, and He has punished sin. But He has punished sin in His Son; and because He has punished Him He does not punish me. I am acquitted. But acquittal is negative. Before I can stand in the presence of God I must have a positive righteousness because God is righteous and holy. So God not only imputes my sin to his Son, He takes His righteousness and imputes it to me. And having put the righteousness of Christ upon me He regards me as just, He pronounces that I am just. John Wesley's translation of Count Zinzendorf's hymn expresses it thus:

> *Jesus, Thy robe of righteousness*
> *My beauty is, my glorious dress;*
> *'Midst flaming worlds, in this arrayed,*
> *With joy shall I lift up my head.*

No one can lay any charge against me because I am arrayed in this righteousness. It is not merely negative; it is positive. The Apostle says the same thing in 2 Corinthians 5: 21: 'He hath made him to be sin for us, who knew no sin; that we might be made the righteousness of God in him.' That is justification! It is a judicial act on the part of God in which He pronounces that because of what He has done in and through the Lord Jesus Christ, whom 'He hath set forth to be a propitiation through faith in his blood', He regards us now as righteous. We are covered and clothed by the righteousness of Christ; not only pardoned and forgiven, but positively righteous. God regards us as just, and pronounces us to be just. The demands of His own Law have been satisfied in this Other, and therefore we are free.

This is the meaning of justification. It is not merely pronouncing an acquittal; it is pronouncing a positive righteousness, a positive holiness in Christ. The Apostle's teaching is that God has made this great proclamation in the resurrection; Christ 'was delivered for our offences, was raised again for our justification' (Romans 4: 25). Furthermore he says that God makes this pronouncement about us once and for ever. He does not make it many times, He makes it once. You cannot be justified many times; God does this once and once only. 'Therefore being justified by faith, we have peace with God through our Lord Jesus Christ.' It is God's statement. He knows the end from the beginning, and once He pronounces a man just, he is for ever just and righteous in the sight of God. It is not something that has to be repeated; it is once and for ever.

The real significance, therefore, of 'Who shall lay anything to the charge of God's elect? It is God that justifies' is that, being justified, we are not cleared against one charge only. The devil may come and make a particular charge, saying, 'This man fell into that sin, is he a Christian?' You are not only cleared against any one charge in justification, you are cleared against every charge – all the charges that can ever be thought of. Justification means that you are cleared, and delivered, and just in the sight of God as regards your past, present, and future. It is a 'once and for all' act. So all conceivable charges are already answered in God's declaratory statement about His having justified us.

But the Apostle's statement goes even further. In a law court there are two barristers arguing a case. The defending counsel has put up his defence and it seems to be very masterly. You feel that the case is finished, that the prosecution has collapsed. But, suddenly, counsel for the prosecution comes forward again and opens a book saying, 'I have an authority here, and my learned friend has forgotten a point. There is a detail in this law, in sub-section So-and-so. It is most unfortunate for counsel for the defence and for the poor prisoner, but here it is in the law.' It may be some little clause that has not been referred to for centuries by any judge, but here it is. He has found it, and this sub-section of a sub-section of a sub-section convicts the unfortunate prisoner of being guilty; and so judgment and sentence have to be passed. What the Apostle is saying here in Romans chapter 8 is that that can never happen in God's court, because God is the Judge and God is the Law-Giver. He knows everything about every possible sub-section. There is never the danger that Satan with all his cleverness and wiliness will be able to come forward one day and produce a clause that brings me under condemnation. God knows it all infinitely better than even Satan does. It is an utter impossibility. God knows all about the Law in its every detail, comma and jot and tittle, so nothing and no one shall ever be able to bring this charge against God's elect. No 'authority' can ever be quoted which is going to shake our position. Because we are justified we have finished with the Law and all its demands, for they have been satisfied on our behalf in what God has done in and through the Lord Jesus Christ. As God's elect we are 'dead to the law'. As far as we are involved in this matter of condemnation the Law is finished. Chapter 7 has reminded us, 'Know ye not, brethren, how that the law hath dominion over a man as long as he liveth? For the woman which hath a husband . . .' (verses 1 and 2). And in verse 4, 'Wherefore, my brethren, you also are become dead to the law by the body of Christ; that you should be married to another, even to Him who is raised from the dead, that we should bring forth fruit unto God'. The material statement is, 'You are become dead to the law by the body of Christ'.

The whole of man's relationship to God, as I said previously, is in legal terms, in terms of Law. No charge can ever be brought against me except in terms of Law. But now, as far as I am concerned, there is no Law. I am out of that realm. I am no longer related to God in terms of Law. Because of what God has done in Christ I am in the new relationship of 'grace'. I am dead to the Law. So should the devil get up and quote any law, the answer to him is, 'Out of court! No case! This man is no longer under law.' Let him do all his research work, let him try to find some little clause which will convict me, it is in vain; the whole of the Law is finished as far as I am concerned; I am 'dead to the law'. 'Ye are no longer under law,' as Romans 6: 14 puts it, 'but under grace.' As it is God who has justified us, and that, in a manner in which He has satisfied His own Law fully, we are therefore dead as far as that Law is concerned. And so it is completely impossible that anyone anywhere can ever rightly bring any charge against us.

Let us now draw some conclusions from all this. How important it is to understand the doctrine of justification by faith only! There is no type of Christian who is so utterly foolish as the one who says, 'I am not interested in doctrine; I have my experience'. The devil can soon shake you and your experience. It is only as you understand the doctrine of justification by faith that you will have security and safety and joy. Doctrine is essential. Have you realized the meaning of justification? You are not merely pardoned and forgiven; you are declared by God to be just in His sight. This is a matter of status, a matter of standing. There is no going back and forth from being justified to not being justified, and then being justified again. God has done this once and for ever, and the Law is ended as far as you are concerned. 'Christ is the end of the law for righteousness to everyone that believeth' (Romans 10: 4). That is the complete answer to any charge that can ever be brought against us. It is the only answer. If you rely on anything else the devil will soon shake you. There is only one answer to give him, and it is, 'God Himself has justified me, so all you say is a lie'.

This, then, is the way to meet the devil and his accusations. If you begin to listen to the devil and say to yourself, 'Well, after all, he is right; I did sin yesterday and I am not as good as I ought to be', you will soon be feeling under condemnation again because you have brought in works once more. You should rather say, 'I know I am unworthy, I know I am sinful; no one knows how bad I am; but God has justified me in Christ. I do not rely upon myself; I am relying utterly, only, absolutely upon the Lord Jesus Christ and upon what He has done on my behalf, and upon God's declaration with respect to me.' Stand on justification by faith only. It is the only ground on which you can stand. We must learn to do this; it is the final answer to the devil. 'It is God that justifieth.'

This is how the Protestant Reformation ever came into being. Do you understand the thrill Martin Luther felt when this dawned upon him? Do you not now see what he meant when he said that this doctrine of justification by faith only is the test of a standing or a falling church? It is the key to everything. And, conversely, do you not see the error of the Roman Catholic Church when she teaches that a man is only justified because he is sanctified? Do you not see the error of that Church also in opposing the doctrine of assurance, and the error of all others who oppose the doctrine of assurance? We are meant to enjoy complete assurance and an absolute certainty concerning our ultimate destiny. We are meant to be able to say without any doubt or hesitation, 'Who shall lay anything to the charge of God's elect?' of which I am one. The answer is, No one, nothing! Why? Because it is God Himself, the Judge, the Law-Giver, who has found a way to satisfy His own Law, and His own holy nature, and His own justice and righteousness, in His only begotten Son, and who has Himself declared that because I believe in Jesus I am just and justified in His sight. Do you answer the devil and every other accuser in that way? It is the only way. Be certain about the meaning of justification, and then use it, apply it, and you will be able to answer every enemy in earth or hell. You will be able to defy them all as Count Zinzendorf did in another verse of that great hymn as translated by John Wesley:

> *Bold shall I stand in that great day,*
> *For who aught to my charge shall lay?*
> *Fully through Thee absolved I am*
> *From sin and fear, from guilt and shame.*

The declaration of our justification is an absolute statement; and there is no conceivable going back on it. Once in Christ, always in Christ! The final perseverance of the saints!

Thirty-four

*

Who is he that condemneth? It is Christ that died, yea rather, that is risen again, who is even at the right hand of God, who also maketh intercession for us.   Romans 8: 34

We have suggested that this and the previous verse should be taken together, because together they constitute the challenge thrown out by the Apostle as to whether it can ever be possible for anyone who is justified to come again into condemnation. The first half of the challenge was 'Who shall lay anything to the charge of God's elect?' The answer was, 'It is God [himself] that justifieth'. Now in the second half the Apostle puts the question in a slightly different form, 'Who is he that condemneth?'

Though there is but little difference between the two, the Apostle varies the expressions because he is anxious that we should be certain of our position beyond any doubt whatsoever. He leaves no stone unturned, he leaves no argument untouched or unconsidered. He knows that we ourselves are ever ready to conjure up possibilities; and still more, he knows that the enemy of our souls is always ready to trip us, to discourage and depress us, and to try to rob us of our confidence and ultimate assurance. So in order to help us, and out of his great pastoral heart, he considers every imaginable and conceivable difficulty and objection.

In this 34th verse the Apostle does two main things. First, he gives proof positive of the fact that it is God who justifies us, and also that God has indeed done so. He is not content with making the statement 'It is God that justifieth', or, 'Is it God who justifieth who is going to bring a charge against us?' Having made the statement he proceeds to give the evidence whereby we can attain to full assurance in these matters. But there is a further point. We are told in many places in the Scripture that judgment has been committed to the Son; so the possible argument may arise, 'Although it is God that justifies, as judgment has been committed to the Son may not the Son condemn us? May not He bring some charge against us because of the way in which He was treated in this world, and so bring us all again into condemnation?' The Apostle shows here that the Son also will bring no charge against us, or be the means of our condemnation, any more than the Father Himself.

But again I would emphasize that above everything else Paul's object in this verse is to demonstrate to us in a final manner that any form of condemnation for believers, the called of God, is quite unthinkable in view of what God has already done for us in and through our Lord Jesus Christ. The Apostle divides this great assertion into four particular statements, and we shall see as we look at them in turn that they are ascending steps; at least steps one, two and three merit this description. I suggest that in many ways the third is really the climax, and later on I shall give what I regard as the Apostle's reason for putting the fourth in that position. Here then are the steps, the particular statements – 'It is Christ that died', 'yea rather, that is risen again', 'who is even at the right hand of God', 'who also maketh intercession for us'. These are statements, propositions, based upon truth which can never be refuted, and which is the ultimate ground of our salvation, and still more of our assurance of salvation.

What we have here is a perfect summary, an astounding summary of our Lord's mediatorial work. If we are to grasp the full import of what the Apostle is arguing here, we must realize that he is not simply concerned to tell us what our Lord has done, or what has been done to Him; he is anxious to stress each one of these points in terms of the fact that each one of them was done 'for us'. That is where the mediatorial aspect comes in. None of these things would have happened to Him in and of Himself; they all happened to Him because of His relationship to us, because of what He had come to do for His people. We must not look at these things merely as incidents in His life story. In all of them He acts as our Mediator, our Representative.

The Apostle's argument is that it is impossible that God who sent His Son to do these things for us and on our behalf should punish us, or that the Lord Jesus Christ Himself who has done them, should in any way be the cause of our condemnation. It is indeed another way of saying what our Lord Himself said, as recorded in the 3rd chapter of John's Gospel, verses 17 and 18: 'For God sent not his Son into the world to condemn the world'; so the Son of God can never be our condemnation. The question is, 'Who is he that condemneth?' It cannot be the Son of God because He was not sent into the world to condemn the world, 'but that the world through him might be saved'. 'He that believeth on him is not condemned: but he that believeth not is condemned already, because he hath not believed in the name of the only begotten Son of God.' This 34th verse of this 8th chapter of the Epistle to the Romans is nothing but a restatement of that truth. God did not send His Son into this world to condemn the world. There is no need of that because the world is already 'under condemnation'. He sent Him in order to save.

Let us follow the Apostle as he divides up that great central statement into these four separate subsidiary statements. First of all, 'Who is he that condemneth? It is Christ that died.' This latter statement can also be put in the form of a question, 'Who is he that condemneth? shall Christ Jesus who died?' That is an equally legitimate translation, and one which perhaps brings out the force of the argument still more powerfully. It is unthinkable that the Lord Jesus Christ should be the cause of our condemnation because it is He who died for us. You may say, 'But I know this already; it is what I learned when I was converted'. I reply that if you claim that you are well aware of this, then you have always had full assurance of salvation, and the devil never makes you feel that you are not a Christian, and you are never troubled when you fall into sin. But is that true of you? The fact is that we constantly need to be reminded of these things. This is the way to answer the accusations of the devil, and the only way to be clear about the fact that we shall never come into condemnation. 'It is Christ that died.' That means, in particular, that in dying our Lord received the condemnation that was due to our sins. That is why He died. He was sinless, no one could bring any accusation against Him. Men tried to do so but they failed. He Himself said just before His death, 'The prince of this world cometh and hath nothing in me'. Nothing at all! Even the devil could find nothing. The Lord Jesus Christ was innocent, He was pure, He had given a perfect obedience to the Law of God, He had not failed in any respect whatsoever. Therefore there was no need that He should ever die, for death is 'the wages of sin', the punishment of sin – 'The soul that sinneth it shall die'. But He had never sinned.

So we have to ask the question, Why did Christ ever die? We have His own answer. When some of His disciples, in their ignorance and their failure to understand, were producing their swords in order to defend Him, He said in effect, 'Put them back, I do not need them'. He had 'set his face steadfastly to go to Jerusalem'. He knew He was going to die, He went deliberately to His death. He said, 'Thinkest thou that I cannot now pray to my Father, and he shall presently (immediately) give me more than twelve legions of angels? But how then shall the scriptures be fulfilled, that thus it must be?' So we find that He went deliberately to His death. There is only one explanation of His death. He died because He took upon Him the guilt of our sins. Or, to look at it from the other angle, God laid the guilt of our sins upon Him and He received our condemnation. His death is the condemnation meted out by God upon sin. He had not sinned; it was for our sins He died. Therefore, says the Apostle, when you look at His death that is the argument you should deduce. He cannot be the cause of our condemnation because His very death proves that He has taken our condemnation upon Himself. How can the One who has taken our condemnation upon Him be our condemnation? It is impossible. *Reductio ad absurdum* once more!

This is the Apostle's way of arguing; it is the only way in which we can defeat the devil, and defeat the thoughts that arise within us as the result of the attacks of the devil. We have to reduce the devil's argument to absurdity, and we do so by looking in the true and the right way at the death of our Lord. We must listen to His statement upon the Cross, 'It is finished'. What is finished? The work He had come to do! What is that? He had already told us in His high-priestly prayer. Even before His death He was able to say, 'I have finished the work which thou gavest me to do', and then He says it again finally upon the Cross – 'It is finished'.

Christ came into the world to do two things – to render a positive obedience to God's Law, and to bear the punishment, the penalty that that Law metes out to sin and transgression. There is an active element, and also a passive element in His work;

and He has fulfilled both. He can say, 'It is finished' on the one hand, and on the other He can assure us that there is nothing left undone. But here particularly He is saying that His work is finished in the sense that the condemnation pronounced by the Law of God upon our sinfulness has been meted out, and He has received it. He has received it to the full, there is nothing left, it is finished. All that the Law has to say about sin, and to do about it, has been said and done in His Person; 'It is finished'. That is what is meant by 'It is Christ that died'. God justifies us because of that; that is the basis of our justification.

As I suggested, the Apostle is here substantiating, proving, what he has laid down in the proposition, 'Who shall lay anything to the charge of God's elect? It is God that justifieth'. It is because He has already condemned our sin and punished it, that God declares us to be just in His sight. It is the only way, I say with reverence, that God could justify us. Thus, as Paul has already told us in the 4th chapter of this self-same Epistle in verse 5, 'But to him that worketh not, but believeth on him that justifieth the ungodly, his faith is counted for righteousness'. God 'justifies the ungodly' and He does so because He has already condemned them and punished their sin in Christ. Justification is a declaration that we are no longer under condemnation.

This means, then, that God's justice is fully satisfied. The Apostle says it again in this manner in order that we may take a firm grasp of it; and therefore we can argue and say that if we who believe in Christ were to be punished now it would be unjust. That is a very strong statement to make, is it not? But it is a statement we must make not only on the basis of what we find here, but on the basis of what we find the Apostle John saying, in his own way, in the first chapter of his 1st Epistle, and especially in verses 8 and 9: 'If we say that we have no sin we deceive ourselves, and the truth is not in us. If we confess our sins, he is faithful and just to forgive us our sins, and to cleanse us from all unrighteousness.'

The two vital words there, of course, are the words 'faithful' and 'just'. John means that God is faithful to His own way of working, to His own statements, to His own promises. Not only so, God is always just. So John says that if we who are believers fall into sin and confess our sins, God's own faithfulness and justice demand that He should forgive us. God has made the statement that in His Son He punished our sins, that His Son took upon Himself our condemnation and our guilt, and that He bore the punishment which we deserved. Justice has already been meted out. So the Apostle John says that we need have no fear. The very truthfulness, the faithfulness, and the justice of God make certain that we are forgiven, because God has already dealt with the sin, has already condemned it, and has already punished it in the Person of His own Son. So we can state the matter in this way, that God's justice now, far from being a source of terror to a Christian believer, should be his greatest comfort, his greatest solace, his greatest security.

This is a vital part of the doctrine of assurance and of final perseverance. When we fall into sin and think of the justice of God, we tend to argue that God would be justified in punishing us, that we deserve nothing else. But we are mistaken. The argument should now be, that the justice, the righteousness, and the truthfulness of God now insist upon, and demand, that we be pardoned completely. This is because of what God has done in Christ. It would be unjust to punish the same sin twice, and God can never be unjust. 'He is faithful and just.' So here we have absolute proof, not only that one cannot be condemned, but that it is because of the death of the Son of God that such condemnation is impossible. For us to be condemned would mean that the sin of which we are guilty and which has already been punished in Christ in our stead should once more be punished in us. That would be injustice. All that justice demands is the punishment of the sin; and as our sin has already been punished, it is already satisfied. Our justification declares that.

The inevitable deduction is that we cannot come under condemnation any more; to do so would imply that God is not faithful and just. It would imply an essential contradiction in God's character. The justice of God is on our side in this matter now. The justice of God demands that whatever sins we fall into be forgiven, and that we be 'cleansed from all unrighteousness', because of what God has done for us in and through the death of Christ. The argument could not possibly be stronger. What is most terrifying to the soul under conviction is the justice, the righteousness, the holiness, the immutability, the truth of God. But the moment you become a believer, God's character and attributes become the greatest guarantee of your security, the greatest proof that you can never come under condemnation.

But we must read on. 'Who is he that condemneth? It is Christ that died, yea rather, that is risen again.' A better translation here is 'yea rather, having been raised again'. The significance of that change is surely obvious. Why does the Apostle say 'yea rather'? Why does he not stop at 'It is Christ that died'? The answer is most significant, most important, and full of reasons and arguments for yet further comfort and assurance.

This addition carries the argument yet further. Indeed we would not have been able to make our first point if we were not sure already of this second one; because it is only in the light of the resurrection that you can truly understand the meaning of our Lord's death. The argument embedded in this phrase is one of the most amazing compressions in the whole of biblical literature. In this one phrase, 'yea rather, that is risen again', you have a synopsis of 1 Corinthians, chapter 15. That is a long chapter, but in a sense it is summarized here in a phrase.

In other words the Apostle is saying that if you could not go on to say 'yea rather, that is risen again', you would be 'yet in your sins', your 'faith is vain', you are still under condemnation. 'If in this life only we have hope in Christ, we are of all men most miserable' (1 Corinthians 15: 19). The fact of the resurrection is absolutely essential to our assurance. Hence those who say that it is immaterial and unimportant that you should believe in the literal, physical resurrection are always people who are without assurance. Indeed they are without a gospel. The Apostle's argument in 1 Corinthians 15, as it is here, is that if you are not sure of the Lord's resurrection, then you have nothing.

The Apostle has already referred to the significance of the resurrection at the end of the 4th chapter, in the words, 'Who was delivered for our offences, and was raised again for our justification'. In summarizing and bringing to a conclusion his argument concerning justification, and particularly in the case of Abraham, he said that these things 'were not written for his sake only, but for us also, to whom it shall be imputed, if we believe on him that raised up Jesus our Lord from the dead; who was delivered for our offences, and was raised again for our justification'. Here, in chapter 8, Paul states the same truth in a different way. He tells us that it was God who raised Christ from the dead; hence my suggestion of the better translation. The Scripture varies in its statements about the Lord's resurrection. Some statements seem to say that our Lord raised Himself; but the majority of references tell us that it was God who raised Him. But here what the Apostle says is, 'It is Christ that died, yea rather, who has been raised again'. It was God who raised Him from the dead.

Such is this Apostle's customary way of stating the matter. We have a notable instance of this in Ephesians, chapter 1, verses 19 and 20: Paul desires that the Ephesians should know 'the exceeding greatness of his [God's] power to us-ward who believe, according to the working of his mighty power, which he wrought in Christ, when he raised him from the dead, and set him at his own right hand'. It was God who raised Him. Similarly, in the reported speeches of the Apostle Paul in the Acts of the Apostles, we find that in preaching at Antioch in Pisidia he states this in a very dramatic manner. He says that men crucified Him, 'but God raised him from the dead' (Acts 13: 30).

Why did God do so? The answer is given in Romans 4: 25: 'He delivered him (to death) because of our offences, He raised him up again (from the dead) because of our justification.' Take note that the resurrection is not the cause of our justification. The death of Christ is the cause of our justification. The resurrection does not justify us. What then does the resurrection do? The resurrection is the proof to us that we have been justified by our Lord's death. Christ had to die because of our sins. He dies 'because of' our sins, He rises 'because of' our justification. The justification takes place before the rising. The rising is the proclamation, the declaration, the assurance of the fact that we are justified and accepted in the Lord Jesus Christ. That is the second point, therefore, which we deduce and use as an argument. God in raising His Son again from the dead is proclaiming to us that He is satisfied with the work that our Lord had done, that He had fully borne the punishment of sin, that everything the Law demanded has been fully accomplished, that there is nothing left to be done, and that every demand of God's holy character and Law has been fully satisfied. For all these reasons God raised Christ from the dead.

But Paul does not stop at this point. We go on to a third argument, a most important one from the standpoint of our comfort and consolation and assurance of salvation. There are five main enemies which, as Christians, we have to fight. Christians in the early centuries of the Christian Church were very much concerned about this, as also was Martin Luther, for he gave it a good deal of emphasis. But we do not always emphasize it as we should. The main thing, of course, in the work of salvation is the satisfaction of the justice of God; but when you consider salvation from the standpoint of assurance, it is good to do so in the light of what has sometimes been called the 'classical' view of the doctrine of the atonement, a view which emphasizes that our Lord's work upon the Cross delivers us from five main enemies that confront us, namely, sin, Satan, the Law of God, death, and hell. And before we can have a full assurance we must be fully satisfied that they have all been dealt with in a final and a conclusive manner.

It is at this precise point that the resurrection helps tremendously. We have seen earlier how sin and guilt and the Law have already been dealt with by the death of Christ. But what about death itself, what about the grave, what about hell? These are powerful enemies and foes that are confronting us. The author of the Epistle to the Hebrews expresses this in his second chapter thus: 'Forasmuch then as the children are partakers of flesh and blood, he also himself likewise took part of the same; that through death he might destroy him that had the power of death, that is, the devil; and deliver them who through fear of death were all their lifetime subject to bondage' (vv. 14 and 15). The fear of death belongs to the entire human race. Whether men always understand it or not, it is with them. The resurrection is a mighty proclamation of our Lord's conquest over death, over the grave, over hell. Death is 'the wages of sin'; 'the sting of death is sin; and the strength of sin is the law'. Hence people are afraid of death. The sting of death includes the sense of guilt, and the fear of what awaits us beyond death. People who call themselves atheists do not like facing death for this reason; and it is innate in the whole of mankind. 'The sting of death is sin', and when you understand the meaning of the Law, the sting becomes stronger, for 'the strength of sin is the law'. So we need to be delivered from this fear. Death comes and tries to shake us and make us doubt our salvation; it tries to bring us under condemnation. The answer is – the resurrection! Christ has conquered death, He has conquered the grave, He has conquered hell, and we can say 'O death, where is thy sting? O grave, where is thy victory?' Christ has led captivity captive, He has conquered all our foes; the devil and all his forces have all been conquered. Even death and hell are conquered, as is shown by His resurrection from the dead. So it is not surprising that the Apostle says, 'yea rather, that is risen again'. The resurrection not only tells me that God is pleased with the work of His Son, and accepts it, and is satisfied with it; it is a final proof to me that every consequence of sin has been dealt with in detail. Christ has triumphed over all, and He rises in proclamation of that fact.

I reminded you earlier that our Lord accomplished all His work and endured all His sufferings as our Representative, our Mediator. He would never have been in the world but for us, He would never have died but for us, He would never have been buried but for us, He would never 'have been raised' but for our sake. And we must draw the inevitable deduction from all this, for this is where assurance comes in. The Apostle has really told us so already in chapter 6, verses 8-10: 'Now if we be dead with Christ, we believe that we shall also live with him: knowing that Christ being raised from the dead dieth no more; death hath no more dominion over him; for in that he died, he died unto sin once: but in that he liveth, he liveth unto God.' That means that He died unto sin once – once and for all – never again! He put Himself under the Law, He came to die, and He died. But that happened to Him once only; He will never die again: 'Christ being raised from the dead dieth no more; death hath no more dominion over him.' He needed to die but once; but He has conquered death in dying once. He will never die again; He is 'alive unto God' – 'in that he liveth, he liveth unto God' – and will live eternally. The resurrection proclaims this great truth. Then the Apostle proceeds to say (Romans 6: 11): 'Likewise reckon ye also yourselves to be dead indeed unto sin, but alive unto God through our Lord Jesus Christ.' Do not let death, and the grave, and hell, frighten you, Christ has conquered them all; He is out of that realm; He came into it for a while in order to save us; He is out of it now and He will die no more. He is alive, and we are in Him, we are joined to Him. The Christian is 'alive unto God', and so nothing can bring him into condemnation. The thought of death should not make a Christian feel condemned, the thought of the grave should not make us feel distressed, the thought of hell should not terrorize us; it has all been dealt with, as the resurrection of Christ proclaims. And we are 'in Him', so what is true of Him is true of us. Therein lies our assurance. 'Who is he that condemneth?' Let the devil come, let sin come, let the Law come, let death come, let the grave come, let hell come; all are answered by 'yea rather, that is risen again'.

We see once more the importance of grasping the great doctrine that the Apostle has already laid down in chapter 6 about our union with Christ. 'How shall we that are dead to sin, live any longer therein?' 'Know ye not, that so many of us as were baptized into Jesus Christ were baptized into his death? Therefore we are buried with him by baptism into death: that like as Christ was raised up from the dead by the glory of the Father, even so we also should walk in newness of life. For if we have been planted together in the likeness of his death, we shall be also in the likeness of his resurrection: knowing this, that our old man is crucified with him.' Note the argument; it explains why the Apostle hurries on to, 'yea rather, that is risen again'. It is by the resurrection that we are made certain that Christ's death was sufficient to deal with our every problem. It is the proclamation of the fact that we are justified and accepted in Him for ever and ever.

We have already seen that in the 11th verse of this 8th chapter the Apostle has hinted at this. He says, 'If the Spirit of him that raised up Jesus from the dead dwell in you, he that raised up Christ from the dead shall also quicken your mortal bodies by His Spirit that dwelleth in you.' The Apostle Peter says precisely the same thing in his own way in his First Epistle, chapter 1, verse 3: 'Blessed be the God and Father of our Lord Jesus Christ, which according to his abundant mercy hath begotten us again by the resurrection of Jesus Christ from the dead.' God said, 'Thou art my Son, this day have I begotten thee' (Hebrews 1: 5) by raising Him up from the dead. And He has 'begotten us again unto a lively hope by the resurrection of Jesus Christ from the dead, to an inheritance incorruptible, undefiled, and that fadeth not away'. Peter says a similar thing in his 3rd chapter, verse 21: 'The like figure whereunto even baptism doth also now save us (not the putting away of the filth of the flesh, but the answer of a good conscience toward God) by the resurrection of Jesus Christ' (1 Peter 3: 21). What gives me a good conscience toward God is the 'resurrection of Jesus Christ'. It is the same argument.

The Apostle Paul states it very clearly once more in Ephesians 2: 5 and 6: 'Even when we were dead in sins, (he) hath quickened us together with Christ, (by grace are ye saved); and hath raised us up together.' We have been raised with Christ. What happened to Him happened for us. It happens to us, as to Him, because He is our Head, our Representative. We are the Body, we partake in all that has happened to Him. So we are 'risen together with him'; and therefore condemnation is a sheer impossibility. He cannot be condemned again, He does not go back again under death; neither do we. We are 'alive unto God' even as He is 'alive unto God'; and that makes any thought of condemnation not only impossible, but utterly ridiculous.

The Apostle is really saying in a different way what he has already said in the 1st verse of this 8th chapter: 'There is therefore now no condemnation to them that are in Christ Jesus.' Therefore, Jesus Christ, the Son of God, can never be the cause of our condemnation. His dying for us makes it impossible, His rising again is a proclamation publicly of its utter impossibility; for it is the proof, the declaration of our justification, our acceptance with God, because of all He has done on our behalf. In rising from the dead 'He has brought life and immortality to light through the gospel' for us, and that makes condemnation a sheer impossibility. In Christ we must 'reckon ourselves to be dead indeed unto sin, but alive unto God'. Or as Paul expresses it in the 13th verse of his 6th chapter: 'Yield yourselves unto God as those that are alive from the dead.'

There is a hymn that expresses all this very nobly:

> *Jesus lives! thy terrors now*
> *Can, O death, no more appal us;*
> *Jesus lives! by this we know*
> *Thou, O grave, canst not enthral us:*
>
> *Jesus lives! henceforth is death*
> *But the gate of life immortal;*
> *This shall calm our trembling breath*
> *When we pass its gloomy portal:*

Romans 8: 34

Jesus lives! our hearts know well
Nought from us His love shall sever;
Life, nor death, nor powers of hell
Tear us from His keeping ever:

Jesus lives! to Him the throne
Over all the world is given;
May we go where He is gone,
Rest and reign with Him in heaven.

The hymn not only sums up the first two steps, it anticipates the remaining two steps. We are climbing a grand staircase here. 'Who is he that condemneth? It is Christ that died.' Have you planted your feet firmly on that step? 'Yea rather, that is risen again.' Are you still with Him? Do you realize what His resurrection means? Do you realize that you are 'risen with Him'? If you do, you will know that there can never be any 'condemnation to them which are in Christ Jesus'. May the Holy Spirit enable us not only to remember these phrases, but to understand their meaning, their significance. May He imprint them on our minds in such power that we shall never again in thought or spirit be brought into bondage, into captivity, into condemnation, into any uncertainty with respect to our ultimate salvation and glorification, and to the fact that we are indeed the 'children of God, heirs of God and joint-heirs with Christ'.

Thirty-five

*

Who is he that condemneth? It is Christ that died, yea rather, that is risen again, who is even at the right hand of God, who also maketh intercession for us.   Romans 8: 34

We have seen that the Apostle in this verse gives a four-fold answer to the challenge he puts up in the words 'Who is he that condemneth?' We have already considered the first two replies, and now we come to the third reply, or third step in the argument, all of which is still designed to prove beyond any doubt or cavil the doctrine of the final perseverance of the saints.

The third statement is, 'Who is even at the right hand of God'. We note once again that each one of these statements concerning our Lord is made specifically with respect to Him in His office as our Mediator. That is the object – to remind us of what He has done for us. He would never have come into the world at all were it not 'for us'. He would certainly never have died were it not 'for us'. 'It is Christ that died', but He would never have died were it not that He had taken our sins upon Him. Everything we are told in the four steps must be considered in terms of His mediatorial work, what He has done, what He does, and what He will yet do on our behalf.

'It is Christ that died, yea rather, that is risen again.' But the resurrection is not the end of the story. The Apostle reminds us now of our Lord's present position; but we note that in doing so he assumes two steps, which he does not actually mention, but which are, of course, of vital importance, and were clearly in the mind of the Apostle. Our Lord not only rose from the grave; following that, after a period of forty days, He ascended into heaven. We term it the ascension. Let us never forget that that is one of the steps, one of the facts, in connection with our Lord's work on our behalf and for our salvation. The ascension!

[426]

It is as much a fact as is the crucifixion, the resurrection, His heavenly session, and the sending of the Holy Spirit. As the author of the Epistle to the Hebrews expresses it, He has 'passed through the heavens' into the very presence of God (4: 14). Or again in the same Epistle (7: 26) He was 'made higher than the heavens'. The result of that, as Paul says here, is, 'Who is even at the right hand of God'.

The present position of our Lord is the answer to the prayer He Himself offered in His great high-priestly prayer as recorded in the 17th chapter of John's Gospel – 'And now, O Father, glorify thou me with thine own self with the glory which I had with thee before the world was'. The Apostle is asserting in our text that God had answered that prayer, and that our Lord has been glorified again with the glory that He had with the Father before the foundation of the world.

How does this statement help the particular argument concerning the final perseverance of the saints? Paul is not merely stating a fact; he is arguing, he is debating, he is reasoning, he is demolishing an opposition. So we must emphasize the exact significance of this statement from the standpoint of this particular argument. It is primarily a reference to our Lord's work on our behalf as our great High Priest. This is the theme which is dealt with at length in the Epistle to the Hebrews. Between the resurrection and His being seated at the right hand of God in the glory our Lord did His work as our great High Priest.

To understand that work we must go back to the Old Testament and study what the high priest had to do under the old dispensation. He had many functions, but his chief function was that once a year, and once a year only, he entered into the innermost chamber of the temple or the tabernacle which was called 'the holiest of all', and there performed an act which he alone was allowed to do. An account of this is given in Hebrews 9: 7–12, 'But into the second' – the second chamber – 'went the high priest alone once every a year, not without blood, which he offered for himself, and for the errors of the people: the Holy Ghost this signifying, that the way into the holiest of all was not yet made manifest, while as the first tabernacle was yet standing: which was a figure for the time then present, in which were offered both gifts and sacrifices, that could not make him that did the service perfect, as pertaining to the conscience; which stood only in meats and drinks, and divers washings . . . But Christ being come an high priest of good things to come, by a greater and more perfect tabernacle, not made with hands, that is to say, not of this building; neither by the blood of goats and calves, but by his own blood he entered in once into the holy place, having obtained eternal redemption for us.'

The high priest once a year took upon him, as it were, the sins of all the people. He had the names of the twelve tribes of Israel on the ephod on his breast, and so acted as their representative. An animal was killed, the blood was collected, and the high priest took it into the 'holiest of all' once a year, and there spread it on the mercy-seat and before the mercy-seat as an offering to God. The people outside were waiting to know whether God had accepted the offering, and when suddenly they heard the sound of the jingling of the bells on the hem of the high priest's robe they knew that God had accepted the offering; when he came out again they knew that their sins were covered and that God would continue to bless them as His people.

That was the chief function of the high priest, and it pictures what our Lord Himself has done on behalf of His people. He did this before He 'sat down at the right hand of God'. Having offered Himself as a sacrifice – He is both the sacrifice and the high priest – He took 'His own blood', He 'passed through the heavens' with it, and entered into the very presence of God in the heavenly tabernacle, and there offered it to God.

This is most comforting doctrine. I have already quoted verses 7–12 in the 9th chapter of the Epistle to the Hebrews, but the author goes on to argue that almost everything in the Old Testament was purified and set apart by blood. 'And almost all things', he says in verse 22, 'are by the law purged with blood: and without shedding of blood is no remission.' Then in verse 23: 'It was therefore necessary that the patterns of things in the heavens should be purified with these, but the heavenly things themselves with better sacrifices than these'. The patterns of things in the heavens are, of course, the earthly tabernacle and the temple that the children of Israel made according to the instructions given by God to Moses. In other words, the earthly tabernacle and the earthly temple were but patterns of the heavenly temple itself. In the Shekinah glory, in the 'holiest of all' of the earthly tabernacle or temple, God in a symbolic manner dwelt and came to meet with the people. But that was only a picture of His dwelling in the heavens. It was essential that the heavenly tabernacle be purified with better sacrifices than the mere earthly representations. 'For Christ is not entered into the holy places made with hands' – that is to say, not into an earthly tabernacle or temple – 'which are the figures of the true; but into heaven itself, now to appear in the presence of God for us' – on our behalf!

Our Lord fulfilled the type between his resurrection and His being 'seated at the right hand of God', and it is a vital part of our salvation, especially from the standpoint of assurance. All the teaching in the Old Testament prefigures what Christ would do. It all has its meaning in Him, and what we are told is, that having offered His life, and His blood having been shed, He took it – His own blood – and offered it to God in heaven itself, in the innermost sanctum even of heaven, where God Himself dwells in His eternal glory.

But that is not all. This being 'seated at the right hand of God' is also a proof of the completion of His work of redemption, for the offering of 'His own blood' to the Father was the last act, the last step, in our redemption. Then, and not till then, did He sit down at the right hand of God in the glory. There are two wonderful statements of this truth, again in the Epistle to the Hebrews. The first is in the 1st chapter, verse 3, where, describing our Lord, the author says, 'Who being the brightness of his glory, and the express image of his person, and upholding all things by the word of his power, when he had by himself purged our sins, sat down on the right hand of the Majesty on high'. He repeats it in the 10th chapter, in verses 11–14, 'And every priest standeth daily ministering and offering oftentimes the same sacrifices, which can never take away sins: but this man, after he had offered one sacrifice for sins for ever, sat down on the right hand of God; from henceforth expecting till his enemies be made his footstool. For by one offering he hath perfected for ever them that are sanctified.'

The word 'sanctified' as used there must not be interpreted in the sense in which it is customarily used. 'Them that are sanctified' refers to those who have been 'set apart for God'. The process of our sanctification is something quite different. In the Epistle to the Hebrews – as indeed so often in other places in the Scripture –

[429]

'sanctified' means 'set apart'. 'He hath perfected for ever them that are sanctified' refers to all who are Christians. All Christians have been 'sanctified' in that sense by the Lord Jesus Christ and His work. The apostle Peter teaches the same truth in the following words: 'Elect according to the foreknowledge of God the Father, through sanctification of the Spirit, unto obedience and sprinkling of the blood of Jesus Christ' (1 Peter 1: 2). We have been set apart by the Spirit – 'through sanctification of the Spirit' – 'unto obedience', 'unto faith', 'unto salvation'.

We see therefore that we are dealing here with very profound teaching. Christ's being 'seated at the right hand of God' tells us, in the first instance, that His work is finished. 'Sitting down' always bears that meaning. We are told that after God made the world He 'rested' on the seventh day. He 'sat down', as it were. Our Lord had completed the work of salvation and redemption, He had completed everything connected with His office in securing our salvation; so, having offered His blood as the final act, He 'sat down'. Sitting down is a sign of finality; it means that nothing further needs to be done concerning our sins. He has done everything. None would dare to say this were it not in the Scripture. 'He hath perfected for ever them that are sanctified.' There is nothing more that needs to be done, there is nothing more that can be done. The author of the Epistle to the Hebrews constantly emphasizes the 'once and for ever' character of our Lord's work. He has 'perfected' it, He has finished it; so He sits down on the right hand of God.

The Apostle's argument is, that in the light of these truths any change as regards our standing is impossible. 'Who shall bring any charge against God's elect?' 'Who is he that condemneth?' It is a sheer impossibility. The work that our Lord has done on our behalf is a 'perfect' work. He has 'perfected for ever' all who are 'in Him', all who are 'the called according to his purpose'. It has been done perfectly by Him once and for ever; therefore it can never change. Condemnation is therefore an utter impossibility for all who are in Christ Jesus.

But we must go on to a third deduction from the statement that Christ is 'even at the right hand of God'. His being 'seated at the right hand of God' is what is described theologically as 'the heavenly session' of the Lord Jesus Christ. Why is He seated at the right hand of God? The answer given in many places in the

Scripture is that He is there as a reward for what He has done. In the Epistle to the Ephesians, chapter 1, verse 19, we read: 'And what is the exceeding greatness of his power to us-ward who believe, according to the working of his mighty power, which he wrought in Christ, when he raised him from the dead, and set him at his own right hand in the heavenly places, far above all principality, and power, and might, and dominion, and every name that is named, not only in this world, but also in that which is to come: and hath put all things under his feet, and gave him to be the head over all things to the church, which is his body, the fulness of him that filleth all in all.'

In the Epistle to the Philippians, chapter 2, verses 9–11, after saying in verse 8 that 'He humbled himself, and became obedient unto death, even the death of the Cross', Paul proceeds to say, 'Wherefore' – because of that; because He humbled Himself; because of the incarnation; because of His obedience; because of His humbling Himself even to the death of the Cross – 'God also hath highly exalted him, and given him a name which is above every name: that at the name of Jesus every knee should bow, of things in heaven, and things in earth, and things under the earth; and that every tongue should confess that Jesus Christ is Lord, to the glory of God the Father'. Notice the 'Wherefore'! He is seated at the right hand of God as a reward for what He has done for us. He has been put into the highest position conceivable. The most distinguished guest is always on the right hand of the host; and the Lord Jesus Christ is exalted to sit at the 'right hand' of God the Father in the everlasting glory. That is His reward for what He has done.

We deduce from this that the work done by our Lord must be satisfactory to God, and that He must be well pleased with it. It must be a complete work which can never fail. And that is precisely what the Apostle wants us to know – that it cannot fail! The fact that our Lord is seated at the right hand of God, and has been rewarded by God in that way for His work, means that nothing can ever go wrong with what He has done for us. The argument runs thus: If God has already rewarded His own Son for saving us in a perfect manner, is it conceivable that anything can go wrong with that salvation? Once more the Apostle reduces any such possibility to utter absurdity. If you are not assured of your salvation and your final perseverance, your real trouble is that you cannot think rightly, or else you do not believe the Scriptures. If you believe the Scriptures you are driven to this conclusion. No other conclusion is possible. But then add this further thought, that all the work which He has done, He has done 'for us'. Not for Himself, but for us, miserable sinners as we are by nature, fallible and failing as we are. He has done it all for us, and He has been rewarded for doing it, in that particular way.

But we can go yet further. His being 'seated at the right hand of God' is also a pronouncement as to what He is, and as to what He is now doing. I say this on the authority of Acts 5: 31, 'Him hath God exalted with his right hand'. What for? 'To be a Prince and a Saviour, for to give repentance to Israel, and forgiveness of sins.' That is what He is doing there! Another statement of the matter is found in the Epistle to the Romans, chapter 14, verse 9: 'For to this end' – for this object, with this intent, with this as its objective – 'Christ both died, and rose, and revived, that He might be Lord both of the dead and living.' This again defines what Christ is doing 'seated at the right hand of God'. Finally we have what our Lord Himself said about the matter, as recorded in the Gospel according to Matthew, chapter 28, verses 18 to 20: 'And Jesus came and spake unto them, saying, All power is given unto me in heaven and in earth. Go ye therefore, and teach all nations, baptizing them in the name of the Father, and of the Son, and of the Holy Ghost: teaching them to observe all things whatsoever I have commanded you: and lo, I am with you alway, even unto the end of the world [end of the age].'

Notice that in each case His work is defined in connection with, and in terms of, *our* salvation. His work there is mediatorial. He has been put into that position not only because He is what He is, and who He is; He has been put there especially as our Representative, as our Mediator, as the One who is the Head of the Body of which we are parts. It all works to one great end, namely the salvation of His people – *our* salvation. He is seated at the right hand of God with all authority and power; and He is using all this authority and power for our benefit, for our salvation, for our sanctification, for our being made more and more perfect in order that we may be prepared for the day when He shall come again. The Epistle to the Hebrews says that 'He sat down at the right hand of the Majesty on high, from henceforth expecting till his enemies be made his footstool' (Hebrews 10: 12 and 13). But while He is there, and waiting, He is doing much on our behalf. He is exercising His great power for our good. 'All things', as we have seen, 'work together for good, to them that love God.' That happens through Him. He mediates all these blessings to us. And this will continue until the appointed time, which is known only to the Father Himself, not even to the Son, when God will send Him back again into this world. He will come, and will judge the world in righteousness. His enemies will be made his footstool; they will finally be destroyed – the devil and all his followers; evil, sin, hell, everything opposed to God will be cast into the lake of final destruction; and He will usher in His great and glorious Kingdom. And we shall be in that Kingdom for ever and ever.

Such is the significance of His being seated at the right hand of God. That is the final guarantee that you and I are ultimately going to be in that glory. We are 'in Him', and He is there as our Representative, 'waiting' until God sends Him to do the final act of introducing 'the new heavens and the new earth wherein dwelleth righteousness', the everlasting glory. And we shall share in that, because He is doing all 'for us'. The Apostle's argument therefore runs: 'Who shall lay anything to the charge of God's elect?' Who shall be able to condemn us? The fact that He is there, and there 'for us', is a guarantee that nothing can ever rob us of the glory which is coming to us.

There is but one further step in this particular argument that we need to take; it is recorded in Ephesians 2: 4–6: 'He [God] who is rich in mercy, for his great love wherewith He loved us, even when we were dead in sins, hath quickened us together with Christ (by grace ye are saved); and hath raised us up together' – if you are 'in Christ' you were crucified with Him, you died with Him, you were buried with Him, and you have been raised with Him – 'and made us sit together in heavenly places in Christ Jesus.' This is not a prophecy of what is yet to happen; it is already true of us. As certainly as we have been quickened and born again and raised with Him, we are seated with Him in the heavenly places.

Can anything or anyone ever remove you from that position in which you are seated in the heavenly places in Christ Jesus?

Can you at one and the same time believe that the Almighty and Everlasting God has raised you to that position, and that there is any power that can ever take you from it? It is an utter absurdity. So it is not a sign of spiritual modesty that you are not sure of your salvation; it is the exact opposite; it is unbelief.

But we now turn to consider the last of the four expressions, 'Who also maketh intercession for us'. Is the Apostle ending on an anticlimax? Why did he add this? The answer, I believe, is that once more the pastor in Paul emerges. He was always a pastor; and never a mere intellectual, or dry-as-dust theologian, or academic man. He was writing to Christian people who were being persecuted and tried, and he wants to give them this absolute assurance and certainty. He takes nothing for granted. He knows how people, even when raised up to the heavens, will go out of a service and say 'Yes but . . .' They did so then, they do so still; and Paul answers them and us before we have had time even to think of saying it. He imagines someone saying something like this, 'I know this is very wonderful, and I have believed in Christ. But what happens if and when I fall into some terrible sin? Does not that make a difference, does it not undo everything?' The Apostle takes up that point and answers it by saying, 'Who also maketh intercession for us'.

For the meaning of that expression we must turn again to the Epistle to the Hebrews – which is the great commentary on this verse – and especially to chapter 7, verses 23–25. He is contrasting the ceremonial in the old tabernacle and temple, carried on by many priests who lived and died and were replaced by others, and he says, 'And they truly were many priests, because they were not suffered to continue by reason of death: but this man [the Lord Jesus Christ], because he continueth ever, hath an unchangeable priesthood. Wherefore he is able also to save them to the uttermost that come unto God by him, seeing he ever liveth to make intercession for them.' This means that our salvation cannot fail, can never come to an end, can never be deficient in any respect. 'He is able to save to the uttermost' – there will be nothing left to be done.

I remember a preacher once saying that 'to the uttermost' means that He is able to save to the 'guttermost'. But that is quite wrong. We are not looking at a gutter, we are looking at heaven and perfection. Saving 'to the uttermost' means saving absolutely, perfectly, and completely until there is not 'a spot or wrinkle or any such thing' left. It includes also the time element. The author of Hebrews makes much of that element. Those other priests, he says, came and then died, and another came; but this Man liveth for ever. We tend to ask very foolish questions and to imagine terrible possibilities. 'What if it suddenly came to an end?' we ask. But it cannot come to an end, because 'He ever liveth'. It is eternal, it is everlasting. Because He is eternal His work will be always the same. So it is a perfect work, and it is a work that can never end, it can never fail, it can never cease. It goes on for ever in all its absolute perfection and glory.

But what does the author of that Epistle mean by saying that 'He ever liveth to make intercession for us?' Here again, unfortunately, some old preachers have greatly abused this truth. They used to dramatize it and picture a great scene in a law-court. God the Judge was sitting on the bench, and there was counsel for the prosecution, the devil, and defending counsel, our advocate the Lord Jesus Christ. The court was in session and our adversary the Devil and accuser was bringing his charge and trying to prove it. But the Lord Jesus Christ got up and answered the charge; and God, having heard the defence, pronounced His verdict. Some of the Puritans started the practice of speaking in that way. But it is unworthy of the truth they were trying to depict.

Let me quote Charles Hodge at this point. In dealing with this very phrase he says, very rightly, 'Of course' – and I like that expression – 'this language is figurative; the meaning is, that Christ continues since His resurrection and exaltation to secure for His people the benefits of His death. Everything comes from God through Him and for His sake.' That is precisely what it means. It cannot carry the other meaning. A verse we have already quoted dismisses that foolish dramatization in a literal sense completely – 'This man, after he had offered one sacrifice for sins for ever, sat down on the right hand of God, ... for by one offering he hath perfected for ever them that are sanctified.' The argument is, that in the old dispensation a remembrance was again made of past sins, and accusations could be brought; hence they had to continue to make their offerings day after day, and every year the high priest had to go again into the holiest, although he had gone in a year before; and this had to be continually repeated. But there is no repetition now, because this Man has done it all, 'once and for ever'. 'It is finished' and the matter can never be raised again.

Actually the first verse of this eighth chapter of Romans has already said it all. 'There is therefore now no condemnation' – there never can be, there never will be – 'to them which are in Christ Jesus.' Imagine that, according to the possibility, every time a Christian falls into sin the court has to meet in heaven; the Devil brings his charge, our Lord gets up and replies as Advocate. Can you not see what would happen? I say with reverence that nothing else could take place in heaven but that, because someone is sinning every moment. So heaven would be a place in which this whole matter of sin was continually being raised, which is ridiculous and absurd; indeed, it seems to me to be a contradiction, as I am trying to show, of the whole teaching of the Scripture. Indeed our Lord Himself has surely settled this matter once and for ever in John 5: 24: 'He that heareth my word, and believeth on him that sent me, hath' – a present possession! – 'everlasting life, and shall not come into condemnation; but is passed from death unto life.'

I say with reverence that there is no need even for our Lord to defend the believer, He has already done so, 'once and for ever'. But in any case, it is God the Father Himself who sent His Son to do the work. There can never be any query or question in God's mind with regard to any of His children. It was He who gave these people to His Son; it was He who sent His Son into the world to die for us and to redeem us. It is God who sent Him to do it all for us. He has told Him that the work is satisfactory, He has approved it by setting Him at His right hand. And yet we are asked to believe that when the devil rises and brings an accusation in the court, God has to hear the defence before He knows what to do with us. It is just a misunderstanding of Scripture. It is foolish literalizing, almost materializing, of something which, as Charles Hodge says so rightly, 'is nothing but a figure'. It is a figure that is used because of our weakness in order to give us understanding.

The Apostle mentions His intercession in order that we may know that we have a sympathetic High Priest. This is stated clearly in Hebrews 4: 14–16: 'Seeing then that we have a great high priest, that is passed into the heavens, Jesus the Son of God, let us hold fast our profession. For we have not an high priest which cannot be touched with the feeling of our infirmities; but was in all points tempted like as we are, yet without sin.' When the devil attacks us and says that we have no right to go to God, we answer him by saying that there is One seated at God's right hand who came into this world for us. 'Ah yes', says the devil, 'but he is God, not man.' We reply that He took on Himself human nature and lived in this world, and that He was 'tempted in all points like as we are, yet without sin'; and so He is able to sympathize with us. As the author of Hebrews has already said in chapter 2, verse 18, 'For in that he himself hath suffered being tempted, he is able to succour them that are tempted'. That is part of what 'maketh intercession for us' means; and we know therefore that in the presence of God always our case is thus presented.

But secondly – and still more important – as Charles Hodges emphasizes: 'The meaning is, that Christ continues since His resurrection and exaltation to secure for His people the benefits of His death. Everything comes from God through Him and for His sake.' In these words Hodge gets to the real truth of the matter. We can state it thus. The object of the high priest in going into the holiest of all once a year was to obtain certain benefits for the people he represented. First and foremost was forgiveness; then, all the blessings needed from God for their daily lives, the goodwill of God and the blessings following the goodwill. Our Lord does exactly the same for us in heaven. So the author of the Epistle to the Hebrews concludes in chapter 4 : 16: 'Let us therefore come boldly unto the throne of grace that we may obtain mercy, and find grace to help in time of need.' The presence of the Lord Jesus Christ at the right hand of God is a guarantee that we can have mercy. It is now 'a throne of grace' to us because He is there. So, knowing that I shall receive mercy, I can go into the presence of God with boldness, with assurance. But I not only get mercy I also get 'grace to help in time of need'. I get everything I need; and that, through the Lord Jesus Christ. In this way He makes intercession for me. All the benefits of God come through Him. God has treasured up in Him all the treasures of His wisdom and grace, and they come to me through Christ the Head. The whole analogy of the body proves it; everything comes from the Head from whom we draw our sustenance and our every need.

One of the greatest proofs of my assertions is what happened on the Day of Pentecost in Jerusalem when the Holy Spirit was 'given'. He was sent by the Son. The Son having achieved our salvation was given the gift of the Spirit by the Father for us, and the Son showered Him forth upon us. That is exactly how it happens. Having gone in as a great High Priest, having made His intercession, He is given the Gift, and He showers the Gift upon us, and the Gift in turn showers graces and gifts upon us.

There are many statements of this truth in the Scriptures. In the Epistle to the Ephesians 1: 3 we read: 'Blessed be the God and Father of our Lord Jesus Christ, who hath blessed us with all spiritual blessings in heavenly places in Christ' – through Christ, by means of Christ! You find it again in Ephesians 4, verses 7 and 8: 'But unto every one of us is given grace according to the measure of the gift of Christ. Wherefore he saith, When he ascended up on high, he led captivity captive, and gave gifts unto men.' Having 'ascended up', and in His high-priestly character – the work having been completed – all the gifts are given to Him, and He gives the gifts to us. '(He) gave gifts unto men.'

In other words, the Father looks upon the Son and He sees us in Him. He sees all our needs. The Father looks upon Him as our Representative, as the One who has done all this for us, the One who is concerned about us; He gives Him everything, and He gives Him everything 'for us'. We receive all these glorious and wonderful gifts in Him and through Him. He is not there simply for His own sake, He is there as our Representative, He is there as our Mediator, and it is through Him that we have 'access' into the presence of God. It is through Him that we pray and go to God; and it is through Him we receive all the blessings of God which are showered upon us as we need them in this sinful, evil, gainsaying world. 'Grace to help in time of need.' Every needed grace comes to us in and through our Lord and Saviour Jesus Christ.

The argument we should deduce is, therefore, that while He is there we shall lack nothing that is essential to our final salvation and glorification. And He will always be there for 'He ever maketh intercession'; 'He continueth ever'. So our final salvation is absolutely guaranteed. 'He is able also to save them to the uttermost that come unto God by Him, seeing he ever liveth to make intercession for them' (Hebrews 7: 25). No day can ever dawn when He will not be there; or when anything or anyone can in any way rob us of the salvation which He has purchased for us. I can throw out this challenge: 'Who is he that condemneth?' The answer is, 'It is Christ that died, yea rather, that is risen again, who is even at the right hand of God, who ever liveth to make intercession for us.' He is there on our behalf, for our good, for our welfare. There is no condemnation conceivable in such a situation – none whatsoever!

Thirty-six

*

Who shall separate us from the love of Christ? Shall tribulation, or distress, or persecution, or famine, or nakedness, or peril, or sword?

As it is written, For thy sake we are killed all the day long: we are accounted as sheep for the slaughter.

Nay, in all these things we are more than conquerors through him that loved us.

For I am persuaded, that neither death, nor life, nor angels, nor principalities, nor powers, nor things present, nor things to come,

Nor height, nor depth, nor any other creature, shall be able to separate us from the love of God, which is in Christ Jesus our Lord.

Romans 8: 35–39

In these verses we come to the end, and to the grand climax of this most marvellous chapter, than which, surely, there is nothing greater or more wonderful in the whole of Scripture. The message of these verses can be sub-divided into two sections. From verse 35 to verse 37 the Apostle issues the last in his series of challenges to the doctrine of the final perseverance of the saints. Then in the last two verses, 38 and 39, he finishes the particular argument, but at the same time he summarizes the argument which began at verse 31. Indeed, he goes even further, and summarizes and brings to a final climax the whole argument of the entire chapter, which, as we have indicated, pertains to assurance, the absolute certainty that all who are justified by faith will arrive at a state of ultimate glorification.

Starting now with verse 35, we remind ourselves that the Apostle has been putting up a series of challenges to the doctrine of Final Perseverance. The first in verse 31 is, 'What shall we then say to these things?', which he answers in the same verse. Then there is the challenge that might come from a possible change or variation in the love of God; he answers that in verse 32. Then comes the possibility of anyone bringing charges

[440]

against us or anyone condemning us; he deals with that in verses 33 and 34.

Now Paul comes to the last challenge in which he considers the possibility that *we* might fail. All these other challenges have been in terms of God's attitude toward us – any weakening of God's power, any lessening of God's love, and the attitude of the Lord Jesus Christ Himself as judgment has been committed to Him. They have all been from that side. But now he takes up an argument from our side, What if *we* should fail? What if we, as the result of trials and troubles and tribulations, should somehow or other fail and thereby be separated from the love of Christ? He takes this up and answers it. Note again his method. He gives a list of the possible things that may come to try us – tribulation, distress, persecution, famine, nakedness, peril, sword. Then to make it complete, he gives us a quotation from the Old Testament: 'For thy sake we are killed all the day long, we are accounted as sheep for the slaughter' (Psalm 44: 22). He means that these trials and troubles and tribulations will come, and do come, and particularly because we are Christians. The New Testament, far from promising us a life of ease, and a life in which there will be no difficulties and problems, rather does the opposite. It says that because we are Christians we are likely to meet additional troubles – 'For *thy sake* we are killed all the day long; we are accounted as sheep for the slaughter'. The early Christians were severely persecuted because they were Christians. They were told that they must renounce their Christianity and say 'Caesar is Lord'. But this involved the denial of Christ and for long years, and for His sake, they were 'killed all the day long', being 'destitute, afflicted, tormented'. Christians must expect tribulations. The ancient Romans used to thresh their corn by means of what they called a 'tribulum', a kind of sledge or wooden platform studded underneath with sharp pieces of flint or with iron teeth; and the impression given here is of a man being beaten, and beaten down, because of his loyalty to Christ. It may include death itself. 'We are accounted as sheep for the slaughter' is a way of describing the possibility of death.

The question the Apostle raises is, How can we stand up to all this? Is it not possible that under tribulation we may somehow fall away and find ourselves as reprobates. For we are weak, we are in the flesh, and these powerful enemies can wear one down mentally, physically, and in every other respect. That was true of Christians in the first century, and it is true again today. Many Christians, probably at this very moment, are being subjected to a process known as 'brain washing'. They are put in cells, a powerful light is made to shine down upon them, they are given inadequate food, and they are interrogated by a series of interrogators without being allowed sufficient sleep, all in an effort to break down their faith.

How can one stand up to all this? The Apostle says in effect: 'I have taught you that nothing shall be able to separate us from God's love; I have told you that if you are justified you are glorified; that these things are certain; I have taught you the doctrine of the final perseverance of the saints.' But can it really be true, can it stand up to this kind of severe trial and testing? The Apostle answers that question, as he has answered every other objection that he himself has put up for the sake of argument. He supplies a twofold answer. We note with interest that he really gives the answer in the very form in which he puts his question. 'Who shall separate us' – *us* – 'from the love of Christ?' The 'us', of course, refers to a particular people only, those who are Christians, those whom God 'foreknew', whom He did 'predestinate', and whom He 'called', and whom He 'justified', and whom he 'glorified'. So the moment he says *us*, in a sense he gives the answer.

The further part of the answer in the very form of the question, 'Who shall separate us from the love of Christ?', is that 'the love of Christ' does not mean our love to Christ, but His love to us. 'Who shall separate us from this love of Christ that has taken hold of us?' That love is the magnet that has taken hold of us. Paul asks, What can pull us away from it? Here, again, is the answer – it does not depend on us at all! He is not asking, Can our love to Christ stand these tests? but rather, Can the love of Christ to us stand these tests? And immediately the situation is entirely changed.

The proof that that is the meaning of 'the love of Christ' in these verses is Paul's answer, 'Nay, in all these things we are more than conquerors through him that loved us'. It is 'through him that loved us' that we triumph. At the very end of the statement we meet the same truth: [none of these things] 'shall be able to separate us from the love of God, which is in Christ Jesus our

Lord'. So, right through, it is not our love to Christ or to God the Father, it is the love of Christ to us, it is the love of God to us. So already we have the answer to the question in the very way in which he formulates his question.

It is interesting and important also to note that the Apostle puts his assertion in the past tense, 'We are more than conquerors', not through Him that 'loves' us, but 'through him that *loved* us. He surely does this quite deliberately. He is reminding us that our Lord and Saviour Jesus Christ died for us, as he has already told us in the 5th chapter: 'For when we were yet without strength, in due time Christ died for the ungodly. For scarcely for a righteous man will one die; yet peradventure for a good man some would even dare to die. But God commendeth his love toward us, in that while we were yet sinners, Christ died for us' (vv. 5–8). Again, in verse 10 of that chapter: 'For if, when we were enemies, we were reconciled to God by the death of his Son, much more, being reconciled, we shall be saved by his life.' The argument is, that if Christ did that for us while we were sinners and enemies and blasphemers and opponents and aliens, how much more will he now, by his life, continue to save us until finally we are glorified. We have already met this argument in verse 34 of this chapter 8: 'Who is he that condemneth? It is Christ that died.' The first reply is, then, that Christ has proved His love to us in that He 'died for us', even when we were in that sorry condition.

But not only so, for, as Paul has reminded us in verse 34, Christ is now in heaven interceding for us. So what he says is that it is Christ's love to us, and the power of Christ, that holds us and guarantees our continuance. Nothing can separate us from that love because it is His love for us, and because it is an all-powerful love.

There is a wonderful statement concerning that love in the 5th chapter of the Epistle to the Ephesians, beginning at verse 25: 'Husbands love your wives, even as Christ also loved the church, and gave himself for it.' Why did He do so? The answer is, 'That he might sanctify and cleanse it with the washing of water by the word, that he might present it to himself a glorious church, not having spot, or wrinkle, or any such thing; but that it should be holy and without blemish.' He died for His church in order that He might ultimately present her to Himself perfect, washed and cleansed and purified. This is what Paul is virtually saying in this 8th chapter in these verses: 'Nay, in all these things we are more than conquerors through him that loved us.'

Christ died for the Church, not simply that she should be forgiven, but that she should ultimately arrive at this absolute perfection – 'without spot, or wrinkle, or any such thing'. He has set His heart on her for that end, and He will not allow anything whatsoever to rob Him of that result. Nothing will be permitted to stand between Him and His purpose for the Church (us), which He shows in His love for the Church. That is the first part of the answer.

Next we must look at this phrase 'more than conquerors'. Not only, says the Apostle, shall nothing separate us from His love to us; in all these things which try to separate us we are 'more than conquerors' with respect to them. This is what he is particularly concerned to emphasize. In every case his argument has been *reductio ad absurdum*. He is not content with merely answering objections, he ridicules them; and he does it here. We are not simply enabled by His love to hold on, and not to fall away and falter; neither is it the case that we just manage to obtain a victory. We are 'more than conquerors', a very strong expression! The Christian is not a man who manages somehow or another just to obtain an entrance into heaven. He is 'more than conqueror'. He not merely stands up to these trials, he demolishes them, he is enabled to overcome them completely. He not merely conquers them, he is 'more than conqueror'. And let us not forget that death is included. Everything that can possibly come against us is included.

But how is the Christian made 'more than conqueror' over all these things by the love of Christ? It is the love of Christ that does it, as I have shown. How does it work? We have already answered, in a sense, in dealing with verse 28: 'We know that all things work together for good to them that love God.' There is virtually nothing new here. Paul is simply stating it in a different way, and repeating it for the sake of emphasis.

How are we made more than conquerors over these things which, when they come to us, help us as Christians to see the nature of life in this world? The greatest danger confronting the Christian is not so much the opposition of the world as the enticements of the world. When the world persecutes us, and deals with us harshly, it makes us ask 'Why is it doing this?', and we have got our answer, 'It is doing this to us because we are Christians'. And that makes us remember that because we are Christians we are receiving the same treatment as Christ received. And as verse 17 has said, 'If we suffer with him', we shall be 'glorified together'. The world persecuted Him, and it is persecuting us. So persecution, far from getting us down, reminds us that we are aliens in the world; we are but 'strangers and pilgrims'; we do not belong to this world; 'as he was so are we in this world'. It already makes us see the real character of this world, and reminds us that we are now the 'children of God, and if children, then heirs', with all the blessings that the word implies.

Trials and tribulations also force us to think of the glory which is awaiting us. In thought, we are back again to verse 18: 'For I reckon that the sufferings of this present time are not worthy to be compared with the glory which shall be revealed in us.' The trials drive us to think in these terms, and in terms of all that follows in verses 19 to 32. They turn our attention to the promised glory, and they make us begin to long for that glory. We know something of the following, 'We ourselves also, which have the firstfruits of the Spirit, even we ourselves groan within ourselves, waiting for the adoption, to wit, the redemption of our body. For we are saved by hope: but hope that is seen is not hope: for what a man seeth, why doth he yet hope for? But if we hope for that we see not, then do we with patience wait for it.' These trials and troubles and tribulations turn our minds to the glory that awaits us, and the moment they do so they become as nothing. So we are 'more than conquerors'.

Furthermore, the trials remind us, as we have been seeing, of our relationship to Him, that we are His people, that His mark is upon us. He has set His heart upon us, He has a purpose for us. Not only so, when we endure these things, He will give us special encouragements. He helps His people, He aids us, He smiles upon us. Most saints have said that times of persecution have been to them blessed times, that they got to know God and the Lord Jesus Christ better when they were in the furnace of affliction than they had ever done before. They all agree with the psalmist in saying, 'It is good for me that I have been afflicted' (Psalm 119: 71). That is their universal testimony.

The Lord also gives us special strength to bear our trials. And beyond that, we can say that even death itself becomes something that ministers to our glory. For what is death to the Christian? If he is like the Apostle Paul he says, 'To die is gain'. 'To be with Christ; which is far better!' So that, even if death comes, it but ushers us into His immediate presence. The Christian can smile in the face of death or anything that precedes it. All these things simply force him to a consideration of who he is, his relationship to God and to Christ, and the glory for which he is being prepared.

In other words, 'All things' do indeed 'work together'; they are made to 'work together for good to them that love God, to them who are the called according to his purpose'. Paul has said all this as far back as the 3rd verse of the 5th chapter, where he says, 'And not only so'. He has just been saying, 'We rejoice in hope of the glory of God'. Then, 'And not only so, but we glory in tribulations also: knowing that tribulation worketh patience; and patience, experience; and experience, hope: and hope maketh not ashamed; because the love of God is shed abroad in our hearts by the Holy Ghost which is given unto us.' Notice how the Apostle repeats himself. Thank God that he does so. It is good for us that these things be brought back to our minds time and time again. Anything as glorious as this is worth repeating; so he keeps on repeating it chapter after chapter.

And not only in this Epistle to the Romans! Paul says the same thing in a very wonderful manner in the Second Epistle to the Corinthians, first of all in the 1st chapter, verse 5: 'For as the sufferings of Christ abound in us, so our consolation also aboundeth by Christ.' Again, in verse 9 of that chapter he says that he has been through terrible trouble: 'We had the sentence of death in ourselves, that we should not trust in ourselves, but in God which raiseth the dead: who delivered us from so great a death and doth deliver; in whom we trust that he will yet deliver us.' He has done so, He is doing so, He will do so. God does it all. And as we suffer these persecutions and trials, we learn lessons that we can only learn in this way. So we are 'more than conquerors'. Again, in chapter 4 of Second Corinthians, verses 17 and 18, you find the same triumphant statement: 'Our light affliction' – he has been describing it in the previous verses – 'which is but for a moment, worketh for us' – produces for us – 'a far more exceeding and eternal weight of glory.' Note the superlatives: 'far more exceeding' and 'eternal' or 'an exceeding, abunddantly exceeding weight of glory'. 'While we look not at the things which are seen, but at the things which are not seen: for the things which are seen are temporal; but the things which are not seen are eternal.' Such is the experience of the great Apostle. 'In all these things we are more than conquerors through him that loved us.'

But is this true only of the Apostle? Take the case of a man called Thomas Browning, who lived at the time of the terrible persecutions under Charles II three hundred years ago. He wrote to his flock from Northampton prison, and this is what he said: 'The cup of afflictions for the gospel is the sweeter the deeper.' The deeper the affliction, the sweeter it is. He adds, 'A stronger cordial the nearer the bottom'. When you get to the very dregs and ultimate of it, the nearer you get to the bottom, the cordial is the stronger. 'I mean', he says, 'death itself.' Here was a man, sixteen centuries after Paul, able to say, 'We are more than conquerors through him that loved us'. There is only one thing to say –

O Love, that wilt not let me go,
I rest my weary soul in Thee.

This love of Christ to us will never let us go; it matters not what happens. He makes us 'more than conquerors'. He enables us even to 'rejoice also in tribulations'. So the Apostle has answered the last possible objection to the teaching concerning the final perseverance of the saints.

Now he winds it all up, he underlines it all in the magnificent final statement in verses 38 and 39: 'For I am persuaded, that neither death, nor life, nor principalities, nor powers, nor things present, nor things to come, nor height, nor depth, nor any other creature, shall be able to separate us from the love of God, which is in Christ Jesus our Lord.' There is nothing fresh in these words, nothing new. But it is a wonderful statement, is it not? It illustrates the secret of the art of writing or preaching. There is nothing new to say in a pulpit every Sunday; it is always the gospel. Some people seem to be surprised at that; people come to me sometimes and say 'Wonderful! The old message; quite simple.' What else did they expect, I wonder!? How people betray themselves by the remarks they make to preachers at the close of services! The Apostle cannot add to what he has just been saying; when you have already said everything, there is nothing to do but to repeat yourself. But listen to what is being repeated! 'For' – he is summing it up, placing it before us once and for ever, giving us a magnificent and glorious statement which should be riveted in our minds and hearts, so that whatever may happen to us it is always there; and it is always more than enough, and always makes us 'more than conquerors'.

Let us examine the statement under a number of headings. He says, 'I am persuaded'. He is not saying all this simply because he happens to have a particular feeling in him at the moment. Neither is he just hoping – hoping against hope. What he says is, 'I am certain'. It is interesting to note that he puts this in the passive, 'I *am persuaded*', which means 'I have come, through a process of persuasion, to a settled conclusion'. That is the true content of the phrase. He does not persuade himself; something else has persuaded him. He is passive. The result is that, as the result of this process of persuasion, he has come to a settled conclusion; he is certain. It is an absolute certainty, beyond any doubt whatsoever.

How has this happened to him? It is as the result of his consideration of the truth as it has been revealed. He has been brought to this conclusion by the evidence that God has put before him – God's purpose and all that he has been saying from verse 28 onwards; indeed all he has been saying in the entire Epistle. He belongs to 'the called according to God's purpose'. That took us back to eternity, to God's eternal plan and all that has happened since. And in the light of all that, Paul has been driven to this inevitable conclusion. No other conclusion is possible.

What is his conclusion? Of what is he persuaded? He is not persuaded that circumstances are about to improve. Many people seem to think that Christianity is a persuasion that things are going to get steadily better. They believe that as Christianity is preached, and as people become more educated by the Christian teaching of the Sermon on the Mount, the world will gradually be changed, trials and troubles will come to an end, and no people will be 'led as sheep to the slaughter'. But this is not the Apostle's teaching. He gives no indication that he expects to be delivered out of his trials, or that they are going to be removed, during the remainder of his earthly life. Actually the Apostle was martyred, as were very many of the early Christians. What he is interested in is that nothing shall be able to separate him 'from

[448]

the love of God which is in Christ Jesus our Lord'; that is his only concern.

Let me emphasize the 'us' again – 'Nothing shall be able to separate *us*', the Christians, those who are 'the called according to God's purpose'. God's love is to them, and to them only. God's wrath is against all others. Such is Paul's teaching. His chief concern is to know that all is well between himself and God; and he is assured that it is. In that he rejoices; that is what makes him happy. Let the world do what it may, he says; I am one of God's people, I am one of Christ's people, I am among 'the called', and nothing else matters. He is 'persuaded' of this, this 'love of God which is in Christ Jesus our Lord'.

Why does he add the words, 'in Christ Jesus our Lord'? He does so because there were people then, as there are people now, who, though not Christians, say that they believe in the love of God. There are many people today who never darken the doors of a place of worship but who say they believe in the love of God. Yet they reject the gospel. They do not believe in a God who is wrathful against sin; a God who must punish sin; a God who sent His own Son to Calvary and smote Him there because of our sin. The thought is terrible to them. They imagine that they believe in the love of God. The Apostle's answer is that no love of God can be known except in and through Christ Jesus our Lord.

No text is more frequently abused than John 3: 16: 'God so loved the world that he gave his only begotten Son, that whosoever believeth in him should not perish but have everlasting life', a statement which shows clearly that the love of God is always in and through Christ Jesus. What most people talk about as the love of God is nothing but their own philosophic conception of love. It is not God's love. God's love is a holy love, a righteous love, a just love, a love always in Christ. No man will ever know the love of God except he believes and trusts himself to the Lord Jesus Christ. He must believe that He is the Son of God, he must believe in His incarnation, he must believe He was 'made of a woman, made under the law, to redeem them that were under the law'; he must believe that He bore the penalty and suffered the punishment of sins not His own, and rose again for His people's justification. This is the only way one can ever know the love of God or ever be involved in it. You must believe the full doctrine the Apostle has announced from the beginning of the Epistle concerning what God has done in and through our Lord and Saviour Jesus Christ. All the love of God is in Him; it comes to us through Him, and through Him alone. That is what the Apostle relies upon; it is of that he is persuaded. This is the basis of his final certainty.

Then again, the Apostle gives us the grounds of this persuasion. Once more it is God's love, manifested to us. 'Nothing shall be able to separate us from the love of God, which is in Christ Jesus our Lord.' The love of Christ and the love of God are one. The Father and the Spirit co-operate in our salvation, as we have been reminded so many times. So you can say, 'the love of God' 'the love of Christ' or 'the love of the Spirit'. What matters is God's love to us, not our love to God. Our love is weak and frail and fallible; it wanes and waxes, comes and goes. Thank God my salvation does not depend on me, but on God's love to me; not upon my frail grasp of Him, but upon His strong grasp of me!

This is not the teaching of Paul only; it is found equally in the teaching of the Apostle Peter. In the 1st chapter of his First Epistle, verses 3 to 5 we read: 'Blessed be the God and Father of our Lord Jesus Christ, which according to his abundant mercy hath begotten us again unto a lively hope by the resurrection of Jesus Christ from the dead, to an inheritance incorruptible, and undefiled, and that fadeth not away, reserved in heaven for you, who are kept [being kept] by the power of God through faith unto salvation ready to be revealed in the last time.' 'Kept by the power of God'! The power of God keeps us; it alone can keep us. Nothing else is strong enough. But the love of God is a powerful love. Peter was so concerned about this that he says a similar thing in his Second Epistle, chapter 1, verses 2 and 3: 'Grace and peace be multiplied unto you through the knowledge of God, and of Jesus our Lord, according as his divine power hath given unto us all things that pertain unto life and godliness, through the knowledge of him that hath called us to glory and virtue' (or 'by his glorious power'). It is God in His great power who has given us everything that pertains unto life and godliness, all that sustains us while we pass through this pilgrimage called life.

But how do we know all this, how can we be assured of this love of God to us? We have God's own word and God's promises. God has said, 'I will never leave thee, nor forsake thee'. Is not that enough? That is God's own word. Hebrews 6: 16–18 tells us that God has confirmed His promises with an oath – 'He swore by himself'. We have our Lord's words also to help us and to encourage us. 'As the Father hath loved me, so have I loved you: continue ye in my love.' In His high-priestly prayer we read, 'That the world may know that thou hast sent me, and hast loved them, as thou hast loved me' (John 17: 23). God has loved us who are Christians as He has loved His own Son. He loves His Son with all His being. Thus John's Gospel, chapter 17, supplies us with a specific statement by the Son of God with respect to God's love to us, confirming the Word of the Father Himself.

But, further, consider the character of the God who has spoken to us. He is unchanging. 'He is the Father of lights, with whom is no variableness, neither shadow of turning.' And He has said, 'I have loved thee with an everlasting love' (Jeremiah 31: 3). There is no end to it. As the hymn-writer puts it, 'Mine is an unchanging love'. That is because God Himself is unchanging. But He is not only unchanging, He is also almighty. Our Lord says about His sheep that they are His Father's, 'and no man is able to pluck them out of my Father's hand'. The Apostle has already said it in verse 31: 'What shall we then say to these things? If God be for us, who can be against us?' He is the Almighty God, and He is 'for us'; He has said so. He does not vary, He does not change, His power cannot diminish.

All this has actually been proved to us already by what our Lord Jesus Christ has done for us. Every argument has already been answered by Him. He has conquered every one of these enemies the Apostle enumerates as being against us. Paul is even persuaded that death cannot separate us from the love of God. How can he prove his words? In writing to Timothy he refers to our Lord as the One 'who hath abolished death' – disannulled it – 'and brought life and immortality to light through the gospel' (2 Timothy 1: 10). Or, as he states it in 1 Corinthians 15, verse 26, 'The last enemy that shall be destroyed is death'. But Christ has already conquered it. 'The sting of death is sin; and the strength of sin is the law; but thanks be unto God, which giveth us the victory through our Lord Jesus Christ.' We can say, 'O death, where is thy sting? O grave, where is thy victory?' As Charles Wesley says:

The Perseverance of the Saints

Stronger His love than death or hell;
Its riches are unsearchable;
The first-born sons of light
Desire in vain its depths to see;
They cannot reach the mystery,
The length, and breadth, and height.

They cannot; it is beyond them! But we can do so in the resurrection, and in the sending of the Holy Spirit on the Day of Pentecost, and in the entire history of the Church and the people of God. Paul has already answered this question concerning death and its power to separate us.

But what of 'life'? Paul lists it after death. Will not life get me down – 'led as sheep to the slaughter all the day long'? The answer is, Christ is the Lord of life. Speaking to John on the Isle of Patmos in Revelation 1: 18, He says, 'I am he that liveth, and was dead: and, behold, I am alive for evermore, Amen; and have the keys of death and of hell'. He is 'Lord of our life, and God of our salvation'. You need not be afraid of life. Life will never separate you from the love of God. The One to whom we belong, and into whom we are incorporated, is the Lord of life. He has the keys of hell and of death. All things are in His hands.

What then of angels, and principalities and powers? Clearly 'angels' here means evil angels. The good angels can never be against us, and would never try to separate us. These are the fallen angels, and the 'principalities and powers' represent the devil and all his forces. Cannot they separate us from 'the love of God, which is in Christ Jesus our Lord'? There is no need to worry, the Lord has already dealt with them. Colossians 2: 15 tells us, 'And having spoiled' (by His death on the Cross) 'principalities and powers, he made an open show of them, triumphing over them in it [by it]'. He has already conquered them on the Cross – all of them together – and He was doing so for us. They can never separate us from the love of God. Or, as the Apostle states it in the 6th chapter of Ephesians, verses 10 and 11: 'Be strong in the Lord, and in the power of his might. Take unto you the whole armour of God, that ye may be able to stand against the wiles of the devil.' And in verse 12: 'We wrestle not against flesh and blood, but against principalities, against powers, against the rulers of the darkness of this world, against spiritual wickedness in high places. Wherefore take unto you the whole armour of God, that ye may be able to withstand in the evil day, and having done all, to stand.' Should all the angels and principalities and powers try to separate you from the Lord, they cannot succeed. He to whom we belong has already conquered them.

What about 'things present'? Paul has already answered that point also. In verse 34 he said, 'Who is he that condemneth? It is Christ that died, yea rather, that is risen again, who is even at the right hand of God'. He is there now, 'waiting until all his enemies shall be made his footstool'; and He has said, 'All power is given unto me in heaven and in earth'. There He is at the right hand of God. He said, just at the end of His life, as recorded in John 16: 'In the world ye shall have tribulation: but be of good cheer; I have overcome the world.' And He has!

> *Things future, nor things that are now,*
> *Not all things below nor above,*
> *Can make Him His purpose forego,*
> *Or sever my soul from His love.*

So we can join the Apostle John in saying, 'This is the victory that overcometh the world [in the present], even our faith' (1 John 5: 4).

What of 'things to come'? Things that lie in the future? Revelation 5: 5 tells us that Christ is the Lord of the future. The book sealed without and within was produced in heaven. It is the book of history, the book of the future. No creature in heaven or anywhere else was strong enough to open it. Suddenly 'The Lion of the tribe of Judah' steps forward, and He is able 'to open the book, and to loose the seven seals thereof'. The future is safe because He is the Lord of History. The future of the whole cosmos is in the hands of the Lord Jesus Christ; He is controlling everything. I am able also to use John Newton's argument –

> *His love in time past*
> *Forbids me to think*
> *He'll leave me at last*
> *In trouble to sink:*
> *Each sweet Ebenezer*
> *I have in review*
> *Confirms His good pleasure*
> *To help me quite through.*

[453]

The Perseverance of the Saints

The Lord's character, and what He has done in the past, are the guarantees of what He will do, because He does not, and cannot change. So I am no more afraid of the future than I am of the present.

But what about 'height'? What of the things that are up there in the heights, beyond where even these astronauts go, and the powers that be? The thought of such heights is stupendous and alarming, but the Lord Jesus Christ still gives me the answer. When God brought Him from the dead, says Paul in Ephesians 1:20, 'He set him far above all principality, and power, and might, and dominion, and every name that is named, not only in this world, but also in that which is to come'. *He* is the exalted One. 'Wherefore', says Paul again in Philippians 2, 'God also hath highly exalted him, and given him a name that is above every name.' There is nothing higher. He is seated at the right hand of God in the glory. Nothing can look down on that level; it is the topmost level. And He is there. So we need not fear any height.

What about 'depth'? Again, happily, we have the complete answer. Paul gives it in Ephesians 4 where he talks about our Lord. He says, 'Wherefore he saith, When he ascended up on high, he led captivity captive, and gave gifts unto men. Now that he ascended, what is it but that he also descended first into the lower parts of the earth' (verses 8 and 9). How awe-inspiring are the depths, and the possibilities that may arise from the depths! What of the things that may rise up out of the inferno? There is no need to fear; Christ has descended into the lowest parts of the earth, and from there He has 'led captivity captive'. So once more William Cowper is right when he describes this love in these words:

> *Mine is an unchanging love,*
> *Higher than the heights above,*
> *Deeper than the depths beneath,*
> *Free and faithful, strong as death.*

Height! Depth! Everything is covered!

'Any other creature', says Paul. He cannot think of another word, so he says 'Any other creature'. 'Nothing shall be able to separate us from the love of God, which is in Christ Jesus our Lord.' Indeed he has already said it all, as I have reminded you, in that great challenge in the 31st verse: 'If God be for us, who can be against us?'

What does the Apostle mean? Let Isaiah answer the question in his 40th chapter, beginning to read at verse 26: 'Lift up your eyes on high, and behold who hath created these things, that bringeth out their host by number: he calleth them all by names by the greatness of his might, for that he is strong in power; not one faileth. Why sayest thou, O Jacob, and speakest, O Israel, My way is hid from the Lord, and my judgment is passed over from my God? Hast thou not known? hast thou not heard, that the everlasting God, the Lord, the Creator of the ends of the earth, fainteth not, neither is weary? there is no searching of his understanding. He giveth power to the faint; and to them that have no might he increaseth strength. Even the youths shall faint and be weary, and the young men shall utterly fall: but they that wait upon the Lord shall renew their strength; they shall mount up with wings as eagles; they shall run, and not be weary; and they shall walk, and not faint.'

These, then, are the grounds on which the Apostle argues that 'nothing shall be able to separate us from the love of God, which is in Christ Jesus our Lord'. Paul was absolutely certain of this. Are you? Can you say, 'I have been persuaded; I have no doubts any longer; I no longer say, "But I am weak and may fall into sin, and my understanding is very poor . . ." ' If you still say that, you have not understood the argument, you have not been persuaded. You are looking at yourself still, whereas the entire argument is to the effect that it is God taking hold of you that matters. Do not look at yourself, do not look at anything else. Nothing can separate you from His power and His love. 'I am persuaded.' Are you? Have I been speaking in vain? Do you still say 'I feel it is presumption to say that I know I am going to heaven'? If you say that, you are still looking to yourself and your life, and what you may do or may not do. Presumption? It is no sign of presumption to talk in the Apostle's terms. It is the exact opposite. The man who fails to do so does not believe the Word of God. Paul says he is sure of all this because he believes God, and has been persuaded by the Lord Jesus Christ. He does not think any longer according to his own feeble understanding; he thinks scripturally.

So reason out these great statements concerning God's purpose, and all He has done to carry out that purpose. Nothing matters but His love to us. We are 'kept', as Peter reminds us, 'by the power of God'. Or as Paul puts it again in Philippians 1:6, 'He which hath begun a good work in you will perform it until the day of Jesus Christ'. And He will do so because He is God. God never starts a process and then gives it up uncompleted. What God starts He finishes. 'His promise is Yea and Amen, And never was forfeited yet', as Toplady reminds us. Salvation – and this is the whole basis of our position – salvation is of God from the very beginning to the very end. That is why it is sure and certain. God's honour demands it. To say that a man whom God starts saving could subsequently be lost would mean that God has been defeated by the devil. That is impossible. God's character and honour demand that a man who has been justified should finally be glorified, and His power guarantees it. So I end with two great statements. The first is from Isaac Watts:

> *Saints by the power of God are kept,*
> *Till the salvation come:*
> *We walk by faith as strangers here,*
> *Till Christ shall call us home.*

The second is from Richard Keen:

> *How firm a foundation, ye saints of the Lord,*
> *Is laid for your faith in His excellent word;*
> *What more can He say than to you He hath said,*
> *You who unto Jesus for refuge have fled?*
>
> *Fear not, I am with thee, O be not dismayed;*
> *For I am thy God, and will still give thee aid:*
> *I'll strengthen thee, help thee, and cause thee to stand,*
> *Upheld by My righteous, omnipotent hand.*
>
> *When through the deep waters I call thee to go,*
> *The rivers of grief shall not thee overflow;*
> *For I will be with thee thy troubles to bless,*
> *And sanctify to thee thy deepest distress.*
>
> *When through fiery trials thy pathway shall lie,*
> *My grace all-sufficient shall be thy supply;*
> *The flame shall not hurt thee, I only design*
> *Thy dross to consume and thy gold to refine.*

Romans 8: 35-39

The soul that on Jesus has leaned for repose
I will not, I cannot, desert to its foes;
That soul, though all hell should endeavour to shake,
I'll never, no never, no never forsake!

As for myself, I am persuaded. I have given in long ago. I am no longer reasoning or arguing, and saying 'What?' 'But', or 'If!' No, no! 'I am persuaded that neither death, nor life, nor angels, nor principalities, nor powers, nor things present, nor things to come, nor height, nor depth, nor any other creature, shall be able to separate us from the love of God, which is in Christ Jesus our Lord.'

With Paul, I am persuaded. Are you?